The Great Wall in Ruins

SUNY Series,
Human Communication Processes

Donald P. Cushman and Ted. J. Smith, III, Editors

The Great Wall in Ruins

Communication and Cultural Change in China

Godwin C. Chu
and
Yanan Ju

STATE UNIVERSITY OF NEW YORK PRESS

Production by Ruth Fisher
Marketing by Theresa A. Swierzowski

Published by
State University of New York Press, Albany

© 1993 State University of New York

All rights reserved

Printed in the United States of America

No part of this book may be used or reproduced
in any manner whatsoever without written permission
except in the case of brief quotations embodied in
critical articles and reviews.

For information, address State University of New York Press,
State University Plaza, Albany, NY 12246

Library of Congress Cataloging-in-Publication Data

Chu, Godwin C., 1927–
  The great wall in ruins : communication and cultural change in
China / Godwin C. Chu and Yanan Ju.
    p.   cm. — (SUNY series, human communication processes)
  Includes bibliographical references and index.
  ISBN 0-7914-1621-6 (acid-free paper). — ISBN 0-7914-1622-4 (pbk.
: acid-free paper)
  1. China —Social conditions—1976– 2. Communication—China.
I. Chü, Yen-an. II. Title. III. Series: SUNY series in human
communication processes.
DS779.23.C473   1993
951.05'8—dc20   93–202
                                                             CIP

10 9 8 7 6 5 4 3 2 1

Contents

Preface ... vii

I: INTRODUCTION

1. Cultural Change in China ... 3
2. Research Methods and Sampling Procedures ... 14

II: RESEARCH FINDINGS

3. Family Relations ... 63
4. Social Relations ... 86
5. Job Preferences and Work Ethic ... 105
6. Organizational Relations ... 131
7. Community Life ... 149
8. Cultural Values: General Perspectives ... 169
9. Cultural Values: Family and Children ... 199
10. Cultural Values: Traditional Precepts ... 220
11. Belief System ... 252

III: CONCLUSION

12. Whither Chinese Culture ... 271

Appendix: Statistical Analysis ... 323
Notes ... 351
References ... 353
Index ... 361

Preface

Cultural change in China has been a topic of personal interest to both of us for somewhat different reasons. It is also an extremely difficult and challenging research task given the traumatic processes of change the Chinese people have gone through in the last four decades. It was a matter of chance encounter that the two of us got to know each other despite our different backgrounds and dissimilar political experiences. And it was also a result of personal perseverance on the part of Ju Yanan that we have been able to bring this field research to fruition.

It is unusual for authors to present their brief biographical sketches in the preface of a book. We do so here because even though our research findings are concrete and our statistical analyses directly verifiable, our interpretations, despite our efforts to be as objective as possible, cannot be completely free of our own value orientations. If some of our views should reflect biases that we are not aware of, we want our readers to know where we are coming from. While the two of us are in full agreement on the main thrust of our conclusion, our personal perspectives are not identical.

Godwin Chu was born and raised in pre-revolution China in a family of gentry background in the larger Shanghai area. From his grandfather, a Confucian scholar of the Manchu Dynasty, he learned to recite the Analects without understanding its meaning. As a child, he participated in the family rituals of ancestor worship during the lunar New Year and other annual occasions. The lunar New Year was particularly a time of joy and excitement, with fireworks and visits of many relatives. These family rituals were dutifully observed even during the Sino–Japanese War, when he followed his parents into interior China to escape the advancing Japanese troops. This tradition was kept after the family moved to Taiwan in 1949. Those rituals were discontinued only after he moved to the United States.

Chu grew up during the perilous years of the Sino–Japanese War. His first encounter with Chinese communism happened when he was living in Zhangding, at one time the Red capital of the Chinese Communists in Fujian province before they embarked on their legendary Long March. In the home of one of his high school classmates, he saw big character slogans left on the walls. His classmate said those were posted by Red soldiers some years before, and his family had not bothered to remove them. Some of his relatives had joined the Red Army and left town when the Communists retreated. A lot had apparently happened to that family when Zhangding was occupied by the Red Army, but his classmate did not wish to discuss it.

Like millions of other Chinese, Chu became aware of the intensely appealing power of Chinese communism after the war had ended. Many of his friends in college were attracted by the ideals of Communism. They put up anti-Kuomintang posters and joined the wild drum dances on campus. They greeted each military setback of the Kuomintang with joy and anticipation. By the summer of 1949, the defeat of the Kuomintang was almost certain. Chu wondered whether he should stay and get a job, but eventually decided to go with his family to Taiwan.

Those early years in Taiwan were a time of tribulation. Life was extremely difficult. He managed to finish college, got married, and joined a newspaper as a reporter. This was when he began his observations of major events in mainland China. What he learned was depressing, especially the Anti-Rightist campaign of 1957. Many of the prominent scholars he read about before 1949 were purged. These were people who had wholeheartedly supported the Communists during the civil war. The year 1958 was even more eventful. This was the year when the Great Leap Forward and the People's Commune movement were started. He wrote a series of news analyses. Perhaps as a result of that, he was offered an Asia Foundation Fellowship the following year for graduate study in mass communication at Stanford University. He received his Ph.D. from Stanford in 1963 and returned to Taiwan to teach.

One question had been lingering in his mind when he was a reporter in Taiwan. What would be the impact of Mao's class struggles and radical social transformation, such as the Anti-Rightist campaign and the People's Communes, on traditional Chinese culture? Because of this interest, he took time to study sociology and anthropology while pursuing his quantitative research program in mass communication at Stanford. After his return to Taiwan, and unable to do research on China, Chu tried out the theoretical concepts and research tools by conducting a study of cultural change in rural Taiwan, which he carried out in two longitudinal surveys over a period of fourteen years from 1964 to 1978.

He returned to Stanford to join the faculty in 1965. One year later the Cultural Revolution began. This was a time of campus unrest because of the Vietnam War, and some of his American students looked upon Mao's Red Guards as heroes. Chu read the news accounts of the Cultural Revolution in disbelief and sadness. He could imagine the sufferings of the Chinese people as the Red Guards applied their destructive hands to Chinese culture. He began collecting materials for a book, which came out in 1977 as *Radical Change through Communication in Mao's China*. He was then on the research staff of the East-West Center in Honolulu. Two years later, he and Francis Hsu edited a volume titled *Moving a Mountain: Cultural Change in China*. This was a time when field research in China was not yet possible. A group of eminent China scholars contributed the best of their research findings. In retrospect, the conclusion that Hsu and Chu wrote on the limited impact of Mao's ideological campaigns on traditional Chinese culture was too modest and too optimistic. Perhaps neither was prepared to face the reality of a crumbling traditional Chinese culture.

In 1979, after normalization of relations between the United States and China, Chu returned to China for the first time in thirty years. He was impressed with the physical infrastructure he saw in Beijing. He had a joyful reunion with members of his family. The Cultural Revolution was one thing they did not talk about. In Shanghai Chu called Fudan University. Perhaps because he spoke Shanghai dialect like a native, he was able to arrange a meeting with the journalism faculty the very same day. This was the beginning of a long and enduring academic exchange between Fudan University and the East–West Center. As part of that exchange program, Ju Yanan came to the East–West Center as a visiting scholar in 1980. This was how the two met and began a rewarding research cooperation leading to this study.

While Chu has had no direct experience under Chinese communism, Ju grew up and received his education under that system and went through an entirely different set of life-course events.

Ju Yanan, when written in Chinese, reads like "living in Yanan." Yanan, as it appears in our manuscript, is the name of the cradle of Mao Zedong's revolution. The first response Ju is likely to get whenever his three-character name is uttered to a Chinese ear is: "Were you born in Yanan?" Which implies, of course, "So, you have a revolutionary background!" And Ju would always happily accept the misunderstanding and decline to explain that the character "Yan" is the line name which means "continuous" and was given to all his brothers and

"An" simply means "peace." Ju's parents had little idea, when they gave this name to their second son, of what Mao and his revolutionary followers were doing in a place called "Yanan."

To what extent this name of "Ju Yanan" helped form people's positive initial perception of Ju as a person in a political environment where the two characters "Yanan" were sacred to the Chinese, he never could tell. But with the full knowledge that he had little family and social resources to depend upon for a politically safe life in those unusual years, including the Cultural Revolution, Ju felt his very name could give him some protection. Maybe it did. He was, for example, enrolled in 1964 in Fudan University, one of the best universities in China, at a time when a revolutionary family background was a main factor influencing a university's decision whether or not to admit a student. Could his name have helped a little bit?

Ju was too young to understand the radical cultural change that Chinese society was undergoing in the 1950s. He was eleven when the Anti-Rightist campaign was launched in 1957. He knew little of the cultural implications of this very important political event in contemporary Chinese history. He had grown into a politically conscious youth when the Cultural Revolution began in 1966. He was right in college, a place where the Red Guard movement did all the extremes to professors, sons and daughters with a "reactionary" family background, cadres labelled as "capitalist roaders," and society as a whole. Unable to join any of the Red Guard organizations on campus because of lack of a revolutionary family background (the name now did not help), Ju witnessed with fear and a very saddened heart what was occurring before his eyes: the burning of books, beating of professors, "reactionary" students forced to kneel before a portrait of Chairman Mao and beg for mercy, and suicides by condemned individuals.

While he could not understand what was happening right in front of him, he often followed the then popular processions of parades showing support for Mao and madly shouting "Long Live Chairman Mao!" Like Lu Xun's "Ah Q," he just could not stand the idea of being left out of the revolutionary process no matter how little he understood it. Soon he travelled to Beijing. He remembers he felt he was the happiest person on earth when he saw Chairman Mao standing in a military jeep reviewing the Red Guards in Tiananmen Square even though he knew he was not supposed to be there because of his non-membership in any Red Guard organization.

His psychology suddenly became twisted when he learned, upon his return on the 15th of January, 1967, from a simulated "Long March" along the Shanghai–Nanjing Railway that one of his closest relatives had just killed herself by jumping into the Huangpu River for fear of further humiliation by the Red Guards. He remembers that in his numerous nightmares those days he often hysterically screamed "Why? Why?" However, while his heart was still bleeding with utter sorrow, Ju again took to the streets, as much encouraged by many of his Red Guard classmates as out of his own willingness, to parade his support for Chairman Mao's revolutionary line, only now with mixed emotions of reverence for Chairman Mao, fear of possible persecution of himself, and sarcasm toward the madness of the Cultural Revolution.

The scar the Cultural Revolution left on Ju's psychology was beyond description. But like many of his contemporaries, he never lost his hope for the system and had all along been struggling to understand what had happened to himself, his family, and the whole country. Partly out of his attempt to get more "Red Safe" protection and partly out of his curiosity about the outside world, Ju went to Africa to be part of an international aid program sponsored by the Chinese government and stayed in an African village for two years and four months.

Mao died in 1976. Ju returned to his academic life in 1978 when he began his advanced degree studies back in Fudan University. Since then, he has visited the United States, Yugoslavia, England, and Australia as an active participant in international conferences, research projects, and academic exchange activities. His broad experiences and enormous opportunities created through his deep involvement in international activities did not shake his continuous conviction in the system, and he wanted to help despite his very much scarred psychology. He returned in October 1983 to teach in Fudan University after his 20-month pre-doctoral studies at the Communication Department, SUNY-Albany. The five years between 1983 and 1988 were the best and the worst years in Ju's life. He sees them as the best because he worked the hardest and produced the most as an academic, and he also saw some healthy signs of cultural rejuvenation, particularly during the 1984–86 period. He also sees them as the worst because once again those worthless political campaigns came back (the Anti-Spiritual Pollution campaign and the Anti-Bourgeois Liberalization campaign) despite the Party's promise that there would never be any more political campaigns. He gradually lost his hope for the system. The Tiananmen killings of 1989 smashed his last dreams to pieces. He now lost all hope, his last hope. And he also lost his cultural identity. He felt dead as a cultural being.

As time went on, wounds began to heal, and his cultural being has regained its consciousness. He feels he is coming back to his culture and his culture is coming back to him. Now in his mid-forties, Ju Yanan is desperately searching for a new cultural identity in his self and a new position in which to land his self in his mother Chinese culture. While he is physically living in the United States, his soul very much wanders toward the Orient. His biggest question now is whether and when he will find his new cultural identity and whether and when his mother Chinese culture will find him.

The first step toward this research was taken in the fall of 1986. Ju had accepted an invitation to come to the East–West Center and joined scholars and policymakers from Thailand and Indonesia to review the initial findings from a study of cultural change in Thailand. This was a time when scholars in China became intensely interested in the future of Chinese culture. Ju was then the Deputy Director of the Center for Cultural and Communication Studies at Fudan University. Impressed with the results from Thailand in particular and the sociological survey approach to the study of cultural change in general, Ju felt that what China needed was this type of empirical research, rather than opinions and debates without concrete data. Upon his return, he convinced his director, Professor Xu Zhen, and other colleagues in Fudan University to undertake a similar survey in the larger Shanghai area. The East–West Center offered methodological advice.

Then came the student demonstrations in January 1987. For a while it looked as if the research would be postponed. It was a reflection of Ju's personal perseverence and persuasive reasoning that his Center obtained approval from the university leadership in April to proceed with research planning. Chu accepted an invitation to visit Fudan University in June. The initial survey instrument Chu brought with him was discussed and extensively revised, and plans were drawn for a pretest in Shanghai and Qingpu. A detailed probability sampling plan was worked out. The pretest results were brought by Ju to Honolulu in late July for review and the survey instrument went through a major revision for a second time. Upon Ju's return to Shanghai, the instrument was revised for a third time. Meanwhile, Ju and his colleagues at Fudan began preparations for the field work, which was completed in December 1987. Results of initial statistical analysis were presented for discussion at an international symposium in Shanghai in August 1988.

Cultural change may be the most imposing subject for research in social science. Not only must one define culture in a way that permits empirical observation, rather than just debate and discourse about culture, but the data must be tied to a body of evidence in a way that demonstrates change. Because both of us have a background in communication research, we want our data to be relevant to the effects of communication. The earlier work in rural Taiwan by Chu came close to meeting these methodological requirements and established the usefulness of longitudinal sociological surveys for the study of cultural change. This is the methodology we are following in our analysis of cultural change in China.

China is probably the most challenging venue for social science research. It was only in recent years that Chinese authorities permitted its academic institutions to conduct research about human behavior. This kind of research, temporarily suspended after the events at Tiananmen, showed signs of return in 1992 as the Chinese government reaffirmed its economic reform and open-door policy. Our research was, strictly speaking, a benchmark survey, to be matched by a follow-up survey some years later for before-and-after comparison. Our survey has academic merits on its own for two reasons. First, in a historical perspective the most important change in contemporary Chinese culture is what has already taken place under the tutelage of Chairman Mao, not what happens in the future. We need to conduct our analysis retrospectively. Although we did not have comparable data from the past for comparison, we get a picture of change by examining our findings in light of our knowledge about traditional Chinese culture. Secondly, because ours was the first empirical survey of Chinese culture ever undertaken, it can serve as a benchmark not only for our own follow-up survey but, we hope, also as an archive data base for other scholars in the future who can make reference for comparative purposes of their own. This is why we have reported our methodology and research findings in detail. The results of multivariate statistical analyses are reported in the appendix. All the comparative results discussed in the text meet the .001 level of statistical significance in the multivariate analysis. Detailed tables of cross-tabulations and the full survey instrument will be made available in a separate volume.

We will be among the first to recognize the limitations of survey research for the study of human behavior. These limitations are even more serious when the survey methodology is applied to something as complex and encompassing as cultural change. Because of this, studies of cultural change in modern societies are not many and have generally been left to scholars who see quantitative, empirical research as inherently inadequate to the task. Through our research we want to demonstrate that survey research not only is objective and replicable, but can also serve as a useful tool for a study of cultural change, that is, if the data are seen in a proper historical perspective. In other words, we can treat the survey data as an objective parameter of evidence within which interpretation about the historical processes of change can be made. The statistical tools of multivariate analysis can illuminate and aid our interpretation. Nevertheless, survey research is only one of the useful tools. Our cumulative knowledge about cultural change in China will rely on research using other innovative methodological approaches, now made possible since China has opened its door in the post-Mao era.

It is difficult to adequately acknowledge the advice and suggestions offered by many of our colleagues. We would particularly express our thanks to Steven Chaffee, Stanford University; Francis Hsu, Northwestern University; Ambrose King, Chinese University of Hong Kong; Anthony Yu, University of Chicago; and Wang Gungwu, University of Hong Kong, for their invaluable contributions in planning this research. Francis Hsu made extensive comments on the first draft, for which we are thankful. Of colleagues at Fudan University, Xu Zhen has been most generous and helpful in his advice. We wish to thank Stanley Rosen, University of Southern California, for his critical reading and for generously making available to us relevant survey findings from China. We are indebted to Donald Cushman, SUNY-Albany, editor of this series, for his editorial advice and counsel. A note of appreciation is due to Deborah Forbis and Michael Macmillan for editorial assistance, Linus Chao for taking the pictures for this book, and Lear Budinger for computer programming for the numerous statistical analyses. The research reported here was supported by a generous personal grant from Mr. and Mrs. Laurance Rockefeller administered by the East–West Center under Victor Li as President and Mary Bitterman as Director of its Institute of Culture and Communication. This research was part of a large project of the Institute on communication and cultural change in Asia. Their support is gratefully acknowledged.

We particularly appreciate the understanding of our wives, Julia Chu and You Qin, for demonstrating in their unique ways the Chinese virtues of patience and tolerance when this manuscript was put together.

Godwin C. Chu
Yanan Ju

Part I

Introduction

Chapter 1

Cultural Change in China

In northern China, starting at the ancient battleground near Fort Shanhai and stretching across wind-swept expanses of virgin mountains and empty deserts nearly all the way to Mongolia, lies the Great Wall. Or more accurately, what is left of that mammoth stone structure put together by Emperor Qin. For some two thousand years, the Great Wall proudly stood guard, protecting the Han Chinese against the nomadic horsemen of the north, and silently watching the rise and fall of many a dynasty.

For people who lived away from the northern borders, the Great Wall was only a fable. Most Chinese never saw the Great Wall. But they knew the folklore about a maiden, Meng Jiangnu, who went on her long journey to look for her husband who had been drafted by Emperor Qin to build the Great Wall. She trekked from one end of the wall to the other, only to be led to the ground where her husband was buried. She threw herself on his tomb and uttered such a loud cry that the Great Wall came tumbling down.

For centuries Chinese were sheltered by another Great Wall. This was not a wall of stones and mortar, but a wall of symbols and ideas, of traditional values and beliefs, that stood just as firm and strong in the minds of Chinese. This cultural bulwark held Chinese society together for milleniums, shielding Chinese life from external encroachment and internal erosion. Just as the stone Great Wall reflected an inward looking mentality of China's ruling elite, the cultural Great Wall had become a mantle that protected the Chinese from innovation and change. The confining consequences became painfully apparent during the last century when China was compelled to open its door to a fast changing world outside.

Traditional Chinese culture began its slow but inevitable erosion in the mid-19th century. The period of political chaos following the fall of the Manchu Dynasty in 1912 created more confusion and initiated a soul searching among Chinese intellectuals. The eight years of war with Japan, from 1937 to 1945, gravely undermined the structural roots of Chinese society and paved the way for the defeat of the Kuomintang and the establishment of the People's Republic of China. It was during the reign of Chairman Mao Zedong that Chinese people, inspired by his idealistic concept of a Communist utopia and propelled by his charismatic leadership, participated in a prolonged and traumatic process of radical social transformation. For the first time in history, traditional Chinese culture was forced to undergo major changes of unprecedented dimensions, all within a short span of decades.

The collapse of the stone Great Wall in answer to the heart-rending cries of maiden Meng Jiangnu was only a fable. The destruction of the cultural Great Wall by Mao and his millions of followers is a reality. But this is a reality that has not been objectively documented. Cultural change in contemporary China has been the topic of much scholarly discourse and public debate in and outside China (Chu and Hsu, 1979; Wang, 1980; Cai, 1987; Li, 1987; Link, 1987; Tang, 1987; Tu, 1987; Xiao, 1987; Liu and Lin, 1988; Liu, 1989; Ogden, 1989; Whyte, 1989; Yang, 1990). *The River Elegy* (Su and Wang, 1988), a controversial six-part television documentary that aired in China in the summer of 1988, touched off a storm of protest as well as waves of ground-swelling support. These discussions and debates (Cai, 1988; Yi, 1989; Yu, 1989) have sometimes taken place in an emotionally charged atmosphere marked by a dearth of concrete data. The research findings which we present in this volume, based on a comprehensive survey undertaken in November and December 1987, illustrate in a manner as objective and concrete as possible the nature of contemporary Chinese culture as it stands today. Using the survey results as a data base, we can assess both the extent and the process of change which traditional Chinese culture has undergone. This is the objective of our research.

Concept of Culture

Empirical studies of cultural change are relatively few, partly because the concept of culture usually carries diverse meanings. In their critical reviews of the concepts of culture up until the early 1950s, Kroeber and Kluckhohn (1952) identified 164 definitions. The monumental work of Kroeber and Kluckhohn has not been updated. Among the more recent contributions are Schwartz and Ewald (1968), Rokeach (1969), Rokeach (1973), Vermeersch (1977), Bernardi (1977), Markarian (1977),

Rokeach (1979), Hall, Hobson, Lowe, and Willis (1980), Melischek, Rosengren, and Stappers (1984), Ball–Rokeach, Rokeach, and Grube (1984), Carey (1989), and Inglehart (1990).

While early works by anthropologists tended to see culture in terms of discrete traits and artifacts, many of the recent theoretical approaches address the concept of culture in more abstract and general terms. Culture is learned and shared and functions as an integrated whole. It is conceptualized as a design for living, a function of social life, a social heritage, an artificial environment, a mode of communication, a set of guiding standards for social behavior, in an imposed arbitrary form. In identifying the common characteristics that apply to the enormous variations of cultures in human life, these approaches generally leave out the substantive features by which a particular culture can be concretely observed. Knowing that culture is a design for living, for example, does not give much direction if one wants to observe and understand the culture of Chinese people.

Because these theoretical concepts examine culture in a general approach, they are not directly appropriate for a concrete study of cultural change. To say that culture is learned and shared and functions as an integrated whole seems to have a timeless basis of universal validity. This general characteristic of culture does not change. To empirically study culture and cultural change, we need to begin by identifying the concrete dimensions and processes of culture, including the manner in which it is learned and shared. These concrete dimensions and processes not only vary from society to society, but change over time. If culture is a set of guiding standards for social behavior, then we need a concrete framework by which we can identify those standards and observe their processes of change.

In the synthesized definition they offered, Kroeber and Kluckhohn moved in this concrete direction when they identified the essential core of culture as consisting of traditional ideas, especially their attached values, as well as patterns of behavior, explicit and implicit. When we treat culture as a phenomenon for empirical observation in the general population of a society, the synthesized definition proposed by Kroeber and Kluckhohn still stands. In his initial analysis of cultural change in China, Chu (1979) took this definition by Kroeber and Kluckhohn as a point of departure and proposed to define culture as an integrated conceptual framework for guiding an empirical study of cultural change.

Chu began by looking at culture as a way of life, a behavioral concept implicit in Kroeber and Kluckhohn. He took an approach similar to a tripartite classification of culture that Kroeber and Kluckhohn identified in the works of Tessmann (1930), Menghin (1931), Boas (1938), and Murdock (1941). The American anthropologist Leslie White (1974) took basically the same approach in his definition of culture, which he considered to exist (1) within human organisms, i.e., concepts, beliefs, emotions, attitudes, (2) within processes of social interactions, and (3) within material objects. Using the self as an anchor point, Chu identified three major components in the life of any self. One consists of the social relations between the individual self and his significant others. Much of our behavior takes place within these social relations, including family relations. Partly by necessity and partly by choice, these social relations are further cast in the context of two other major components:

(1) materials and objects in the physical environment that the self relies on for survival and that, through the extent of technology, mediate social relations, and

(2) ideas, including ideology, values, and religious beliefs—both cognitive and evaluative—that (a) influence the way the self perceives the social and physical environments and (b) set priorities for social relations and the pursuit of materials and objects in the physical environment. The three major components Chu has proposed are similar to the social, material, and spiritual culture identified by Menghin and used by Tessmann in his study of East Peruvian tribes.

The relationships between the self, on the one hand, and the significant others, materials and objects, and ideas, on the other, are represented in figure 1.1.

The bold lines represent the direct relations, that is, how the self interacts with the significant others, how the self uses the materials and objects in the physical environment and is in turn influenced by them, and how the self embraces certain ideas as relevant for social and material relations. The thin lines represent perceived relations, or

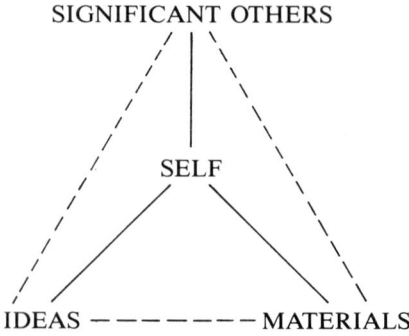

Figure 1.1 Paradigm of Cultural Components

linkages, that exist in the perceptual field of the self. They are important even though they may not fully correspond to reality, because it is often the perception rather than reality that influences our behavior. Are the significant others seen as endorsing the same ideas the self embraces? Are the significant others seen as cooperating or competing with the self in the pursuit of material gains? Is the self's pursuit of materials and objects seen as consistent with the prevailing ideology?

Culture, expressed as a way of life, encompasses the totality of these complex relations, both substantive and perceptual, which regulate the behavioral patterns of a cultural group. These relations are so intricately intertwined that they tend to be fused at the observational level. Conceptually, they are distinguishable and can serve as a cogent framework in which we sort out and organize our empirical observations.

These relations form a holistic structural entity. The social relations, which are the human ties that hold a cultural group together, are built upon two other components as cornerstones: The material component is essential for physical survival and nurture, and the ideological component sets these relations in a normative frame of order and at the same time gives life a measure of meaning. It is in the context of social relations that material life is sustained and ideologies are maintained. Human culture is unique because both social relations and material life are influenced and regulated by our ideas, that is, knowledge, beliefs, and values which very much dominate our way of life. What makes one culture distinctively different from others stems primarily from the domain of ideas, even though the differences become manifest in both social relations and material relations at the observational level.

Cultural Change—A Structural–Functional Perspective

We follow a structural–functional perspective in analyzing the processes of cultural change. Function as a concept refers to the manner in which the social processes in an institution contribute to the operation of (a) the individual role players who participate in the institution, and/or (b) other structural components in the broad social system of which the institution is a part. Aberle et. al. (1950) have proposed certain functional prerequisites which they consider essential for all societies. Merton (1961) speaks of manifest and latent functions. Because the theoretical writings of Parsons (1951), Radcliffe–Brown (1952), Levy (1952) and others focus on the interrelated nature of various structural components of a social system, the structural–functional approach is sometimes mistaken for espousing a static view of society. This structural interrelatedness, however, refers not to a static equilibrium, but to a moving dynamics, in the sense that change in one structural component is likely to be followed by changes in some other components. The concept of change is thus inherent in the structural–functional approach, as made clear by Parsons (1951) and Smelser (1968) when they discuss processes of change of social systems. In fact, even in the early writings of Malinowski (1922, 1938, 1945), his functional theory of culture was centrally concerned with change. Among recent works, Chu (1977) has followed this perspective in his analysis of the roles of communication in bringing about radical structural change in Mao's China. Almond, Powell and their colleagues (1984) have applied the structural–functional approach in their comparative analyses of the political systems and change in Europe, Russia, China, Mexico and Africa.

From a holistic functional point of view, culture can be seen as a system of collective survival. As such, culture has two salient features. It must be adaptive to changes in the external environment and internal conditions. A culture that fails to adapt to these changes will run the risk of extinction. Thus, change is very much an inherent characteristic of any culture. However, a culture must also be resistant to change, at least to some extent. A culture that is readily adaptive to every change in the environment will have no basis for stability and continuity. Resistance to change, ironically, is as necessary for survival of a culture as is adaptability. It is these two seemingly contradictory features that make the study of cultural change both fascinating and difficult.

In a structural perspective, a cultural system, whether its social relations, material relations, or the ideological domain, consists of constraining components and incentive components. Constraining components, by and large, are those that prevent people from reaching what they want. Incentive components are those that motivate people to reach what they want. Together they regulate human behavior and maintain social order. Constraining and incentive components can be either structural or ideological, figure 1.2.

Many constraining components are structural in nature. One particular constraining component is the legal system. Other than that, most structural components are embedded in the class structure and apply unevenly to different social classes. The land-tenure system in most traditional societies is an example. For tenants who toil on the land and receive a meager income there is almost no chance for them and their children to break out of their bondage of poverty. Another common constraining component resides in the division between men and women.

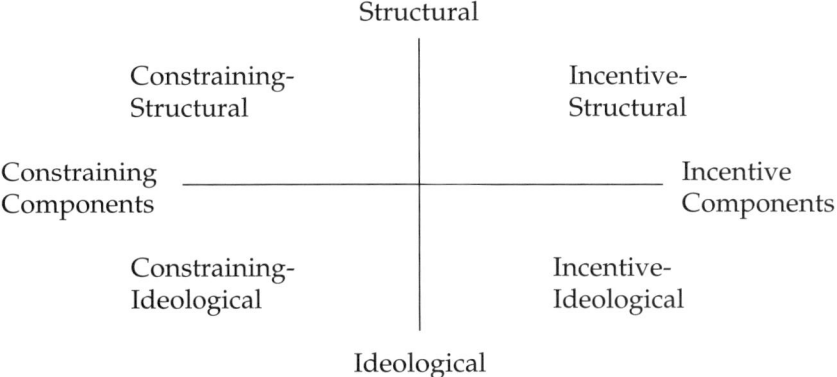

Figure 1.2 Structural and Ideological Constraints and Incentives

But constraining components can be rooted in the ideological domain, functioning as a cognitive foundation of the structural components, sometimes in a powerful way. The traditional Chinese belief that one's life was destined by fate made it easier for most people to accept their state of misery without challenging it. Similarly, the Buddhist belief that people have power and wealth because of their karma lends support to a popular conception, that is, the way to deal with power is to appease it, rather than challenge or confront it, because one cannot fight karma. The belief in fate and karma becomes a powerful ideological constraint that reinforces the existing social structure.

Some incentive components are structural. In traditional Chinese society, except for the offspring of a few despised occupational groups, such as prostitutes, opera players who were female impersonators, and bath-house attendants who scrubbed the customers' backs and manicured their toenails, all male children were allowed to take the state examinations, which opened the door to upward mobility. In Chinese history many rose to high positions by this route.

Other incentive components are ideological. The traditional Chinese belief that one must bring glory to one's ancestors served as a powerful incentive for Chinese to excel in whatever they were doing. We have suggested that the Buddhist belief in karma can be seen as an ideological constraint. By accepting one's karma, one endures inequities even though one may not approve, because one's personal condition at any moment in time is believed to be the result of one's past actions and thoughts. An integral part of the Buddhist belief in karma is the notion of merit making. If one makes merit, generally by offering food to monks or making contributions to temples, there is the hope that the accumulated merits may overbalance the bad deeds and thoughts of the past and bring about a change for the better, for the next life if not for this life. Thus the belief in karma, as embodied in the custom of merit making, gives people incentive to endure the current life conditions, no matter how miserable, with the expectation that their next life will be endowed with riches, power, and prestige. The Buddhist belief in karma, in this instance, serves both as ideological constraint and incentive.

It is easy to see why incentive components are necessary. Whether structural or ideological, they provide rewards—material or symbolic—for carrying on life and performing those tasks that are essential for collective survival. Yet in the perspective of social order and cultural stability, the constraining components are equally important. By setting up constraints on social relations and on the pursuit of material ends, these structural and ideological components minimize conflicts and contribute to the maintenance of order in society.

The constraining and incentive components in a culture may seem just as contradictory as are adaptability and resistance to change. But they must co-exist. Both perform important system-sustaining functions. The specific manner in which constraining and incentive components coexist in a particular culture and the conditions under which they maintain a delicate balance of system-sustaining functions will be fascinating topics for research. If that delicate balance is destroyed, contradictions between the constraining components and incentive components will be accentuated, and the result could be system destroying rather than system sustaining.

A culture responds to changes in either the external environment or internal conditions. Cultural change can be seen as an interplay between initial changes in the constraining and incentive components on the one hand, and individual and institutional responses to such changes on the other (see figure 1.3).

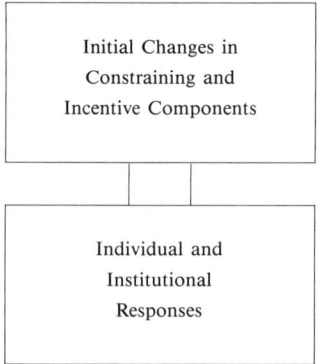

Figure 1.3 Processes of Cultural Change

Hypothesis

Following our conceptual framework of culture and cultural change, we propose this general hypothesis:

> In traditional Chinese culture there were constraining components and incentive components. Some were structural, others ideological. As these constraining and incentive components are altered, Chinese people change their social relations, material relations, values, beliefs, and attitudes to adapt. Thus Chinese culture changes. A number of factors, such as age, sex, education, economic status, and urbanization mediate in the way individuals relate to both the old and new constraining and incentive components, and thus have an impact on the nature of cultural change.
>
> In China, communication plays a central role in the processes of cultural change in two major perspectives. Political communication was used intensively in the days of Mao Zedong to change the ideological foundation of traditional Chinese culture. In the post-Mao years of economic reforms under Deng Xiaoping, the Chinese mass media has become a conduit for Western influence on Chinese culture.

Major events in China since 1949 can be seen in the perspective of structural changes in constraining and incentive components. The agrarian land reform and the expropriation of urban business removed the landlords and businessmen from China's social class and lifted two major structural constraints from rural peasants and urban workers. However, China's Communist Party placed them under equally confining structural constraints in the People's Communes and state enterprises. Landlords and business owners, stripped of their properties, completely lost their power and authority, which were taken over by Party cadres. It took the Cultural Revolution to remove the Party cadres from their positions of authority. Chaos lasted for years. Although order was eventually restored, the traditional Chinese concept of authority was cast in doubt.

Political communication has played a major part in the change process. Beginning in the early 1950s, the Party started a series of ideological campaigns to attack traditional cultural values and beliefs. These campaigns came one after another, culminating in 1966 with the Cultural Revolution as a traumatic climax. Confucian teachings were criticized in many of these campaigns. Toward the end of the Cultural Revolution decade, a direct attack was made on Confucius himself as part of an internal power struggle. An overall objective of the ideological campaigns was represented by Chairman Mao's motto: "if you do not destroy (the old), you do not establish (the new)." Mao wanted to destroy the old so that he could establish a new set of Communist-inspired ideologies. Mao's strategy seemed to have left a distinctive impact on Chinese culture not because his new ideologies were found appealing to Chinese people but because his class struggle tactics of accusations and confrontations set up behavioral patterns that proved to be contrary to the traditional Chinese way of moderation and harmony. Mao's idea that government should wholeheartedly serve the people did not seem to be embraced by the Chinese. Instead, highly restrictive ideological confines came to dominate the economic, social, and political life of China for some three decades. The results, it seems, were the destruction of the old without the establishment of something new and positive.

From these events, it appears that old structural constraints were replaced with new limitations, possibly somewhat more restrictive. If the traditional Confucian ideology set clear boundaries on Chinese social behavior, then the ideological tenets of Mao seemed to put up new barriers that were just as rigid, if not more so. What seems a curious parallel between the old and the new was their similar lack of cultural incentives, both structural and ideological. In traditional China, the state examination system was one of the few established avenues of upward mobility. Education in Mao's China, however, did not necessarily serve this same function. A college degree was not a guarantee for a desirable job assignment and promotion. During the Cultural Revolution, a degree could be the source of a social stigma branding the educated as "stinky No. 9" and relegating them to the bottom of China's social ladder. A sure way to distinguish oneself, at considerable risk of retaliation if not handled skilfully, was to severely attack others during criticism campaigns. Getting ahead often meant participating in an intense internecine warfare as part of China's organizational life. This new structural incentive offered reward for competition through destruction.

In olden day China, people were motivated to excel by a desire to bring glory to their ancestors. This traditional value served as one of the few ideological incentives of the past. The Party's attack on ancestors, however, particularly during the Cultural Revolution, has put this Confucian value under a dark cloud. Because Mao's ideal of wholeheartedly serving the people did not seem to receive much more than lip service, the Chinese were left without any strong ideological incentives of their own, until the arrival of a new ideology from the West in the early 1980s as Deng Xiaoping introduced his economic reforms (Whyte, 1989).

As popularly perceived by Chinese people, Western ideology is not a set of clearly articulated principles and standards. Rather, it is presented as a lifestyle of unmistakable affluence, marked by a high standard of material comfort and a remarkable degree of personal freedom, which Chinese audiences have seen in American films and television programs. This lifestyle is somehow associated with words like "capitalism" and "democracy," even though few Chinese understand how capitalism works in the United States or how democracy is practiced in the West. It is nevertheless an ideology because it consists of captivating images and powerful ideas. What seems to have vividly impressed Chinese people is a sharp contrast between what they see around them in their own lives and what they see on the video screens. Some forty years of dedication and toiling labor under their Communist leadership has brought them not the socialist utopia that has been promised but little more than a bare subsistence. Yet this strange world outside—even though it has been corrupted by the evils of capitalism, as the Chinese have been repeatedly told—presents a dazzling array of just about everything they would like to have. This new Western ideology, imprecise and unclear as it may seem, enters Chinese society in the context of an ideological vacuum, as it were, and finds an audience, especially the young, at a moment when they are particularly vulnerable to its influence. This influence is difficult to resist because its validity seems to be well established by what people can see. Whether it corresponds to reality does not seem to matter.

This is, in short, the new social and political environment in which Chinese people find themselves today. How they adapt to this complex mixture of constraining and incentive components, some old and some new, and how they respond to an array of messages, some Communist and some Western, is reflected in their social relations, material relations, values, beliefs, and attitudes. These, in turn, will vary among Chinese according to different age groups with their dissimilar socialization experiences, male and female characteristics, urban versus rural areas, diverse educational and income levels, and different accesses to official mass media and Western cultural influence.

Our research provides concrete data to help us understand contemporary Chinese culture as well as assess its processes of change.

Chapter 2

Research Methods and Sampling Procedures

Methods for Studying Cultural Change

How do we study culture and cultural change? To answer this question requires not only defining and examining the very nature of culture, but also measuring and assessing cultural change on a longitudinal, comparative basis. Any attempt at a comprehensive study of culture needs to consider such topics as the patterns of relations between the self and significant others, including family relations in particular and social relations in general, our relations with the material environment, generally cast in the perspective of the work ethic and economic relations, and our cultural values, religious beliefs, and social attitudes. We need to consider the appropriate methods to be used for studying the various components of culture. For a study of cultural change, we need to consider the assessment of both the process and direction of change by introducing a time dimension to our investigation. Methodological difficulties will be further compounded when the study of culture and cultural change is applied to a huge, complex modernizing society rather than a primitive tribe with a small population.

Generally speaking, three approaches have been used: participant observation, the analysis of written materials including popular literature, and until more recently, the use of sample surveys. Each approach has its strengths as well as its limitations.

A major approach to the study of culture has been through the field work of participant observation. By living among the people whose culture one wants to study, the researcher can participate in the different facets of their daily life, make observations in an ideally unobtrusive manner, and collect additional data from selected informants to aid his interpretation. This method has been used extensively by anthropologists with fruitful results. In China, the two classic studies of traditional culture, one by Fei Hsiao-tung in eastern China just before World War II (Fei, 1939), and the other by Francis Hsu in Yunnan during the war (Hsu, 1949), both relied on participant observation. When Bernard Gallin went to Taiwan in 1957–1958 to study changing village life in southern Taiwan (Gallin, 1966), he primarily used participant observation aided by historical documents. Based on what he reconstructed about the past from informants, Gallin was able to make some inferences about changes in Chinese culture in rural Taiwan. William Klausner's insightful study of contemporary Thai culture (1983) draws largely from his own participant observations while living in Thailand during the last three decades.

Another way is to analyze written materials about a culture, not only historical documents but also popular media such as novels, vernacular dramas, folk tales, and even folk songs. These materials reflect elements of a culture. Selective passages can be used for illustrative purposes, sometimes enlivened with anecdotes from personal observations. Ruth Benedict's classic study of Japanese culture, *The Chrysanthemum and the Sword* (1946), was based entirely on analysis of written materials. So was her study of Thai culture and behavior (1952), also undertaken during World War II. The more recent works of Francis Hsu (Hsu, 1953, 1981) on Chinese culture, after his well-known *Under the Ancestors' Shadow*, are based on both personal observations and analysis of written materials. Insightful interpretations have been made by Hsu following this approach on outstanding characteristics of traditional Chinese culture.

The contents of popular media have been analyzed in depth in their own right to enunciate various aspects of a culture. Godwin Chu and his colleagues have examined short stories, comic books, revolutionary operas, and folk songs during the days of Mao Zedong (Chu, 1978) in order to elaborate on the major themes of the new Chinese culture which Mao wanted to construct for China. Herbert Phillips (1987) has surveyed modern Thai literature, including short stories, for major themes that illustrate religious practices, family relations, and the deterioration of traditional Thai life in the process of development. Benedict Anderson and Ruchira Mendiones (1985) have probed popular Thai short stories to shed light on the changing political culture in Thailand.

Both of the above methods have been used creatively and productively. But like all research methods, they suffer from certain limitations. One is the generalizing of inferences made from the results. Participant observation is limited to a small locality where the researcher can spend a considerable length of residence. This was true with the two classic studies of Chinese culture by Fei and Hsu. Here one problem is the sampling of locations. Generalizations can be made only if we assume that observations made in the particular locations were representative of Chinese culture as a whole. The rituals of ancestor worship which Hsu observed in a small town in Yunnan were largely the same elsewhere. The adoption of a "child wife" by a family for a young boy, which Fei observed in a village in eastern China, was practiced in other parts of China. In fact, Gallin found the same practice in his village in southern Taiwan some twenty years later. However, if the phenomenon we observe is not homogeneous in the entire population, then the selection of one particular location for observation can create a problem of sampling bias.

Another kind of sampling bias that will limit generality may be more serious, because participant observation is often not only confined to one location, but is usually limited to a small number of people whom the researcher can interact with and observe. Problems may arise due to selectivity. If the research objective is to ascertain whether a practice such as "child wife" exists, then the problem may not be too serious. If "child wife" is widely practiced, it is not likely that the researcher will choose a rare location where this practice does not exist. But if the researcher wants to demonstrate how widely this practice is being followed in a community, then observations based on a few selected cases will not offer a valid basis for generalization. This is why the participant observation method is productive when the phenomenon being observed is widespread, such as ancestor worship in traditional China, or if the purpose is to illustrate the processes of a certain practice, such as how the "child wife" custom is implemented, but not the relative prevalence of such a practice.

Observer bias is a problem with all research methods, but can be particularly troublesome with participant observation. It is well known that the presence of an observer can influence the phenomenon that is being observed, no matter how unobtrusive the observer tries to be. If culture consists of a set of ready-made definitions for our behavior, as Kluckhohn and Kelly (1945) have suggested, then the presence of an outside observer will most probably change the definition of a particular situation, especially if the observer becomes an active participant. What the participant–observer sees may not be the untainted phenomenon he wants to record. This kind of observer bias will be more serious for informal patterns of interactions such as family relations than for formal rituals such as ancestor worship.

Other than the impact of observation on the behavior being observed, perhaps far more troublesome is the possible subjective selectivity of the observer. Few researchers would deliberately introduce bias into their data. Most researchers want to maintain a high degree of objectivity. But when one's time is limited, and when there is so much to observe within a fixed amount of time, selective attention becomes almost inevitable. There is the possibility of selective perception to see what the researcher wants to see, and to skip what he does not want to notice. The problem becomes even more serious because in a participant–observation situation, there is usually no possibility for verifying inter-observer consistency. This is why sometimes two researchers observing the same culture can come up with entirely different impressions. What was originally presented as a fascinating psychological study of primitive youth in Samoa (Mead, 1928) turned out to be little more than a misguided myth (Freeman, 1983). This problem is further compounded when we add a time dimension to study cultural change. If observations are made at two different points in time, we do not know whether the culture has indeed changed, or whether the results simply reflect different perceptive biases of the two observers.

There is also the possibility of informant bias. When a researcher lives in a community for an extended period of time and actively participates in many of its activities, he will make friends, some of whom will be his informants. Usually they know why he has come to live in their community. The possibility exists that some of his informants will tell him what they think he wants to know, either by elaborating on a phenomenon beyond reality or exaggerating the importance of an event for more than it is worth. Informant bias can be particularly serious when the researcher relies on his informants to reconstruct the past, about which he may know next to nothing. A well-trained field worker must be always on guard against such tendencies on the part of his informants, by seeking cross validation whenever possible, but this is easier said than done. The experience of Mead well illustrates this point. If informant bias is introduced into the data unknowingly, there is usually no readily available way for other researchers to detect it. Derek Freeman's carefully documented disavowal of Margaret Mead's classic Samoan study was the exception rather than the rule. The Samoan myth persisted for more than half a century until Freeman set the record straight.

There are two other limitations with the participant–observation approach. Human behavior is rarely uniform. Part of the objective of any research is to document the extent of variability. Indeed, cultural change is generally reflected not in the existence or nonexistence of certain behavioral patterns and cultural values, but rather in their *changing patterns of variability*. Take divorce as an example. In Chinese society, divorce existed forty years ago as it does today. The change is in the varying rates of divorce, now compared to the past. Participant observation is unable to measure the full range of variability. By the same token, this method is not appropriate for establishing covariation, which is essential for demonstrating relationships among behavioral and attitudinal patterns. If the observations are based on a small number of cases, as they typically are, they cannot be used to make reliable inferences about patterns of covariation.

Participant observation is particularly suited for illustrating rituals and ceremonies (Hsu, 1949; Gallin, 1966) as well as patterns of interpersonal relations in a small-group setting (Whyte, 1943), because these are concretely observable processes. As William Klausner has observed from his thirty years of fieldwork in Thailand (1989), participant observation can be a highly productive means of identifying the personal agenda of a people, of gaining insight into rhythms of their life initially unaffected by an imposed research agenda. Eventually the researcher must begin probing the sociocultural depth of their life in terms of his own research objectives. However, through unobstrusive observation, much can be gained by flowing with their current life and thoughts and their priorities. As Klausner has pointed out, the participant–observation method can be fruitfully used to assess the attributes of the cognitive world of a people, not only through inferences from concrete behavior, but also from paying careful attention to their dialogues, proverbs and gossip, and listening to lullabies, folk tales, sermons, etc. Participant observation can produce valuable insights. However, this method is not highly productive when one wants to systematically document a wide range of values, beliefs, and attitudes of a people.

The analysis of literature and other written contents has one salient virtue. These novels, short stories, dramas, and folk tales were not written for the benefit of researchers, and thus are free from the kind of intended informant bias we are concerned with here. One cannot blame the author of *The Dream of the Red Chamber* for painting a distorted picture of family life in China. It simply was not his purpose to present a representative picture in the first place. If a researcher wants to analyze *The Dream of the Red Chamber* for an understanding of family life in China in the olden days, he must keep this point in mind. By the same token, another well-known classical novel, *The Golden Lotus*, was not written by its author to illustrate typical husband–wife relations in traditional China. This novel is fascinating in its revelation about an unrestrained quest for sadistic sexual pleasure by the hero, in a society where sex was a taboo topic. Given these limitations concerning the major themes, however, popular novels like these vividly portray the ordinary lives of the many minor characters in a way that reveals much about Chinese culture in those days, and therefore can be analyzed as such.

Other than the absence of the particular kind of informant bias that we have defined, the analysis of written materials shares most of the common problems with the participant–observation approach. One concerns the sampling of authors. When there are many authors available, which ones should be chosen? Then there is the problem of sampling the works of a particular writer. The criteria of selection usually present enormous problems for the researcher. One particular problem concerns the experience of an author. Most authors are middle class in background and they write for a literate population. The generality of their audience appeal and the values they represent may be questionable.

Far more serious is the possibility of observer bias, that is, the subjective judgment of the researcher in interpreting the meanings of the contents. *The Dream of the Red Chamber,* for example, has been analyzed by many Chinese writers, including the noted philosopher Hu Shih. Few agreed on the messages intended by the author. Observer bias may present an unsolvable dilemma with the use of this research method. Take the thematic analysis of a popular novel as an example. One implicit assumption in this kind of analysis is that the novel's themes reflect some aspect of social reality, as seen by the author. It is the task of the researcher to capture the author's perception of reality. Because of the potential observer bias, we do not know whether the perception is the author's or the researcher's, or whether the perception reflects any reality at all. In China's case, observer bias may be further compounded by political bias, because we do not know whether we are dealing with the author's perception of reality, or the Party's prescription of what reality should be. Because of these limitations, the assessment of cultural change based upon an analysis of written materials should be treated with caution.

In our discussion we are referring to the analysis of written contents in a *qualitative, interpretive* mode. We are not referring to *quantitative* content analysis, which involves certain particular assumptions and requires entirely different analytical techniques (Berelson, 1952; Holsti, 1968). It is obvious that this kind of qualitative analysis does not lend itself to an assessment of variability of behavioral patterns or cultural values. Nor can it be used to establish patterns of covariation among different components of a culture. Qualitative analysis of this kind, however, can be highly productive in illustrating cultural values, beliefs, and attitudes, that is, if we bear in mind those limitations that we have discussed.

The application of survey research to the study of culture and cultural change has been a relatively recent phenomenon. The first such major attempt was Daniel Lerner's classic *Passing of Traditional Society* (1958), based on surveys conducted in several Middle East countries. Florence Kluckhohn and Fred Strodtbeck (1961) were among the first to employ survey research for an insightful study of dominant and variant value orientations in five communities in the American Southwest. In Japan, the Institute of Mathematical Statistics has been conducting since the mid 1950s periodical surveys of Japanese national character, which basically cover cultural values, attitudes, and beliefs. These surveys have been conducted under the direction of Chikio Hayashi, using a cohort analysis known as the Hayashi method (Hayashi, 1981, 1987; Hayashi, Suzuki, and Hayashi, 1984). Jean Stoetzel (1955) surveyed a sample of young Japanese after World War II in his *Without the Chrysanthemum and the Sword* that sought to update Ruth Benedict's classic study of Japanese culture. Alex Inkeles and David Smith (1974) used survey research in their studies of individual modernity in six developing countries. Godwin Chu and Gin-yao Chi (1984) did a fourteen-year longitudinal study of cultural change in eight villages in northern Taiwan, using repeated interviews with the same respondents as a before-and-after comparison. Chu, Alfian and Wilbur Schramm (1985) conducted a six-year longitudinal study of the impact of television on Indonesian culture through the use of repeated surveys of national samples in rural areas. Recently, the National Opinion Research Center in the United States (NORC, 1986) has been conducting periodic national surveys on cultural values and social attitudes of American people.

In his important empirical studies of cultural change in industrial nations in Europe, Inglehart (1990) analyzed data from both longitudinal surveys, the Euro-Barometers that regularly measured values and social attitudes in twelve Western nations from 1970 to 1986, and the World Value surveys conducted in twenty-five countries in 1981–1982. Using both the individual and the nation as his units of analysis, Inglehart detected a shift from an overwhelming emphasis on material well-being to a concern for the quality of life.

Yet the use of sample surveys for a study of culture is sometimes received with skepticism. A basic concern is whether verbal responses to a question can be taken as valid indicators of behavioral patterns and attitudes. Indeed much of the current research in social psychology and also in sociology rests on the assumption that verbal responses may be taken as valid indicators, within certain limits. This is a long-standing issue, first addressed more than half a century ago by LaPiere (1934). During one summer, LaPiere travelled with a young Chinese couple throughout the United States. They stopped at 66 hotels, auto camps, and tourist hostels and ate at 184 restaurants and cafes. They were refused service only once. LaPiere sent a questionnaire to all those places later, and asked whether they would accept Chinese as guests. Half of the respondents returned the questionnaire. Over 90 percent of them said no. The discrepancy between actual behavior and verbal responses about "what would you do" in this case illustrates the relation between behavior and attitudes. Attitudes—we include here values and beliefs—are relevant to our behavior but are not rigid indicators of how we behave in actual situations (McGuire, 1968; Scott, 1968). We must take into account situational factors. Those hotel and restaurant owners who said they would not admit Chinese probably had in mind laundry men and waiters. When they saw an attractive, young Chinese couple, accompanied by an older, respectable looking American, they behaved differently. This does not mean, however, that attitudes are not important, or that LaPiere's survey was invalid. The fact that over 90 percent of those who responded said "no" clearly indicated the racial prejudice against Chinese prevalent in America in those days. Any Chinese old enough to remember should know.

Once this point is kept in mind, it should be clear that criticism of survey research because the results do not match scattered anecdotal observations is usually not well informed. Indeed half a century of survey research, initially in America and now expanding at an accelerating rate in Europe, Asia, and Latin America, has demonstrated beyond a doubt the usefulness of this quantitative methodology in studying human behavior and its attitudinal correlates. Its widespread uses in public opinion polling, attitude research, marketing assessment, and mass communication research are among the better known applications. In China itself, many surveys have been conducted since the early 1980s following the opening of China's door to the outside world. Some of the methodological problems and ideological constraints have been discussed by Stanley Rosen and David Chu (1987). On the whole, survey research is regarded positively in China.

The survey methodology has its limitations, just as there are limitations to other research methods such as participant observation and analysis of written materials. Survey research is not free from observer bias, which occurs when one asks a leading question. A competent researcher takes steps to minimize this bias. Indeed the phrasing of a productive question for a field interview is as much an art as science (Cannel and Kahn, 1968). Once a variable is identified, there are different ways of asking questions that will highlight that variable in a way to ensure validity. Clear conceptualization is a must. Simple language is preferred. There must be a common frame of reference between the researcher and the respondent. The question must be phrased in a way that the respondent is able to answer. Each question must tap only a single idea. Pretesting is essential. The prior work of other researchers can help. But much depends on the researcher's own judgment. Experience counts a great deal in survey research, just as research using participant observation depends very much on the experience of the field worker. One crucial point is: If observer bias exists in a survey, it is open to inspection by all other researchers.

Nor is survey research free from respondent bias, comparable to the informant bias we have discussed earlier. This happens when the respondent gives what he thinks is the "correct" answer. Over the years techniques have been developed to minimize this tendency. In explaining the purpose of the survey to the respondents, it is always emphasized that there are no right or wrong answers. The researcher is interested only in what the respondent thinks or feels. Anonymity is assured. Sensitive topics are avoided. Questions are phrased in such a way as to avoid the slightest suggestion of preferred answers. To each question, a variety of response categories is offered to indicate to the respondent that any answer is acceptable. The respondent is also allowed to provide an answer beyond the given alternatives. Projective techniques are used whenever appropriate. Though respondent bias exists in any setting, it can be a particularly serious problem in a society like China, where it is likely to be compounded with the political climate. In our own research we were fully aware of this problem, and believe that we found a way to minimize it. This will be discussed later.

A major strength of survey research is its broad scope of generality. A sample survey seems to be the only feasible way to capture the full range of data variability that exists in any large population. It is also the only way to conduct quantitative measures of covariation as the first step toward establishing causal relations. The use of partial and multivariate analysis reduces the potential spuriousness of the covariation, and the introduction of a time dimension to data analysis further strengthens the validity of causality. Longitudinal surveys using identical questions, such as those Hayashi and his colleagues used in Japan and those asked by Chu and Chi in rural Taiwan, can provide an appropriate and revealing means of documenting concretely the direction and extent of change of cultural values, religious beliefs, social attitudes, work ethic, and family and social relations.

Figure 2.1 Suzhou River runs through metropolitan Shanghai.
(*Photo courtesy of Linus Chao*)

While survey research is particularly suited for measuring behavioral indicators and attitudinal attributes, including values, beliefs, and perceptions, it is typically unable to portray interactional processes. For that, participant observation and the analysis of novels and dramas are far more productive. The study of culture and cultural change must therefore not be limited to any single method. The various methods that we have discussed all have their strengths and limitations, and thus complement each other. The main body of data for this report comes from a sample survey conducted in eastern China as a cooperative research project between East–West Center in Honolulu and Fudan University of Shanghai. As part of the larger project, we were conducting an in-depth study of social and cultural change in one rural community, Qingpu, in which we used a variety of data collection methods, including participant observation, extended interviews with knowledgeable informants, life histories, and analysis of documentary evidence. We were also analyzing a selection of short stories published in China during the period from 1978 to 1987 to throw additional light on the values, aspirations, and agonies of a people caught in a whirlpool of traumatic social and political change. The Qingpu in-depth study and the analysis of short stories will be reported elsewhere. This manuscript covers only the survey findings.

Research Sites and Sampling Procedures

Our research sites were Shanghai, China's largest metropolis with a population of nearly seven million in 1985, and Qingpu, a rural county outside Shanghai. Sometimes referred to as "Paris in the Orient," Shanghai used to be one of the most glamorous cities in Asia. During the war with Japan, many refugees crammed into Shanghai's International Settlement and French Concession, which were off limits to Japanese forces until Pearl Harbor. Most of these refugees stayed after the war ended. After the founding of the People's Republic, Shanghai lost much of its international atmosphere and developed into a huge industrial city. It achieved prominence during the Cultural Revolution as the home base of the Gang of Four. Except for Chairman Mao's wife, Jiang Qing, the three other members of the Gang began their careers in the Party from Shanghai.

Qingpu is one of ten rural counties in the larger Shanghai area. It is situated in the water country of east China, close to the village community where the sociologist Fei Hsiao-tung (1939) did his classic field study just before the Sino–Japanese War. In 1987 it had a population of over 440,000. In economic development, Qingpu occupies a middle ground among the ten counties around Shanghai. Two paved highways now replace the many little canals that for centuries served as Qingpu's main linkages with the outside world. Although agriculture and fishing are still important, the economic basis of Qingpu has been gradually shifting to cottage industries supplying big factories in Shanghai, and in recent years even some limited tourism business. The county seat is in Qingpu Town, first established in 1542 and located about 50 kilometers southwest of Shanghai. It was included in our survey. In addition to the county seat, another town, Zhujiajiao, situated next to scenic Lake Dingshan, was also included in our survey. There are twenty rural districts in Qingpu.

We drew a stratified probability sample of 2,000 respondents, including 1,199 from metropolitan Shanghai, 304 from the two towns in Qingpu, and 497 from twenty villages in four of the twenty rural districts.

There are twelve urban districts in metropolitan Shanghai. The 1985 population figures and the subsample sizes are given in table 2.1.

We did not include Minghang and Wusong in our sample because these two outlying districts were added to metropolitan Shanghai only in recent years and their populations were small. In terms of degree of urbanization they were more like the towns around Shanghai rather than metropolitan Shanghai itself. Transportation costs of getting approximately 50 interviews from these two districts would have been

Figure 2.2 Qingpu County, outside Shanghai, is in China's fabled water country. (*Photo courtesy of Linus Chao*)

Table 2.1 Population and Sample Sizes of Shanghai

DISTRICTS	POPULATION SIZES	SUBSAMPLES
Huangpu	683,700	123
Nanshi	757,400	136
Luwan	480,400	88
Xuhui	658,100	120
Changning	492,000	90
Jingan	496,500	90
Putuo	658,500	120
Zhabei	665,500	118
Hongkou	818,900	146
Yangpu	974,600	168
Minghang	117,500	—
Wusong	179,900	—
Total	6,983,000	1,199

disproportionately high. Since our research objective was not to make a projection of the administrative area of Shanghai, but rather to compare a metropolitan area with small towns and rural villages, we made a decision to draw our sample from the ten old districts only. The sampling ratio in Shanghai was approximately 1 over 5,600.

Relying on personal knowledge of district officials, who were intimately familiar with their districts, we divided the subdistricts of each district into four strata: high, upper middle, lower middle, and low, randomly drawing one subdistrict from each stratum. A subdistrict in China is called *jiedao*, or street committee. A jiedao in China is the lowest urban administrative unit, generally supervising from 10 to 15 neighborhood committees, which are self-administered coordination units. A neighborhood committee may have anywhere from a couple of thousand to as many as ten thousand residents. Cooperation by jiedao officials was required for any type of research. We randomly selected one neighborhood committee from each subdistrict. Since the residential areas within a subdistrict are largely homogeneous in social and economic characteristics, a random selection of one was considered representative. Thus in each district, we began with an initial sample of four neighborhood committees selected from four subdistricts each representing one stratum.

We visited each of the neighborhood committees and obtained the registry of the complete list of the households and individual members within that neighborhood. We excluded those who were under 18 years of age and those who were above 65 years of age. A person reaching 18 is eligible to join the work force. We used 65 as the upper limit because if we return for the follow-up survey five years later this person would be 70 years old. Ten years later he or she would be 75. We divided the subsample size of that district by four to get the number of interviews from each neighborhood committee. In Huangpu, for example, where we intended to interview 123 respondents, we assigned 31 to three neighborhood committees, and 30 to the remaining committee. For each neighborhood committee we randomly drew two lists of 31 each. We would call on the 31 individuals on the first list. If some of them were ill, or out of town, or for other reasons unavailable, we would draw from the second list until we reached 31 respondents. A cadre from the neighborhood committee accompanied us when we called on the respondents.

At this point we considered a major decision regarding the nature of the interview. During the pretest it became apparent that in a personal interview situation most people were reluctant to answer questions which might be considered sensitive. Assurance of anonymity did not seem to alleviate their hesitation. But when they were put in a small group and asked to fill out the questionnaire anonymously on their own, they had no hesitation in giving their rather frank answers. After considerable discussion we decided to use the small group self-administered approach, rather than the personal interview approach. (We have subsequently learned that because of China's political climate, this small group approach is commonly used for assessing public opinion on issues touching on government policies.) The small group approach would assure the respondents of complete anonymity, but we would have to eliminate those who were illiterate or nearly illiterate. The illiteracy rate in the general Shanghai area was estimated at about 10 percent in 1987. We felt that even if we should lose those 10 percent of people, the small group approach would be appropriate because we would be able to get more accurate data.

We thus consulted the neighborhood committeee personnel again and with their help we identified those on our lists who were illiterate. They were removed from our initial lists. Only those who could read were included in our sample. In each neighborhood committee we gathered the respondents in one or two small groups of about 15 to 25 in size. We explained the objectives of the research, the organization of the questionnaire, and the use of check marks to indicate answers. We emphasized that there were no right or wrong answers, and that we wanted to have their honest responses. At each group session one faculty member and one or two graduate students were present to answer questions. The respondents were asked to proceed when all their questions had been answered.

Almost identical procedures were followed in Qingpu Town, which is the county seat, and Zhujiajiao Town, except we went directly to the neighborhood committees. Of the 16 neighborhood committees in Qingpu Town, we took the 8 even number committees. Of the 10 neighborhood committees in Zhujiajiao Town, we took the 5 even number committees. The residential areas in those towns were highly homogeneous and a systematic random sample of half of the neighborhood committees would be representative. From the household registry list we randomly selected two lists of 25 respondents from each neighborhood committee (in Qingpu Town) after we had eliminated those under 18 and those over 65. The neighborhood officials helped us identify and remove the illiterate residents. A total of 25 residents were called from the remaining names in each neighborhood committee. For Qingpu Town, the sample was 201. For Zhujiajiao Town, the sample was 103 (20 to 21 respondents in each neighborhood committee).

From each rural district we randomly chose five villages. In each village we selected 25 respondents by systematic random sampling. Village officials knew each household. In case we had chosen someone

Figure 2.3 Zhujiajiao, one of our research sites in Qingpu, sits on a busy canal. (*Photo courtesy of Linus Chao*)

Figure 2.4 An old village home in Qingpu. Boat is essential for transportation. (*Photo courtesy of Linus Chao*)

who was ill or out of town, this person was skipped and we went to the next person. For the rural districts the sample sizes ranged from 123 to 125, making a total of 497 for the four rural districts. The same procedures for selecting those between 18 and 65, and the same literacy identification by village officials were followed. Because of the literacy requirement, the rural sample was much younger than the urban sample, as we shall see later. Each selected respondent was visited by a village official and invited to participate in this research. Participation was highly enthusiastic in the villages. Even in urban areas the respondents showed great interest in the survey. Many neighborhood committee officials and rural district cadres volunteered to fill out the questionnaire and asked to be informed of the results so that they could compare themselves with people in their areas. In both metropolitan Shanghai and Qingpu County, we gave the respondents a small present as a token of our appreciation.

Sample Composition

We divided the ten districts in Shanghai into two strata. The upper stratum consisted of five districts that previously belonged to the International Settlements (administered by the British), the French Concession, and the Japanese Concession before they were returned to Chinese jurisdiction following the end of World War II. They were: Huangpu, Luwan, Xuhui, Jing'an, and Hongkou. By and large these districts used to have better roads, more convenient transportation facilities, more adequate water supply, and better housing. Most residential areas in these districts had modern toilet facilities. The lower stratum consisted of five districts that had traditionally been under Chinese administration even before World War II. They were: Nanse, Changning, Putuo, Chapei, and Yangpu.

We compared the two strata in metropolitan Shanghai with the towns and villages in Qingpu County according to average monthly income of household members (table 2.2). This figure was reported by the respondents as the total income of the household divided by the number of individuals in the household. Average monthly income was measured at five levels: below 59 yuan, 60–89 yuan, 90–119 yuan, 120–149 yuan, 150 yuan and above. For cross-tabulations, we classified the total sample into three groups: 20.1 percent with average monthly income below Y59, 46.2 percent from Y60 to Y89, and 33.7 percent earning Y90 and above.

Even though there have been newspaper stories and anecdotes about the so-called Y10,000 families in rural areas, that is, rural fami-

Table 2.2 Income in Urban and Rural Areas

	HIGH SHANGHAI	LOW SHANGHAI	QINGPU	VILLAGES
Y59 and below	9.9%	11.4%	21.1%	41.9%
Y60–89	51.0%	47.5%	47.4%	38.2%
Above Y90	39.2%	41.1%	31.6%	19.9%
Total Cases	567	632	304	497

Chi-Sq. = 222.1   D.F. = 6   p < .001

lies now earning more than Y10,000 a year under the new agricultural production policies, we found the average income in the villages to be far below the level in the cities. While only about one in ten families in Shanghai had an average monthly income below Y59, the corresponding figure was as high as 41.9 percent in the villages. The two towns in Qingpu were in between, at 21.1 percent. On the other hand, approximately four in ten families in Shanghai reported an average monthly income of Y90 and above, but only two in ten families in the villages had income that high. There is no question that even in the general Shanghai area, where many opportunities exist for villagers to earn extra money by selling their produce at the open market in the city, the income of rural people is way below that of the urban residents.

What was most interesting, and a surprise even to our Chinese colleagues, was the finding that the "higher" and "lower" strata in Shanghai were about even as far as their average income was concerned. If anything, people in what was previously the lower stratum reported a slightly higher average income than people in the higher stratum. It is quite clear that the egalitarian wage policy adopted in China since 1949 has eliminated the class-based income differentiation of the old society.

The urban versus rural disparity was even more pronounced in terms of education. Even though we had eliminated the illiterates from our sample, the educational level of the village subsample was much lower than those of Shanghai and Qingpu towns. Education was measured at seven levels: no schooling, some elementary schooling, elementary school graduation, junior high school graduation, senior high school graduation, college graduation, and graduate school completion. For purpose of cross-tabulations, we classified the respondents into three educational levels: 22.9 percent low (8.9 percent up to some

Figure 2.5 Traditional farming has not changed much.
(*Photo courtesy of Linus Chao*)

elementary school and 13.9 percent elementary school graduation), 38.4 percent middle (junior high school), and 38.7 percent high (28.3 percent senior high school and 10.4 percent college). Even in villages in the general Shanghai area, where the level of education was considered higher than much of the rest of the country, as many as 47.9 percent of the rural respondents were in the low group, compared to 23.7 percent in Qingpu towns and about 12 percent in Shanghai. On the other hand, more than half of the Shanghai respondents versus only 9.1 percent of the rural respondents were in the high education group (table 2.3). Again the higher and lower strata in Shanghai were quite close in their educational levels. Because of the homogeneity of the two former strata, we combined all ten districts in Shanghai into one subsample for further analysis.

Age was measured at six levels: below 20 years old, 20–29, 30–39, 40–49, 50–59, 60–65. As we have explained before, we did not include in our sample anyone above 65 years of age. For cross-tabulations, we divided our sample into three age groups: younger group (29 years old and below), middle age group (30 to 49), and older group (50 to 65). As we included only those who were literate in our sample, the rural subsample was much younger than their urban counterparts. While fewer than one in five in the Shanghai sample was in the younger age

Table 2.3 Education in Urban and Rural Areas

	HIGH SHANGHAI	LOW SHANGHAI	QINGPU	VILLAGES
Low	11.6%	13.1%	23.7%	47.9%
Medium	32.6%	37.7%	43.4%	43.1%
High	55.7%	49.2%	32.9%	9.1%
Total Cases	567	632	304	497

Chi-Sq. = 385.3   D.F. = 6 p < .001

bracket, as many as 44.3 percent of the rural respondents were in that group. In the Shanghai subsample, over one third were 50 years old and above, as compared to only 6.2 percent in the village subsample (table 2.4). Obviously this was because many of the older rural people were illiterates and had been excluded from our sample. The two towns in Qingpu were in between. Just slightly more than half of the total sample were men (52.8 percent), and 47.2 percent were women. The females in the sample were slightly younger than the males (table 2.5). The reason that the females were just under 50 percent and a little bit younger than the males, we think, is because we eliminated the illiterates, and there were slightly more older females who were illiterate. There were no statistically significant differences in gender in the urban and rural areas (table 2.6).

Age was closely related to education (table 2.7). Of those up to 29 years of age, only 11.2 percent were in the low education group, while 44.3 percent had gone to senior high school and above. This finding indicates the considerable success of China's programs in popular education within the Shanghai area. Even among those 50 years old and above, only about one third was in the low education group, with the remaining respondents almost evenly divided between the middle and the high education group. We need to bear in mind that these findings apply only to the literate population.

While the younger people are better educated, it is the older people who reported more average earnings in their families (table 2.8). Of those 29 years of age and below, 21.6 percent reported an average monthly income under Y59, as compared to only 8.7 percent in the 50-65 age-group. More than half of the older people reported an average monthly income of Y90 and above. The corresponding figure among the younger group was 30.8 percent. The middle-aged group was in

Table 2.4 Age Distributions in Urban and Rural Areas

	HIGH SHANGHAI	LOW SHANGHAI	QINGPU	VILLAGES
Below 29	18.5%	16.5%	26.6%	44.3%
30–49	47.4%	48.6%	56.6%	49.5%
50–65	34.0%	35.0%	16.8%	6.2%
Total Cases	567	632	304	497

Chi-Sq. = 225.8   D.F. = 6 p < .001

Table 2.5 Gender and Age Distributions

	MALE	FEMALE
Below 29	23.7%	27.6%
30–49	52.1%	47.1%
50–65	24.2%	25.3%
Total Cases	1056	942

Chi-Sq. = 6.1   D.F. = 2 p < .05

Table 2.6 Gender Distributions in Urban and Rural Areas

	HIGH SHANGHAI	LOW SHANGHAI	QINGPU	VILLAGES
Male	52.2%	51.4%	51.3%	56.3%
Female	47.8%	48.6%	48.7%	43.7%
Total Cases	567	632	304	497

Chi-Sq. = 2.8   D.F. = 3 n.s.

between. One possible explanation is that young people are likely to have small children, and this will bring down the average income. Even allowing this possibility, the data clearly show that older people have much more disposable income in their families, perhaps a reflection of the weight of seniority in China's wage system.

Table 2.7 Education in Different Age Groups

	BELOW 29	30–49	50–65
Low	11.2%	22.9%	35.1%
Medium	44.5%	38.7%	31.7%
High	44.3%	38.3%	33.3%
Total Cases	510	994	496

Chi-Sq. = 80.5   D.F. = 4 p < .001

Table 2.8 Income in Different Age Groups

	BELOW 29	30–49	50–65
Y59 and below	21.6%	24.8%	8.7%
Y60–89	47.6%	48.7%	39.5%
Above Y90	30.8%	26.5%	51.8%
Total Cases	510	994	496

Chi-Sq. = 116.5   D.F. = 4 p < .001

Higher education does not appear to contribute to higher income. When we cross-tabulated education with income, there was initially a close relationship (table 2.9). Of those in the high education group, only 11.8 percent reported average monthly income of Y59 and below. The corresponding low income percentage rose to 21.7 percent in the middle education group, and 30.9 percent in the low education group. Nearly four in ten in the high education group had an average monthly income of Y90 and above, as compared to only 27.9 percent in the low education group. These findings, however, are largely due to the fact that people in rural areas had lower education and lower income. When we analyzed the data separately for Shanghai, Qingpu towns, and the villages, there was no significant relationship between education and income. The egalitarian wage policy in China apparently does not give special consideration to high education.

Traditionally very few Chinese women learned to read, a reflection of a Chinese belief that lack of knowledge was a source of virtue for women. Only men were allowed to take the state examinations.

Table 2.9 Income in Different Educational Groups

	LOW	MEDIUM	HIGH
Y59 and below	30.9%	21.7%	11.8%
Y60–89	41.2%	46.6%	48.7%
Above Y90	27.9%	31.7%	39.5%
Total Cases	459	769	772

Chi-Sq. = 69.2   D.F. = 4 p < .001

Traditional schools, whether in towns or villages, enrolled only boys who learned Confucian classics. This discrimination against women in education was abolished after the Chinese republic was established in 1912, but real change proceeded rather slowly. Even in big cities very few girls went beyond high school. The first major breakthrough came during the Sino–Japanese War (1937–1945) when many teenage boys and girls left home to join the war effort in the interior and enrolled in state universities and colleges. Statistics for those days were not avail-

Figure 2.6 University co-ed dorm—eight girls sharing one room. (*Photo courtesy of Linus Chao*)

able, but perhaps no more than 15 to 20 percent of college students were women. The situation today is very different. We found that the gender disparity in education had greatly diminished (table 2.10). The percentages of men (21.8 percent) and women (24.2 percent) in the lower education group were close. There were more women (42.3 percent) than men (35 percent) in the middle education group, and more men (43.2 percent) than women (33.5 percent) in the higher education group. By and large men still had a higher level of education, but the differences were no longer as lopsided as they used to be.

We sense the magnitude of social change in just one generation when we compare the levels of education of our respondents with those of their fathers and mothers. In the general Shanghai area, the rates of illiteracy (among those 12 years old and above) was dropping from 20.91 percent in 1964 to 14.36 percent in 1982. Within a span of eight years, with the passing of the older generation, the rate of illiteracy was cut by 6.5 percent. Assuming that the same trend has continued, the illiteracy rate in Shanghai in 1987 would be about 10 percent. Because we have excluded the illiterates from our sample, we can approximately reconstruct the educational distributions in Shanghai in 1987 by including 10 percent illiterates for both men and women and giving a weight of .90 to the existing percentages in the sample. We compared the weighted distributions of education of our respondents with the educational levels of their fathers and mothers based on reports by the respondents. The results are presented in table 2.11.

Although the 10 percent estimate of illiteracy was for the general population in the Shanghai area, and the rate among women in 1987 would be higher, perhaps 14 or 15 percent, it would certainly be nowhere near the 54.7 percent illiteracy a generation ago. Whereas one generation ago only 4.7 percent of the women had attended senior high school, the corresponding figure now was 23.6 percent, five times as

Table 2.10 Gender and Education Distributions

	MALE	FEMALE
Low	21.8%	24.2%
Medium	35.0%	42.3%
High	43.2%	33.5%
Total Cases	1056	942

Chi-Sq. = 21.5   D.F. = 2 p < .001

high. The improvement of education among men was almost as impressive as among women.

In terms of occupation, nearly three out of four respondents in rural villages were engaged in agricultural work as one would expect (table 2.12). Indicative of the trends of social change in that part of China was the finding that nearly 8 percent of the rural respondents were working in village factories. In metropolitan Shanghai and

Table 2.11 Comparison of Education of Men and Women with Their Parents

	MEN	WOMEN	FATHERS	MOTHERS
Illiterates	10.0%	10.0%	25.7%	54.7%
Some primary school	7.6%	8.5%	22.6%	17.8%
Primary School graduates	11.8%	13.0%	21.3%	12.5%
Junior High	31.4%	38.4%	15.7%	8.5%
Senior High	27.2%	23.6%	8.7%	4.7%
College	12.0%	6.5%	6.0%	1.8%
Total	100.0%	100.0%	100.0%	100.0%

Table 2.12 Occupations in Urban and Rural Areas

	SHANGHAI	QINGPU	VILLAGES
Agriculture	.5%	1.7%	73.2%
Business	7.5%	17.2%	1.9%
Office	11.7%	11.9%	4.7%
Factory	31.6%	35.3%	7.7%
Education	13.6%	11.6%	.8%
Political	7.5%	9.9%	2.2%
Retired	21.0%	6.9%	1.1%
Self-employ	.9%	1.7%	4.4%
Other	5.7%	4.0%	3.9%
Total Cases	1199	304	497

Chi-Sq. = 1332.4   D.F. = 16 p < .001

Qingpu towns the largest occupational category was factory work, which comprised more than 30 percent of the respondents. Many respondents in Shanghai (21 percent) were retired, largely due to the early retirement age for women at 55 versus 60 for men. The rural respondents were much younger. As farmers they were not on government payroll and were not bound by the official retirement age. In Qingpu towns, some (17.2 percent) were engaged in small business and thus were less affected by the retirement age requirement.

We see clearly that agricultural work generated much lower income (table 2.13) than other types of work. Otherwise, no particular line of work provided unusually high income. This is clearly an outcome of the egalitarian wage policy in China. An interesting finding is that retired people, mostly in metropolitan Shanghai, were living on a fairly good income. Generally, older people in China who are retired have adult children living with them, and therefore the average family income would be quite high. By and large, farmers had a lower educational level, while office workers, political cadres, and school teachers had higher levels of education (table 2.14).

A rather striking finding was the nearly equal occupational status of men and women (table 2.15). This may be considered one of the

Table 2.13 Occupation and Income Distributions

	Y59 AND BELOW	Y60–89	ABOVE Y90
Agriculture	38.2%	10.6%	7.5%
Business	5.3%	9.4%	7.6%
Office	8.6%	11.3%	10.1%
Factory	25.3%	31.0%	24.3%
Education	5.8%	11.4%	12.8%
Political	5.6%	6.4%	8.2%
Retired	5.3%	13.1%	22.4%
Self-employ	2.5%	1.5%	1.6%
Other	3.3%	5.3%	5.6%
Total Cases	400	923	677

Chi-Sq. = 246.6   D.F. = 16 $p < .001$

distinctive accomplishments of the occupational structural change introduced in China since 1949. Women and men in our sample were gainfully employed to the same extent. More men worked in factories and held political jobs than women, while more women worked as school teachers. Because of the different retirement ages, more women were retired. Otherwise, there were hardly any differences in occupations between men and women.

Figure 2.7 A villager making clay tiles in a traditional way. (*Photo courtesy of Linus Chao*)

Table 2.14 Occupation and Education Distributions

	LOW	MEDIUM	HIGH
Agriculture	35.4%	15.1%	3.6%
Business	6.9%	10.8%	5.9%
Office	4.5%	9.4%	14.4%
Factory	16.1%	36.6%	25.4%
Education	1.2%	3.7%	22.5%
Political	3.7%	4.3%	11.0%
Retired	25.5%	14.0%	9.9%
Self-employ	3.5%	1.9%	.7%
Other	3.2%	4.3%	6.7%
Total Cases	459	769	772

Chi-Sq. = 516.6   D.F. = 16 $p < .001$

Table 2.15 Occupation and Gender Distributions

	MALE	FEMALE
Agriculture	15.2%	14.2%
Business	7.0%	9.1%
Office	10.4%	10.4%
Factory	29.3%	25.7%
Education	9.4%	12.4%
Political	9.6%	3.8%
Retired	10.5%	19.8%
Self-employ	3.1%	.1%
Other	5.5%	4.5%
Total Cases	1056	942

Chi-Sq. = 84.0   D.F. = 8 $p < .001$

Age differences (table 2.16) reveal a trend of social change unfolding under China's new economic policy. Many of the farmers were young because of the way the rural sample was chosen under the literacy requirement. More than half of those above 50 were retired, as expected. Thus fewer older people were found in the active occupational categories. Other than those obvious differences, what is inter-

Figure 2.8 A fisherwoman in Qingpu. Economic independence has given rural Chinese women a new social status.
(*Photo courtesy of Linus Chao*)

Table 2.16 Occupation and Age Distributions

	BELOW 29	30–49	50–65
Agriculture	23.7%	16.2%	4.3%
Business	10.2%	8.6%	4.9%
Office	10.2%	14.4%	2.6%
Factory	33.0%	33.7%	11.2%
Education	7.0%	12.5%	10.8%
Political	2.6%	8.8%	6.9%
Retired	.5%	.3%	55.2%
Self-employ	3.5%	1.2%	1.2%
Other	9.3%	4.2%	2.9%
Total Cases	510	994	496

Chi-Sq. = 968.9   D.F. = 16   p < .001

esting is a rather clear trend of fewer young people entering a political career and more of them getting into small business or making a living through self-employment. More young people were in the "other" category, which included students and those without a job who were waiting for work.

Survey Instrument

The survey instrument consisted of 185 questions, some having as many as 11 sub-items. Altogether there were 360 items. Most of the questions had multiple choice answers. A few were open-ended, and the responses were content-analyzed for tabulations. On average it took slightly less than two hours for respondents to answer a complete questionnaire. Some finished in one hour and a half, but a few took as long as three hours. The faculty supervisors and graduate assistants stayed until everyone had finished. The supervisors checked the answers for completeness. In case some questions were skipped, the respondents were asked to fill them in, unless they preferred not to answer. After that, the questionnaires were scrambled to guarantee complete anonymity. Very few questions were unanswered.

The questions were organized into three sections that were considered to be most readily comprehensible to local government officials who had to approve the survey, and to the respondents who answered the questions. The first section was on family life, which most people would have no difficulty answering. Extensive surveys of this kind had never been attempted in the Shanghai area before. Asking questions about family life first seemed to be an appropriate way to get the respondents sufficiently interested and motivated to complete the questionnaire. Next was a section on work within an organization. Except for the very old who had retired, nearly everybody was employed by some organization. So questions about job performance and its relationship to an organization were highly relevant. By that time, the respondents were already comfortable with the questionnaire format. The last section pertained to society. These were more difficult questions about goals in life, values, religion, meaning of life, concept of success, community participation, and economic reform, ending with a section on the use of mass media.

The survey instrument was developed following a lengthy process. Because no such extensive survey of Chinese culture had ever been undertaken, we had to start almost from scratch. Godwin Chu had done a survey of Chinese culture in villages in northern Taiwan, but it covered only a few aspects of village life. Villages in northern Taiwan were quite different from the social and economic system in China. Thus in June of 1987, a workshop was convened at the East–West Center in Honolulu to prepare a first draft of the Chinese survey instrument. The workshop was attended by Francis Hsu, an anthropologist, Ambrose King, a sociologist in Hong Kong, Anthony Yu, who has done extensive work on religion in China, and Wang Gungwu, a historian in Hong Kong. All are extremely knowledgeable about traditional Chinese society and culture and well informed about major events in China over the last four decades. Steve Chaffee, a survey researcher with many years of experience who had done no prior work on China, joined to provide a fresh perspective and offer methodological advice. Chu served as coordinator. The group took a survey instrument developed by Chu and his Thai colleagues for a study of cultural change in Thailand in 1986 and deleted questions that seemed to be irrelevant to contemporary China. They then constructed new items that covered important elements of traditional Chinese culture as well as new features introduced since the founding of the People's Republic in 1949.

Chu took this first draft to Shanghai in July 1987. He and his colleagues at Fudan University, including Ju Yanan, critically examined the draft. Some items were deleted, others revised, and new items were added. After several rounds of revisions, a second draft was prepared which was quite different from the first draft developed in Honolulu. This draft was then given a pretest by Fudan faculty members through personal interviews with 30 respondents in Shanghai and 20 respondents in one village. The reactions of the respondents were recorded in detail. This was when Fudan faculty members discovered that personal interviews were not workable and experimented with the small group approach. The pretest results were brought to Honolulu by Ju Yanan for review. On the basis of the pretest results, the survey instrument was revised again. A number of questions were either deleted or simplified. It was during this review session that a decision was made to use the small group approach rather than individual personal interviews. A major improvement was the inclusion of 18 traditional Chinese values. It was felt that while many questions addressed Chinese cultural values in concrete terms, we needed a more concise assessment of value changes. With the help of Tu Weiming, a Confucian scholar from Harvard, we developed a scale of 18 traditional values. The second draft was taken back to Shanghai for another review, and was used as the final survey instrument with only a few minor changes in wording.

While various attitudinal scales were available, we did not use any of them for our survey largely because few of them were considered relevant to the Chinese people. Also the general scaling format of asking whether a respondent strongly agrees, agrees, has no opinion, disagrees or strongly disagrees to a generalized statement sounded odd and artificial when rendered into Chinese. At any rate people in China were not used to this type of survey technique. In general we followed a technique developed by Chu (1964) from his interview experiences among rural respondents in Taiwan.

First, inasmuch as possible we phrased our questions in concrete behavioral terms, rather than abstract statements. Next, instead of presenting a statement, such as "Children have an obligation to look after their aging parents," and then asking whether the respondent agrees or disagrees, we turned it into a simple question that contained two realistic alternatives: "Do you think children should look after their aging parents, or do you think parents should take care of themselves?" This way the respondents would not feel obligated to say yes. Unless we wanted to force them to make a difficult choice, as we occasionally did, we allowed "it depends" as a third alternative, and asked the respondent to elaborate. These questions were made as relevant as possible to the Chinese reality.

To measure cultural values, we used a variety of techniques. Sometimes we used vignette-type questions, asking the respondents to place themselves in a hypothetical situation and indicate what they would do. Other times we listed a number of options that were all desirable in some way, and asked the respondents to choose no more than two, three or five, depending on the question. In our traditional value scale, we presented to the respondents a list of traditional Chinese values, and asked which ones they were proud of and which ones they would want to see discarded, or whether they were not sure. Sometimes, we presented a commonly known Chinese cultural characteristic, and asked how important the respondents considered it to be. A few items were adapted from surveys of Japanese national character conducted under the direction of Chikio Hayashi of the Institute of Mathematical Statistics in Tokyo. Respondents' use of mass media was measured by their frequency of reading, listening and viewing, and by the categories of the media content used.

Perhaps because the questions addressed real life issues made easily comprehensible, the interest on the part of the respondents was unusually high. The respondents were serious in answering these questions. When the faculty supervisors and graduate assistants walked by them during the sessions, they would cover up their answers. As we have mentioned earlier, local government officials were extremely interested in this survey, and many asked to fill out the questionnaire themselves so that they would know where they stood on these issues in comparison to the general findings.

Data Generality

In our data presentation we considered the question of weighting but decided against it. Metropolitan Shanghai is not completely representative of other big cities in China. The small towns and villages in the larger Shanghai area are much more prosperous and have greater access to urban markets and other facilities than many other small towns and villages in other parts of China. Since our objective was to select a sample with sufficient variability for statistical analysis, rather than as a representative of the Chinese population, it would be inappropriate to project the findings from the Shanghai area to China as a whole. Weighting the percentages from our survey in Shanghai by adjusting the data according to proportions of urban and rural residents in the Chinese population at large would therefore not be justifiable. In this monograph we present the data as they are without weighting.

The overall percentages of answers to a particular question by respondents in metropolitan Shanghai, small towns, and villages need to be viewed with this perspective in mind. However, this does not mean that our findings have no general implication to areas outside eastern China. Rather, we would argue that they do have considerable generality for the majority of Chinese people who are of Han origin. There are several reasons. First, through a long historical process of assimilation Chinese people of Han origin have become highly homogeneous. Regardless of their geographical and dialectic dispersions, they share many common customs, values, and beliefs.

Two episodes illustrate this point. During the war with Japan, many people in the Shanghai area followed the government and migrated to Chongqing, the wartime capital in the upper reaches of the Yangtze River. The dialects were very different, and there were petty quarrels due to conflicts between natives and outsiders. But the Shanghai migrants and the Chongqing natives shared almost identical ways of life. They observed the same festivals and followed the same rituals for childbirth, ancestor worship, marriage, and funeral. In contemporary China there are two classic studies of Chinese culture, one by the sociologist Fei Hsiao-tung and the other by the anthropologist Francis Hsu. Fei did his study in a fairly prosperous rural community not far from Shanghai just before the war with Japan. Hsu did his anthropological fieldwork during the war in a rather backward rural community in Yunnan, a border region in Southwest China. In terms of economic standing and access to modern facilities, the two communities were very different. But the way of life, as analyzed by Fei and Hsu, was again very much the same.

The homogeneity of Chinese culture today not only has a historical root, but seems to be reinforced by the rather drastic measures of revolutionary structural change which have been introduced in a highly uniform manner since the founding of the People's Republic in 1949. In the vast rural areas, beginning in the early 1950s, whether it was the agrarian land reform, the mutual aid movement, the agricultural cooperatives, or the People's Communes of 1958, these structural changes were rigidly enforced throughout the country. If the policy was to "cut the tails of capitalism," meaning to disallow the smallest deviation from state-directed collective agricultural production plans, then every village, no matter where it was located, must "cut the tails of capitalism." In urban areas, following the total takeover of private enterprises during the Public–Private Joint Management movement of 1956, all industries and businesses were operated by the state whether they were in big cities like Shanghai or large towns. Only in recent years have some small private businesses been allowed, and only on a very limited scale. In short, to the extent that these revolutionary changes have had an impact on Chinese culture, their impact has been felt rather similarly throughout the country.

Another source of the homogeneity of contemporary Chinese culture is the tightly controlled, ever-present Chinese mass media, operated entirely by the Party. Every rural village, no matter how remote, is connected to the state-wide mass media system by wired broadcasting. Public speakers are set up in village squares and offices, as well as connected to many peasant homes, to broadcast a variety of music, news from the official Xinhua News Agency, and public announcements. In recent years these speakers have been augmented by transistor radios, and where electricity is available, by television. Every village office has a copy of the official *People's Daily*. In towns and cities, newspapers are readily available, including the *People's Daily* and provincial or municipal papers. Radio, and now television, have reached all towns and cities where electricity is available. While each individual medium has its unique technical characteristics, the basic message is largely the same. The impact of this overwhelming amount of information is felt all over China.

Because of these factors, some historical and others structural or media-related, we believe that what we have found in urban Shanghai and small towns and villages in eastern China does reflect, with some qualifications, the general dimensions of contemporary Chinese culture elsewhere in China. We expect urban Shanghai to be somewhat similar to most other big cities in China. The two towns we surveyed will approximately represent small cities and towns elsewhere. Where we find major differences between Shanghai and adjacent villages, we would expect villages in more remote areas to depart still further. We want to make clear that we are not suggesting that the descriptive findings from this survey can be taken as typical of China as a whole. We do suggest, however, that our findings allow us to gain a valid overall picture, in a general but not a literal sense, of what contemporary Chinese culture looks like, especially when it markedly deviates from what we know about traditional Chinese culture.

Other than descriptive findings broken down by urban versus rural residency, we performed correlational analyses with demographic factors and media influence variables. Given our probability sample covering a wide spectrum of respondent characteristics, the results of these correlational analyses can be validly projected to the literate Chinese population at large. If we find that people of high education differ widely from people of low education in Shanghai with respect to some cultural values, we expect such differences to hold in other areas as well. Because we have included only those who were literate, our sample was somewhat curtailed as far as education was concerned. This curtailment of sampling distribution will tend to lower the degree of correlation between cultural variables and education, and indirectly any other variables associated with education. In this sense, the correlations we report in this study will be conservative estimates of what we might find in the population as a whole.

Longitudinal and Correlational Analysis

We follow two strategies of data analysis in our study of cultural change in China. First we want to show, after we have had an opportunity to conduct a follow-up survey ten years later, whether there are concrete changes in the various dimensions of Chinese culture, and whether the directions and rates of change are different in the three types of residential environments. Perhaps some changes are more noticeable in metropolitan Shanghai while with other cultural values the villages move ahead at a faster pace. Also we want to demonstrate whether varying rates of changes can be traced among people of different age and educational levels, and among men and women. These are empirical questions for which we have no clear hypotheses as yet. This type of analysis will be done after the longitudinal before-and-after surveys have been completed.

For the benchmark survey itself, we focus on another perspective of data analysis. Beginning with the survey data now, we look back to our general understanding about traditional China and ask in what ways our empirical assessment of contemporary Chinese culture represents a change from its traditional past. Furthermore, we analyze the ways in which respondents of different educational and income levels and from different age groups and different urban and rural settings vary in different cultural values, beliefs, and social relations at this moment. We examine the manner in which attitudes of men are different from those of women.

Education and income are major demographic variables generally introduced for cross-tabulations in survey research. People of higher education generally have a perspective of life different from people of lower education. Income variations may represent different outlooks to opportunities and constraints in a changing society.

People at different stages of the life circle can be expected to have somewhat different values and goals. This is generally true in any society. But age in China has a special significance. Because the last four decades in China have been marked by extraordinary events, such as the Cultural Revolution, which placed many people in traumatic and painful situations, people in various age groups have had vastly different exposures to such events. As a result they may be responding to the revolutionary changes in the sociopolitical environment in remarkably different ways.

Figure 2.9 A street in Shanghai. Banner ad sells washing machines now used in many Shanghai homes. (*Photo courtesy of Linus Chao*)

Gender is an important factor because of the greatly improved roles of women in Chinese society. We have already seen the enormous advancement in education among Chinese women today compared to their mothers. Another major difference is found in their occupational roles. Before 1949 very few women had a job outside their homes. Today, whether in cities or villages, men and women are engaged in productive work almost on an equal basis, although most of the senior positions are still held by men.

Urban residency in China has a unique significance not usually found in other developing countries. We see urbanization, in this case the experience of living in metropolitan Shanghai, as a far broader experience than being a resident in a congested city contrasted to an inhabitant in a sparsely populated rural setting. We recognize that living in metropolitan Shanghai means better educational opportunities, more stable income as a wage earner than a rural land tiller, and easier access to mass media. But urban living in China also means something else. It provides better access to modern facilities such as running water, flush toilet, and mass transit transportation. It also offers a different kind of social environment characterized by less personal relations and more interaction with people of diverse backgrounds, more rapid diffusion of innovative ideas and greater room for deviance from

Figure 2.10 A village ferry provides the only connection with Quinpu Town. Slogan says: "Happily go to work. Safely return home." (*Photo courtesy of Linus Chao*)

traditions because peer group pressure tends to be mitigated by a buffer of impersonal surroundings. It creates more opportunities for upward mobility beyond what is available in rural villages, and therefore more intense competition. These are among the characteristics which distinguish an urban setting from a rural one. When we compare metropolitan Shanghai with small towns and villages over and beyond education, income, and media exposure, we are casting all these differences, some identifiable and some not, into our comparison. We are simply using the urban–rural dimension in a very broad sense as a "locator variable," much as age and sex are treated in social research. Just as age does not refer to the actual number of years a person is physically living, and just as sex does not refer to merely biological differences, we treat urbanization as that whole range of characteristics that is significant but not completely identifiable. Following this broader perspective, if we find a clear relation between urbanization and a cultural value, it tells us something about urban living that is more than education, income and mass media exposure.

If such a significant relation is found, can we then assume a direction of casuality between urbanization and certain cultural values? Normally in most developing countries we cannot. If people who live in urban areas are different from rural villagers, it is possible that some of them are different in the first place and they simply are attracted in large numbers to move to urban areas. This is a phenomenon one finds in many developing countries, where large scale migrations of rural villagers into urban centers are accelerating. But this is not the situation in China. For a span of two generations since the founding of the People's Republic, the government in China has imposed a strict ban on physical mobility to other residential areas. Some of the urban residents, largely students and public servants, are now and then transferred to rural areas and small towns for job assignment and permanent settlement. But rural villagers and small town residents are not allowed to move to urban areas. With very few exceptions the residents in Shanghai, Qingpu, and the villages have been living where they are, literally in the same housing units because of a housing shortage, during their entire lives. This situation approximates what may be considered a quasi-experimental treatment. People are permanently assigned, by birth, to live in a certain environment. They have been exposed to different social and physical environments throughout their lives. We may therefore observe the behavioral and attitudinal consequences of living in either an urban or a rural setting, and impute a causality to the broad but different living environments.

Roles of Communication

In addition to these demographic factors, we are interested in the roles of communication in bringing about cultural change in China. One type of communication refers to the massive political campaigns launched under the tutelage of Mao Zedong, especially during the ten years of the Cultural Revolution. These campaigns started as early as the summer of 1957 during the Anti-rightist movement right after the abortive Hundred Flowers movement in that spring. They represented Mao's main effort to change the ideological foundation of Chinese culture. The concerted uses of all communication channels, including the communication media, mass campaigns, organizational networks, and small group criticism sessions have been analyzed by Berstein (1977, 1979), Cell (1977, 1984), Chang (1979), Chu (1977, 1979), Dittmer (1979), Goldman (1979), Lieberthal (1984), Liu (1975), Parish (1979), Whyte (1974, 1979), and Yu (1964, 1967). In our survey we were not able to include questions on such political communication campaigns for two reasons. First, these campaigns ended with the death of Mao in 1976, more than ten years before we conducted our survey. Second, we decided not to ask any politically sensitive questions in order to facilitate the review of our survey instrument by local authorities.

For data interpretation on the impact of communication on cultural change, we relied on variables considered to be associated with the respondents' participation in these communication campaigns. First is age. People who were 29 years of age and below at the time we conducted our survey were too young to be affected by the peak of the Cultural Revolution. Someone who was 29 in 1987 was only eight years old when the Cultural Revolution started in 1966. Second is the urban vs. rural dichotomy. Generally speaking, those living in urban centers such as Shanghai were more severely affected by these communication campaigns than those residing in rural villages (Barnett 1979). Education could be a third factor, as these campaigns were by and large directed more at those of higher education. We keep these factors in mind in our data interpretation.

In our survey we specifically measured two sources of influence on Chinese culture that seem to be particularly relevant in this age of rapid communication. One has to do with access to current news information from the official mass media, including newspapers, radio, and television. Because of the mass media's extensive reach into the life of nearly everyone, including the rapid expansion of television in the reform years, these official information sources may have an effect in redefining the perceptual fields of Chinese people and therefore leave an impact on their values, goals, and beliefs. The other source of influence stems from exposure to Western ideas and lifestyle as presented in television, radio and movies in the last ten years since China opened its door to the world outside in 1978. During the 30 years from 1949 till 1978, American movies and television programs were totally banned in China. This ban was lifted when Deng Xiaoping assumed power and introduced his economic reform programs in 1978. American movies, such as Sound of Music, and television programs, such as Hunter, are carefully screened by the Chinese authorities before they are presented to the general audience. Regardless of their specific contents, however, they still present a lifestyle and a degree of affluence very much different from what the Chinese people are used to experiencing in their own surroundings. We want to know whether people who have greater access to official news information and people who are more heavily exposed to Western cultural influence through the mass media are different from others in their values and attitudes.

To measure the use of news information, we have constructed an index consisting of four items: (1) reading national events and (2) reading world events in newspapers, (3) watching major domestic news and (4) watching world news on television. Each item was measured by a 5-point scale: a lot, some, not much, very little, and not at all. In Chinese language, "some" was clearly understood to be more than "not much." A person was given a score of 1 each if he (or she) reads "a lot" of national events (37.6 percent) and world events (27.1 percent) in the newspapers, and watches "a lot" of major domestic news (52.3 percent) and world news (46.4 percent) on television. As we see, people get more news information from television than from newspapers, and more people learn about domestic events than world events. The media information scale had scores from 0 to 4. As it turned out, 32.5 percent of the sample had a score of 0, that is, they did not get a lot of news information about either national or world events from either newspapers or television. The remainder of the sample was distributed as follows: 16 percent (scored 1), 20.8 percent (2), 17.2 percent (3), and 13.6 percent (4). About one out of seven got a lot of national and world news from both newspapers and television. The media information scale had a reliability (alpha) coefficient of .73.

The media information index was significantly related to gender, education, urbanization, and age (multiple R = .27, p < .001). Those more heavily exposed to official news information are more likely to be men, better educated, living in Shanghai and towns in Qinpgu, and somewhat younger (tables 2.17 to 2.20).

For Western cultural influence, we selected four items covering television, radio, and movies. Items about television and radio were measured by a 5-point scale: a lot, some, not much, very little, and not at all. A person was given a score of 1 each if he (or she) watches "a lot" of Western films (26.6 percent), watches "a lot" of Western dance shows on television (6.5 percent), listens to Western music "a lot" on radio (11.8 percent), and prefers Western movies (38.2 percent), mostly Hollywood films, to Chinese movies. For movies, we asked about their

Table 2.17 Gender and Use of News Media Information

		MALE	FEMALE
Low Use	0	26.9%	38.7%
	1	14.6%	17.5%
	2	20.1%	21.5%
	3	19.6%	14.4%
High Use	4	18.8%	7.7%
Total Cases		1056	942

Chi-Sq. = 77.5   D.F. = 4 p < .001

Table 2.18 Education and Use of News Media Information

		LOW	MEDIUM	HIGH
Low Use	0	40.5%	32.5%	27.7%
	1	19.4%	17.4%	12.6%
	2	20.9%	20.0%	21.4%
	3	11.3%	18.1%	19.7%
High Use	4	7.8%	12.0%	18.7%
Total Cases		459	769	772

Chi-Sq. = 64.4   D.F. = 8 p < .001

Table 2.19 Use of News Media Information in Urban and Rural Areas

		SHANGHAI	QINGPU	VILLAGES
Low Use	0	30.4%	31.3%	38.2%
	1	13.6%	14.5%	22.7%
	2	21.4%	23.0%	17.7%
	3	18.7%	18.1%	12.9%
High Use	4	15.8%	13.2%	8.5%
Total Cases		1199	304	497

Chi-Sq. = 50.1   D.F. = 8 p < .001

preference as something stronger than just exposure. The Western cultural influence scale also had scores from 0 to 4. About half of the respondents (50.7 percent) scored 0, that is, they were not much exposed to any of these Western cultural contents in the media and did not prefer Western movies. The others included: 27.3 percent (scored 1), 13.1 percent (2), 6.5 percent (3), and 2.6 percent (4). It seems that even in the larger Shanghai area, relatively few people are heavily exposed to Western cultural influence. The Western influence scale had a reliability (alpha) coefficient of .63.

Like the media information index, the Western cultural influence index was also significantly related to age, education, urbanization, and

Table 2.20 Age and Use of News Media Information

		BELOW 29	30–49	50–65
Low Use	0	30.8%	31.9%	35.5%
	1	20.6%	13.7%	15.9%
	2	17.6%	21.3%	22.8%
	3	16.7%	18.4%	15.1%
High Use	4	14.3%	14.7%	10.7%
Total Cases		510	994	496

Chi-Sq. = 21.8   D.F. = 8 p < .01

Table 2.21 Education and Exposure to Western Cultural Influence

		LOW	MEDIUM	HIGH
Low Exposure	0	75.4%	52.9%	33.7%
	1	15.7%	28.0%	33.4%
	2	6.3%	11.1%	19.0%
	3	2.4%	6.2%	9.2%
High Exposure	4	.2%	1.8%	4.7%
Total Cases		459	769	772

Chi-Sq. = 218.6   D.F. = 8 p < .001

gender, but in a different order, and of a much larger magnitude (multiple R = .48, p < .001). Those more heavily exposed to Western cultural influence tended to be much better educated, much younger, and living in metropolitan Shanghai. Men seemed to come under somewhat greater Western cultural influence than women (tables 2.21 to 2.24).

While the media information index and the Western cultural influence index were related, one by no means subsumes the other (table 2.25). Of the 1,013 respondents who scored 0 on our Western cultural influence scale, only 389 also scored 0 on the media information scale. The remaining 624 had scores on the media information scale ranging from 1 to 4. Of the 650 respondents who scored 0 on the media

Table 2.22 Age and Exposure to Western Cultural Influence

		BELOW 29	30–49	50–65
Low Exposure	0	37.3%	47.5%	70.8%
	1	26.7%	31.1%	20.2%
	2	17.8%	14.2%	5.8%
	3	13.5%	5.0%	2.2%
High Exposure	4	4.7%	2.2%	1.0%
Total Cases		510	994	496

Chi-Sq. = 174.3   D.F. = 8   p < .001

Table 2.23 Exposure to Western Cultural Influence in Urban and Rural Areas

		SHANGHAI	QINGPU	VILLAGES
Low Exposure	0	40.5%	51.3%	74.8%
	1	31.4%	26.3%	17.7%
	2	16.2%	13.5%	5.2%
	3	8.3%	6.6%	2.0%
High Exposure	4	3.6%	2.3%	.2%
Total Cases		1199	304	497

Chi-Sq. = 176.4   D.F. = 4   p < .001

information scale, 261 had scores on the Western cultural influence scale ranging from 1 to 4. As we shall see later, these two indices often had opposite relations to some of the cultural values and beliefs which we measured in our study.

Stages of Analysis

We conducted our data analyses in two stages. First we conducted multivariate statistical analysis. We had seven independent variables:

Table 2.24 Gender and Exposure to Western Cultural Influence

		MALE	FEMALE
Low Exposure	0	47.5%	54.1%
	1	28.2%	26.1%
	2	13.3%	12.8%
	3	7.7%	5.2%
High Exposure	4	3.3%	1.7%
Total Cases		1056	942

Chi-Sq. = 14.9   D.F. = 4 p < .01

Table 2.25 Use of News Media Information and Exposure to Western Influence

		LOW USE				HIGH USE
		0	1	2	3	4
Low Exposure	0	59.8%	60.9%	45.1%	43.4%	34.2%
	1	25.4%	21.9%	28.2%	30.6%	32.4%
	2	10.0%	11.3%	16.6%	13.7%	16.2%
	3	3.4%	5.6%	6.7%	9.9%	10.3%
High Exposure	4	1.4%	.3%	3.4%	2.3%	7.0%
Total Cases		650	320	415	343	272

Chi-Sq. = 112.4   D.F. = 16 p < .001

age, gender, education, income, urbanization, official media information, and Western cultural influence. Gender is dichotomous. For urbanization we have created two dichotomous variables: Urban (Shanghai 1, others 0), and Rural (Villages 1, others 0). Other independent variables were measured by ordinal scales.

We have already seen how the media information index and Western cultural influence index were related to other independent variables. Some of these independent variables were intercorrelated as well. People in metropolitan Shanghai, as we recall, are better educated, have higher income and, because of the literacy requirement in the sampling procedures, older than villagers in rural areas. In the first stage of statistical analysis, for each dependent variable we want to identify those independent variables with which it is related in a nonspurious manner. For those dependent variables that were measured by ordinal scales, we used the multiple regressional analysis. For those dependent variables that were measured by nominal scales, we used the discriminant analysis. Both regression analysis and discriminant analysis stipulate as a minimum requirement that the independent variables are either measured by ordinal scales or dichotomous. The difference in these two types of multivariate analyses is in the way the dependent variable is measured.

We did not include occupation in our multivariate statistical analysis because while all other independent variables were either dichotomous or ordinal in nature, occupation was measured by a nominal scale (of nine categories) and thus not feasible for either multiple regressional analysis or discriminant analysis. We did not consider it helpful to use occupations for bivariate analysis, such as the Chi square test, because the question of spurious relationship would be unresolved. Not including occupation as an independent variable for multivariate analysis, we think, did not result in a serious loss of information because occupational variations, curtailed in terms of income and status under the current Chinese system, were closely associated with four demographic variables, that is, urban vs. rural residence, income, education, and age (tables 2.12, 2.13, 2.14, 2.16) and also slightly related to gender (table 2.15) and thus would have relatively little to contribute to the multivariate analysis.

We used the two multivariate statistical methods only as a heuristic device to identify those independent variables that are meaningfully related to the dependent variables. They were not used to test any specific hypotheses. Because of our large sample size, a relatively small correlation could be statistically significant at the .05 level. In order to minimize capitalization on chance and the Type I error, we adopted .001 as our level of significance, rather than the conventional .05. If an independent variable has a beta coefficient significant at the .001 level in a regressional analysis, or if it is a key variable in a rotated discriminant function significant at the .001 level in a discriminant analysis, this independent variable is considered to be meaningfully related to the dependent variable. All the independent variables we discuss in the text meet the criterion of the .001 level of significance. The details of the multivariate statistical analyses, such as the multiple correlations, beta coefficients, eigan values of discriminant analysis and rotated discriminant functions, are presented with brief explanations in an appendix at the end of this book. They are not repeated in the text for the sake of readability.

In the second stage, independent variables that meet our criterion are retained for cross tabulations with the dependent variable. Chi square tests are conducted even though the significance of those independent variables has already been established at the .001 level in the regressional analysis and discriminant analysis. These tables of cross-tabulations are presented in a separate volume. The findings are discussed in the text. From the cross-tabulations we gain an overall picture of relationships between each dependent variable on the one hand and the demographic factors, use of official media information, and Western cultural influence on the other. From both the multivariate analyses and cross-tabulations we see the relative importance of the independent variables, in an approximate sense, as they are related to the dependent variable.

To summarize at this point: In our study of cultural change in China, we are following two research designs, one explicit and the other implicit. In the explicit research design, we will compare the results from the benchmark survey with the follow-up survey several years later for a measure of change. In the implicit research design, which is being followed now, we use the results of the benchmark survey for an implicit comparison with our knowledge about traditional Chinese culture of the past. Such a comparison will give us a general picture of the nature and direction of cultural change up to the present.

From correlational analysis of the cultural variables with the independent variables, including both the demographic variables, official media information, and Western cultural influence, we can draw inferences about factors contributing to cultural change. In making our inferences, we are relying on general patterns of relationships rather than specific relationships involving particular variables. Guided partly by the general patterns of these statistical analyses (rather than specific details) and partly by our own understanding of traditional Chinese culture, we derive our interpretation of the current status of contemporary Chinese culture as well as the trend for change.

Using our empirical data as the general parameters, we then follow a sociological, historical perspective for an analysis of the major changes of constraining and incentive components, both structural and ideological, and assess their roles in the processes of cultural change in China. We will discuss the implications of the changing Chinese culture on major institutions, including the family, the work place, the community, and the political institutions. Our interpretation is aided by our knowledge of major events that have taken place in the social, economic, and political domains in China since 1949, seen in the perspective of modern Chinese history. Any interpretation of the dynamics of cultural change that goes beyond the immediate domains of survey data inevitably carries a certain degree of subjectivity. We do not claim that ours is an exception. What we do want to emphasize is that our interpretation is not one based on personal observations, but rather, is grounded in concrete data from a broad-based cross-sectional sample seen in a historical and sociological perspective.

The major findings are presented in the following chapters. To use an analogy, the specific findings in each of the chapters may be seen as the trees of contemporary Chinese culture. Because this was the first time such a comprehensive survey was ever conducted in China, either before or since 1949, we need to examine the trees in considerable detail. In the concluding chapter, we will present an overall picture of the forest, so to speak, identifying the most salient features of contemporary Chinese culture and discussing the processes by which traditional Chinese culture has been transformed to its current form.

Part II

Research Findings

Chapter 3

Family Relations

For thousands of years, close family relations have been a major cornerstone of traditional Chinese culture (Hsu, 1949). While this cornerstone has survived numerous social revolutions including one of the most recent, the Cultural Revolution, Chinese family relations have not remained static. The Cultural Revolution was believed to have inflicted wide-ranging damage on the Chinese family. The bitterly torn family relations were dramatically portrayed in a popular short story, "The Scars" (Lu, 1978). Written by a young college student in 1978, this story tells of the agony and remorse felt by a high school girl in Shanghai who had denounced her mother and volunteered for farm labor reform in a remote village in order to prove her ideological dedication to Chairman Mao. When she returned to Shanghai after the Cultural Revolution, she wanted to tell her mother how much she regretted her behavior and to beg forgiveness. But it was too late. Her health ruined by torture during the Cultural Revolution, the mother had died the day before.

    This simple realistic tale caught the imagination of writers all over China and started a new wave of novels and short stories known as the "scars literature." The march of history introduces a new literary genre and also ushers in new challenges, the most recent one being economic reforms. To what extent have the Cultural Revolution and the recent economic reforms affected, on a tangible level but in their different ways, Chinese family relations? If the Cultural Revolution had temporarily distorted Chinese family relations to suit the ideological dictates of the Gang of Four, have the economic reforms accentuating a shift toward a cash economy even in a limited sense, and bringing in a tide of rising material aspirations, affected family relations in any adverse manner?

Are family relations as close as before? What are the general family interaction patterns? What role does television play in family interactions as this new electronic medium begins to penetrate family life in China, opening the eyes of the Chinese to a dazzling outside world of vastly different lifestyles? As China undergoes the growing pains of social and economic reforms, family life is facing new tensions. What kinds of family disputes occur most often? How about husband–wife relations? If a husband and wife find it extremely difficult to get along with each other, should they file for a divorce? Or should they try to keep a broken marriage together? These questions will be addressed in this chapter. Our data analysis will be divided into the following sections: family interaction, parent–child relations, family disputes, and divorce.

Family Interaction

We first asked: "Are you living with your parents?" This question might sound a bit odd to Westerners, as many people would assume that grown-ups do not live with their parents. But it was extremely important in the Chinese context for two reasons. First, traditionally, grown-up children and even married children tended to live together with aging parents in order to form a three-generation or four-generation family. Second, due to China's formidably large population, housing was very hard to find in urban areas, forcing grown-up children, married or not, to live with their parents even if they preferred otherwise.

This question was answered by 1,658 respondents whose parents were still living. About two-thirds of them (65.4 percent) said they were living with their parents. Rural villagers were definitely more traditional than urban dwellers. Almost four out of five villagers (77.7 percent) said they were living with their parents. We do not think this is because they had more serious housing congestion. Farmers living on the outskirts of Shanghai had much less severe housing problems than those who lived in the city proper. Rather we think this is because they chose to live together. It is interesting to note that less than half of the townspeople (45.5 percent) were living with their parents, compared to 64.7 percent of the Shanghai residents. Apparently housing problems were less serious in Qingpu towns than in crowded metropolitan Shanghai. These findings suggest a new trend in urban areas: if housing conditions permit, such as in small towns, more people choose to live away from their parents. On the whole, more people live with their parents than do not.

Age was found to be a relevant factor. As many as 78.1 percent of the young group lived with their parents. It was extremely difficult, if not entirely impossible, for unmarried young people to find a separate apartment. What did surprise us, however, was that over half of the old (53.8 percent) and three-fifths of the middle-aged (61.6 percent) were still living with their parents even though the majority of them were married.

Although we think these findings show that the traditional way of family life still prevails to a large extent, congested housing conditions are definitely a factor, as suggested by the findings on income distribution. Of those with an average monthly income below Y60, 70.4 percent were living with their parents. As income increased, the percentage declined. In the top group earning an average monthly income above Y90, only 60.6 percent were living with their parents.

We then asked a follow-up question: "If you are not living with your parents, when was the last time you visited them?" Almost half (45.8 percent) of the 537 respondents who answered this question said their last visit was two or three days before. More than one-fifth (21.6 percent) said one week before and others (14.2 percent), two weeks before. Relatively few made their last visits from one month to half a year before. These findings show that a large majority of our respondents had frequent or fairly frequent interaction with their parents even though they were not living together. It is safe to say at this point that vertical family ties were still very close.

The parental visit pattern was consistently similar in most groups; only age made some difference. We found that young people visited their parents more frequently than the middle-aged group and the old group. This is not difficult to understand, as many of the young had probably just left their parents to live on their own after marriage and would have more emotional and material need to visit the "old home" as often as they could.

Living together does not necessarily mean being together all the time. As another indicator of family togetherness, we wanted to know how often the whole family (those who lived under the same roof) got together. So we asked: "Other than having a meal together, is there a time during the day the whole family gets together?" The term "the whole family" emphasized all members of the family, not just some members. About two-thirds of the respondents (64.6 percent) said that their whole family got together almost everyday. It is clear that interaction among family members was quite close. Age is a relevant factor. Young and middle-aged people reported more frequent family get-togethers (66 percent and 67.8 percent almost daily respectively) than old people (48.2 percent). It is possible that older people live in families of larger sizes, and it is more difficult for everybody to get together everyday. Rural people reported family get-togethers more frequently (71.4 percent almost daily) than urban dwellers (60.4 percent).

We asked: "When the whole family gets together, what do you do?" We listed seven activities and asked each respondent to choose no more than two.

It is interesting to note that the most popular family activity was watching television, a phenomenon that did not exist in the 1960s or even early 1970s when television sets were not widely available in China. Figure 3.1 is a list of the seven activities in order of decreasing popularity.

Considering each of these family activities, we examined the correlations between the independent and dependent variables.

Watch television: We were at first surprised to find that more villagers (60.8 percent) than Shanghai residents (56.5 percent) or townspeople (50.7 percent) watched television when the whole family got together. Upon further reflection, we felt it was quite understandable. First, farmers in the ten rural counties surrounding metropolitan Shanghai were much more affluent than those who lived in the interior of the Chinese countryside. Television sets were no longer a luxury for them. More than half of the village families we surveyed (56.5 percent) had black-and-white television sets, compared to 60.9 percent in Qingpu towns and 60.6 percent in metropolitan Shanghai. Another 12.5 percent of rural families had color sets versus 31.3 percent in Qingpu and 51.2 percent in Shanghai. Second, cultural life at night in these rural villages was much more limited than in metropolitan Shanghai. Before, when the villagers had nothing to do in the evening, they went to bed; now they watched television. It is amazing to find that television has not only brought a new element into the family interaction patterns in urban areas; it has also changed the life of the villagers—not yet those living in the inner parts of the country beyond the reach of electricity, but definitely villagers who have had an opportunity to explore this twentieth century media marvel.

More older people (62.5 percent) than their younger counterparts

watch television	56.7%
chat	40.6%
do household work	39.1%
discuss something	24.7%
read, study	13.9%
play cards or chess	5.6%
visit friends and relatives	3.7%

Figure 3.1 Family Get-together Activities

Figure 3.2 In cities and villages alike, television has become the focal point of family life. (*Photo courtesy of Linus Chao*)

(52.8 percent) reported that watching television was the activity they were engaged in when the whole family got together. We also found more women (60.8 percent) than men (52.9 percent) mentioning television viewing.

Chat: This was the second most popular family activity, which was traditionally cherished in Chinese culture. We were somewhat surprised that urbanites (44.5 percent) were more gregarious than villagers (30.0 percent). It is also interesting to note that the young (47.3 percent) reported chatting more often than the old (39.8 percent). A plausible explanation is that the urbanites and the young probably had more to talk about than the villagers and the old.

Household work: Villagers were found to be much busier than urbanites: almost two-thirds of the village respondents (64.5 percent) said they did household work when the whole family got together, compared to only 29.2 percent of Shanghai residents. This is understandable as villagers did not have a clear-cut work schedule; they worked whenever they wanted to. In village life, there is probably more work to do around the house.

Discussion: Only media news exposure was found to have a significant correlation: more people with high media news exposure (30.1

Figure 3.3 Mahjong, played by Chinese around the world, was banned during the Cultural Revolution. It has returned to Shanghai. (*Photo courtesy of Linus Chao*)

percent) than their low-exposure counterparts (21.4 percent) said this was something they did when the family got together. Apparently, people who had more exposure to media news had more things to talk about.

Read, study: Here education was the only relevant factor. In families of the better educated, people spent more time reading and studying than those who had only limited education. About one-fifth of the former (18.4 percent) said they read and studied when the family got together, compared to only 9.8 percent of the latter.

Playing cards and chess and visiting friends and relatives were the two least popular family activities.

The data we presented in this section seem to suggest that family ties in China are still very close despite the damage inflicted on numerous Chinese families during the Cultural Revolution. Family members interacted with each other frequently or fairly frequently. One immediate impact of the economic reform was the growing accessibility to television sets. As family income rose and prices of television sets dropped, many families had acquired television. Television seems to have become an irresistible social force. It has assumed a predominant role in family interaction patterns and has affected the life of the rural population who could afford to have television sets. The specific nature of the impact of television, particularly its Western programming, will be discussed later.

Parents' Concern Over Children: Excessive Interference?

The close tie between Chinese parents and their children can be vividly demonstrated in how parents are concerned about their children. First, what are they concerned about? Second, to what extent? Is their concern justified? Or is their concern excessive? Based on our knowledge of contemporary Chinese society, we would assume that Chinese parents would be concerned with just about everything that might have an effect on their children's future, ranging from education to their dating behavior and marriage. Whether parents today are concerned so much as to be interfering we did not know.

To start with, we asked this question: "Do your children consult you on their problems?" Of the total sample, 290 had no children. Another 538 said their children were too small to consult. This question was answered by the remaining 1,172 respondents. About half of them (51 percent) said their children often consulted them on their problems. Two-fifths of them (39.2 percent) said their children sometimes did. Only 8.8 percent said that their children rarely consulted them, and 1 percent said they were never consulted. These findings again point to the close parent-child relations in present-day China. Our findings are consistent with the results of a recent survey of Chinese college students (Li, Ou, and Hou, 1987). When asked whom would they consult when there were difficulties in their lives, 61 percent of the respondents named their parents. Schoolmates ranked a distant second (18.3 percent), followed by friends (8.9 percent) and political counselors (6.3 percent). Parents were even consulted on questions relating to love and romance (22.9 percent) and also on future plans of the young people (27.9 percent).

Somewhat as expected, mothers (55.9 percent at the "often" level) had more consultation requests from their children than fathers (47.7 percent). But the difference was not dramatically large. Traditionally Chinese children have been closer to their mothers than to their fathers, who usually maintain a distance from their children.

Children consulted their parents presumably because the latter had more experience and were ready to help. It was also a show of their respect. In traditional Chinese society, children were not supposed to object to their parents' decisions, opinions, or even suggestions. These were often interpreted as "orders" which children must listen to. In

China today, the parents' words may not carry the weight of "orders." But are they still important in their children's eye? We asked: "Generally speaking, when you ask your children to do something, do they talk back?" Again this was a question for those who had children.

This question was answered by 1,340 respondents whose children were old enough to talk back. One-third of them (33.9 percent) said their children hardly ever talked back when asked to do something. Half of them (51.1 percent) said sometimes they did. Only a small percentage (15.0 percent) complained that their children talked back under most circumstances. The findings here suggest that Chinese parents still enjoyed, to a large extent, the filial obedience of their children.

However, the results of analysis by age indicate that this filial obedience is being challenged as time passes. The younger the parents, the more likely their children will talk back. As many as 41.6 percent of the old group said their children hardly ever talked back. This percentage decreased with age and dropped to 25 percent among young parents. With the remaining 75 percent of young parents, their children talked back either sometimes or most of the time.

We were interested in how the parents would enforce "filial obedience" to maintain discipline. What was the most favored method of discipline when children failed to behave the way the parents wanted them to behave? We had this question: "If your children (not yet grown up) behave badly (such as smoking, drinking), what would you do?" This question was directed to everybody.

It is interesting to note that, on the whole, discipline would not be strictly enforced. About three-quarters of the sample (73.5 percent) said they would advise their children, which few people would doubt was a more positive way to educate children. Whether this represents a dramatic change, or whether the notion about strict parental discipline of the past was just a fiction, we do not know. We had no comparable data from the past for comparison. Almost one out of five (18.4 percent) would resort to spanking if talking proved to be of no use. Very few people (3 percent) considered outright scolding or spanking to be a healthy way of education. The more liberal method of doing nothing and letting children learn the lesson themselves also received a very weak endorsement (5.1 percent).

The old were found to be more patient than the young in educating their children: 85.1 percent of the old said they would advise the ill-behaved children, compared to 70.3 percent of the young and 69.3 percent of the middled-aged. Very few old people (7.8 percent) would resort to spanking when advising proved futile. In contrast, 18.9 percent of the young and 23.4 percent of the middle-aged group would lose temper and resort to spanking.

Spanking is seen as a form of child abuse in some Western societies, a concept that did not exist in traditional Chinese culture. As an old Chinese saying goes, a filial son grows out of a spanking stick; chopsticks (i.e., knowing only how to feed him well) would only spoil him. In their classic study of village and family life in Southern China, Parish and Whyte (1978) found relatively little change in the practice of corporate punishment of children. While this may still be a firm belief held by many people, our findings showed that the majority in the general Shanghai area would resort to neither a spanking stick nor chopsticks as an effective way of raising their children; they would rather use communication to guide a healthy growth of their children.

One of the most important decisions of Chinese parents used to be the selection of a mate for a son. This decision was made in the past almost entirely by the parents, particularly the father. In most cases, the two young persons did not know each other. Astrology was always consulted to ensure a good match. Whether the young couple would actually get along after marriage was left to fate. Following the influx of Western ideas at the turn of the century, things began to change slowly, especially in big cities like Shanghai and Beijing. Occasionally, the son was consulted, and a get-together of the two families was arranged so that the two young persons could meet before the final decision was made by the parents. A major change came after 1949, when more and more young women left the family to join the work force, where they worked alongside young men. This change in occupational structure, along with the elimination of the traditional upper and middle classes, has brought about a new phase in parent–child relations. Parish and Whyte (1978) found more freedom of mate choice and initiative by young people in marriage in villages in Southern China. Parents no longer have the power to make ultimate decisions regarding their children's marriages. But children do not have complete freedom of choice either. In a recent survey of Chinese women in Chengdu, Sichuan, Xu and Whyte (1990) found the role of parents to have declined sharply, while young people increasingly dominate the process of spouse selection.

We wanted to know the situation in the Shanghai area. We asked: "If you have a son, will you let him find his own mate, or will you find one for him?" An overwhelming majority of our respondents (90.3 percent) said they would let the son find his own mate. Very few people (5.9 percent) would try to find one for him. The others were not sure. Age was the only relevant factor. The old were still a little more traditional: 8.5 percent of them said they would find a mate for their son, contrasting with 3.9 percent of the young.

How about the daughter? Did the Chinese treat their sons and daughters differently, as they used to? So we further asked: "If you have a daughter, will you let her find her own mate, or will you find one for her?" The results were almost the same: the more democratic way of letting the daughter find her own mate received a slightly weaker endorsement (88.3 percent) than in the case of son. Again only age made some difference. The old were found to be a bit more traditional than the young: 11.3 percent of the former said they would find a mate for their daughter, compared to only 5.3 percent of the latter.

Thus most Chinese would now let their sons and daughters find their own mates under normal circumstances. Indeed, marriage is very important to Chinese because it is a lifelong commitment. What if the child wants to marry someone with bad reputation? In this instance, the consequences were considered to be more serious for a daughter than for a son, because in traditional China once a daughter was married, she was like "spilled water," that is, lost forever. The water must not be "spilled" into the wrong hands. So we asked: "If you have a daughter and she wants to marry someone who is a bad character, what will you do?"

Many parents or would-be parents were opposed to such a marriage. More than one-third of the respondents (37.6 percent) said they would express their opposition firmly. Another 30.9 percent were a bit more patient, saying they would try to persuade their daughter not to do it. It is interesting to note that a sizable minority (29.6 percent) were so liberal as to be willing to let the daughter make her own decision.

The young were found to be much more liberal than the old: as many as 42.9 percent of the young said they would let the daughter make her own choice; in contrast, only 22.5 percent of the old took this liberal position. This is not difficult to understand. People with higher education, however, turned out to be far more conservative than their lower-education counterparts. While only 18.9 percent of the better educated would allow their daughter to make her own decision, as many as 43.0 percent of the lower education people would not hesitate to do so. This excessive concern with the marital well-being of a daughter used to be largely a middle-class phenomenon, and it seems to remain so today, related to those who have higher education.

As one might expect, women were more concerned about their daughter's future happiness than men: 42.4 percent of the females were resolutely opposed to her marrying a man of bad character, compared to a third of the male sample (33.2 percent).

Other than mate selection for children, are parent–child relations overly restrictive or generally supportive? We asked this general question:

Do you think your parents express so much concern as to be interfering; or often give you appropriate suggestions;

or express concern but do not interfere;

or show not much concern;

or others (please specify)?

The question in Chinese applied equally well to present and past situations.

A large majority of our respondents expressed a positive feeling toward their parents' concern about their lives. Many (41.5 percent) thought their parents often gave them appropriate suggestions, and about the same number (43.3 percent) said their parents would express their concern, but did not interfere. Only a small number of people (7.6 percent) complained that their parents gave them too much concern, so much as to be interfering. Very few respondents (5.4 percent) reported that their parents did not show much concern at all.

Villagers were more positive toward their parents than urban residents: over half of the rural respondents (51.3 percent) said their parents often offered them appropriate suggestions. The implication here is that if the suggestions are considered appropriate, they are most likely followed. In contrast, only 36.0 percent of the Shanghai residents said so. However, this does not mean that urbanites were unhappy with their parents. More urbanites (47.5 percent) than villagers (34.4 percent) said their parents did express concern, but did not interfere. It seems that urban parents allow their children a little more freedom. More of them expressed their concern without suggesting what their children should do.

Over half of the lower-education group (51.5 percent) considered their parents' suggestions as appropriate. In contrast, less than a third of those with higher education (32.9 percent) thought their parents often gave them appropriate suggestions. This is not difficult to understand as often better-educated people think they have good judgment themselves and would look at their parents' advice with a more critical eye. But here in our case, they still showed their appreciation, as half of the better educated (50.3 percent) reported that their parents had concern for them but did not interfere.

The picture we have presented here in this section is clear: parent–child relations are still close in China. Children seem to respect their parents much the way they used to and consult them often. On the other hand, parents no longer dominate the lives of their children as before. On such an important matter as mate selection, the parents tend to allow their children a wide latitude of freedom. Parents are perceived to be caring and understanding even when they think their children are going to make a grave mistake, such as marrying a bad character. In general, the parents' concerns are not seen by their children as interfering.

Family Disputes

Close family relations do not prevent disputes. Probably the opposite is true: the closer the relations are, the more often family disputes will occur. It would be interesting to know what kinds of family disputes were more common in China's current context of social and economic changes. Through the kinds of disputes that frequently happened, we could have a better knowledge of the kinds of problems Chinese families were confronted with and the manner in which these problems would affect their relations.

We asked this question: "Disputes are inevitable in families. Among your relatives and friends, which disputes occur more often?" We did not directly ask about disputes in their own families. The respondents might not want to admit to them. Rather we asked for their observations. We listed nine problem categories that often generated family disputes in China and allowed each respondent to name up to five.

We were amazed to find that disputes involving mother and daughter-in-law friction were the most frequent. The nine disputes are presented in figure 3.4 in order of decreasing frequency.

The top three dispute categories were mother and daughter-in-law relations, housing problems, and children's education. The first

mother and daughter-in-law	54.4%
housing problems	53.4%
children's education	49.1%
character incompatibility	40.8%
daily expenses	34.9%
caring for old parents	33.0%
lifestyle issues	23.5%
property disputes	20.0%
entertainment	10.7%

Figure 3.4 Frequencies of Family Disputes

two categories may be related to each other in that much of the friction between mother and daughter-in-law could be caused by "unfair" (as seen by one party or both) division of the extremely limited home space. Housing problems in metropolitan Shanghai were extremely serious; many of the newlyweds had to share space with the parents, often the husband's parents, in their already very small apartment. When mother and daughter-in-law were thrown into a situation like that, disputes were almost inevitable.

Mother and daughter-in-law disputes can also involve value confrontations due to a generation gap. While an old mother would complain about her young daughter-in-law's lack of respect or her being less obedient than expected, the daughter-in-law would accuse her mother-in-law of being unbearably authoritarian and unreasonable. Such complaints and accusations were often heard of in both metropolitan Shanghai and rural villages. Value confrontations seem to surface more in a mother versus daughter-in-law relationship, particularly when they live under the same roof, as each side is often intolerant of what she sees to be the other's unwelcome behavior with regard to the same man—the mother's son and the daughter-in-law's husband.

In-law disputes seemed to be uniformly widespread in most groups. No differences were found between urban and rural areas. Education was the only relevant factor. Those of lower education reported fewer in-law disputes (45.5 percent) among their relatives and friends than the middle (57 percent) and higher-education (56.9 percent) groups. It seems that education widens the generation gap. Family disputes about housing were far more frequent in Shanghai (61.1 percent) than in Qingpu towns (36.6 percent) or the villages (44.8 percent).

We were not surprised that family disputes over children's education came third. This again points to the fact that children occupied a central position in the family. It is one more piece of evidence that family relations were on the whole very close. Such disputes occurred more often in Shanghai (50.2 percent) and Qingpu towns (56.1 percent) than in villages (42.1 percent). It seems that urbanites take children's education more seriously than rural villagers.

Frequent disputes over character compatibility between husband and wife are a new phenomenon. Such disputes were relatively rare in the past, not because married couples got along well, but because a distant relation prevailed to prevent such disputes from surfacing. The diffident position of the wife in the family was such that the issue of character compatibility hardly arose. Our findings therefore are highly significant. They indicate a major change in the Chinese family. Not only is character compatibility a relevant factor in husband-wife relations, but also the position of the wife has apparently improved so much that she is now able to make an issue of it. Character disputes between husbands and wives appear to be not only frequent but also widespread. Age is a relevant factor. Young people reported such disputes far more (49 percent) than old people (33.1 percent), suggesting the tension among the younger generation in this time of unsettled transition. Another relevant factor is the area of residence. Rather surprisingly, villagers reported more such disputes (49.1 percent) than Shanghai residents (36.8 percent). One plausible explanation is that marriages are brought together with less consideration for character compatibility in rural areas, and thus more disputes occur.

That one-third of the respondents reported family disputes about daily expenses bespeaks the difficulties Chinese people have in making ends meet. Although we had no parallel data from the past, our impressions are that such disputes were much less frequent. Disputes about daily expenses were even more frequent in rural areas (44.7 percent) than in Shanghai (31.9 percent) and Qingpu towns (30.9 percent), undoubtedly because the income level was much lower in the villages. The finding that nearly half of the rural respondents reported such disputes indicates a rather serious situation.

Disputes about caring for old parents, reported also by about one-third of the respondents, points to another deep-seated social problem. Such disputes were generally considered to be rare in the past. The situation is different today. On the one hand, the traditional concept of filial piety requires that grown-up children physically look after their aging parents. But the prolonged life span of the parents, due to improved health conditions, and the extremely crowded housing facilities combine to create a burden for the children. The result is one more kind of arguments in the Chinese family. Such arguments were reported to be more frequent in rural villages (44.3 percent) than in Qingpu towns (32.3 percent) and Shanghai (28.4 percent). As we recall, more people were living with their parents in rural villages than in metropolitan Shanghai or the towns, and thus there were more occasions for such bickering.

Lifestyle disputes are largely a matter of generation gap. Young people prefer rock music and flashy clothes, something the old people frown upon. We suspect that such disputes are a relatively recent phenomenon, brought about largely by the new open door policy of the early 1980s. What came as a surprise was that lifestyle disputes were reported by nearly one out of four respondents. Age was the only relevant factor, not surprisingly. Such disputes were reported more by the young (29.4 percent) than the old (20.8 percent).

Property disputes were largely a rural phenomenon, reported far more frequently in villages (32.3 percent) than in Shanghai (15.6 percent) and Qingpu towns (17.2 percent). This is because relatively few people in urban areas own any property, whereas in rural villages most people own the houses they live in and have other property such as cattle and farm instruments.

We included entertainment to see whether this was a potential family dispute because first radio listening and now television viewing have become a problem in a crowded small apartment. Only about one out of nine respondents reported such squabbles, much more by the young (17.3 percent) than by the old (6.7 percent).

Divorce

For a long time, divorce was an issue that Chinese husbands and wives rarely talked about or even thought about. In traditional China, the husband had the indisputable right to dismiss his wife for a number of reasons, including inability to bear a male heir, disobedience of parents-in-law, and adultery. The wife, however, could not ask for a separation for any reason. After the end of the Manchu dynasty in 1912, the position of the wife improved somewhat. But divorce was still considered to be something bad or even shameful. Like its predecessor, the government of the People's Republic discouraged divorce, as it considered divorce harmful to social stability. If a couple could not get along, the neighborhood committee would do its best to work out a compromise.

With the introduction of the open-door policy and economic reforms, divorce rates in the country were reported to be rising in the past decade, from 341,000 in 1980 to 800,000 in 1990 (WuDunn, 1991), mostly in big cities. We wanted to know how our respondents looked at the issue of divorce. So we asked: "If a husband and a wife have great difficulty getting along, and they have no children, do you think they should get a divorce?"

A large majority of the sample (76.4 percent) said they should get a divorce, with a stronger endorsement in metropolitan Shanghai (82.9 percent) than in rural villages (59.6 percent). More than one-third of the villagers (35.8 percent) wanted to keep the relationship going even though they knew it didn't work. Divorce was also seen as not desirable by more than one-third of the lower-education people (36.4 percent). Only three-fifths of them (59.3 percent) supported the idea of divorce. In contrast, an overwhelming majority of the higher-education group (86.7 percent) thought the troubled couple should get a divorce. Western cultural influence also made a difference, though it was not dramatically large. More people under strong Western cultural influence (86.3 percent) than those little influenced (68.7 percent) agreed that divorce was the solution to a crippled marriage. Women were more in favor of ending an unhappy marriage (79.1 percent) than men (73.9 percent). The difference is not large, but indicative of the improved status and autonomy of Chinese women in their new roles in the family as well as the occupational structure.

It seems that the old notion that divorce was bad or shameful was being challenged, more so among urban residents, the well-educated, and people under heavy Western influence than among villagers, people with limited education, or under little Western influence.

Notice that having no children was part of the condition of the previous question. We asked this follow-up question: "If a husband and a wife have great difficulty getting along, but they have children, do you think they should get a divorce?"

Children changed the whole picture. The high percentage of endorsement for divorce recorded in the preceding question dropped to a low 34.8 percent. More than half of the respondents (55.2 percent) now gave a definite no to the question. They would rather keep children and maintain a crippled relationship than have a new life. The others were unsure.

Villagers were found to be even more concerned about children than urbanites: more than two-thirds of the rural respondents (69.6 percent) said divorce was not acceptable when the unhappy couple had children, compared to 49.9 percent of Shanghai residents. With children involved, the attitudes of women changed. More females (61.5 percent) than males (49.5 percent) hated to see children suffer from a broken family, saying the couple should not get a divorce.

People with limited education cared about children much more than their higher-education counterparts. The latter presumably cared more about their personal happiness than the former. As many as 72.3 percent of the lower-education people said no to divorce, contrasting with a weak 42.9 percent of those who had higher education.

As before, people under heavy Western cultural influence cared much more about their own happiness than those with little Western influence: over half of the former (56.9 percent) said the troubled couple should get a divorce even though they had children; in contrast, only 27.2 percent of the low-influence group took this position. As many as 63.6 percent of the low-influence people objected to divorce, compared to only one-third of the high foreign exposure group (33.3 percent).

To sum up, in dealing with the divorce issue, urban residents, men, the better educated, and people under heavy Western cultural influence were less traditional than villagers, women, and people either with limited education or little exposure to Western culture. Another strong message we got from the data presented above was that children had a really important position in Chinese families. Few other types of family relations, including husband–wife relations, seem to be as important as the parent–child relations.

Discussion

One of the most significant findings in this chapter is that the family, a cornerstone of Chinese culture, has survived the turmoils of the Cultural Revolution. During the height of the Cultural Revolution, children were incited to denounce their parents. Husbands and wives accused each other for their own survival. For a time, when Mao's struggle theory went into full play, fears spread across the country that traditional Chinese family relations, which had been valued for thousands of years, would finally fall apart. Such fears proved to be unfounded. The chaotic effects of these ten destructive years proved to be transitory.

From our study, we found that family relations remain stable, as demonstrated in close family interaction patterns, in parents' concern over their children's well-being, and above all, in warm feedback from the children. It appears that the disruptive forces aroused by the Cultural Revolution were ideologically superficial and politically unstable. They failed to remove the soil in which Chinese family had been planted. Once the Cultural Revolution ended with the death of Mao and the arrest of the Gang of Four, these forces quickly lost ground. Their traumatic impact on the Chinese family proved to be short-lived and soon faded.

However, this is not to say that the Chinese family has remained unaffected. Indeed, the impression we get from our findings is that changes have been phenomenal, though not directly traceable to the Cultural Revolution. Parental dominance, traditionally strong in China, is mostly gone. Children consult their parents often, but seem to be given a great deal of independence, as indicated by their unusual freedom of choice in mate selection. Previously, such decisions were made exclusively by the parents. Child-rearing practices are no longer authoritarian, and there does not seem to be rigid enforcement of discipline over such undesirable behavior as drinking or smoking. Total filial obedience appears to be fading, especially in the families of young parents.

Whether the denunciation of parents during the Cultural Revolution had some residual impact on parent–child relations is not certain. Perhaps the changes we have documented in family relations are largely due to modifications in both the family structure and the occupational structure. The disbanding of the extended kinship structure, following the rural land reform and urban economic reorganization in the fifties, effectively removed a deep-rooted source of authority in the Chinese family. In some areas, such as the village in North China which Cohen (1990) studied in 1986–87, the lineage kinship structure still provided a context for visiting and feasting during such festivals as the lunar New Year. But the kinship structure is no longer a basis of economic resources and power. With the kinship structure very much weakened, there is not much left beyond the nuclear family to back up the authority of the father.

The total reorganization of work in both urban centers and rural villages further elevated the positions of children and, conversely, diminished the authority of parents. The organizational structure of work has undergone several major changes in the last forty years. But the basic patterns of state control have remained unaltered since the late fifties. In urban areas both parents and children work for the state and receive wages. In rural villages, parents and children used to labor in production teams under the communes and received work points. Now with the commune system abolished, they till the small patch of land which has been recently leased from the state. Under rather complicated terms known as the "responsibility system," they submit a portion of their crops to the state without compensation, as a sort of lease fee, and receive cash compensation for the remaining portion. In both cities and villages, parents and children have nearly equal status before the ultimate source of employment authority, namely, the state. The economic contributions of the children have brought them a considerable degree of autonomy within the family.

Similarly, husband–wife relations have undergone an enormous change. Previously the wife was totally dependent on her husband and his family. She had no role of her own beyond the family. Married women in cities and towns did not have an independent economic role to play. Even village women, who used to bear a major share of the family's productive labor, had to obey their husbands and other male elders in the extended family. All this has changed. Whether in cities or villages, sex roles have become less differentiated and men and women receive comparable wages and other benefits.

The improved status of women is in part reflected in rather liberal attitudes toward divorce that are vastly different from the past. Previously, the concept that a wife could ask for a divorce did not even exist in the world of Chinese women. While most Chinese still value long and sustained marriages today, people seem to have become increasingly aware of the tragic nature of unhappy marriages. The old notion that divorce was bad and shameful is being discarded. The rather cautious approach to divorce when children are involved fully suggests the central importance of children in the Chinese family.

Another dramatic manifestation of the improved status of women in relation to their husbands, though superficially cast in a negative light, is the high incidence of disputes about character incompatibility. Such disputes were nearly unheard of in the past, not because husbands and wives were always compatible, but because the wife had to submit to her husband no matter what. The fact that now a woman can engage in a dispute with her husband over a matter of character compatibility clearly demonstrates that their positions in the family are nearly equal.

While we think the manifest disruptive effects of the Cultural Revolution on the Chinese family were short-lived, we see the possibility of a different type of impact that is latent but may have some long-term implications of a troublesome nature. We are referring to the unusually high incidences of family disputes of various sorts reported by our respondents. Even though we have no comparable empirical data from the past for reference, our general impression is that under the traditional cultural value of treasuring harmonious relations, such family disputes were relatively few in the past.

One is initially tempted to attribute these frequent family squabbles to the overly crowded housing facilities. Indeed, when a whole family, sometimes containing as many as three generations, huddles under the same roof in a space no larger than two rooms, it is relatively easy to get on each other's nerves. The frustration can easily lead to quarrels or even fights. However, we do not believe the housing situation is the sole factor, because housing facilities are much less crowded in Qingpu towns and the villages, and yet people living there quarrel just as frequently as those in metropolitan Shanghai. Another major factor, we suspect, is traceable to the Cultural Revolution. It seems that the open confrontations and merciless accusations, which were officially orchestrated to be the predominant style of human interactions during the Cultural Revolution in a concrete demonstration of Mao's struggle theory, are leaving an unintended but lasting mark on Chinese society. In traditional China, a buffer zone of interpersonal harmony acted as a strong deterrent to highly contentious family relations. As part of the traditional culture, this buffer zone was difficult to break. But once it is broken, as it was during the Cultural Revolution, then it becomes difficult to patch it up. This seems to be the current situation today. The kind of contentious approach to human relations that we have documented can be expected to aggravate the social dislocations that usually accompany economic development, such as what China is pursuing in its current drive toward modernization.

We now consider the impact of the current economic reform on Chinese family relations. While programs of economic reform in China have been multifaceted, here we discuss only two aspects, both related to television. A number of factors reflected in both increased supply and expanding demand have brought television to many homes. The economic reform, especially in its initial years, brought about an increase of family income, particularly in rural areas. At the same time, production of television sets increased substantially. Prices came down, more for color sets than for black-and-white models. Under the reform policy, China opened its doors wider to the Western world. Foreign programs were introduced, primarily from American producers. Domestic programs toned down their ideological slant to enhance entertainment appeal. Television audiences grew quickly. When a family had some savings, usually the first major purchase was a television set.

Our data showed that television now occupies a dominant place in family life in the area we studied. When family members get together, the most popular activity is to watch television. (The viewing

Figure 3.5 Talk shows in entertainment center used to be highly popular among Shanghai residents. Their place is being taken over by television. (*Photo courtesy of Linus Chao*)

patterns will be discussed in a separate paper.) But regardless of what they watch, the fact that a family now spends hours in front of the television set during the evening suggests that family life will not be the same as before. This may be considered a "channel" effect of mass media, meaning that the introduction of a new channel will have some impact regardless of the programming contents. The specific nature of the channel effect in urban and rural areas in China would require a separate study. Studies in other Asian countries suggest that with television, interactions within families generally decrease (Chu, Alfian, and Schramm, 1985).

Other than the channel effect, we consider the effects of one particular kind of programming content. We are referring to the findings on Western cultural influence, emanating partly from films and radio but largely from television.[1] We summarize the results in table 3.1.

As we see, people heavily exposed to Western cultural influence through the media have consistently more liberal attitudes toward divorce, whether or not the couple have children, than those under little influence. Even when children are involved, more than half of those heavily exposed found divorce acceptable. Although the marriage law promulgated in the early fifties permits divorce, in practice divorce has been discouraged by the government. Only in recent years have divorces been reported in significant numbers. Thus divorces in China are a relatively new phenomenon, and liberal attitudes toward divorce a very recent development. Given the correlations between Western cultural influence and attitudes toward divorce, it is unlikely that people with prior liberal attitudes toward divorce are attracted to view television programs and films that reflect Western influence. Probably few people had such prior liberal attitudes. It is rather more likely that the lifestyle that they have seen in these television programs and films helps them form their new liberal attitudes. Thus, if China continues to keep its door open to the West, and if the influx of Western cultural influence maintains its current pace, we would expect more changes in husband–wife relations than in parent–child relations. The latter, as we

Table 3.1 Western Cultural Influence and Divorce

	WESTERN INFLUENCE	
	High	Low
Divorce OK with no children	86.3%	68.7%
Divorce OK with children	56.9%	27.2%

have seen in our findings, are not related to Western cultural influence. In other words, husband–wife relations, particularly among young couples, would be less stable than parent–child relations. Indeed, we would expect many rocky marriages to be saved only by concerns for children.

Exposure to official news information, as another communication content, had little effect on family relations, except one particular instance. Those heavily exposed reported more discussions in the family (30.1 percent) than those least exposed (21.4 percent). It seems that news information from the official media, regardless of its level of credibility, tends to bring family interactions to a more active and participatory level.

Another impact of the economic reform on family relations may also be indirectly related to television. We are referring to the rather high incidence of family disputes over daily expenses, more so in rural villages than in urban Shanghai. A family may quarrel about children's education, or in China's current situation, about housing. But for so many families to have frequent quarrels about daily expenses suggests there is something fundamentally wrong about the allocations of income and expenditures. Since most families in China live on fixed incomes, this can only mean that those families are spending beyond their means. In China, housing is subsidized by the state and does not cost much. The rent, including water and electricity, is usually less than ten yuan. Rice is a staple food supplied by ration and costs little. At the time we did our survey in late 1987, prices of meat and vegetables were still relatively stable, though already much higher than in the early 1980s. An average family of two adults with children in Shanghai could expect a combined monthly wage of about 150 to 200 yuan. This amount, although not sufficient for a comfortable life, does provide the bare essentials. Why would family finances be in such serious difficulty that something as basic as daily expenses would become a matter of constant dispute?

One plausible explanation is that the rapidly rising material aspirations, partly due to what people have seen in television programs and commercials, are outpacing the limited increase of family income. Many families are spending heavily on expensive consumer goods such as color television, refrigerator, washing machine, camera, and stereo set. Our survey found high percentages of families, in both metropolitan Shanghai and rural villages, that owned these luxury items. Since the economic reform programs were launched, many factories have retooled their production lines to turn out refrigerators and washing machines. Others produced color television sets. These items are advertised on television as well as on roadside billboards. People have developed high expectations for a better life, most likely beyond their limited means. In the general Shanghai area, it has become a craze for a family to own these items, whether or not it can afford them. After so many years of austerity, the sudden outburst of material aspirations seems to be so powerful that people neglect to consider the limitations of their budgets. The burden can be even heavier on rural than on urban families because by and large family income in the countryside is much lower. Many newlyweds in the larger Shanghai area go heavily into debt with their purchase of modern appliances, which they proudly show off to relatives and friends. Their marital happiness is doomed before it is given a chance. Unless this adverse trend is relieved, either by higher wages (which is most unlikely) or by scaling down material aspirations to a more realistic level, these disputes about daily expenses may be a forerunner of serious family instability in the years to come.

Chapter 4

Social Relations

Social relations here are defined as relations that are initiated, developed, and maintained through interactions in the larger social system beyond the immediate family structure. They include relations with relatives, friends, neighbors, or individual members of any other social groups. Some of these relations, such as those with relatives, are extensions of the kinship network, and others, such as those with friends, though beyond the kinship structure, could also be colored by such a structure. In traditional China, for example, one often created simulated kinship relations to cement friendship. Friends addressed each other as "brother" while acquaintances of one's father or uncle were called "uncles." These terms of address suggest that social relations in China could be better understood in comparison with the familial and kinship structure. But kinship structure is not the whole picture, nor is it sufficient to explain all human relations in contemporary Chinese society. Social relations in China today are also governed by other factors, economic, political, and cultural. How they are governed by these and other factors will be discussed although they are not the main concern of our empirical research. We wanted to illustrate what various kinds of social relations looked like in contemporary China. We wanted to obtain a descriptive picture first, albeit a rough one. Based upon this descriptive picture, we will proceed with more in-depth analytic interpretation.

Relations with Relatives

Relatives used to be an important part of the traditional kinship network in China. The radical structural changes introduced in both rural and urban areas in the 1950s, through the land reform and state acquisition of private enterprises, destroyed the economic foundation of the traditional kinship networks and greatly weakened kinship ties. It is not clear to what extent relatives still play a role in the lives of Chinese today. One such measure is the frequency with which people interact with their relatives. So we asked: "Do you have an opportunity to see relatives who do not live with you?"

One-third of the sample (33.3 percent) reported that they saw their relatives quite often, more people (39.9 percent) said several times a year, and the rest (26.7 percent) only once or twice a year. Even though we had no empirical data from the past for comparison, our general impression is that formerly Chinese people saw their relatives much more frequently.

The area of residence was found to be the only relevant factor. Rural villagers (42.7 percent saying they saw their relatives quite often) were found to have more frequent interactions with their relatives than urban residents (27.0 percent). This seems to suggest that the kinship network was more closely maintained in rural areas than in large cities such as Shanghai.

In order to get a sense as to how solid such relations were, we designed this question: "What will you do if a relative wants to borrow Y200 from you?" Mutual financial assistance was a major obligation among members of the kinship network in the past. We wanted to know whether and to what extent this obligation is still being honored. Two hundred yuan is a sufficiently large amount, roughly twice the monthly wage of an average level worker.

Well over half of the respondents (61.8 percent) said they would lend the money to the relative. In contrast, only 2.5 percent gave a flat no. Some (12.2 percent) said "it depends" without specifying the condition. It is interesting to note that a sizable number of people (13.5 percent) said they would lend the money if it is for a proper purpose.

In this response, two relevant factors were the area of residence and age. Villagers were more generous to their relatives than urbanites: a large majority of the former (80.4 percent) said they would lend the money to the relative, compared to only 54.3 percent of Shanghai residents. While not many villagers (5.0 percent) thought about conditions of lending, 15.3 percent of the urban sample said "it depends." It seems that urbanites were more hesitant and cared about the relative's purpose for borrowing money more than villagers: 17.6 percent of city residents said they would lend the money if it was for a proper purpose. In comparison, only 4.4 percent of rural residents cared about the purpose. These findings support our previous assertion that villagers had better and closer relations with relatives than city dwellers.

Figure 4.1 A family dinner in honor of a visiting scholar, Professor Linus Chao (center), from the United States
(*Photo courtesy of Linus Chao*)

It is a surprise to us that the young people were found to be much less particular than the old: as many as 70.2 percent of the young were willing to lend the money without asking about details, contrasting with only 44.7 percent of the old. Quite a few old respondents (22.7 percent) wanted to know if the requested money was for a proper purpose. Only 7.7 percent of the young people put this down as a condition.

A very important ingredient of Chinese social relations is known as *renqing*, which may be translated as "personal obligations and affections." It was largely this feeling of renqing that bound together many of the basically reciprocal social relations in traditional China. A practical manifestation of renqing is the asking and giving of a favor. This can mean an obligation between two persons. But more typically, it requires one of the parties to ask for a favor on behalf of the other from a third party.

We asked the following question regarding renqing obligations toward relatives: "Suppose a relative wants your help to ask someone to do something. You are able to do it, but it will give you some inconvenience. What will you do?" The key element here is whether a person is willing to incur some inconvenience in order to honor a renqing obligation for a relative.

Quite consistent with their answers to previous questions, over two-thirds of the sample (70.9 percent) would offer to help under those circumstances. Very few (8.0 percent) would decline. Some others (5.1 percent) said they would help if the request was for a good purpose. The rest said "it depends."

Here age and education were relevant. Again the young appeared to be more willing than the old: 75.0 percent of the young said they would help, compared to 63.0 percent of the old. More old respondents (19.1 percent) than their young counterparts (9.8 percent) said "it depends." We found a slightly higher percentage among people with lower education (71.9 percent) than among those with higher education (66.1 percent) who would be willing to help.

The general picture we derive from the data is that people had relatively frequent interactions and maintained relatively close relations with relatives, much more so in rural villages than in urban areas.

Relations with Friends

For a comparative purpose, we also asked this question: "What will you do if a friend wants to borrow Y200 from you?"

It is interesting to note that less than half of the sample (43.9 percent) said they would lend the money to the friend. Quite a few (16.6 percent) said "it depends," and another sizable number of people (18.3 percent) wanted to know if the money was for a good purpose. Only 4.6 percent of the respondents said no. The others gave miscellaneous answers.

Area of residence, age and education were three relevant factors. Again, villagers were more generous than urbanites: more than two-thirds of the village sample (68.8 percent) were willing to lend the money no matter what, contrasted with only 33.9 percent of Shanghai residents. More urbanites (21.7 percent) and townspeople (20.1 percent) than villagers (8.9 percent) wanted to make sure that the money was for a proper purpose.

Once again, young people were more willing to help. Over half of the young (53.5 percent) said they would lend the money, compared to only 28.5 percent of the old who agreed to do so without asking about the details. Almost half of the old respondents said either "it depends" (23.0 percent) or that they would do it if the money was for a proper purpose (25.7 percent).

People with lower education were more willing to help than those with higher education. While more than half of the former (54.3

percent) were positive about lending the money, only a bit over one-third of the latter (36.4 percent) would help. A considerable number of the better-educated people (22.3 percent) would refuse to help unless they knew that the money was for a proper purpose, as compared to only 9.9 percent in the lower-education group.

We asked a similar question on renqing for friends. "Suppose a friend wants your help to ask someone to do something. You are able to do it, but it will give you some inconvenience. What will you do?"

About two-thirds of the respondents (64.3 percent) would offer to help. Quite a few (15.5 percent) said "it depends," and 11.4 percent said no. It is interesting that people's willingness to help friends was weaker than their willingness to help relatives. We will return to this point later.

The area of residence and age had significant correlations with the dependent variable. Once again, villagers (74.4 percent) were found to be more willing to help than urbanites (60.7 percent). In contrast, urbanites and townspeople were more concerned about the "nature" of the requested help than villagers. Consistent with their earlier answers, the old again appeared to be more prudent than the young. Almost one-third of those over 50 years of age said either "it depends" (20.8 percent) or "if the request is for a proper purpose" (10.2 percent). The percentages for the young (below 29) were 12.0 percent and 2.6 percent respectively.

The previous question involved a third person, which could make the situation a bit complicated. We then designed a simpler question about renqing that involved "you" and your "good friend" only: "You are tired after a whole day's work, and you want to take a rest. A good friend comes along and wants you to do something, which is very important to him. Will you help him?"

An overwhelming majority of the sample (90.2 percent) said they would help. This percentage is much higher than the 64.3 percent when honoring a renqing requires a favor from a third person. Only a few (7.9 percent) said "it depends." And very few (1.9 percent) would be mean to their "good friend" and refuse. Clearly most people were ready to put aside their own physical well-being to do a renqing favor for a good friend.

Interestingly, gender was the only relevant factor here. We found more women (92.9 percent) than men (87.9 percent) willing to offer help unconditionally. One out of ten men (10.2 percent) said "it depends," compared to 5.3 percent of women. It seems that Chinese women are somewhat more accommodating than men.

What if honoring a renqing obligation would place the person in a situation of role conflict? We chose to investigate a conflict between a personal obligation and the duty of a citizen to vote. We asked this question: "An election is coming up. Suppose a good friend wants you to vote for someone you know nothing about. Will you agree?"

A large majority of our respondents (82.2 percent) would refuse to vote for somebody they knew nothing about even though it was a request from their good friend. However, some (12.0 percent), though not many, would sacrifice a matter of principle to uphold their friendship.

Age was the only relevant factor. Again, the older people would adhere more closely to principles than the younger people. While only 5.0 percent of the old would agree to vote as their friends told them to do, as many as 16.1 percent of the young would do so.

Recall that we asked two similar questions about relations with relatives and with friends. We now consider the data in table 4.1.

This list indicates clearly that relations with relatives, which fall into the kinship structure, occupy a consistently more important place in the lives of Chinese than relations with friends. In other words, traditional kinship networks are still playing a role, perhaps much more limited than before but nevertheless still significant, even though their economic foundation has basically been destroyed. To double check, we asked this question: "If you are in need of money, where would you go to borrow it?" We asked this question because in China borrowing money is considered something very personal; such help usually comes from relatives or friends, not banks.

Not surprisingly, those who said they would go to relatives to borrow money represented the highest percentage (42.2 percent). About one-third of the respondents (32.2 percent) would borrow

Table 4.1 Renqing Obligations to Relatives and Friends

ITEMS	TO RELATIVE	TO FRIEND
Asked to borrow		
lend	61.8%	43.9%
not lend	2.5%	4.6%
depends	35.7%	51.8%
Asked to help, inconvenient		
help	70.9%	64.3%
not help	8.0%	11.4%
depends	21.1%	24.3%

money from their friends. The rest would go elsewhere for the needed money.

Here the four relevant factors were area of residence, age, education, and Western cultural influence. About two-thirds of our village sample (64.5 percent) said they would go to relatives for help, compared to only 31.8 percent of the urban residents. In metropolitan Shanghai, we found a slightly higher percentage (34.3 percent) who would go to friends to borrow money rather than go to relatives for help. But the main message here was that villagers seemed to enjoy closer relations with relatives than urban dwellers.

Age made an interesting difference here. While an overwhelming majority of the young people would go to either relatives (45.1 percent) or friends (41.1 percent) for the needed money, the older people, though they would also rely heavily on relatives and friends, mentioned their work units as a major source of financial assistance (27.2 percent). Not many young people (6.6 percent) wanted to go to them for help. It seems that older people have more seniority and higher standing in their work units. It is also possible that the work units, which have played a dominant role in the lives of Chinese for some forty years, are losing their influence on the young.

Over half of the lower-education group (55.1 percent) said they would seek financial help from relatives; in contrast, only a third of the higher education group (33.1 percent) would do so. This latter group would rely more on friends (39.3 percent) than on relatives.

People under heavy Western cultural influence would also rely more on friends (51.0 percent) than on relatives (23.5 percent). In contrast, only about a quarter of those under low Western cultural influence (26.2 percent) chose to borrow money from their friends, while almost half of them (47.6. percent) would seek such help from relatives.

The data we have reported here suggest that while relations with relatives are still generally closer than those with friends among Chinese people today, such processes as urbanization, education, and Western cultural influence are pulling people away from their traditional kinship networks and pushing them toward what we may call nonfamilial social interactive networks. The age differences we have found are rather interesting. It is possible that older people are more prudent and would respond to requests for financial help more cautiously. But the results on voting would suggest that compared to the old, the young people are, relatively speaking, more conscious of friendship and less concerned about such matters as voting under the current political system.

Figure 4.2 Two grandmas having a mid-morning chat.
(*Photo courtesy of Linus Chao*)

Relations with Neighbors

Generally, as urbanization speeds up and the rhythm of social life accelerates, people have less time to interact with those who live in the same neighborhood, hence relations with them become less close than they used to be in agricultural societies. How true is this pattern in China with its traditional culture emphasizing close social relationships, particularly in congested cities like Shanghai where people are forced to live physically close?

We asked this question: "Do you often chat and spend leisure time with your neighbors?" Rather surprisingly, almost half of the sample (47.5 percent) reported that they hardly ever chatted and seldom spent leisure time with their neighbors. Neighborhood relations on the whole did not seem to be very close at the interactional level, despite the fact that people literally lived next to each other in extremely crowded housing units. Only a quarter of them (25.8 percent) said they did so almost everyday. The rest were split among three other options: once in two/three days, once in a week, and once in half a month.

The area of residence, education, and age were three factors with significant correlations. We found a large difference between villagers and urbanites in their interactions with neighbors. Even though villagers lived in more sparsely populated areas, they interacted with their neighbors much more frequently than urbanites did: as many as two-fifths of the former (40.3 percent) said they chatted and spent leisure time with their neighbors almost everyday, compared to only 19.8 percent of the latter. Over half of the urban sample (56.1 percent) hardly ever talked to their neighbors; in contrast, a little over a quarter of village respondents (27.6 percent) reported the same behavior. These findings clearly show that rural residents in China, just as elsewhere, live a slower life and have closer relations with their neighbors.

Education as a variable is negatively related to the frequency of interaction with neighbors. Well over half of the higher-education group (58.1 percent) said they hardly ever chatted and spent leisure time with their neighbors, constrasting with 35.9 percent of the lower-education group. While over one-third of the latter group said they did so almost everyday, only 17.8 percent of the former group followed that pattern. This seems to suggest that in addition to urbanization, a better-educated population will be characterized by less intimate neighborly relations regardless of where they live.

It is interesting to note that people over 50 years of age appeared busier than those under 29: over half of the former (53.7 percent) reported they hardly ever interacted with their neighbors; in contrast, only 37.3 percent of the latter could not find any time to have such interaction.

One way to measure one's relation with another person is to see if he can approach that person to borrow money. In China, as we have noted, people do not go to banks for loans; they go to their work units or personal friends or relatives to borrow money. So we asked this question: "If you urgently needed Y70-80, could you approach your neighbors to borrow it?" This sum is not a trivial amount. It is the monthly wage of a young worker who has just joined a factory.

Over half of the respondents (53.1 percent) claimed that they could approach their neighbors for the money. What is really interesting is the enormous difference between rural villagers and urbanites. While an overwhelming majority of the village sample (84.5 percent) said they could borrow that amount from their neighbors, only 41.8 percent of the urban respondents said they could do so. There were many more urbanites (52.0 percent) than villagers (13.9 percent) who could not approach their neighbors to borrow money. This is solid evidence that people had closer relations with neighbors in rural areas than in cities.

It is commonplace in metropolitan Shanghai that four or five or even more families live in one single old-style house, which could be so crowded that physical friction would often generate disputes among neighbors. In rural villages, people living next door to each other may also quarrel. It would be interesting to know how people would handle quarrels, and particularly heated ones. We asked: "What will you do if you have a quarrel with a neighbor and receive verbal abuse?"

Over half of the respondents (57.2 percent) said that in a situation like that they would control themselves. Quite a sizable number of people (31.4 percent) had respect for the neighborhood committee, saying they would go there for a settlement. What is interesting is the uniform influence of the neighborhood committee in both urban and rural areas. The percentages who would take their disputes to the neighborhood committee were identical, 31.4 percent, for metropolitan Shanghai, the two small towns, and the rural villages. The neighborhood committee is a new element introduced into the lives of the Chinese since 1949. It is a government presence that directly reaches every family. Our findings show that this institution has already established itself in the local neighborhood. It has taken over the functions of elders in mediating disputes. In contrast to those who would control themselves or take the case to the neighborhood committee, only a few (7.7 percent) would lose temper and curse back.

Age was a relevant factor. As one might expect, the young were found to be less patient than the old: about one out of nine of the former (11.6 percent) said they would curse back, compared to only 1.8 percent of the latter who would do so. The old seemed to trust neighborhood committees much more than the young. More than one-third of those over 50 (36.0 percent) said they would go there for a solution; in contrast, only a quarter of those below 29 (25.0 percent) would seek help from the neighborhood committees. In Shanghai city, where living conditions were much more congested, people were less patient than rural villagers: 55 percent in Shanghai would control themselves compared to 62.2 percent in the villages. But even in an extremely crowded living environment, such as the one we found in metropolitan Shanghai, people on the whole seemed to take a rational attitude toward neighborhood quarrels.

The strongest message emerging from the data presented in this section is that neighborhood relations in China are in a process of change. Interaction among neighbors used to be very close in this society with a traditional emphasis on cordial ties. Despite the extremely congested living quarters, the evidence shows that neighbors strive to keep their distance today. If there is an emergency financial need, many still can count on their neighbors for help. There seem to be a number of contributing factors. Our data show clearly that urbanization, even in its mild form in China, is introducing an impersonal element to human relations in a very dramatic way. Villagers definitely have much closer relations with people who live in their neighborhood than urban residents. Education is another factor. It seems that as people become better educated, they broaden both their interests and their circle of friends beyond the immediate environment. Their interaction with neighbors decreases. Another factor, we think, lurks in the background. This is the social climate in which Chinese people have lived in the last forty years. The Cultural Revolution and many other political campaigns have made people wary of what they say to others who are not close relatives or intimate friends. We will come back to this point with some concrete data later.

Relations with Older People

One of the values cherished in traditional Chinese culture was respect for age. One way to show such respect was to restrain oneself from arguing with or even expressing opinions different from those of a senior person. We wanted to know if this is still true. First we asked: "Do you think that younger people should show proper respect to older people?"

Almost all our respondents (97.4 percent) said "definitely yes" or "yes." Out of the 1,994 valid responses, only 14 said there was "no need" for showing respect. This shows that the value of respect for the old was very much alive in Chinese society. In their study of village and family life in Southern China, Parish and Whyte (1978) also found little change in the respect for the aged. In our survey, it is interesting to note that people with high media news exposure were firmer supporters of this value than those who had low media news exposure. Almost half of the former (47.1 percent) said definitely yes, compared to 30.1 percent of the latter. The difference is rather pronounced and unexpected. It is possible that those with high media news exposure identified themselves more closely with the political system and thus had greater respect for authority, including those senior in age. Nearly all the top leaders in China are old.

We found this traditional value to be upheld more firmly in the villages, where 43.1 percent of the respondents answered "definitely yes," than in Shanghai or the towns, where only 34 percent felt this way.

However, what is meant by "proper respect"? There could be many ways to show proper respect. One traditional way was to refrain from expressing disagreement. So we had this question: "If you do not agree with the opinions of someone who is senior, will you express your different opinions?"

We were rather surprised that an overwhelming majority of the sample (94.0 percent) said either "definitely yes" or "yes." This suggests that while people still uphold the value of respecting the old, they seem to be practicing much less self-control and deference than before when it comes to expressing their opinions.

The area of residence and media news exposure were two relevant factors. Rather unexpectedly, villagers were found to be more affirmative about the expression of different opinions than urbanites: about one-third of the former (32.2 percent) said they would "definitely" express their different opinions; in contrast, only 19.5 percent of the latter took this position. People with high media news exposure (28.4 percent definitely yes) also gave a stronger endorsement to the expression of different opinions than their low-exposure counterparts (19.3 percent).

If the different opinions were expressed in a polite way, the old probably would not feel too offended. But what about having an argument with them? Our next question was: "If you do not agree with what older people tell you, would you argue with them?"

Now a different attitude was revealed: about two-fifths of the respondents (39.3 percent) reported that they would not *argue* with them. This is a much higher figure than the percentage who would rather not *express* their different opinions (6 percent). However, we should by no means underestimate the weight of 53.1 percent of the total sample saying they would not hesitate to argue with the old if they disagreed. This seems to be a rather dramatic change in attitudes toward relations with those who are senior. In traditional China, it was unthinkable for a young person to argue with someone senior in age.

While those who were young and better educated tended to be more assertive, interestingly the most prominent factor was the influence of Western culture. Those who were under heavy Western cultural influence were more likely to argue (60.8 percent) than those under little Western cultural influence (49.2 percent).

The combined message from responses to the three questions above is that the value of respect for the old is still positively held in principle among the Chinese people, but this value has taken on a different meaning. Showing respect does not mean silence or acquiescence. In fact more than half of the respondents would not hesitate to argue if they disagreed. This is a most significant change from the past. While those with heavy media news exposure tend to show more respect for age, they are also more vocal in expressing their different views. Although Western cultural influence has been present in China for only about ten years since the door was opened to the outside world in 1978, it already seems to have made a difference. Those under heavy Western cultural influence appear to be far more outspoken.

Relations with Others in General

In this section, we discuss relations with others in a general way. We look at patterns of advice seeking, factors that influence social interaction patterns, ways of handling relations in an ambiguous setting, and the traditional concept of reciprocity.

One kind of interaction is the seeking of advice. We asked: "During the last month have you consulted others (excluding your family members) on something?"

One-third of the sample (33.1 percent) said yes. The area of residence, education, gender, and age were relevant factors. We found urbanites (40.8 percent), people with higher education (44.1 percent), men (38.4 percent) and the middle age group (35.2 percent) consulting with others more than villagers (18.0 percent), people with lower education (21.3 percent), women (27.1 percent), and the old (28.3 percent).

What did they consult about? Over half of the respondents (53.6 percent) said they talked about work. The rest of the responses were divided among such topics as children, housing, prices of daily necessities, family problems, etc., none of which represented more than 7 percent. No significant correlations were found between these topics and any of the independent variables.

We then changed the direction of the first question by asking: "During the last month have other people (excluding your family members) consulted you on something?" In communication research, those more frequently consulted by others are considered "opinion leaders."

A little more than a quarter of the sample (27.7 percent) gave a positive answer, slightly lower than the 33 percent who consulted others. This time, the area of residence, education, and Western cultural influence were relevant. As one might expect, urban residents (34.3 percent) and people with higher education (38.6 percent) were consulted far more than rural villagers (8.4 percent) and people with lower education (16.7 percent). What is interesting is that those under heavy Western cultural influence (40.4 percent) were also consulted much more than those under little Western cultural influence (20.6 percent). Exposure to media news, which has been found to be correlated to opinion leadership in other countries, showed a small and positive correlation, but this correlation disappeared when other factors were controlled.

What were people consulted about? Work (43.9 percent) again ranked highest among all topics. Though marriage and family issues (12.9 percent) represented the second highest percentage, it was much lower than work issues. Also none of the demographic factors were found to have correlations with the topics of consultation.

So it was work, a topic that was generally considered to be less personal, about which people consulted or were consulted most. Remember that in our questions we excluded family members as the providers or recipients of advice. This means that people discussed with non-family members things that were less intimate. More personal issues, such as children, marriage, and family, it seems, would be topics for consultation mainly among family members.

We wondered what general factors influenced people's relations with others in Chinese society. So we asked this question: "In our society today, what factor do you think most influences our relations with others?"

Over half of the sample believed that friendship (26.3 percent) and money (25.6 percent) influenced social relations most. Face and feelings (22.8 percent), traditionally important, ranked a close third. The findings are listed in figure 4.3.

The fact that money almost tied with friendship as the most important factor points to a much talked-about assertion that Chinese society has recently turned highly materialistic under the current drive toward economic reform. Forty years of revolution has failed to suppress people's desire for money. On the contrary, money seems to have become something very important in Chinese social life.

Different groups of people had different perceptions. In this case, one's area of residence and education were found to be related to the perceptions of social relations. It is most interesting that while more villagers (39.9 percent) than urbanites (22.4 percent) saw friendship as the factor that influenced social relations most, more Shanghai resi-

friendship	26.3%
money	25.6%
face and feelings	22.8%
social position	13.3%
public interest	10.7%
others	1.2%

Figure 4.3 Factors Influencing Social Relations

dents (30.7 percent) than those in rural areas (16.3 percent) perceived money to be the most important factor. As a matter of fact, friendship ranked first in the rural list, but among the urban residents money topped the list. This is not too surprising as we know that Shanghai is a commercialized metropolitan city, and market economy experiments in the past few years seem to have enhanced greatly people's consciousness of money.

It is even more amazing to find that among people with higher education, money (31.9 percent), not friendship (20 percent), was perceived to be the factor that influenced human relations most. In contrast, those who had lower education believed that frienship (35.1 percent) played a more important role in maintaining social relations than money (18.5 percent). The traditional concept among the educated Chinese that one should strive to find peace in poverty has largely vanished.

The percentages we report here do not necessarily represent reality; they represent people's perceptions of reality. If we postulate that the perceptions of urbanites and people with higher education are closer to reality because they are in a better position to see reality more objectively, then money would be the most important factor influencing people's relations with others in China of today.

In discussing social relations with neighbors, we have suggested that the social climate in China seems to have had a constraining effect. We now look at some data that bear on this point. The degree to which people trust strangers could be an indicator of how open or guarded they are in interacting with each other in a society. We asked this question: "When you meet someone for the first time, what should you do?" We offered three options: trust him first; don't trust him until you come to know him better; do not trust him, he may very likely use you.

Surprisingly, an overwhelming majority of the respondents (84.5 percent) said they would not trust the stranger until they got to know him better. Only a small number of people (12.4 percent) would choose to trust him first. These findings suggest that there exists an unusually high degree of mutual suspicion among Chinese meeting for the first time, quite different from the traditional concept of hospitality even for strangers. This is probably partly due to the lesson that people learned from the ten years of the Cultural Revolution, when there were numerous instances of people betraying their colleagues, close friends, and even immediate family members in order to protect themselves from persecution by the Gang of Four.

What is equally surprising is that this mutual suspicion is widely shared. Neither age, nor education, nor area of residence, nor any other factors were found related to the cynical way people regard strangers.

In dealing with social relations in traditional Chinese culture, people emphasized the ethic of repaying kindness shown to them by others. The Confucian teaching that kindness must be repaid with kindness was ingrained in the Chinese mind. How do people look at this Confucian ethic now? We asked: "In our society today, how important is it that we repay the kindness shown to us by others?"

A large majority of the sample still considered this ethic to be either "very important" (25.4 percent) or "quite important" (56.7 percent). Though very few (1.3 percent) perceived it in an entirely negative way (not important at all), quite a number of people (16.6 percent) were moderately negative toward this ethic, saying it was "not very important." Apparently this traditional value is still present, but far less significant than before.

The area of residence and media news exposure were relevant factors. As we would expect, villagers were found to be far more traditional than urbanites. Almost two-fifths of the rural sample (38.8 percent) said that it was very important to repay kindness, compared to only 20 percent of the urban residents who said so. In contrast, we saw more urban dwellers (18.5 percent) than villagers (11.5 percent) dismissing this value as being not very important. The fact that nearly one out of five urban residents considered this traditional value not very important is a rather shocking finding. Media news exposure made a difference: people with high media news exposure (31.5 percent saying very important) seemed to respect this value more than those with low exposure (19.8 percent).

Generally, relations with others appear to be much less intimate than those with relatives; they tend to be superficial. Money seems to become increasingly important as a factor influencing social relations. And there is a surprisingly high degree of mutual suspicion among initial acquaintances. However, the traditional value of repaying kindness, a very important cornerstone of social relations in China, is still largely honored, although there are clear signs of erosion in urban areas.

Discussion

Despite the many social upheavals in the past forty years, relations with relatives, who still hold membership in the kinship network, seem to remain relatively close among the Chinese people. Even though the formal dimensions of the kinship structure, especially its economic foundation, have been destroyed, the affiliative ties among relatives are still moderately strong. But urbanization, education, and now an influx of Western culture may activate the kind of impersonal social processes that further erode the traditionally solid kinship structure which has been the mainstay of Chinese culture.

We see this trend in our findings that urbanites, people who are better educated, and those under heavy Western cultural influence tend to develop more of their relational ties beyond the kinship network. In other words, people in these categories have a more flexible perspective on human relations and show an increasingly stronger preference for developing social networks outside the kinship boundaries to enlist social and psychological support. This trend is particularly strong among those heavily exposed to Western cultural influence through the media,[1] as we see in table 4.2.

Those heavily exposed to Western cultural influence not only tend to rely on friends rather than relatives for financial help, they are more inclined to argue with elders when they disagree. This behavioral pattern would not be tolerated under the kinship system. Interestingly, those individuals are far more likely to be consulted by others in their role as "opinion leaders," as if what they have learned from Western cultural programs in the mass media has some instrumental value in the new changing social and economic environment.

While there appears to be a steady shift toward social relations outside the kinship structure, these diverse human ties are definitely less close and more unstable than family relations or extensions of the kinship network. This probably has been one of the salient characteristics of Chinese culture for ages, and therefore is not something new. What is new are two powerful elements injected into the picture only in recent years. Social relations in traditional China were largely based on the kinship network and often expressed in simulated kinship terms. The kinship structure lent to them a measure of stability. Now that the formal kinship structure has been disbanded—except for

Table 4.2 Western Cultural Influence and Relational Ties

	WESTERN CULTURAL INFLUENCE	
	High	Low
Source of loan		
Ask friends	52.0%	26.2%
Ask relatives	24.0%	47.5%
Argue with elders	60.8%	49.2%
Consulted by others	40.4%	20.6%

social visiting and feasting in some rural areas during such festivals as the lunar New Year, as Cohen (1990) has observed in one village in North China—social relations in China today are searching for a new anchor. There are indications that social relations in China now function in a state of ambiguity.

In other words, the weakening of the kinship basis does not mean that social relations are freed from their traditional bondage and are therefore improving in quality. Probably the opposite is true. One such clear indication is the extraordinarily high mutual suspicion among new acquaintances. This is largely due to the radical structural changes in society, which have destroyed many of the familiar social bearings, and the frequent political campaigns that have served to alienate people not only from the prevailing social system in general but also from individuals in various social groups. Wary of the many unseen pitfalls in the social environment, and unsure of the intentions of those one interacts with in one's surroundings, a person tends to be on guard most of the time.

The other new element is the heightened consciousness of money in the midst of the current economic reform. Money was something of a mixed blessing in traditional China. No one could deny that money was useful. Yet there was the traditional notion that money "stinks." Educated Chinese, especially refined scholars, considered themselves to be above money. They searched for life's meaning and a sense of peace in poverty. The much-cited story of the poet Tao Yuan-ming illustrates that given a choice between dignity in poverty and richness in humiliation, Chinese traditionally chose poverty.

The culturally conditioned emphasis on poverty was reaffirmed during the first thirty years of the People's Republic. Especially during the height of the Cultural Revolution, poverty was elevated to the status of a supreme virtue. But all this has abruptly changed in the last ten years. Under the Four Modernizations campaign, the country is now supposed to get rich. Since China's door has been opened, Chinese people have been dazed to find how rich people are in the world outside. In this environment of abrupt change, as our data showed, money, or rather the desire for money, has begun to play an increasingly prominent role in initiating, developing, and maintaining social relations. The old types of social relations built on shared traditional values and beliefs seem to be giving way to relations formed largely on the basis of practical interests and utilitarian concerns. As a current popular saying goes, the eyes of Chinese are supposed to look forward, but in reality they are set only on money. In Chinese language, "looking forward" and "looking only at money" are both pronounced as *xiang qian kan*.

If the traditional social relations were a significant force of societal integration in China of the past, then their erosion may usher in a period of prolonged and chaotic adjustment, possibly with a lasting impact on Chinese society and culture.

Chapter 5

Job Preferences and Work Ethic

Organizational values and work relations were a second major part of our Shanghai survey. The Chinese call their work organizations *danwei*, where one works eight hours a day and six days a week and earns, besides one's salary or wage, almost all one's social benefits, including medical care and family-planning allowances. Danwei rewards when one performs a heroic deed and punishes when one commits a serious mistake. One lives in a housing unit provided by one's danwei. Quite often one's children go to the school run by the danwei. One makes friends among those working in the same danwei. One's lifelong association with danwei ends only with death. The family gets a wreath from the danwei. It is not an exaggeration to say that the danwei culture represents a large portion of contemporary Chinese culture.

The benefits of the danwei incur a responsibility: one is expected to perform at his best, theoretically as a contribution to the socialist national reconstruction. In reality, the opposite seemed to be true up until recently. Because there was no occupational mobility, and because job performance was not associated with reward under China's egalitarian wage policy until it was recently modified, the traditional Chinese concept of diligence was replaced by a practice known as the "iron rice bowl." Once a person got a job, it was like an iron rice bowl, which was unbreakable and would feed him forever. Regardless of one's performance or lack of it, one received the same reward as everyone else. This practice, cultivated by the collective economic system before 1976, has been challenged in the past few years under the economic reform. Other changes in work organizations included small-scale experiments in the free flow of labor, by balancing government assignments with some individual choices. These new experiments permitted some limited occupational mobility.

We wanted to know to what extent the recent economic reforms had brought changes to Chinese organizational life at the workplace. How do people feel about their work? What preferences do they have about their jobs? Has there been a revival of the traditional Chinese work ethic? How do they feel about some of the new measures introduced to their work environment, primarily the requirements for work evaluation? Just as family relations reflect cultural values in that intimate core of one's life, the work ethic and work relations can reveal values in that important sphere of activities that provide subsistence for individuals and survival for the social system as a whole. These topics will be analyzed in this chapter. Organizational relations will be discussed in chapter 6.

Job Preferences

Were people content with their present jobs? How did they attach practical importance to different categories of jobs? If they were allowed to choose from among several job opportunities, what kind of job would they prefer?

We first asked a simple and direct question: "Do you like your present work?" Somewhat to our surprise, the respondents were more or less evenly divided between "like very much" (43.3 percent) and "like somewhat" (56.2 percent). Almost none of them (0.6 percent) said "do not like." Even more surprising was that more than half of the young respondents (55.2 percent) said they liked their work very much, compared to only 23.9 percent of the old folks who said so. It seems that under China's current occupational structure, although jobs do not pay well and occupational mobility is extremely difficult if not impossible, holding any job offers a high degree of security and thus a fair amount of satisfaction. Young people who have recently joined the work force are probably quite happy that they have found a place in what may soon become an increasingly tight job market. Older people, on the other hand, who have been doing the same jobs for years without any chance of promotion or job change, are understandably less happy with their current job situations.

Education was also found to be a significant factor: there were more higher-education people (46.5 percent) than lower-education respondents (35.7 percent) who said they liked their jobs very much. This is understandable as normally the jobs held by well-educated people would be better than those held by people with limited education.

If old people didn't seem to be as excited about their work as their young counterparts, then how about their attitudes toward retirement? We asked this question: "If you retire now and can get enough pension to live comfortably, do you want to continue to work, or do you want to retire now?"

As many as two-thirds of the sample (65.0 percent) would rather continue to work than retire and live comfortably. What's interesting is that despite the fact the old people were less happy about their work than the young, they were in no mood to retire. In fact, slightly more older people (68.7 percent) would want to continue to work than the young (65.4 percent). It is perhaps true across all cultures that retirement, which is often coupled with a sense of diminished accomplishment and limited involvement in the larger social life, is less appealing than work. But in China there are also practical reasons involved: retirement would, in most cases, be followed by less pay, fewer fringe benefits and most important, fewer privileges for those who used to hold important positions. Whatever the reasons, people seemed to want to hold on to their jobs.

Figure 5.1 Retired persons practice Taichi in the morning. (*Photo courtesy of Linus Chao*)

The more one works, the more one gets. This has become more a reality than a theory in China's rural areas since the commune system was abolished and land was reallocated among the farmers in the early eighties. We were not surprised to find that an overwhelming majority of the villagers (84.0 percent) wanted to continue to work, compared to 59.0 percent of the urban residents. Also, unlike urban workers, farmers have no pension to count on. To say that they can retire and live comfortably probably does not make sense to them.

A rather interesting implication is the finding that people under heavy Western cultural influence were less eager to continue to work than those under low influence. Over half of the former (51.0 percent) said they would like to retire and live comfortably, compared to only 26.7 percent of the latter.

How would the generally positive attitude toward work relate to pay? How important is pay as part of the Chinese people's conception of work now that the "iron rice bowl" is pushed aside, at least for the time being? Do people want to work because they are concerned about pay or because they find their work interesting? We designed this question: "Which kind of job do you prefer?" We presented two options: a job that is boring but pays well, or a job that is very interesting but pays less.

Perhaps not surprisingly, the better-paid, boring job clearly received a higher endorsement (61 percent) from our respondents than the less-paid, interesting job (39.0 percent). So pay was more important than interest on the whole. The young considered pay even more important than the old: 65.7 percent of the former would rather choose a better-paid boring job, compared to 49.5 percent of the latter. This is not difficult to understand. The young people need money badly, for example, to get married. In the Shanghai area, a wedding ceremony may cost a young worker five years of wages in present-day arrangements. Even in the hinterlands which Unger and Xiong (1990) studied, a son's marriage can cost more than a year's income of the whole household. In the Shanghai area, the young people are particularly attracted by many of the modern consumer items, such as television, stereo sets, cameras, videocassette recorders, and so forth, all of which are expensive.

Gender seldom appears to be a significant factor in our analysis, but in this question it is. We were amazed to find that women valued interest more than men: almost half of the female respondents (47.7 percent) said they would rather have "a job that is very interesting but pays less," compared to only 31.1 percent of the male sample. The majority of the men (68.9 percent) preferred a well-paid, boring job to an interesting but poorly paid job.

Figure 5.2 Under the economic reform policy, private stores are doing profitable business. (*Photo courtesy of Linus Chao*)

Media news exposure as a variable also shows its significance here: as many as 76.8 percent of the high media news exposure people preferred "a job that is boring but pays well," compared to 51.6 percent of their low-exposure counterparts. If anything, all the media publicity in recent years about people who achieved an annual income of 10,000 yuan seems to have left its mark on its audience.

In order to further test whether pay was still the first consideration in our respondents' choice of jobs when elements other than interest were included, we asked this question: "If there was an opportunity to choose another job, what would be your top priority?" In reality, people in China have few opportunities to chose another job. We offered seven options to see what their preferences would be.

Of the seven choices, "high income" was the most popular among the respondents (36.6 percent). "Opportunity for career accomplishment" came second (27.4 percent) and "interest" dropped to third place (19.0 percent). The rest of the sample was divided among the other choices, none of which indicated a high percentage, as shown in figure 5.3.

Our data are consistent with the research findings of Lin and Bian (1991). A representative sample of the working population in

high income	36.6%
opportunity for career accomplishment	27.4%
interest	19.0%
more leisure time	6.1%
more promotion opportunity	5.6%
good collegial relations	4.2%
miscellaneous	1.1%

Figure 5.3 Criteria for Job Preferences

Tianjin showed that state agencies and enterprises were the preferred routes of career attainment. They offered both better income and opportunities for career advancement. An earlier study by Lin and Xie (1988) showed essentially the same pattern.

In our survey, villagers were found to be more money conscious than urban residents: half of the former (49.7 percent) chose the "high income" option as against 34.0 percent in Shanghai and 25.2 percent in Qingpu towns. The high rural preference for income was possibly caused by the farmers' craze for building new houses in the past few years. On the contrary, urban dwellers (19.9 percent) and townspeople (23.6 percent) emphasized "interest" more than villagers (14.0 percent). For urban residents, building one's own house was nearly impossible.

Quite unexpectedly, we found more women (40.0 percent) than men (33.6 percent) making "high income" their top priority. This may sound inconsistent with their answers to the pay versus interest question. In that question, the female respondents were less money-conscious than the males when asked to make a choice between good pay and interest as a criterion for job preference. However, in this question the "high income" option was set against several other factors, including "opportunity for career accomplishment." Far more men (33.5 percent) than women (20.7 percent) selected "opportunity for career accomplishment" as their top priority, reflecting perhaps some deep-rooted structural constraints against career advancement for women even in contemporary China. With the door to career advancement partly closed, "high income" thus became a bit more attractive, relatively speaking, for women than for men. It may be noted that women still preferred interest slightly more (20 percent) than men (18.1 percent).

The same phenomenon was observed when media news exposure was introduced as an independent variable. When it was a matter of a simple choice between high pay and an interesting job, people with high news exposure wanted well-paid, boring jobs more than their low-exposure counterparts. When more options were offered, including "opportunity for career accomplishment," more people with high news exposure (37.4 percent) selected career accomplishment as their top priority than those with low exposure (20.4 percent). We think this is because those who keep themselves informed on news from the official media identified themselves more with the current system and saw greater opportunity for career advancement. In relative terms, given their perception of limited career opportunities, those with low media news exposure (39.6 percent) found "high income" more attractive than those with high exposure (27.4 percent).

We are quite clear at this point about people's job priority considerations. Income, career opportunity, and job interest were the top choices. In order to obtain additional information about job preferences of our respondents, we asked this question: "Which kind of work do you prefer? A high position, with a heavy responsibility, or an ordinary position, but with a responsibility not so heavy?"

This is a measure of career aspirations in a sociopolitical climate where responsibility sometimes carries risks of uncertainty. Slightly more than half of the sample (52.4 percent) said they preferred "high position, but heavy responsibility." Rather interestingly, people under heavy Western cultural influence did not want a high-position job that involved heavy responsibility. As many as 71.9 percent of the heavy influence group preferred to have an "ordinary position, but responsibility not heavy," compared to 41.6 percent of their low-influence counterparts. This is more evidence that people under Western cultural influence seem to detach themselves from the current system.

It is interesting to note that villagers liked high-position and heavy-responsibility work more than urban residents. Three-fifths of our village sample (60.8 percent) said they preferred this kind of work, compared to 48.8 percent of the Shanghai respondents. It seems that in the rural environment, responsibility means primarily dealing with a small circle of individuals in a more personal setting. There is probably a little more local autonomy in rural areas. In urban centers, any position with heavy responsibility would require interaction with a complex bureaucracy and thus become less appealing to urban workers than their rural counterparts.

Young people did not enjoy responsibility as much as the old: more people in the old group (62.4 percent) preferred high positions with heavy responsibility than in the young group (48.6 percent). It could be that young people are not yet ready for heavy responsibility. Young people are also more heavily exposed to the influence of Western culture, which does not seem to contribute to a sense of high responsibility.

Other than the intrinsic rewards of jobs, such as income, career opportunity, and interest, preferences of specific job categories in a society can reflect both the social status attached to a particular occupation and the general trend of values. In traditional China, scholars and officials were held in high esteem, while merchants were by and large not highly regarded even though they had more wealth. We wanted to know what were the preferred occupational categories today. We asked: "What ideal job would you like to do?" We offered eight categories and asked the respondents to select only one.

The "managerial" position received the highest endorsement and that of "political, Party cadre" the lowest. Figure 5.4 shows the list in order of decreasing endorsement.

There are some important implications. First, the list seems to suggest that Chinese society is turning toward a more materialistic and pragmatic-oriented society. This is not only reflected in the high percentage of those choosing the "managerial job," which many believed could earn more money than other jobs in China today, but also is seen in the fact that the job of college/high school teacher received a very weak endorsement. College/high school teachers used to be a profession highly respected and very much envied by the Chinese. There was the traditional belief that teachers deserved high respect. This profession no longer appears to be attractive. We know that teachers' social status has dropped to a very low level. And their financial plight is even worse. A college professor, for example, now makes 200–250 yuan (about $55 to $70) a month, and an average high school teacher makes much less. Given the high inflation rate, life is difficult for them.

Under the current economic reforms, someone who is self-employed stands a good chance of making considerable money. But

managerial	27.0%
research or scientific personnel	22.9%
ordinary worker, service personnel	18.3%
service industry that has lots of contacts with foreigners	10.0%
artist	5.4%
college/high school teacher	5.2%
self-employed worker	4.7%
political, Party cadre	4.1%

Figure 5.4 Choices of Ideal Jobs

Figure 5.5 A roadside barber, typical of the new individual small enterprises now encouraged by the government.
(*Photo courtesy of Linus Chao*)

why was the enthusiasm for self-employed occupations so low? Self-employed money-making entrepreneurs do not enjoy high social status for various cultural and social reasons. They are categorized as petty merchants, who have never been highly regarded in Chinese society. They have no formal affiliation with any organization, when such affiliation is important in a status-conscious China. But this is only part of the story. In recent years, private enterprises, with their dynamism unseen in state-owned organizations and their creative flexibility in management and marketing, have become an important addition to the still-changing economic system. They have helped ease

Figure 5.6 A well-managed grocery store in Qingpu Town, a sign of change. (*Photo courtesy of Linus Chao*)

the unemployment problem of the young in some tangible ways and supply the market with what consumers cannot get from state-owned enterprises. However, life is not easy for these "little bosses," as Chinese people now call them. They could easily be caught in a jam if they do not know how to handle things the way the establishment wants them handled. Such factors as frequent government policy changes and cuts in supply of raw materials from state channels could all affect the smooth functioning of private enterprises, many of which are small and fragile with a limited amount of capital. In addition, private entrepreneurs do not receive free medical care, which all workers of state-owned organizations enjoy, and they have no pension benefits.

That more than one out of five respondents considered research and scientific work an ideal career can be seen as an encouraging sign for China's drive toward modernization. There has been an intensified interest in science and technology in recent years, and special newspapers devoted to these topics now enjoy phenomenal circulation.

One of the most significant findings was the extremely low endorsement of the profession of "political, Party cadres." During the Cultural Revolution, and even in the years before that, going back to

Figure 5.7 Making a living by sharpening knives and scissors: a new private enterprise in Zhujiajiao. (*Photo courtesy of Linus Chao*)

the Great Leap Forward of 1958, political and Party cadres wielded enormous influence in China. The early debate in the 1950s was between the Red and the expert, meaning whether political ideology or technical expertise was more important. Chairman Mao and other top leaders put the emphasis on the Red. If a Party cadre knew how to follow Mao's directives faithfully and manipulate his way in the huge bureaucratic maze, it did not matter whether he or she had any technical knowledge required for the job. The current economic reforms shifted somewhat back toward an emphasis on technical expertise. Our findings showed clearly how low the position of political, Party cadres has sunk in the eyes of the people. When there was not much political work to do, the cadres lost their usefulness. Because many of them had abused their power during the Cultural Revolution, they apparently incurred extreme resentment from the public.

Our findings are consistent with the results of two surveys of occupational preferences conducted among Chinese university students in the late 1980s. In one survey (n = 445) conducted in Xian (Zhao, 1989), other than "students studying overseas," which received the highest preference, the top two choices were staff members in a foreign trade company and administrative cadres in an enterprise. These were comparable to the managerial positions in our survey. Both offered good income and career opportunity. In a similar survey of university juniors and seniors (n = 197) in Beijing, Shanghai, Nanjing, Jinan and Qingdao (Teng and Yin, 1988), the three top ranks were identical. In both surveys, self-employed work was ranked low, next to the bottom in the Xian survey, and at the very bottom in the other survey. University teachers also ranked low.

In our data analysis, we found three variables to be significant in differentiating the responses regarding occupational preferences: area of residence, education, and Western cultural influence. Regarding the two top choices, that is, "managerial" and "research and scientific personnel," we saw higher percentages among Shanghai respondents (28.7 percent and 27.2 percent) than among villagers (20.2 percent and 16.5 percent). This is quite understandable as there were more such job opportunities in Shanghai than in rural villages. Interestingly, the third most popular choice, "ordinary worker, service personnel," received a much higher endorsement from the villagers than from the urban residents. Almost one-third of the village sample (31.3 percent) said their ideal was to be ordinary workers or service personnel, compared to only 12.6 percent of the Shanghai respondents. Apparently, the positions of workers and service personnel, which urban residents seem to take for granted and sometimes complain about because they want higher wages, are very attractive to village people who must till the land to earn a living and face all the uncertainties of an unpredictable natural environment.

Education definitely would affect people's occupational preferences. It is only natural that the more educated respondents (31.9 percent) compared to their less-educated counterparts (14.7 percent) saw "research personnel" as the most ideal job. The lower-education people would be happy just to be ordinary workers or service personnel: more than one-third of this group (35.0 percent) selected this option, while only 5.4 percent of the higher-education category did so. In the eyes of the well-educated people, self-employed occupations were low: hardly any of them (1.8 percent) wanted to be self-employed. This is indicative of the traditional low regard for petty merchants among people of the upper social class. The percentage among their lower-education counterparts was 9.0 percent, not too low a figure.

The profile for the heavy Western cultural influence group is revealing. Regardless of Western influence, many would like to be research or scientific personnel or managers. Western influence was not a factor. The work of artists, with its opportunity for creative expression under the open-door policy, seemed to be particularly attractive to those under heavy Western influence despite the low income usually associated with this profession. In the high-influence group, 22 percent chose artist as their ideal job, compared to only 2.8

percent in the low-influence group. On the contrary, those under heavy Western influence did not find the position of ordinary workers at all appealing. Only 6 percent made this their ideal choice, in contrast to 25.8 percent among those under little Western influence. Those under heavy Western influence wanted to have nothing to do with the work of cadres. Not a single one (a rare zero percent) wanted to be a Party cadre.

Workmate Preferences

What people consider to be ideal jobs reveals some aspects of their values. So does the concept of an ideal workmate. Workmate preferences could reflect, from a unique angle, an organization's work climate and the work attitudes of its members. We had this question for our respondents: "What kind of person do you prefer as your workmate? Someone with a high ability even though not a close friend, or a close friend who does not have a high ability?"

An overwhelming majority of the respondents (92.0 percent) would like a workmate to be one with outstanding work ability even though not a close friend. Only 8 percent wanted to work with a close friend who had poor work ability. The findings suggest that most people were serious about their work.

Age and media news exposure were found to be significantly related to how people answered this question. More old people (96.6 percent) than young (87.2 percent) preferred one with keen work ability even though not a close friend. It seems that for young people, friendship is relatively more important than for old people. The percentage of the high media news exposure group (92.6 percent) choosing work ability was a little higher than that of the low exposure group (89.6 percent). We also asked this somewhat difficult question: "What is the most important quality you look for in your colleagues?" We gave three equally attractive choices and allowed only one. Figure 5.8 is the order of qualities our respondents cited.

Age was the only relevant factor. To the young people, the quality of "friendly, easy to get along with" was the most important and

has strong sense of responsibility, completes tasks	(39.2%)
friendly, easy to get along with	(32.1%)
lofty character, highly respected	(28.7%)

Figure 5.8 Preferred Qualities of Workmates

friendly, easy to get along with	(46.8%)
lofty character, highly respected	(27.9%)
strong sense of responsibility, completes tasks	(25.3%)

Figure 5.9 Workmate Qualities Preferred by the Young

that of "strong sense of responsibility, completes tasks" the least. Figure 5.9 is the order for our younger respondents.

For the old people, the preferences were the other way round, shown in figure 5.10.

These findings seem to suggest that the young and the old were very different in their preferences for colleagues: the former emphasized close human relationships, while the latter were more task-oriented, attaching greater importance to responsibility and task completion.

In order to have a better sense of what kind of persons people would like to have for their workmates, we also asked this question: "If you want to pick a co-worker, which one would you prefer?" The two choices were: someone who works very hard, but has no sense of humor; or someone who does a minimum of work, but is a lot of fun.

A large majority of our respondents (78.5 percent) did not care much if their co-workers had a sense of humor or not; they would like to see them work hard. However, we found that the Western cultural influence made a big difference in their preferences for workmates. Almost half of the high Western influence group (49.0 percent) would rather have a co-worker "who does a minimum of work, but is a lot of fun," compared to only 12.5 percent of the low-influence subjects who did so. We will discuss this point later.

Again age made a difference. An overwhelming majority of the old group (92.4 percent) wanted their co-workers to work hard; whether one had a sense of humor was not important. The young did not quite share this attitude: more than one third of them (36.1 percent) said they wanted their colleagues to be a lot of fun; work was secondary in importance.

strong sense of responsibility, completes tasks	(48.3%)
lofty character, highly respected	(35.5%)
friendly, easy to get along with	(16.2%)

Figure 5.10 Workmate Qualities Preferred by the Old

Figure 5.11 The boat is both their home and their means of living. (*Photo courtesy of Linus Chao*)

There was a small gap between urban residents and rural farmers. Farmers seemed to be a bit more serious toward work in the choice of their co-workers. Those in the villages who wanted their co-workers to be fun only and did not care much about work accounted for 15.4 percent. One quarter of the Shanghai residents (24.6 percent) were found to be this way. Apparently, in Shanghai most people worked for state organizations, and it was relatively less important to have co-workers who took work seriously. In the villages, now that the People's Communes have been abolished, the situation is different. People work primarily for themselves, and one cannot afford to have co-workers who are a lot of fun to have around but do very little work.

Selecting a co-worker is a little different from hiring someone. With the former, one engages in a horizontal relationship; with the latter, one eatablishes a vertical relationship. But both could be included in the larger category of colleagues. The following question was similar to the previous one: "If you want to hire someone to work for you, which one would you prefer?" The same two choices were: someone who works very hard but has no sense of humor, or someone who does a minimum of work but is lots of fun.

We assumed that the percentage who selected the "work hard" option would be even higher than in the previous horizontal co-worker situation. Indeed it was: 88.4 percent of the sample were for the hard working type; only 11.6 percent chose the fun type.

Again age and Western cultural influence were relevant factors. Just as before, while only 5.5 percent of the old group would hire a fun-type person, 19.3 percent of the young would do so. Of the high Western cultural influence group, 22.0 percent wanted the fun type, compared to only 7.9 percent of the low-influence people.

Based on the findings from these questions, we were quite sure that generally people emphasized such qualities as high work ability, diligence, and strong sense of responsibility in their preferences for workmates. We also saw clear evidence that the young people and those under heavy Western cultural influence deviated from the mainstream.

Work Attitudes

While the previous two sections cover topics that may be put in the larger category of work ethic, this section deals specifically with work attitudes. Particularly, we wanted to know to what extent the economic reforms may have affected people's attitudes toward work. We wanted to know what the general work ethic was after so many years of "eating out of the same big pot" in China. We first asked a direct question: "What is your attitude toward work?"

Over half of the sample (52.2 percent) said they would try to do much more than others. One out of five (21.2 percent) said they would do a little more than others. The rest of the respondents were divided between the two less positive attitudes: "I do as much as others do" (12.0 percent) and "I do as much as I feel like doing" (14.7 percent). That is, the majority of the people (73.4 percent) held positive or relatively positive work attitudes.

Age, Western cultural influence, and media news exposure were found to have significant correlations with attitudes toward work. Quite consistent with previous answers, a large 71.4 percent of the old group claimed that they were holding the most positive work attitude, saying they would try to do much more than others, compared to a weak 41.3 percent of the young who had the same attitude. It is also understandable that more young people (23.2 percent) than old (9.1 percent) said they would do as much as they felt like doing.

People with high Western cultural exposure did not seem to be as enthusiastic about work as their low exposure counterparts. While as many as 60.3 percent of the low-exposure group took the "do much more than others" attitude, only 33.3 percent of the high-exposure people did so. The difference was rather pronounced.

On several questions we found people with high media news exposure taking a somewhat more positive stand toward various issues. Here again we found them to be a little more positive toward work than their low-exposure counterparts. While 56.1 percent of the former said they wanted to do much more than others, only 49.5 percent of the latter said so.

As Western cultural influence and exposure to official media news were related to work attitudes in opposite ways, we combined the two media variables into one scale to assess their cumulative effects.[1] The results are presented in table 5.1.

The most positive work attitudes were found when the use of official media news was high and Western cultural influence was low (b). Two-thirds of the respondents said they would try to do much more than others. People were least enthusiastic about work when they were under heavy Western influence and did not make much use of media news information (c). The difference between (b) and (c) was as large as 27.3 percent. Western influence seemed to have a strong suppressant effect. Even when the use of media news was high, heavy Western influence brought the level of work enthusiasm down to 47.2 percent (d), some 19 percent below the level in (b). When Western influence was low, even in the absence of heavy use of media news (a),

Table 5.1 Western Influence, Media News, and Efforts to Do Much More

WESTERN INFLUENCE	NEWS LOW	NEWS HIGH
low	56.0% (a)	66.0% (b)
	(582)	(427)
high	38.7% (c)	47.2% (d)
	(385)	(599)

56 percent of the respondents had highly positive work attitudes.

In order to obtain more accurate information about our respondents' attitudes toward work, we designed a more concrete question involving a hypothetical episode: "If you are doing an important job, but your friend asks you to go out and play, what will you do?"

Consistent with their answers to the previous question, most of the respondents (79.1 percent) said they would decline the invitation. Some (17.3 percent) would go out but still think about work. Only a tiny percentage of the sample (3.6 percent) said "just go out and have a good time."

Also consistent with their formerly expressed attitudes toward work, an overwhelming majority of the old group (92.1 percent) placed work above play and declined the invitation, as compared to 71.4 percent of the young respondents. We were not at all surprised to find that more low Western cultural influence people (84.9 percent) than their high-exposure counterparts (54.9 percent) took this positive attitude. Of those under high influence, 41.1 percent would accept the invitation and go, as compared to only 14.1 percent of those under low influence.

For a double check, we asked a similar question: "Suppose you are the leader of a unit (such as village head or factory manager). You have a lot of official business to handle. A very close friend invites you to attend his baby's 'full month' celebration. Will you put down your official business and go, or will you not go?"

The condition was devised to make it sound somewhat difficult for the respondent not to accept the invitation. However, not too small a majority of the respondents (69.9 percent) decided not to go. One out of five (19.5 percent) could not stand the temptation and said they wanted to go. The rest (10.7 percent) said "it depends."

Age was the only relevant factor. As many as four out of five (80.6 percent) among the old group would not go, compared to 64.1 percent of the young who took this option. This is consistent with the previous findings. The young people took work less seriously than the old.

Probably it is easier for one to discipline oneself than to discipline others. But work attitudes could also be reflected, in some way, in how one deals with somebody who has violated work discipline. So we had this question: "Suppose you send someone to do a job. The job is not finished, but he has gone out to play. What will you do?"

Of the four options we gave, "criticize him" was generally considered to be a severe but positive response. A bit to our surprise, a large majority of the sample (83.6 percent) took this harsh stand. Very few (2.6 percent) said "leave him alone." Of the others, 7.1 percent would punish this person, and 6.7 percent would forgive him. Of the independent variables, only education was found to be statistically significant: it made a small difference. People who had higher education appeared a little bit tougher than those who had lower education: 10 percent of the former were for "punishment", compared to 4.1 percent of the latter.

It seems that, on the whole, people had very positive work attitudes. Those who deviated from the mainstream were again these two groups: the young and those under heavy Western cultural influence.

Work Evaluation

One of the goals of China's economic reforms was to get rid of the "iron rice bowl" practice, which had to a large extent plagued workers' morale. Under such a practice, no vigorous work evaluation was necessary. As long as one could prove that politically he had "no problem," he did not have to worry about losing his "rice bowl" no matter how bad his work performance. It would be interesting to take a look at how people viewed work evaluation after almost a decade of economic reforms. We asked this question: "What is your attitude toward work evaluation? Do you support rigorous work evaluation once a year?" Four responses were offered: rigorous evaluation once a year, routine evaluation once a year, evaluation once in several years, and no need for evaluation.

An overwhelming majority of the sample supported either "rigorous evaluation once a year" (76.3 percent) or "routine evaluation once a year" (14.3 percent). Those who said "evaluation once in several years" or "no need for evaluation" accounted for very small percentages (3.6 percent and 5.8 percent respectively). This seems to suggest that people supported the new economic system that was being tried out and wanted to see a more competitive working environment.

Western cultural influence and exposure to official media news were found to be relevant, again in opposite ways. We found those under heavy Western cultural influence to be less enthusiastic about rigorous work evaluation than those under little influence. While as many as four out of five among the low-influence group (80.4 percent) said they were for "rigorous evaluation once a year," only 62.7 percent of the high influence group wanted it this way. We found more people under heavy influence (11.8 percent) than under little influence (3.9 percent) saying "no need for evaluation." It is usually the case that people who do not work hard hate to have rigorous work evaluation; they would rather see no evaluation at all.

The impact of media news exposure went just the other way, though not quite as pronounced. Those with high exposure were more positive about rigorous work evaluation than the low-exposure group. Over four-fifths of the former (82.7 percent) endorsed "rigorous evaluation once a year," compared to 74 percent of the latter.

We combined these two media variables into one scale to measure their cumulative effects. We present the results in table 5.2.

People were most positive about work evaluation when they made heavy use of official news information and were not under strong Western influence (b). Conversely if they were heavily influenced by Western culture and did not make much use of news information, their attitudes were least positive (c). The difference was nearly 16 percent. When Western influence and use of media news were both high (d) or both low (a), they seemed to counterbalance each other.

A key issue related to work performance in China during the last four decades has been the nature of incentives. A debate at the top policy level ever since the mid-1950s has centered on the relative weight of material incentives versus symbolic incentives. Chairman Mao leaned heavily on symbolic incentives. Beginning with the Great Leap

Table 5.2 Western Influence, Media News, and Rigorous Evaluation Once a Year

WESTERN INFLUENCE	NEWS LOW	NEWS HIGH
low	77.9% (a)	83.8% (b)
	(580)	(425)
high	68.2% (c)	74.7% (d)
	(384)	(598)

Forward of 1958, many production campaigns were waged to mobilize the Chinese people to join the gigantic task of socialist reconstruction. Mass rallies, public parades, banners, and honor rolls were extensively used to motivate the peasants and workers. Material incentives were kept at a minimum. The results have been mixed. At the height of a campaign, under the watchful eyes of campaign organizers and the local media, people generally performed at a high level. After a campaign was over, they went back to their practice of "eating from a big pot." Since performance was unrelated to reward, it made little difference whether or not one worked hard. The current economic reforms have been trying to change that by restoring some of the material incentives. A chief incentive has been the selective distribution of merit pay raises.

The work evaluation process supplies references to be considered for pay raises. We wanted to know what criterion was considered the most important by our respondents for the purpose of evaluation. We asked: "Under the present circumstances, which of the following should be the most important consideration for getting a raise in wage?" We offered three criteria and asked the respondents to choose only one: work performance, good human relations, and qualifications.

Consistent with their attitudes reflected in our discussions above, a large majority of the sample (81.6 percent) said "work performance" should be the most important consideration. Another 9.9 percent said "good human relations," and 8.6 percent mentioned "qualifications."

Age, education, and gender were relevant factors though the correlations were not high. We found a higher endorsement of "work performance" among the old group (90.0 percent) than among the young (78.0 percent). Young people, on the other hand, cared a little more about "good human relations" (10.2 percent) and "qualifications" (11.8 percent) than old people (3.0 percent and 6.9 percent respectively).

Better education means better qualifications. Therefore, even though the majority of the higher education group (78.2 percent) supported "work performance" as the most important pay raise consideration, 10.4 percent of them were for "qualifications," compared to 5.9 percent of the lower education group. People of lower education (89.1 percent) attached greater importance to "work performance."

It is interesting to see that slightly more male respondents (83.1 percent) endorsed "work performance" than female subjects (79.8 percent), and more women (11.2 percent) than men (6.3 percent) felt qualifications should be the most important criterion for pay raises.

The data we have presented here in this section showed rather clearly that a more competitive environment brought about by the economic reforms would heighten people's consciousness of work performance and eventually break them of the habit of "eating from a big pot." People generally wanted regular evaluation which would get their performance properly recognized so that they could receive their due rewards.

Discussion

Overall our survey shows a society of people who like their work and support a strong work ethic; they also favor rigorous work evaluation and equitable recognition of their job performance. This is a picture quite different from that of a multitude of people "eating out of a big pot." We do not know for sure to what extent the "big pot" practice still prevails. That practice is deeply imbedded in the Chinese economic system. Until the system is completely overhauled, we suspect that some residual of the "big pot" practice will linger on. Some initial improvement has already been made. China's limited success with economic recovery in the last few years would not have been possible if the "big pot" practice had not been in some way corrected. What our data have shown is that the economic reform programs, even in their current entangled form, were reintroducing a relatively healthy work ethic which had been destroyed by Mao's former egalitarian system.

Good morale and a healthy work ethic, however, need to be continuously matched by a responsive economic system. If the system is not responsive, sooner or later the people's morale and work ethic will die again. The system—not the people—should be held responsible for the current lag in productivity.

From our data, it is also evident that, possibly as a result of economic reforms and the open-door policy, some fundamental changes are occurring in cultural values that are related to the Chinese perception of the material world. Traditionally the Chinese people lived in a world of limited resources and a harsh natural environment. They had to work hard to survive. Their inhospitable environment also taught them to be contented with a sparse material life. They learned to live with few material aspirations. The traditional concept of striving to find peace in poverty best captures this mentality. It enabled the Chinese people to accept what they were not able to change.

Our data reflect a new Chinese concept, one that is becoming increasingly materialistic in orientation. In chapter 4, we saw money to be a prominent factor for social relations in China. This trend is also reflected in people's occupational preferences. To our respondents, pay seemed to be more important than any other factors in choosing an occupation. High income weighed more heavily than anything else.

A boring job that pays well was overwhelmingly preferred to a job that is interesting but pays less. Managerial positions, generally with high wages, were the top choice. Very few people wanted a teaching job, which used to be highly respected but now does not pay well and predictably carries low social status.

Another sign of change, which may have important implications, is the nearly total rejection of political and Party cadres as a desirable career choice. This is probably partly because a low-echelon Party cadre enjoys very few privileges under the current reform programs and yet runs the risk of losing his job whenever there is some structural change. We wonder whether this disinterest in a career as a political cadre might not have an ideological basis. In a recent survey of high school students (n = 569) in Shanghai (Shanghai jiaoyu keyan, 1989), when asked about their ideals, only 6 percent mentioned Communism. The top ranking value was the right to have freedom of choice, chosen by 59 percent.

In the same context, it is hardly surprising that news information from the official media had only a moderate effect, as we see from the summary in table 5.3.

In spite of the repeated pleadings of the official media for Chinese people to support the Four Modernizations by working hard, the results appeared to be rather marginal. Most respondents supported rigorous work evaluation and preferred a workmate who was not a friend but had high ability. Heavy exposure to the official news information only slightly strengthened these attitudes. What impressed them more, it seems, was not the spirit of sacrifice and dedication as exemplified by model Communist Party members like Lei Feng, but the news stories told of ordinary people who made it rich during the economic reform years. People who were heavy consumers of official news information overwhelmingly preferred boring jobs with high pay.

Two variables, age and Western cultural influence, consistently stand out as important factors. When these findings are put together, two very distinct profiles emerge. One is the young group and the

Table 5.3 Exposure to Official News and Work Attitudes

ITEMS	HIGH EXPOSURE	LOW EXPOSURE
Support rigorous evaluation	82.7%	74.0%
Prefer workmate of high ability	92.6%	89.6%
Prefer boring jobs with high pay	76.8%	51.6%

other, the group under heavy Western cultural influence. We first look at the young, table 5.4.

From these responses, we see a picture of young Chinese with a high degree of consistency but not reassuring as far as their work ethic is concerned. Compared with the old, the young people have a weaker sense of responsibility and a less strong work ethic. They are more oriented toward fun and less serious about work. They take work performance less seriously. They are less inclined to accept responsibility.

Are these traits largely a reflection of youth, something they will outgrow as they become mature? Or do we have a young generation of Chinese who are fundamentally different from their parents because of their vastly different life experiences? We are inclined to think it is more likely the latter case because of the influence of Western culture, to which these young people have been more heavily exposed. Generally, those under heavy Western influence are predominantly young, urban, and better educated. Their profile is shown in table 5.5.

Table 5.4 Contrasting Work Attitudes of the Young and the Old

ITEMS	YOUNG	OLD
Prefer what jobs		
responsibility not heavy	51.4%	37.6%
Prefer what kind of workmate		
someone having strong sense of responsibility	25.3%	48.3%
Workmate: hardwork type or fun type		
someone who does no work, but is a lot of fun	36.1%	7.6%
Work attitudes		
do much more than others	41.3%	71.4%
Asked to go out and play when doing important job		
decline	71.4%	92.1%
Criteria for pay raise		
emphasize work performance	78.0%	90.0%
emphasize good relations	10.2%	3.0%

Table 5.5 Western Cultural Influence and Work Attitudes

	WESTERN INFLUENCE	
Items	High	Low
Continue to work or retire		
retire and live comfortably	51.0%	26.7%
Prefer what jobs		
responsibility not heavy	71.9%	41.6%
Workmate: hardwork type or fun type		
someone who does no work, but is a lot of fun	49.0%	12.5%
Work attitudes		
do much more than others	33.3%	60.3%
Asked to go out and play when doing important job		
decline	54.9%	84.9%
Work evaluation		
rigorous evaluation once a year	62.7%	80.4%
no need for evaluation	11.8%	3.9%

These people under heavy Western cultural influence are similar to the young: they show a weaker sense of responsibility, a less hardworking spirit, and less strong work ethic. If they had the opportunity, many of them would rather retire and live comfortably. They are more fun-oriented and take work evaluation less seriously. People who have no firsthand knowledge about Western societies, particularly the American society, can be superficially impressed with the kind of lifestyle seen in American television programs and Hollywood films. What is rather striking is the finding that the differences between the high and low Western cultural influence groups (average 27.6 percent) are much greater than the differences between the young and old (average 21.3 percent). This finding suggests that Western cultural influence, rather than the immaturity of youth, is most likely the predominant factor.

With multivariate analysis of this kind, we know these relationships are not spurious. We know some kind of causality exists, but the results of correlational statistical analyses themselves do not specify the direction of causality. We gain an understanding about causality by applying additional knowledge about the data. Given the relationship between age and the work ethic, we know for sure that the direction of causality is not that people are young because they do not have a strong work ethic. Young age cannot be the consequence of a poor work ethic. Rather, people lack a strong work ethic because they are young, or because they have certain experiences associated with being young. Our data suggest that exposure to Western cultural influence is most likely part of those experiences that make young people in China develop a weak work ethic.

Chapter 6

Organizational Relations

Organizational relations are an important aspect of China's work units as they shape the climate in which the members perform their assigned tasks. Supportive and healthy relations between superiors and subordinates and among collegues make a more productive organizational atmosphere. The Cultural Revolution, unleashing merciless struggles among countless groups of people, poisoned organizational relations in China to a great extent as work units became a primary stage where many of the painful dramas of conflicts were performed. Both vertical and horizontal relations within organizations were clouded by mutual suspicion, distrust, and hostility during the ten long years of chaos.

Recent economic reforms were said to have injected new blood into China's organizations, lubricating both vertical and horizontal relations. According to Chinese press reports, organizational relations had become not only more smooth, but also healthier. Promotions within organizations, for example, used to be judged not on the basis of performance, but on how servile and politically loyal a worker was in the eyes of the leadership. In 1987 promotions were reportedly based more on one's work ability and performance than on his relations with the boss. How true these reports were we did not know. So in our survey we asked a number of questions on the general topic of work relations within China's organizations. We present our findings under three headings: vertical relations, horizontal relations, and promotions.

Vertical Relations

Vertical relations here refer to superior-subordinate relations within an organization. How was this type of relations perceived by our respondents? We first asked this question regarding their perception of the potential impact of the open-door policy begun in the early 1980s: "In your opinion, as we proceed with opening up to the outside world, what will become of relations between superiors and subordinates in organizations?" Under this new policy, there seemed to be a shift in many organizations toward greater emphasis on task performance. The challenge of a common task could bind superiors and subordinates more closely together, resulting in more harmonious relations. On the other hand, a change of work routines, if not handled properly, could generate conflicts and impair relations between superiors and subordinates.

Over half of the sample (52.8 percent) were quite optimistic, saying that relations between superiors and subordinates would be more harmonious as China proceeded with the open-door policy to attract more foreign business. The rest of the respondents were more or less evenly divided between those saying "more tense" (22.2 percent) and those saying "same as now." (25.0 percent). It is interesting to note that the young people appeared less positive about the future prospects of the open-door policy than the old. As many as 67.5 percent of the old believed that superior–subordinate relations would be more harmonious, compared to only 47.3 percent of the young. More than half of the young respondents said such relations would either become more tense (24.7 percent) or remain the same (28.0 percent). The young sounded more skeptical than the old about the success of the government's reform programs.

Media and gender were the two other relevant factors though the differences were not large. People with high exposure to official media news were more optimistic about the open-door policy than those who had low-exposure: 58.0 percent of the former said superior–subordinate relations would be more harmonious, compared to 50.2 percent of the latter. Slightly more women (55.5 percent) than men (50.0 percent) were hopeful about more harmonious relations between superiors and subordinates.

In work organizations in China, subordinates call their superiors "leaders." In China's social context, where the concept of due process is unknown, it is advisable to be on good terms with one's leaders. This was particularly true during the Cultural Revolution years. How has the situation changed? We had this question: "Suppose you are working at home on something important to you. The leader of your unit comes and asks you to help him with something urgent. What will you do?" We left the situation somewhat vague so that respondents could project their own interpretations.

Not surprisingly, a large majority of our respondents (78.4 percent) were willing to put aside whatever they were doing and go to help their leaders. Some (12.5 percent) said "it depends." Only 9.2 percent decided that their own matters were more important, so their answer was not to help.

Villagers were more willing to do a favor for the leader than urban residents: 88.1 percent of the villagers said "help him," compared to 75.2 percent of the urbanites. More urbanites (15.5 percent) than villagers (4.6 percent) said "it depends." While about the same percentage of the old (13.1 percent) and the young (13.3 percent) said "it depends," the latter did not care about their leader's problem as much as the former: 12.9 percent of the young would refuse to help, compared to only 5.6 percent of the old. The male–female picture looks much like the young–old dichotomy: more women (84.7 percent) than men (72.8 percent) were willing to help. Quite a few male respondents refused to help the leader (11.1 percent) or said "it depends" (16.1 percent). In contrast, only 6.9 percent of the women did not want to help and 8.4 percent said "it depends."

We wanted to know what qualifications people were looking for in their leaders. We asked a carefully designed question: "In your unit, what qualifications should a good leader have? Please select (from the list below) three you consider most important and three you consider least important." We listed eleven qualifications for our respondents to choose from.

For each qualification, we took the difference between the percentage saying "most important" and the percentage saying "least important" as an index of net importance. The eleven qualifications in terms of net importance are presented in table 6.1 in three categories: three that were highly positive, three that were highly negative, and five in between.

This is a most revealing picture. The top three qualifications, having indices above 30, were "technical expertise," "decisive, resolute," and "bring benefits to workers." The three least important qualifications, from the bottom up, were "seniority," "good (revolutionary) class background," and "good outside connections, know a lot of people," all having clearly negative indices. The others were in between. Let us take a close look at the three most important and the three least important qualfications.

Technical expertise. This was the most popular choice made by our respondents. More than two-thirds of the sample (70.7 percent) said technical expertise should be one of the three most important qualifications for a good leader. In contrast, hardly anyone (2.8 percent) regarded it as one of the least important qualifications, yielding a net positive index of 67.9 percent. There is no question that under China's reform policy, people look for technical expertise in their lead-

Table 6.1 Most and Least Important Leadership Attributes

QUALIFICATIONS	MOST IMPORTANT	LEAST IMPORTANT	NET INDEX
technical expertise	70.7%	2.8%	67.9
decisive, resolute	39.5%	5.0%	34.5
bring benefits to workers	39.3%	6.6%	32.7
fair to workers	36.9%	9.2%	27.7
serious, responsible	32.9%	7.0%	25.9
respected, liked by workers	28.1%	4.6%	23.5
good judgement	21.9%	5.0%	16.9
sincere toward colleagues	15.8%	14.3%	1.5
good outside connections, know people	7.8%	59.1%	-51.3
good (revolutionary) class background	1.4%	87.0%	-85.6
seniority	1.2%	88.5%	-87.3

ers. As this quality became increasingly important, old cadres who did not have a sound educational background risked being replaced by younger and better-educated individuals as leaders of various organizations, a phenomenon rarely seen before economic reform was started. This was one of the main reasons why the young and better educated were more enthusiastic about reform than old cadres with limited education.

Interestingly, more villagers (76.5 percent) than urbanites (69.6 percent) and townspeople (65.5 percent) saw technical expertise as an important qualification for a good leader. This is not difficult to understand as the new rural economic system demanded that production leaders have technical expertise which could directly affect farmers' income. We also found that people with high media news exposure had a more positive feeling toward this qualification than their low-exposure counterparts: 75.5 percent of the former endorsed it as one of the three most important, compared to 66.9 percent of the latter. It may be noted that the mass media in China at the time we did our survey were generally under the control of the reform group in the Party. News coverage by and large favored unit leaders with technical expertise.

Decisive, resolute. About two-fifths of the respondents (39.5 percent) identified this as one of the three most important qualifications for a good leader. Only 5.0 percent of the sample said this was one of the three least important, putting the index of net importance at a positive 34.5 percent.

People with higher education considered this qualification far more important (50.4 percent) than their lower-education counterparts (26.1 percent). To be decisive and resolute was more important to leaders in urban areas than in rural villages. These two attributes were rated more highly by Shanghai urbanites (44.7 percent) and Qingpu townspeople (42.1 percent) than by rural residents (25.2 percent). They were somewhat more important to the old (42.5 percent) than to the young (31.4 percent). The fact that together they were rated as the second most important leadership qualification suggests that economic reform was introducing a more competitive environment. Rather than dutifully following orders from above, as they did in the past, unit leaders often had to make their own decisions, which would affect the performance of their organizations. Leaders who lacked this quality could easily be beaten by others in a competitive environment. People of higher education and those living in urban environments seem to be more keenly aware of the importance of this attribute. It may be noted that having good judgment was also rated as a positive qualification.

Bring benefits to workers. This was considered just as important as being decisive and resolute. Two out of five (39.3 percent) endorsed this qualification as one of the three most important. Only 6.6 percent said this was least important. The net index is 32.7 percent, the third highest. The young were found to be more concerned about their benefits than the old: 41.8 percent of the former endorsed "bring benefits to workers" as most important, compared to 25.4 percent of the latter. More urbanites (44.5 percent) than villagers (26.0 percent) said this characteristic was most important. Quite a few villagers (10.7 percent) regarded it as one of the three least important, compared to only 5.3 percent of the Shanghai residents. It may be noted that under the new rural economic system, villagers were quite independent and relied less on their organizations for benefits than before.

Bringing tangible fringe benefits has been an active concern of Chinese workers only in the last ten years or so. While benefits were always welcome, during the Cultural Revolution a good leader was supposed to emphasize ideological education, and not openly advocate material benefits. Our findings suggest that leaders who care more about ideology than real benefits for workers will lose popularity in their organizations.

Seniority. One of the most interesting findings was that seniority received the weakest endorsement as a qualification of a good leader. An overwhelming majority of the respondents (88.5 percent) saw it as one of the three least important qualifications. In contrast, only 1.2 percent considered it to be one of the most important, putting the index at a surprisingly high negative mark (-87.3 percent). The rejection of seniority as a leadership attribute was stronger among people of higher education (89.4 percent) than among those of lower education (85.2 percent), though the difference was not large. Education was the only relevant factor. Otherwise, the negative feelings against seniority were unanimous in all demographic groups, whether male or female, young or old, urban or rural, high or low income.

This response came as a total surprise because we never thought that people would be so negative toward this traditional value of Chinese society. Our data represented a candid, unambiguous vote against this current practice in China, in which leadership positions at various levels depended primarily on seniority. It is quite obvious that people were unhappy with their senior leaders who possessed little technical expertise and probably cared very little about the well-being of the masses.

Good class background. In the unique Chinese context of the past four decades, a person with a "good class background" was someone born from families categorized as workers, poor peasants, or revolutionary cadres. This kind of revolutionary class background had been an important consideration since the founding of the People's Republic. It became the single most significant qualification for leaders of all organizations during the Cultural Revolution. Leadership positions at all levels were filled exclusively by individuals recruited from the revolutionary classes. Whether or not they had technical expertise was secondary.

Our research findings indicated that this political ideology was now totally rejected. Almost nine out of ten respondents (87.0 percent) regarded it as one of the least important qualifications. In contrast, only 1.4 percent said it was one of the most important. The index of net importance is a solid negative -85.6 percent. The negative ratings were much higher among the high-education people (92.2 percent) than among their low-education counterparts (75.6 percent). This is quite understandable as the better educated people suffered most under the previous policy during the Cultural Revolution. They apparently thought that a leader's ability had nothing to do with one's revolutionary class background; rather it should relate more to one's education. Only one out of 771 high education respondents took a different stand, saying "good class background" should be one of the three most important qualifications for a good leader. In contrast, 3.7 percent of the low-education respondents said it was one of the most important.

People under heavy Western cultural influence rejected this qualification even more strongly: 96.1 percent of them said this was least important, compared to 82.8 percent of those under little Western influence.

Good outside connections, know a lot of people. This was one of three leadership qualifications clearly given a negative rating. Over half of the respondents (59.1 percent) said this was one of the least important attributes. Only 7.8 percent of the sample endorsed it as one of the three most important, putting the index of net importance at -51.3 percent. Urbanites seemed to be more negative about this attribute than villagers: nearly two thirds of the former (64.7 percent) placed this qualification among the three least important, compared to 43.5 percent of the latter. It is interesting to note that more villagers (17.5 percent) than urban dwellers (4.2 percent) saw having good outside connections and knowing a lot of people as one of the three most important qualifications for a good leader. It seems that rural villages rely heavily on these connections to get materials and supplies that are needed.

The past few years saw a rampant surge in backdoor dealings in businesses and other sectors of life. People used personal connections, instead of normal channels, to get things done. A work organization without a leader who had good outside connections and knew a lot of people would often find itself isolated. Managers had to deal with a whole range of thorny issues, such as cuts in supply of electricity or gas or water, or trivial matters like the purchase of monthly bus passes for their workers. One heard such exaggerated remarks as "the whole society is running on the wheel of connections," which was not totally groundless. So why is it that leaders who have good connections are rated so negatively? We think that the highly negative rating of this qualification was not so much a reflection on the leaders themselves, but rather a condemnation of the widespread current practice. While everybody was playing the game, many deplored it. Seeing the whole society plagued by this social epidemic, people hated the behavior of leaders who used connections deviously to serve either organizational or their personal purposes.

We asked the two previous questions mainly from the subordinate's perspective; we wanted to know how a subordinate would treat his superior and what kind of leadership a subordinate was looking for in his superior. We reversed our questioning to see how one would treat his subordinate. We asked: "Suppose someone in your work unit is not qualified for the job. How would you handle the situation?"

Most workers in China are state employees with lifetime job security. A supervisor has very few options in dealing with someone who is unfit for work.

Not surprisingly, over half of the sample (58.7 percent) would first advise the person to improve, and if he didn't, transfer him to another unit. Quite a number of respondents (28.6 percent) still wanted him to stay, but would move him to another job. Only one out of ten respondents (10.0 percent) said just "transfer him to another unit," a measure considered to be harsh and unkind. Very few people (2.7 percent) were willing to take a "no action" position. In present-day Chinese organizations, dismissal was not an option.

Age was the only relevant factor. Responses of the young represented extremes, either more punitive or a bit more irresponsible than the old. More young respondents (15.0 percent) than their old counterparts (4.9 percent) wanted to have the unqualified worker transferred to another unit. And 3.7 percent of the young said "in a situation like this, no action is necessary," compared to only 1.6 percent of the old group expressing the same view.

Horizontal Relations

Healthy collegial relations depend largely on attitudes that colleagues hold toward each other. What then was the general attitude reflecting relations at the workplace? Was it mainly constructive and cooperative? Or was it indifferent or even antagonistic? We asked: "If one of your co-workers is lazy and does not want to work, what will you do?"

A large majority of the respondents (72.5 percent) said they would "talk to him." Some (10.5 percent) sounded harsh, saying they would report him to the supervisor. Others (7.3 percent) would conceal his poor work habits by helping him do his work, or (7.6 percent) take a hands-off attitude and leave him alone. Very few (2.1 percent) would protest by refusing to work hard.

The young and the old seemed to have very different approaches to this problem. The young (66.1 percent) were less willing to talk than the old (81.7 percent). Almost none of the old (0.4 percent) would resort to a retaliatory reaction by refusing to work hard. In contrast, 4.5 percent of the young would do so. It is also interesting to note that quite a few young respondents (10.0 percent) said they would "leave him alone," compared to only 2.0 percent of the old who took the same attitude. In general, the young were less accommodating and less patient than the old.

Western cultural influence was found to be a significant factor. Those under heavy Western influence seemed to be less helpful and less responsible than those under little influence. While the high-exposure people were less willing to talk to the lazy co-worker than their low-exposure counterparts (52.9 percent vs. 77.5 percent), the former were also more harsh than the latter: one out of five (19.6 percent) among the heavy-influence group wanted to report him to the supervisor, compared to only 9.7 percent of the low-influence group. At the same time, quite a few heavy-influence people (17.6 percent) took the irresponsible position of "leaving him alone." Only 3.9 percent of the low-influence group would do so.

In dealing with human relations, face-saving used to be very important to the Chinese. This is discussed in more detail in another chapter. Was this traditional concept also important in social relations at the workplace? How was it weighed in dealing with collegial relations in organizations? This was our question: "If someone in your work unit has done something he should not have done, would you consider his face before you talk to him?"

Apparently face-saving is still important: 22.4 percent of the sample said they "would consider a lot," and 64.7 percent "would consider some," making a total of 87.1 percent. Western cultural influence and gender were found to have small correlations with the dependent variable. The heavy-influence group seemed to consider saving face more important than the low-influence group: 29.4 percent of the former said they would weigh face-saving carefully before they talked to the troubled person; in contrast, 20.3 percent of the latter would. While 6.9 percent of the low-influence people would not consider face at all, only 2.0 percent of the heavy-influence respondents would follow this approach. Women were slightly more concerned about face-saving than men. While more than a quarter of the women (24.7 percent) said such considerations were important, one out of five of the men (20.3 percent) agreed. For both Western cultural influence and gender, the differences were not large.

Differences of opinions among colleagues are a common occurrance in organizations. In the past Chinese people generally tried to avoid open confrontations. We were interested in knowing how people would behave today. We asked this question: "If you have a difference of opinion with someone in your work unit, how would you handle it?"

Two out of five of the respondents (39.4 percent) said they would directly bring up the difference with the person. This was the most popular response, quite different from what one would expect from the traditional approach, which would require one to keep silent. The least popular solution was to "ask a third person to mediate" (10.0 percent). The rest of the sample were divided between "best not say anything, let time take care" (28.4 percent), which came closest to the traditional way of conflict avoidance, and "ask the leadership to mediate" (22.3 percent), which reflected the influence of the Party leadership that seemed to permeate all organizations in China.

Education and Western cultural influence were found to be relevant factors. More than one-third of the high-education people (35.1 percent) felt the best way to solve the problem was to keep silent and let time be the healer. In contrast, only 20.4 percent of the low-education respondents felt the same way. Low-education people relied on leaders more than their high-education counterparts: 31.1 percent of the former said "ask leadership to mediate," compared to only 15.0 percent of the latter. The high-education people seemed to be more cautious on the one hand, reflecting perhaps their more painful exposure to criticism campaigns in the past. On the other hand, they seemed to be more detached from the Party-dominated leadership hierarchy than those who had lower education.

People under heavy Western cultural influence took a somewhat less positive attitude toward such an issue: almost half of them (47.1 percent) would choose to say nothing. Only 23.0 percent of the low-influence group took this traditional attitude. In this sense, those under heavy Western cultural influence acted much like those having higher education. We saw more of the low-influence people (27.8 percent) than their high-influence counterparts (15.7 percent) relying upon the Party-dominated leadership for solving the difference of opinions. Western cultural influence was negatively related to a confrontational style of conflict resolution. Those under little Western influence were more likely to confront the other party directly (40.4 percent) than those under heavy influence (27.5 percent).

Promotions

As we have mentioned earlier in this chapter, promotions within Chinese organizations used to be largely determined by how good one's relations were with the organization's leaders and how hard one studied politics. In the Chinese context, the term "study politics" means that one seriously studies Marxist–Mao Zedong thoughts. Work performance counted little, if at all, during the time when the practice of "eating out of the same big pot" was a dominant work ethic. A major objective of economic reform was to change the "big pot" practice. How were promotions perceived now? What did our respondents think should be the most important criteria for promotions? We asked this question: "Of the following criteria for promotion, please select two that you consider to be most important, and two that you consider to be least important." We offered seven criteria.

Again we took as an index of net importance the difference between the percentage endorsing a criterion as one of the two most important and the percentage that rated it to be one of the two least important. The results are presented in table 6.2 in descending order of importance.

This list of criteria is highly revealing about what people considered to be important and unimportant for promotion. By far the most important was the criterion of "diligent, hardworking," followed at a distance by "eager to help others" and "outstanding performance." These were the only three criteria to earn positive scores. We were surprised that "outstanding performance" did not figure more prominently. The general attitude seemed to be that if someone worked hard and was eager to help others, then he deserved a promotion. People were not so sure how to measure themselves against "outstanding performance" although this was something they considered to be positive.

The other four qualifications were rated negatively, with "seniority" at the bottom of the list. The strong rejection of "seniority" as a promotion criterion was consistent with the highly negative rating which seniority received as a leadership quality. These findings can be taken as an expression of resentment against the current system, in which nearly all top positions of organizations were occupied by individuals with long term service, including those who joined the Communist move-

Table 6.2 Most and Least Important Promotion Criteria

CRITERIA	MOST IMPORTANT	LEAST IMPORTANT	INDEX
Deligent, hardworking	87.2%	2.1%	85.1%
Eager to help others	33.3%	9.9%	23.4%
Outstanding performance	34.3%	11.7%	22.6%
Study politics seriously	9.3%	29.1%	-19.8%
Good collegial relations	10.3%	37.9%	-27.6%
Good relations with superiors and subordinates	13.1%	49.3%	-36.2%
Seniority	7.8%	46.9%	-39.1%

ment in the 1930s and early 1940s. It is also clear that people no longer felt that one's good relations either with colleagues or superiors and subordinates should be an important factor for their promotion. Perhaps not surprisingly, the criterion of "study politics seriously," which used to be extremely important, did not receive a positive endorsement at all. Chinese people seemed to have had enough of political indoctrination which was part of their lives for some thirty years.

We look at some of the correlations for each of the listed criteria, also in order of their decreasing net importance.

Diligent, hardworking: Education was the only variable found to have a significant correlation. This criterion received a stronger endorsement from the high-education group (89.6 percent) than from the low-education group (83.4 percent), although the difference was not large. Otherwise, this criterion was unanimously rated high by all groups.

Eager to help others: No major differences were recorded across different groups except that more young respondents (12.0 percent) than the old (5.8 percent) regarded this criterion as one of the two least important.

Outstanding performance: Two-fifths of the high-education group (40.5 percent) endorsed this qualification as one of the two most important, compared to 27.0 percent of the low-education group, a finding which is not difficult to understand. Age also made a difference: more of the old (38.5 percent) than of the young (27.8 percent) emphasized outstanding performance as a highly important promotion criterion. It is interesting to note that quite a few villagers (17.3 percent) said this qualification was least important. In contrast, only 8.7 percent of urban residents in Shanghai said so.

Study politics seriously: We found some very interesting correlations here. This criterion received a much weaker endorsement from the high-education group (4.9 percent) than from the low-education group (17.6 percent), from urbanites (6.7 percent) than from villagers (16.1 percent), and from the young (8.0 percent) than from the old (12.7 percent). People under heavy Western cultural influence were found to resent this criterion most: over half of them (58.8 percent) said this was one of the two least important factors for promotion. In contrast, only one out of five in the low-influence group (20.2 percent) felt this way. We also found more young respondents (30.0 percent) than their old counterparts (18.8 percent) saying this was least important. The difference with age was considerable, but not as dramatic as the difference with Western cultural influence. These findings tell us, in clear and unambiguous terms, that the young, the urbanites, those who were better educated, and particularly those under heavy Western cultural influence resented studying politics. Again in China's revolutionary history, studying politics means "studying Marxist and Mao Zedong Thoughts."

Good collegial relations: On the whole, the majority of the respondents did not see it as an important promotion criterion. But interestingly, we found more young respondents (13.3 percent) than old (4.4 percent) endorsing it as one of the two most important. In contrast, 42.9 percent of the old said this was least important, as against only 30.6 percent of the young. Rural villagers valued good collegial relations somewhat more than urbanites: 15.5 percent of the former considered it to be most important, compared to 7.8 percent of the latter.

Good relations with superiors/subordinates: In the Chinese context this criterion refers to someone who is smooth and knows how to please superiors and at the same time handle subordinates in a nice way. In short, a good company man. The endorsement of this criterion was rather weak, with only 13.1 percent of the respondents saying this was one of the two most important. It is interesting to note that more people under heavy Western cultural influence (23.5 percent) considered this criterion one of the most important than those under little influence (10.0 percent). This finding is puzzling. Is it possible that people under heavy Western cultural influence were so eager to get promoted that they did not hesitate to act obsequiously with their superiors, even though the general attitude seemed to be against such behavior?

Education was a relevant factor. Over half of the high-education group (53.8 percent) said that good relations with superiors and subordinates was one of the two least important, compared to 42.5 percent of the low-education group. The findings here suggest that people were generally not happy with promotion being determined by one's personal relations with superiors or subordinates. People with higher education resented this practice even more.

Seniority: As we recall, of all the seven promotion criteria, seniority received the most negative rating from our respondents. Opinions were almost identical among the different groups except that villagers disliked seniority slightly more than urban residents: over half of the rural sample (51.7 percent) said this should be one of the two least important promotion criteria, compared to 43.0 percent of the urban sample. This is not unusual as agricultural work would require physically strong and healthy leaders.

Promotion in China is something that is decided upon by one's superiors. Using Chinese jargon, it is the leadership of the work organization that decides who will be promoted. The workers themselves have relatively little to say. However, different workers adopt different approaches to advance their chances. Some act aggressively by going directly to the superior to ask for a promotion. Others do nothing, hoping that the superior will finally recognize his merits. Still others solicit the help of a trusted colleague to send a message in his favor. What tactics would our respondents use? We asked: "If you have met the qualifications for promotion, what will you do?"

A large majority of our respondents (74.4 percent) said they would leave it to their supervisor to decide. This would seem to be a safe approach in a tightly controlled organizational environment. About one out of ten (10.8 percent) would try to explain their situation to the supervisor in the hope that the supervisor would recommend them for promotion. Another 10.9 percent were more aggressive, saying "they would directly ask for a promotion." Very few people (3.9 percent) wanted to use a third person to convey a message, which seems to make sense as promotion is something rather personal.

Western cultural influence was found to be a significant factor. People under heavy Western cultural influence were far more aggressive than their low-influence counterparts in their approach toward promotion: more than one-fourth (27.5 percent) of the former group said they would directly ask for promotion, in contrast with only 5.0 percent of the latter. The correlation was strong and clearly linear. The higher the Western influence, the more aggressive the attitude toward promotion. These findings are most revealing. While people under heavy Western influence were found (in this chapter and elsewhere in our report) to be less responsible and less hardworking, they became extremely aggressive when their personal interests were at stake.

Similarly, the young were more aggressive than the old: 15.2 percent of the young versus 3.9 percent of the old would directly ask for a promotion. The old people (82.3 percent) were more inclined to leave the matter to their supervisor than the young (67.5 percent).

Discussion

We have presented data relating to vertical and horizontal relations and promotions within organizations. Our research suggests that the environment of human relations at the organizational level was largely favorable to many of the reform ideas put forward since the new open-door policy was adopted at the beginning of the 1980s. We know that ten years of Cultural Revolution adversely affected organizational relations in China, and yet with the passing of time and positive reinforcement from reform programs, Chinese people still had positive feelings toward human relations within organizations.

As China proceeded with its reform policies, vertical organizational relations were expected to be more harmonious than tense, and people were generally optimistic about the future. This may be taken as evidence that the Chinese supported reform, which they believed would bring even healthier superior–subordinate relations. The fact that people on the whole felt positively toward the vertical relations does not mean that they did not expect their leaders to exhibit laudable traits. Our findings clearly indicate that people commended leaders who had technical expertise, were resolute in making correct decisions, and were able to bring tangible benefits to workers. To them, seniority and good revolutionary class background were no longer important, even though these were attributes favored by the Party leadership. They also wanted their leaders to be honest and to handle business and other matters according to principles.

In his research on managerial behavior in the reform era, Walder (1989) found that an effective factory manager must pay special attention to cultivating not only vertical relationships within the bureaucracy, but also non-market exchange relationships with other enterprises. While these external connections may be necessary for effective functioning within China's current political and economic system, our survey findings point to considerable resentment among the people. A leader's connections outside were not, in their opinion, a guarantee of organizational efficiency and prosperity. Instead, excessive manipulation of network connections in business transactions could easily lead to corruption, as it was made clear by numerous reports publicized in the past few years.

The three important qualifications that people were looking for in their leaders were, indeed, qualifications that were usually possessed by young, educated, and caring people. Currently Chinese people want their leaders to be to be younger, better-educated, and more caring, not, as in the past, identified by seniority, a good revolutionary class background, and skills in waging political campaigns and making connections.

The picture of horizontal organizational relations was not discouraging either. The attitude that people took toward their colleagues was generally constructive. When there was a problem involving collegial relations, most were willing to talk and tried to solve the problem through communication. People also seemed to respect each other; they would, for example, think about the feelings of their colleagues, something the Chinese call "face," if and when the latter had done something they should not have done. When they had difference of opinions with each other, which is not uncommon within any organizations, they tended to bring up the difference directly with the persons involved, again a constructive attitude even though it was a deviation from the traditional way of the past.

Our data on promotion criteria proved to be highly revealing. Most interesting to us, as a matter of fact, was not the negative endorsement of "seniority" as a promotion criterion. Rather, it was that "outstanding performance" ranked as a weak third as the most important criterion for promotion, well behind the top choice of "diligent, hardworking" in terms of net importance. This suggests that work attitude was considered to be more important than work efficiency or production results. In competitive market economies, what counts as the most important criterion for promotion in organizations should be a worker's performance which would directly affect the outcome of production. The fact that outstanding performance was rated as much less important than "diligent, hardworking" suggests that Chinese people's mindset has not moved beyond the rigid value confines that were partly traditional and partly promoted by the Party leadership to suit a non-competitive, centrally planned economy.

We found exposure to news information in the official media to have only moderate effect on how the respondents felt about organizational relations, as summarized in table 6.3.

The differences, though not pronounced, were by and large in a direction desired by the official policy. The official media had promoted the notion that Deng Xiaoping's open-door policy would contribute to better relations between the Party leadership and the people. Expertise and decisiveness were among those attributes which Party cadres in leadership positions should possess in order to carry out the Four Modernizations.

Although the profiles of the young people and of those under heavy Western cultural influence drawn from our data in this chapter were not as prominent as in some other chapters, we still found them quite striking. We present a profile comparing young and old in table 6.4.

Table 6.3 Effect of Official News on Work Relations

Responses	EXPOSURE TO NEWS INFORMATION[1]	
	High	Low
See superiors/subordinate relations as more harmonious	58.0%	50.2%
Leadership qualities		
expertise	75.7%	66.0%
decisiveness	49.3%	35.4%

Table 6.4 Work Attitudes of Young vs. Old

RESPONSES	YOUNG	OLD
See superior/subordinate relations as more harmonious	47.3%	67.5%
When asked by supervisor, refuse to help	12.9%	5.9%
Leaders should bring benefits to workers	41.8%	25.4%
If worker is unqualified, transfer him out	15.0%	4.9%
If co-worker fails to work,		
talk to him	66.1%	81.7%
leave him alone	10.0%	2.0%
also refuse to work	4.5%	0.4%
Performance as promotion criterion	27.8%	38.5%
Good collegial relations as promotion criterion	13.3%	4.4%
How to handle promotion:		
directly ask	15.2%	3.9%
leave it to supervisor	67.5%	82.3%
Reject political studies	30.0%	18.8%

Young people are less optimistic about harmonious work relations as a result of the open-door policy, and less patient with their co-workers. If a co-worker does not do his share, the young are less inclined to be friendly and helpful. They appear to be more forceful, relatively speaking. If someone is not qualified for the job, more young people would choose the rather drastic course of transferring him out of the unit. Their approach to promotion is more straightforward. More young people would ignore the prevailing norm of inaction and directly ask for a promotion. Compared to the old people, they look more actively for leaders who can take care of their practical benefits. Conversely, they are less concerned about outstanding performance as a promotion criterion. They are more emphatic in rejecting political studies as a criterion for promotion.

Very much like the young group, people under heavy Western cultural influence[2] are quite different from those under little influence, as we see in table 6.5.

We found those under heavy Western cultural influence to be less willing to talk to their colleagues in the interest of group productivity. If a co-worker refuses to do his share, they would more likely either pass on the case to their supervisors or take a nonconstructive and hands-off attitude. They are less inclined to discuss deficiencies with lazy co-workers. If different opinions develop with their colleagues, they are more apt to keep silent and let time take care, while those under little Western influence would either directly confront the situation or rely on their unit leaders to resolve the differences. On the whole, they have less constructive attitudes toward collegial relations than their low-influence counterparts. However, when their personal interests are involved, such as their own advancement, then those under heavy Western influence would act differently. They would become altogether aggressive and directly ask for their promotion. They also emphatically reject political studies as a promotion criterion, far more so than those under little Western influence.

Table 6.5 Western Cultural Influence and Work Attitudes

Responses	WESTERN INFLUENCE High	Low
Class background denounced	96.1%	82.8%
If co-worker fails to work		
talk to him	52.9%	77.5%
report to supervisor	19.6%	9.7%
leave him alone	17.6%	3.9%
How to handle difference with colleagues		
say nothing, let time take care	47.1%	23.0%
confront directly	27.5%	40.4%
rely on leadership	15.7%	27.8%
Reject political studies	58.8%	20.2%
How to handle promotion		
directly ask	27.5%	5.0%
leave it to supervisor	62.7%	81.1%

Chapter 7

Community Life

In this chapter we examine those patterns of interaction and related values that lie beyond the family, the intimate circles of friends and neighbors, and the workplace. They help define the life of Chinese people in their communities and in society at large.

Community life in China is not what it used to be half a century ago, before the war with Japan. At that time, the forces of modernity had barely progressed beyond the limits of big cities. When one of the authors arrived in 1935 in Wuchang, the cradle of the 1911 revolution, the city had no paved roads. Only a small segment of the city had electricity. The city had only one newspaper, with a small circulation. There was no radio at that time. News travelled slowly. People lived in a world of perceptual confinement. Life in the community moved at a leisurely pace. There was relatively little involvement by most people beyond their extended families. The local people in Wuchang with ample spare time took great pleasure in eating. Whether rich or poor, a family sat down for three meals and two snacks a day. The role of the government was unclear. The Chinese were no longer living in a state where "heaven is high above, and the emperor is far away." There was no emperor. And whatever the government did, or did not do, seemed remote and of little concern to the people. Community life in those days was defined by the boundaries of the immediate neighborhood.

The last forty years have seen limited economic development and urbanization and a phenomenal growth of the mass media in China. The pace of life is much faster. From the official mass media people receive much more information about events in China and abroad than ever before. Their perceptual world has been greatly enlarged. The most dramatic change is perhaps the expanding role of the government. Now the presence of the government is everywhere, constantly demanding sacrifices by the people for the collective good that extends not only to their own communities but also to the nation as a whole. The state controls all major resources. These different forces of change have acted to push community life in China in a direction that is as yet unclear. The situation is further complicated due to the experiences that many Chinese suffered during the Cultural Revolution. People learned to be cautious when dealing with others beyond their immediate family circles. The political environment loosened considerably following the reforms and open-door policy of the early 1980s, but experiences as traumatic as the ten years of the Cultural Revolution could hardly be forgotten.

So how was community life in China during the recent reform years? What did people do to get around the omnipotent presence of the government in nearly every aspect of their life? What was their perception of the rights and responsibilities of the individual in relation to the government? How did they see the overriding issue of public interest versus individual interest, which directly affected the way they lived? To what extent were they prepared to participate in community affairs?

Connections versus Law

A dilemma that confronts nearly everyone in China when he tries to deal with the social environment beyond the immediate circles of his family and friends is whether or not to avail himself of the personal connections he has developed. Whether one wants to get a train ticket to Beijing, or to buy a refrigerator, or to get one's son transferred back to Shanghai from the interior, or to secure an apartment room, one has to deal with some branch of the government. Following the government's established rules and procedures will take a long time and the results may not be positive. But if a person knows someone with connections, he may prevail upon this benefactor to help get what he wants. A dilemma arises when he must choose between following government rules and finding a way to bypass them and secure his objectives.

It seems that nearly every Chinese has his network of connections, known as *guanxi* (King, 1985, 1991), and this network could include a friend, a neighbor, a former teacher, a relative, a former superior, or any relationship one may find useful someday. The general rule is: the more key government offices and social sectors a person's network covers, the more social influence he has at one's disposal, and the more easily he can get things done. Because nearly everybody seems to be using his network of connections, anyone who faithfully follows the established rules and procedures will be putting himself at a disadvantage. So the temptation to use one's connections seems almost irresistible.

Access to the material resources and opportunities that exist in Chinese society is very much regulated by one's relative positions in the highly complex and entangled networks of personal connections. Not everyone has useful connections. If an individual's aunt is selling tea-leaf eggs on the street, he cannot expect to get much help from her in the purchase of a train ticket. On the other hand, a government official has considerable resources at his disposal, and he will find it advantageous to selectively use these resources to expand his influence and enlarge his social network. Thus, connections in China function to reinforce a system of inequitable distribution of resources and status.

To get a sense of how people perceive network connections, we asked a general question: "Some people say that in Chinese society, network connections have their importance. What do you think?" An overwhelming majority of our respondents said either "very important" (42.7 percent), "important" (26.9 percent), or "somewhat important" (22.8 percent). Only a few (4.9 percent) said "not very important," and still fewer (2.6 percent) said "not important at all." These findings point to the enormous practical importance of network connections in Chinese society, a fact acknowledged by an overwhelming majority of our respondents. Such data may be seen as an indication that most people know that China today is still very much governed by man, not by law.

It is interesting to note that younger people seemed to attach greater importance to network connections than older people, a finding we did not quite expect. Almost half of the young (46.0 percent) said "very important," compared to 35.1 percent of the old. Only 5.0 percent of the young said either "not very important" or "not important at all," compared to 13.6 percent of the old. It seems that the young people, who are still on the fringe of social networks, realize more concretely the important part such connections play for their career advancement and access to the extremely scarce material resources.

Interestingly, the only other relevant factor was Western cultural influence. More people under heavy Western influence (54 percent) considered network connections very important than those under little influence (37.8 percent). The relationship was consistently linear. The greater the Western cultural influence, the higher the percentage endorsing the importance of network connections, from 37.8 percent to 46.0 percent, 47.7 percent, 52.3 percent till it reached 54.0 percent. One plausible explanation is that people under heavy Western cultural influence are more attracted by the material amenities they have seen in foreign films and television programs. Network connections thus assume a greater importance to them in order to fulfill their material aspirations.

Recognizing the importance of network connections does not necessarily mean people will actively use them. So we asked this question: "Suppose you have a problem. If you follow the normal channels, it will take a long time, and the result may not be satisfactory. Do you think you should first try to go through some connections?" Over two-thirds of the respondents (71.7 percent) said they "should first try some connections." Only one out of five (19.6 percent) would rather follow normal channels, saying they "should not try connections." The remaining 8.8 percent were not sure. These findings confirm the prevalence of this particular practice in Chinese society today. An interesting question may be asked. Were most Chinese people unethical in their approach to life, or was the practice of using network connections so widespread and so deeply intertwined with daily life in China that one simply could not avoid them? We do not have a clear answer. But our research suggests that the practice of network connections has lowered the standards of social ethics and morality, and it has spread through Chinese society like an epidemic.

Again we found age and Western cultural influence to be relevant. Consistent with the earlier findings, a substantial 75.7 percent of the young said they should first try some connections, compared to 54.4 percent of the old. About one-third of the old group (32.5 percent) were against trying connections, while only 14.9 percent of the young took this stand. It seems that the young cared more about getting things done or getting what they wanted regardless of the means they employed.

Quite consistently, we found more of those who had high exposure to Western cultural influence (84.3 percent) saying they would first try some connections. The corresponding figure in the low-influence group was 64 percent. One out of four low-influence respondents (25.9 percent) were against trying connections, compared to only 7.8 percent of the high-influence group. Quite possibly, people under heavy exposure to Western cultural influence have higher material aspirations and they rely more on connections to get them. Also, it seems that these people have less confidence in the normal channels for getting things done.

As we suggested earlier, China is still very much a country where man looms larger than law. While network connections are widely used, how do our respondents look at the function of law? This was our question: "People have two different views about law. Which is more important to you?" The two views were: Law helps people get along with each other, and law brings justice to society. The former is a more pragmatic perspective and can be more readily reconciled with the widespread use of network connections. The latter implies a more universal application of justice to all segments of society.

A bit to our surprise, an overwhelming majority (92.2 percent) identified themselves with the statement that law brings justice to society. We could hardly find any differences across the seven independent variables with the exception of sex, which turned out to be a statistically significant factor. However, the difference is not large: 90.6 percent of male respondents said law brings justice to society, compared to 94.0 percent of the females. This perception of law suggests that despite the widespread use of network connections in society, there is a nearly universal wish among the Chinese people that the country be ruled by law because they believe "law brings justice to society."

Rights and Responsibility of the People

In a country where all major decisions are made by the Party and the government, the role of the public and people's perception of this role are interesting topics to examine. The "mass line" philosophy of Chairman Mao had a prominent role for the "public," identified as the "people." The people were considered to be the inspiration for the Party's policies, the implementation of which was to be guided by constant feedback from the people. The mass line was intended to be distinguished by intensive two-way communication, from top down and from bottom up. In reality, at least during the years of the Cultural Revolution and even before, the Party hierarchy not only made all major decisions, but also unilaterally decided for the people what they had a right to know and what they should not know. It was the people's responsibility to learn what they were required to learn about major policy decisions and to express their full support.

Had economic reforms and the open-door policy in the past decade brought about any change in the people's perception of the rights and responsibility of the public? How did our respondents look at the functions of government? Who should decide upon public affairs, the government or the public? And who should be responsible for community development?

First we asked: "Some people say how a local govenment spends its money is the government's own business. Others say this is something we have a right to know. How do you feel?" Somewhat to our surprise, a large majority (74.2 percent) said the public has the right to know. However, the number of those saying it is the government's own business (25.8 percent) was quite sizable. Although we had no data from the Cultural Revolution years for comparison, our findings clearly suggest that nearly a decade after the reform policy was put into practice, Chinese people have developed a keen awareness of the right of the public to be informed on matters that affect them.

Interestingly enough, we found two factors were relevant: sex and exposure to news information from the mass media. It seems that men were more conscious of the right of the public than women: 78.2 percent of our male respondents said the public has the right to know, compared to 69.8 percent of the females. This is not surprising. Chinese women have always been more oriented to life within the family than to public affairs. In traditional China, a woman's world was strictly confined within the walls of the family residence. Our finding that seven out of ten women said the public has the right to know demonstrates how drastically the roles of women in China have changed.

Equally interesting is the finding that people with high exposure to media news had a higher awareness of the right of the public to know than the low-exposure group. As many as 82.0 percent of the high media exposure respondents said the public has the right to know, while those of the low-exposure group who said so accounted for 66.5 percent. These findings raise a question of considerable theoretical importance. The mass media in China operate under strict supervision of the Party. Even though there was a trend toward some liberalization in the early 1980s, the news presented by the Chinese media by and large reflected the official perspective of the Party. Yet this official dose of news was able to stimulate a demand for more information about public affairs, and intensify the people's perception of the right of the public to know. It seems that dissemination of information, no matter what, begets a demand for more information.

In order to further test people's perception of the rights of the public and the process of decision making in public affairs, we asked this question: "Do you think that public affairs should be left to those who have influence and experience, or do you think these matters should be discussed by the people before decisions are made?" Surprisingly, an overwhelming majority of the respondents (89.4 percent) said public affairs should be discussed by the people before decisions are made. Only one out of ten people (10.6 percent) preferred to leave public affairs to those who have influence and experience. The findings were unambiguous and clearly reflected Chinese people's heightened awareness of the rights of the public and the importance of a democratic decision-making process. Here was one of those rare occasions when majority views were universally endorsed by all social and demographic groups. We found no differences whatsoever in any of the seven independent variables. Whether they lived in metropolitan Shanghai or rural villages, whether they had high or low education, whether they were old or young, male or female, of high or low income, and whether they were heavily exposed to media news and Western cultural influence, a uniformly high percentage of our respondents wanted the government to allow open discussion of public affairs before decisions were made.

We wanted to know how people looked at the issue of responsibility for community development. We phrased the question this way: "Who do you think should assume responsibility for the development of your community?" Four options were offered:

people in the community
enterprises in the community
government
others (please specify)

Over two-thirds of the respondents (69.8 percent) said the government should assume responsibility. The rest of the respondents were evenly split between those who mentioned "people in the community" (15.9 percent) and those who said "enterprises in the community" (14.2 percent). These findings represent a major change from the traditional concept of government viewed by Chinese. Throughout China's history, the government seldom played a major role in community development. Beyond collecting taxes and other forms of levies, the government did little for the benefit of local communities other than maintaining law and order by its bureaucratic presence. Justice was often tempered by influence. Chinese people generally wanted to be left alone and expected little from their government. This pattern of "governing by noninvolvement" was broken by the People's Republic. Ever since the early 1950s, the Chinese government has launched one movement after another that usually involved almost the entire population. Some of the movements were political, such as the Anti-rightist movement in 1957, the Four Clean-ups movement in the early 1960s, and the Anti-Confucius movement in the early 1970s. Others, such as the People's Commune movement of 1958, required major reorganization of productive activities. Whatever the government did in reality, in theory the role of the people's government was to serve the people.

Our findings suggest that after some forty years of intensive penetration by the government in their daily life, the Chinese people have developed a new perception of its role, by putting the government right where it claims to be. While they want to be informed and consulted, they expect their government to serve the people and improve life through concrete development programs. There is an important message here: when the people are aware of their own rights and the responsibility of the authorities, they can pose a challenge or even a threat to an unresponsive government at whatever level. In other words, a government that wants to have the support of the people must not forget its own responsibility and the rights of the public.

Two variables were found to be statistically significant: area of residence and education. More urbanites (74.0 percent) and townspeople (75.7 percent) than villagers (56.2 percent) said the government should assume responsibility for community development. It is interesting to note that quite a large number of our village respondents said that enterprises in the community should be held responsible. This seems to point to the fact that newly established enterprises in rural areas, whether run by local collective units or private groups, were in rapid growth and were seen as having the potential to contribute to community development projects.

Four out of five high-education people (80.4 percent) said the government should assume responsibility for community development, compared to 55.1 percent of the low-education group. Almost one out of four low-education respondents (24.6 percent) put the responsibility on the shoulder of the people and 20.4 percent of them felt that local enterprises should be responsible. This shows that education raises people's consciousness about the constructive functions of the government.

Public versus Individual Interest

For centuries the Chinese were taught from childhood that public interest should be placed above individual interest. "One must endure sufferings before anyone else under the heaven has begun to suffer, but one can enjoy life only after all people under the heaven have already enjoyed it." This couplet by an ancient Chinese patriot, Fan Zhongyan, was often used by the rulers of China to inculcate among the Chinese a firm belief that one must place public interest above individual welfare. This tradition has been followed by the current government. In every campaign since the founding of the People's Republic, Chinese were exhorted to sacrifice their individual benefit for the sake of public good. It would be interesting to see how people now viewed the issue of public interest versus individual interest. So we asked this question: "Which one of the following do you agree with?"

In order to protect public interest, sometimes it is necessary to sacrifice individual interest.

In order to protect individual interest, sometimes it is necessary to sacrifice public interest.

An overwhelming majority of our respondents (90.8 percent) agreed with the first statement, sacrificing individual interest in order to protect public interest. Only 9.2 percent of the sample were more concerned about individual interest. This is an example of a long historical tradition endorsed by the Party and received with nearly universal acceptance by the Chinese people.

As an independent variable, age again seems to reveal its fascinating impact. As many as 95.3 percent of the old were willing to sacrifice individual interest in order to protect public interest, but only 82.8 percent of the young took the same position. About one out of six of the young (17.2 percent) said public interest should be overruled when it is necessary to protect individual interest. We consider this to be extremely important evidence. Against the overwhelming weight of a traditional heritage, and despite the unanimous voice of the Party propaganda apparatus, a sizable minority of the young have stood up to defend their individual interests.

Media news exposure was also found to be statistically significant. Of those under heavy exposure to media news, only 4.8 percent would sacrifice public interest to protect individual interest. On the lower end of news exposure, the figure was as high as 12.3 percent. It is not difficult to accept the notion that exposure to news from the official media helps raise one's public consciousness.

Western cultural influence reflected the opposite direction. Of those under little Western influence, only 6.6 percent would sacrifice public interest. On the higher end of Western cultural influence, as many as 17.8 percent wanted to put individual interest above public interest. The implications of this finding are enormous if China continues to keep its door open to the outside world.

We combined media news exposure and Western influence into one scale to assess their cumulative effects.[1] The results are presented in table 7.1.

Relatively speaking, the spirit of individualism was the highest when people were under strong Western influence and did not make much use of official news information (c). Nearly one out of six respondents would sacrifice public interest in a society still dominated by collectivism. The lowest level of individualism was found when people made heavy use of official information and were not very

Table 7.1 Western Influence, Media News, and Collectivism versus Individualism

	WESTERN INFLUENCE	
	Low	High
Sacrifice public interest		
News low	8.5% (a)	15.2% (c)
	(576)	(381)
News high	4.0% (b)	9.7% (d)
	(424)	(598)

much influenced by Western culture (b). The difference between (c) and (b) was 11.2 percent. When Western influence and use of media news were both high (d) or both low (a), they seemed to counterbalance each other.

On the whole, Chinese people seem to cherish a strong public interest even though we see the beginning of change under Western cultural influence. But how readily is this positive public spirit translatable into real action? Are people really willing to sacrifice individual interest for the public good? We had no way of making actual observations. So we asked a more specific question: "If other people want to elect you to serve as a member of the neighborhood committee or village committee, would you agree to serve?" This was a test of people's willingness to serve the public. These committee assignments carried virtually no power under the reform policy, but could take up precious time from individual productive activities. Only slightly more than half of the respondents (55.7 percent) said yes, and the rest (44.3 percent) said no. This should not be a surprise. But interesting differences showed up with four independent variables in our analysis: area of residence, education, Western cultural influence, and media news exposure.

Urbanites seemed much less willing to serve the public than rural villagers. Over half of our Shanghai respondents (52.0 percent) said no, compared to only 24.4 percent among the villagers. Three-fourths of the village folks (75.6 percent) would like to sit on some committee, while less than half of the city residents (48.0 percent) shared the willingness to serve.

Is it true that the more education one gets, the more willing one would be to serve the public? Our findings say no. While 71.3 percent of the low-education group said they were willing to serve, only 43.1 percent of the high-education people took this positive stand.

Much as we expected, three-fifths of those under heavy Western cultural influence (60.8 percent) were not interested in serving on those committees, compared to only 36.7 percent of the low-influence respondents. There seems to be a clear pattern: people who enjoy Western culture are less willing to serve the public.

Though statistically significant, the differences were not as big with media news as an independent variable: 57.8 percent of the high media exposure group said yes, compared to 52.3 percent of the low-exposure people.

Again we combined the two media variables to assess their cumulative effects. We present the results in table 7.2.

Here we see evidence of predominant and negative Western cultural influence as far as public service is concerned. People's willingness to serve was relatively low when they were under heavy Western influence (c and d) whether or not they made extensive use of official news information. When Western influence was low, people were more ready to serve (a), and heavy use of news information (b) brought the level even higher.

To serve on some committee is probably easier than to legally challenge one's friends or neighbors in order to protect public property, an action that demands much more courage on the part of the challenger. To test this assumption, we asked: "Suppose your neighbor or friend illegally takes something. If you do not report it, nobody will know. What will you do?" Somewhat to our surprise, more than three-fifths of the sample (62.6 percent) said they would report the theft, 25.2 percent would not, and the rest (12.2 percent) had different ways of handling the situation, including "ask them to return, otherwise

Table 7.2 Western Influence, Media News, and Readiness for Public Service

	WESTERN INFLUENCE	
	Low	High
News low	60.2% (a)	48.7% (c)
	(576)	(381)
News High	67.4% (b)	47.6% (d)
	(426)	(599)

report," "depends on how expensive it is," "depends on whether my interest is affected," and "it is excusable if done just once."

Only two factors are relevant: age and Western cultural influence. As many as 77.6 percent of the old group chose to play tough on their neighbors and friends, compared to 58.0 percent of the young who were ready to sacrifice friendship or neighborhood relationships. It is interesting to note that almost one out of three young respondents (31.0 percent) would rather protect their neighbors and friends, compared to 11.8 percent of the old who chose not to report.

It is most interesting to find that over half of those under heavy Western cultural influence (54.0 percent) said they would not report, three times as high as those of the low-influence group (15 percent) who chose not to report. An impressive majority of the low-influence group (76.5 percent) said they would report, compared to only 24.0 percent of the high influence people. This means that a majority of those under heavy Western cultural influence would rather sacrifice public property than risk destroying their relationships with neighbors or friends.

Participation in Community Life

The degree of participation in community life is an important indicator of how deeply people care about their neighborhood. We asked this question: "Have you ever been so concerned with things in your district that you really wanted to do something about them?" Half of our respondents (50.5 percent) said they occasionally felt that way, and the rest of the sample were split between "quite a few times" (22.8 percent) and "hardly ever" (26.8 percent). This suggests that despite all the years of official communication that presumably encouraged active participation, there existed only a marginal degree of concern for participation in community life.

Four factors were found to be relevant: age, education, exposure to media news, and Western cultural influence. Not to our surprise, more old respondents (30.7 percent) than the young (17.1 percent) said they wanted to do things for their district quite a few times. Almost one-third of the young (31.4 percent) said hardly ever, compared to 18.0 percent of the old. The young were clearly less interested in participating in community activities than the old.

About the same number of high-education people (26.5 percent) and low-education respondents (25.6 percent) said they hardly ever wanted to do things for their district. Over half of the high-education group (57.9 percent) said they did occasionally, compared to 40.2 percent of the low-education group. However, one-third of the low education people (34.2 percent) said quite often, and those of the high-education respondents who did so represented a low 15.6 percent. In terms of willingness to participate, the low-education people looked a bit more active than their high-education counterparts.

High media news exposure people should be more actively involved in community life than their low-exposure counterparts, we assumed. The findings supported our assumption. We found 27.7 percent of the high-exposure group saying that they quite often wanted to help, versus only 18.8 percent of the low-exposure people. Of the low-exposure respondents, 30.9 percent said hardly ever, compared to 20.7 percent of the high-exposure group.

Consistent with our earlier findings, people under heavy Western cultural influence were less inclined to participate in community affairs than their low-influence counterparts. One-third of the former (33.3 percent) hardly ever were concerned enough to want to do things for their district, compared to 22.8 percent of the latter. It seems that those under heavy Western cultural influence were more concerned about themselves than about the community at large.

We combined the two media variables as we did before to assess their cumulative effects. The results are presented in table 7.3.

Table 7.3 Western Influence, Media News, and Concern with District Affairs

	WESTERN INFLUENCE	
	Low	High
News low:		
Quite a few times	23.1% (a)	15.5% (c)
Occasionally	50.1%	51.3%
Hardly ever	26.9%	33.2%
	(577)	(386)
News high:		
Quite a few times	36.7% (b)	17.3% (d)
Occasionally	46.1%	53.3%
Hardly ever	17.2%	29.3%
	(425)	(600)

People were most actively concerned when they made extensive use of official news information and were not under strong Western influence (b). They were least concerned and least ready to help if they were heavily influenced by Western culture and did not make much use of media news (c). If we take "quite a few times" as an index, the difference between (b) and (c) was as large as 21.2 percent. We see evidence of the predominantly negative influence of Western culture (c and d). Whether or not the use of official news information was high, if people were under heavy Western influence, their concern for district affairs was low.

Having asked a question about people's readiness to get involved in community service, we now wanted to know if they participated in interpersonal communication concerning local district affairs. We asked: "Do you discuss things in your neighborhood district with your neighbors and friends?" Two-thirds of our respondents (60.5 percent) said they discussed only occasionally, with the rest of the sample being split between "discuss regularly" (15.9 percent) and "do not discuss" (23.6 percent). These findings suggest rather limited participation in informal local communication. The caution that people developed during the years of the Cultural Revolution still lingers on. Education and media news exposure were found to be two relevant factors. Of the high-education group, 67.2 percent discussed occasionally, compared to 51.4 percent of the low-education people. However, we found an impressively higher percentage among the low-education group (27.0 percent) than among the high-education respondents (9.6 percent) who regularly discussed neighborhood affairs. So in terms of participant communication, low-education people seemed to have a deeper involvement than their high-education counterparts. The latter seemed to be more cautious.

We were not surprised to find a higher percentage among the low media news exposure group (27.1 percent) than among the high-exposure respondents (19.6 percent) who did not discuss matters about their neighborhood district at all. More of the high-exposure respondents (65.3 percent) said they discussed occasionally than the low-exposure respondents (57.7 percent). Those who discussed regularly numbered the same between the high (15.1 percent) and the low-exposure (15.2 percent) groups.

We asked another question: "Have you ever thought about doing something good for your neighborhood?" An impressive majority of the sample (84.7 percent) said yes, with the rest (15.3 percent) saying no. Four independent variables were found to be statistically significant: area of residence, age, education, and media news exposure.

Urbanites appeared busier about their own affairs and had less time thinking about the neighborhood than village people. Of the former group, 17.4 percent said they never thought about doing something good for their neighborhood, compared to 12.3 percent of the latter. But the difference was not large.

As we expected, there were more older people (91.7 percent) than younger respondents (80.3 percent) who said yes. It seems to be a common phenomenon in China that the old have a deeper involvement in community life than the young.

Low-education people not only talked more about neighborhood affairs, but also thought more about doing good things for their district. We found an overwhelming majority of them (91.4 percent) saying they thought about doing good things for the neighborhood, compared to 80.0 percent of the high-education respondents.

People with high exposure to media news were found to be slightly more thoughtful about community affairs than low-exposure people. Of the former group, 87.5 percent thought about doing good things for their district, compared to 81.1 percent of the latter. This is another indication that media news exposure raises people's consciousness about what is going on around them.

Discussion

Chinese society has been traditionally characterized by "rule by man" rather than "rule by law." Particularistic considerations, depending on the status and positions of the individuals, generally carried more weight than the universal application of specific rules. Network connections were important, but probably never reached the extraordinary dimensions that they have developed in China today. A number of historical differences may be noted.

Material resources have always been scarce in China. But the situation has become far more acute now because of an expanding population, compounded by rapidly rising aspirations since China opened its door to the outside world. When the supply of material amenities is severely limited, the natural tendency is to use whatever means are available. The imbalance between supply and demand, we suspect, is only one factor among others. We think the widespread abuse of network connections, now reaching epidemic proportions, is largely due to the dominant role of the government in controlling the distribution of goods and resources.

In traditional China, the government had relatively little direct control over material resources. Other than taxes and levies, the government at one time or another monopolized the sales of salt and iron, but left the distribution of most amenities in the hands of traders. If one had money, one could buy almost anything one desired. The roles of the government were rather limited. For example, the government had no control over the major means of transportation. In China today, the government's presence is everywhere, reaching into virtually every aspect of one's life. This monolithic control by a centralized bureaucracy is not administered with rules that are clearly enunciated and evenly enforced. Whether a person can get what he wants, whether it is a train ticket or a color television set, depends on who he is and whom he knows. Organizations are not exempt from this dilemma. If a factory does not have the right connections, it may not be able to get its supply of raw materials. This situation has directly contributed to the widespread practice known as "going through the back door." Our survey confirms the seriousness of this situation.

If the abuse of network connections is limited to the distribution of material goods alone, the situation would be undesirable but probably not disastrous. Although we did not ask questions that directly involved the political life, we assume, based on the data and our general knowledge of Chinese society, that the "network" phenomenon is embedded in politics as in other sectors of life. Our concern is that this contagious practice of network connections will pose a major threat to the institutionalization of the basic economic and political processes needed by a society in transition. These widespread abuses oppose the nearly unanimous wish of the Chinese people to have laws that uphold social justice.

We are now convinced that Chinese people are well aware of the right of the public to know what government is doing and of government's responsibility to solicit opinions from the public before decisions are made. The evidence is clear and forceful. Ironically, many years of political campaigns and ideological indoctrination seem to have produced a quite unintended effect. What particular rights the people of China want to exercise, we did not ask. However, this increased awareness may eventually lead to a higher demand for a government system that is more responsive to public needs. Our survey suggests that if the process of political reform is too slow, it will widen the gap between the government and the public. A more responsive system, though unlikely to appear in the foreseeable future, is the only way to resolve this political dilemma.

While people usually feel more comfortable in saying that in order to protect the public interest it is sometimes necessary to sacrifice individual interest, their willingness to participate in public affairs remains rather marginal. The revolutionary belief in suppressing individual interest used to be strong, but it is being modified more and more by a pragmatic-minded public who are increasingly conscious of their own needs as against the needs of a collective society. It is largely a misconception that people who live in socialist China, where the government places collectivism and public interest above individualism and individual interest, are less concerned about their welfare than people in Western countries.

When we organize our findings by four major variables, that is, age, Western cultural influence, exposure to news information in the official media, and education, we see distinctively different profiles. The age differences are presented in table 7.4.

The analysis presented here suggests that the young, in a relative sense as compared with the old, are more interested in trying network connections rather than normal channels to get what they want, less concerned about public interest, and less willing to participate in community affairs. They seem to be more detached from the current social and political systems and more conscious of their own individual interests. Are the young people in China more self-centered than the old? There could be some truth in this presupposition. However, we believe that our data also suggest something else. It seems that the young people, for reasons that deserve in-depth probing, identify

Table 7.4 Contrasting Values of the Young versus the Old

ITEMS	YOUNG	OLD
When having problem,		
try connections	75.7%	54.4%
should not try	14.9%	32.5%
Which to sacrifice?		
sacrifice public	17.2%	4.7%
sacrifice self	82.8%	95.3%
Know friends or neighbors stealing		
report	58.0%	77.6%
Concern about district affairs		
hardly ever	31.4%	18.0%
quite often	17.1%	30.7%
Ever thought of doing things for neighborhood		
yes	80.3%	91.7%

themselves less closely with the current collective system. They seem to have a mind of their own. Their higher education and greater exposure to Western cultural influence may be important factors, table 7.5.

Our analysis shows that people under heavy Western cultural influence, compared with their low-influence counterparts, are more interested in trying connections to get what they want, less willing to serve the public, and less concerned about community affairs. Like the young, those under heavy Western influence are more indifferent about collective interests and more concerned about their own welfare. Like the young, they also seem to be more detached from the system and perhaps more self-centered.

These findings, however, raise a question about causality. The findings about age are unambiguous. People do not become young because they are detached from the current system. They become detached because they are young or because of their different life experiences associated with being young in the current social and political contexts. The relationship with Western cultural influence is not so clear-cut. Does their detachment come first or does exposure to Western cultural influence come first? Probably it has been more of an interactive process rather than a linear cause–effect relationship. It is quite possible that those who feel alienated from the current social and political system may be more attracted to the Western cultural pro-

Table 7.5 High Western Cultural Influence versus Low Influence

Items	WESTERN INFLUENCE High	Low
When having problem,		
try connections	84.3%	64.0%
should not try	7.8%	25.9%
Willingness to serve on		
neighborhood committee	39.2%	63.3%
Know friends or neighbors stealing		
report	24.0%	76.5%
not report	54.0%	15.0%
Concern about district affairs		
hardly ever	33.3%	22.8%
quite often	21.6%	28.8%

grams on television and in films. Exposure to such foreign cultural influence in turn makes them more indifferent to the collective system.

Participation in community life is one of the few cultural aspects where exposure to news information in the official media seems to have a consistent impact. Although the differences were not large, the trend is clear (table 7.6). On the one hand, the heavy consumers of news are more actively concerned with community affairs. They discuss community issues more with their neighbors, and are more willing to serve on neighborhood committees. They want to do something for their community. If there is a conflict between their individual interest and the public interest, they are more inclined to sacrifice the former for the public good. On the other hand, while they are willing to give more, they also expect more from their government, believing that the public has a right to know how the local government spends its money.

Table 7.7 shows an interesting trend: while the high-education people have a higher awareness of the government's responsibility than their low-education counterparts, this awareness is not translated into more active concern for public interest. Rather the better-educated people are less concerned about public affairs and less willing to participate in community life than the less well educated. Here we think the direction of causality is quite clear. One does not seek higher education because one feels indifferent about the current system. Rather,

Table 7.6 Exposure to News Information in Official Media

ITEMS	EXPOSURE HIGH	EXPOSURE LOW
Government spending public has right to know	82.0%	66.5%
Which one to sacrifice individual interest	95.2%	89.4%
Willingness to serve on neighborhood committee	57.8%	52.3%
Concerned with district affairs quite often	27.7%	18.8%
Discuss community affairs do not discuss	19.6%	27.1%
Ever thought of doing things for community	87.5%	81.1%

Table 7.7 High-education versus Low-education Group

ITEMS	HIGH EDUCATION	LOW EDUCATION
Who should assume responsibility for community development		
government	80.4%	55.1%
Willingness to serve on neighborhood committee	43.1%	71.3%
Concerned about district affairs		
quite often	15.6%	34.2%
Discuss community affairs		
regularly	9.6%	27.0%
occasionally	67.2%	51.4%
Ever thought of doing things for community		
yes	80.0%	91.4%

people become indifferent, or even feel alienated, because of what they have learned from higher education, or because their education now enables them to see things differently.

Our survey indicates that China today is undergoing enormous change. As the older generation passes, as Chinese people become better educated, and as the influence of Western culture spreads, the people of China are becoming more conscious of their own individual welfare and less inclined to devote themselves to the collective system in its current form. We want to emphasize the collective system in "its current form" because our data clearly suggest that Chinese people are not highly individualistic and strongly self-centered. Rather, our data show that Chinese people today are quite willing to place public interest above individual interest, provided that the public interest is formulated and articulated in consultation with them. Those who are heavy consumers of official news information seem to be more inclined to participate in the management of community affairs provided that the political system maintains an open attitude toward their participation.

Chapter 8

Cultural Values: General Perspective

Cultural values, according to Clyde Kluckholn (1951), are conceptions of the desirable which influence the selections of ends, means, and modes of actions. The distinction between ends and means is relatively clear, even though the goals of one society can be the means in another. What may be an end in one historical period could be a means at another point in time. Milton Rokeach (1968–1969, 1973) has offered what he calls terminal and instrumental values. The former are ends while the latter are means.

The mode of action is an ambiguous concept. To Kluckholn, mode refers to the style in which an instrument is used. The example he gives is the manner in which foreigners speak English as a means of obtaining a position abroad. Someone may speak English softly, and others loudly. Applying this concept to cultural values, however, runs into problems. Honesty, for example, may be considered an instrumental value. Do cultures differ in the styles in which honesty as a value is applied? Are there specific characteristics of style which can be identified for instrumental values?

These are difficult questions. It seems that the concept of mode as a cultural value needs to be clarified further before it can become a useful research tool. For our analysis, we concentrate on desirable ends and means. We will touch upon the modes only when appropriate.

Other than the ends versus means distinction, cultural values can be classified in a functional perspective. Some values function primarily as guiding principles for maintaining social relations that are essential for group solidarity and societal stability. The traditional Chinese values of harmony and tolerance are examples. They are important elements from the social aspects of traditional Chinese culture. Other values, such as diligence and ambition, are more directly relevant to task performance, generally involving the material aspects of culture. Many of the Chinese cultural values we have discussed belong to the social domain, clearly pointing to the general ethos of Chinese culture.

In the previous chapters we have touched on various cultural values in contemporary Chinese society. In the following three chapters, we focus attention on certain particularly salient values in Chinese culture. In this chapter, we discuss a few prominent Chinese cultural values in a general perspective. We explore the concept of a good person in Chinese society today. We assess the important goals in life and the perceived likelihood of achieving these goals. We probe the concept of success and the meaning of life. We consider the importance of "face" as a Chinese cultural value, and evaluate the perception of human nature as a reflection of fundamental value orientation. Chapter 9 addresses several important Chinese cultural values within the family context. In chapter 10 we discuss a full range of traditional values influenced by Confucianism.

Concept of Good Person

One way to understand the cultural values of a society is to see how people define a good person. This definition is particularly relevant to understanding the Chinese because in vernacular Chinese language there is a special term for a "good person," *haoren*, as distinguished from a "bad person," *huairen*. Haoren is someone to be trusted while huairen is someone to avoid. The values Chinese people aspire to can be identified by the attributes they assign to a good person.

We asked our respondents a simple question. What kind of person do you consider to be a haoren? This was an open-ended question and the respondents wrote in their own answers. The responses were content analyzed and classified into eight categories. Six may be considered to reflect traditional Chinese attributes of a good person. They were:

> Honest, decent
> Kind
> Helpful
> Dedicated to friends
> Frugal
> Promoting harmony

The remaining two seem to be more relevant to contemporary China in its current drive toward modernization: law abiding and educated.

More than one out of four respondents (26.5 percent) did not answer this question. Another 9.3 percent said they didn't know, or were not sure, or gave miscellaneous answers that were irrelevant. Altogether more than one-third of the respondents either gave no answers or were unsure. Is it possible that after nearly four decades of class struggle and numerous criticism campaigns, many Chinese have lost a clear sense of what constitutes a good person? The results of a discriminant analysis of the no answers and "not sure" seem to lend some plausibility to this hypothesis. Education was not a factor, suggesting that it was not because of their low education that some people failed to answer this question. Only two factors were found relevant: urban residence and age. In metropolitan Shanghai, where class struggles were pursued more vigorously, 42.5 percent of the respondents were in this category of no answers or "not sure," as compared to 25.7 percent in Qingpu towns and rural villages combined. The difference was nearly 17 percent. The corresponding figure of no answers and "not sure" was much higher (46.2 percent) among those 50 years old and above, who by and large suffered more during the class struggles, than among the middle-aged and younger groups (33.1 percent and 30.8 percent respectively). The younger people, many of whom were not even born when the Cultural Revolution began in 1966, did not have much personal experience with class struggles. The age differences were almost as large as the one between urban and rural respondents. Given these findings, their traumatic experiences with class struggles seem to be the common element that distinguished the urban residents and older people on the one hand, from the rural inhabitants and younger and middle-aged people on the other.

The results from the 1,285 respondents who gave specific answers are presented in figure 8.1.

Being honest and decent is the topmost attribute of a good person. Being helpful rates a distant second, followed by being kind, law abiding, educated and cultured, and others.

Frugality has long been recognized as a traditional Chinese virtue. Chinese children were taught to be diligent and frugal, because survival in traditional China very much depended on these qualities. But frugality was mentioned by only a few as indicative of a good person. From the way our respondents answered this question, it seems that the characteristics of a good person in Chinese society by and large refer to how one relates to other people, while frugality reflects the way one relates to the material environment.

Honest, decent	65.1%
Helpful	15.4%
Kind	7.4%
Law abiding	6.3%
Educated, cultured	3.0%
Promoting harmony	1.2%
Dedicated to friends	0.9%
Frugal	0.7%

Figure 8.1   Attributes of Good Persons

Nor was promoting harmony considered by our respondents to be a prominent characteristic of a good person. In traditional China, however, harmony in social relations was considered to be extremely important. People were admired and respected if they could play an effective role in resolving disputes and maintaining social harmony. They were called "harmony makers," or peacemakers. They were usually older persons who were able to use their positions in the community to work out a compromise. Very few people in our sample thought of a good person as someone who was good at promoting harmony. Apparently that role has lost its social significance in contemporary Chinese society.

A highly valued personal attribute in traditional China was dedication to friends, known as *yi*. Yi means going out of one's way to help friends when they are in dire need, even at the risk of sacrificing one's own personal interests or even one's own life. This kind of behavior was expected of close friends who were sworn brothers. An example well known to most Chinese was Song Jiang, in the legend of the *Water Margin*. Song Jiang was a court clerk in a county close to the Water Margin. One day he received a warrant for the arrest of his sworn brother Zhao Gai. Instead of executing the arrest, he held up the warrant and rode to Zhao Gai's village to forewarn him. This gave Zhao Gai and his gang just enough time to get away before the soldiers arrived. Song Jiang did that with the full knowledge that his behavior could be exposed. That is Yi. It is a much stronger dedication to a friend than just being helpful. This kind of personal attribute, however, would be counter-productive during a mass criticism campaign. Incidentally, the historical figure of Song Jiang was the center of an attack during Mao's campaign that criticized the Water Margin in the early 1970s. Fewer than 1 percent of our respondents mentioned Yi as an attribute of a good person.

The Chinese have traditionally put a high premium on education. Because education was out of reach for most people, someone who was educated and could read usually received high respect in the community. An educated person was generally perceived as possessing the quality of a good person. The situation appears to be rather different today. Education has become far more popular as many more people have been able to attend school. It is less of an elite quality, so to speak. On the other hand, the ruling elite throughout the years tended to treat the highly educated with suspicion and distrust. Particularly during the Cultural Revolution, the college-educated were broadly labelled "the stinky No. 9," a vernacular phrase reserved for those with the lowest social status. This social stigma has been partly lifted since 1979, but the position of intellectuals remains ambiguous. Whatever the reasons, education no longer figures prominently in the minds of Chinese today as something that distinguishes a good person.

Another omission deserves mention. Traditionally, the concept of a good person was closely associated with good deeds. Someone who made a special effort to help the needy, especially during times of famine or natural disaster, was considered to have the virtue of being a haoren. Among Chinese Buddhists, this was considered to be one way of accumulating merit to ensure happiness and prosperity during the next life. The concept of "good person and good deeds" is still prominent in Taiwan, where an annual campaign, known as Good Persons and Good Deeds, is staged to pay tribute to people in each community who have performed exemplary deeds. Although being helpful was a recognized attribute, there was no mention at all of doing good deeds as a quality of a good person.

The major traits mentioned were honesty, decency, kindness, and helpfulness. These personal attributes have been part of the traditional Chinese core of virtues for centuries, and they are still important today. "Law abiding," cited by relatively few, seems to be a new concept, and may reflect the government's recent campaign to educate the people on respecting the law as a measure to counter the chaotic disorder inherited from the Cultural Revolution in many parts of the country.

A second discriminant analysis examined the specific concepts of a good person. The results showed these concepts to be relatively uniform among our respondents. Urbanization was the only factor that made a difference in the sense that rural villagers (19.5 percent) were more likely to consider being helpful as a salient quality of a good person than people living in urban areas (about 14 percent). The difference was not large but statistically significant. It seems that life in rural villages depends more on mutuality, and someone who is willing to extend a helping hand is more highly valued. Other than the urban–rural division, the specific responses to this question were not related to age, gender, education, or income. Neither Western cultural influence nor use of media news information was a relevant factor.

Goals in Life

Other than personal attributes, another way to assess cultural values is to find out what people consider to be important goals in their lives. We asked a simple question: What do you want most in life? We gave the respondents a list of 14 desirable goals, and asked them to select no more than five. Their choices are presented in descending order in figure 8.2.

The most important goal in life was a warm and close family. Four out of five respondents said this was what they wanted most in life. The older people (84.8 percent) considered family warmth slightly more important than the younger people (76.1 percent) even though the latter also considered it highly important. This finding confirms the paramount importance of family in Chinese society today.

Successful children was the next most important goal. Here people above 30 attached much greater importance (74.9 percent to 70.7 percent) to successful children than people below 29 (44.9 percent). The younger people are apparently preoccupied with other concerns.

Warm and close family	79.8%
Successful children	66.2%
Career accomplishments	60.1%
Comfortable life	57.5%
Harmonious (family) relations	53.2%
True love	27.1%
Education and knowledge	22.8%
Building a house	22.2%
True friendship	19.0%
Contribution to country	18.9%
Starting own business	12.3%
Going abroad for education	9.1%
College degree	8.0%
Adventure and initiative	2.1%

Figure 8.2 Important Goals in Life

Under China's late marriage policy, many of them may not yet have children. Successful children are more important to women (71.7 percent) than to men (61.4 percent). They are equally important to urban and rural residents.

Career accomplishments were highly valued and nearly as important as successful children. In most other societies one would expect education to be related to this particular goal, in the sense that people of higher education would more likely consider career accomplishments to be important. This is not so in China. There was no difference whatsoever between the high (60.2 percent) and low (60.9 percent) education groups. This finding confirms the general observation that high education in contemporary China does not lend itself to career accomplishments. Nor were career accomplishments as a goal related to age, gender, urbanization, or income. The only two relevant factors were use of new media information and Western cultural influence, with contrasting results. Those who made heavy use of news media information (72.4 percent) were far more likely to consider career accomplishments an important goal than those who made little use (53.6 percent). On the other hand, those under heavy Western cultural influence from the media (51 percent) considered career accom-

Figure 8.3 School children in Shanghai line up for an excursion. (*Photo courtesy of Linus Chao*)

plishments much less important than those under little influence (63.2 percent).

We combined the Western cultural influence scale and the news information scale into one in order to assess the cumulative effects of these two types of media content.[1] The results are presented in table 8.1.

When Western cultural influence and news information use were both low (a) or both high (d), they seemed to counterbalance each other. The percentages of those who selected career accomplishments as an important goal were about the same as the overall percentage. The main difference was between (b) and (c). Among those who were heavy users of news information but under little Western influence, a much higher percentage valued career accomplishments than among the non-heavy users of news information who were under heavy Western cultural influence. The difference was 15 percent. It is clear that Western cultural influence tends to steer people away from career accomplishments as a goal in life, while use of news information will accentuate this goal.

A comfortable life was desired by nearly six out of ten respondents. This goal seems to be evenly shared by Chinese people. Only Western cultural influence was found to be a relevant but weak factor. A comfortable life is slightly more important to those under heavy Western cultural influence than those under little influence.

Harmonious relations were the only other goal endorsed by more than half of the respondents. A more faithful translation of the Chinese phrase would be "getting along harmoniously," which primarily refers to harmonious relations within the family. This goal was far more important to women (61.9 percent) than to men (45.6 percent), and even more important to older people (68.5 percent) than to younger (48.9 percent) and middle-aged people (47.8 percent). This

Table 8.1 Western Influence, Media News, and Career Accomplishments as Important Goals

	WESTERN INFLUENCE	
	Low	High
News low	60.4% (a)	51.9% (c)
	(583)	(385)
News high	66.9% (b)	60.4% (d)
	(429)	(601)

was one of the recurring instances where a clear division was found between those 50 years old and above, and those 49 years old and below.

We now move to goals endorsed by less than 30 percent of the respondents. First was "true love," a romanticized idea generally traceable to the West. It was important to 27.1 percent. As expected, age was the most relevant factor. Nearly half of those below 29 (48.5 percent) considered true love to be something they wanted most, compared to only 10.9 percent among those above 50. The greater the Western cultural influence, the more important true love was. Those under heavy influence (41.2 percent) were twice as likely as those under little influence (21.2 percent) to want true love. Exposure to official news information was again related in an opposite way, though not as strongly. Those who made heavy use of news information (25.4 percent) were less likely to want true love than those who made little use of it (29.8 percent).

We again combined the Western influence scale and news information scale into one for analysis as we did for career accomplishments.

True love was much more important to those under heavy Western cultural influence, especially if they were not heavy users of news information (c). A strong reliance on official news information (d) brought down the endorsement of this romantic goal slightly, from 37 percent to about 31 percent. Among those under little Western influence (a), true love was much less important (about 25 percent). If they made heavy use of news information (b), they tended to regard true love as even less important, down from some 25 percent to about 17 percent. Here we have one more clear demonstration of the impact of Western cultural influence on Chinese cultural values.

Table 8.2 Western Influence, Media News, and True Love as Important Goal

| | WESTERN INFLUENCE | |
	Low	High
News low	24.5% (a)	37.0% (c)
	(584)	(386)
News high	16.8% (b)	30.6% (d)
	(429)	(601)

Figure 8.4 Junior high school students learn how the heart functions. Science, not revolutionary ideology, is now emphasized in school curriculum. (*Photo courtesy of Linus Chao*)

Education and knowledge were an important goal to about one out of five respondents, appealing more strongly to those of high education (26.8 percent) than those of low education (15.7 percent), and more attractive to younger people (26.5 percent) than to older people (16.7 percent).

Building a house was primarily a goal for people living in rural villages (46.1 percent), where land is available, than for people in urban areas (7.9 percent in Qingpu and 15.9 percent in Shanghai). Interestingly, people who made heavy use of news information were less concerned about building a house (11.4 percent) than those who made little use (27.1 percent). To the former, there were other important goals, such as career accomplishments.

True friendship was relatively unimportant, chosen by 19 percent. Western cultural influence was the only relevant factor. Those under heavy influence (27.5 percent) tended to consider true friendship to be more important than those under little influence (15.2 percent).

Overall, contributions to the country did not stand out as an important goal for our respondents. Only 18.9 percent endorsed it. Relatively speaking, this collective goal is more important to men (24 percent) than to women (13.2 percent), and more important to frequent users of official news information (22.8 percent) than to non-frequent users (14.2 percent). A prominent factor is Western cultural influence. Those under heavy Western influence (average 10.5 percent for two top levels) considered contributions to the country much less important than those under little influence (23.5 percent). This goal was less important to the younger (15.3 percent) and middle-aged people (16.8 percent) than to the older people (26.6 percent), another instance where age 50 seems to draw a clear line. It was less important to residents in Shanghai (15.9 percent) than to those living in Qingpu towns (23.4 percent) and the villages (23.1 percent).

Until recent years when the Chinese government began to allow some small individual private business, it was not possible for anyone to start a business of his own. It is therefore understandable that very few (12.3 percent) considered this an important goal. Relatively speaking, men (16.4 percent) were more attracted to this new opportunity than women (7.6 percent). Younger people (15.3 percent) took this twice as seriously as older people (6.7 percent).

Figure 8.5 Raising ducks, previously prohibited as an evil of capitalism, has now become a profitable business in rural Qingpu. (*Photo courtesy of Linus Chao*)

Going abroad for education is hardly a feasible idea for more than a tiny fraction of people even in the Shanghai area. Yet as many as 9.1 percent chose this as one of their important goals. This finding shows how appealing this possibility must be to some Chinese. Going abroad for education is primarily a goal for those under Western cultural influence, of higher education and younger. If someone is under heavy Western influence, he or she is about six times as likely (27.5 percent) to want to go abroad as someone under little influence (4.4 percent). A senior high school or college education increases the aspirations about 4.5 times (15.6 percent for high education versus 3.5 percent for low education). Those under 29 years old (13.7 percent) were about six times as likely as those above 50 (2.2 percent) to want to study overseas.

A college degree was important to only 8 percent. Age was the only relevant factor: a college degree was important to 12.2 percent of those under 29 years of age versus 2 percent of those above 50.

"Adventure and initiative" was the least important of all the goals we presented to the respondents, more or less as expected. What the Chinese phrase means is to adventure into something unknown, use initiative at some risk so that one might achieve major success. This spirit of adventurism was not part of the Chinese character in the old society. It certainly has received little encouragement under the rigid structural constraints of the current socioeconomic system. It is not surprising that only 2.1 percent listed this as one of their important goals. Most interestingly, we found that the greater the Western cultural influence, the more likely one will endorse adventurism as an important goal. Of those under little influence, only 1.2 percent mentioned this goal. This goal became more important as Western influence increased until it reached a sizable 9.8 percent among those most heavily influenced.

Likelihood of Goal Achievement

How likely did they think they would be able to achieve these goals? We did not ask the respondents to assess the likelihood for each goal they had identified. We simply asked: How likely is it that you will be able to accomplish your goals?

On the whole, the respondents were highly optimistic: their answers were "very likely" (27.4 percent), "likely" (61 percent), "not very likely" (9.3 percent), and "not likely at all" (2.2 percent). Rather interestingly, rural villagers were most optimistic and Shanghai residents least so. The percentages for "very likely" were 37.1 percent for villages, 27.6 percent for Qingpu towns, and 23.3 percent for Shanghai.

It seems that under China's current policy, rural villages are enjoying more opportunities and benefits from economic reforms while urban residents are still earning pretty much the same wages as before. Even though in absolute terms the average income was higher in urban areas, our survey revealed, in a relative sense the rural people have seen more improvement and are therefore more optimistic. Men (24.7 percent said very likely) were less optimistic than women (30.4 percent).

We cross-tabulated the perceived likelihood with each of the goals endorsed. Three popular goals—career accomplishments, warm and close family, and successful children—were positively related to the perceived likelihood (significant at the .01 but not the .001 level). That is, those respondents who identified those three goals were more likely to say they would be able to accomplish their goals than respondents who did not identify those goals. Only two goals, both low on the popularity scale, were significantly related to the perceived likelihood at the .001 level, and both in a negative way. Those who wanted to go abroad and those who wanted to build a house were less confident about accomplishing their goals than others who did not have those goals. It is clear that even though some people were entertaining the idea of going abroad or building a house, they realized that the odds were heavily against them.

We further asked: If your children work hard, will they be able to reach their goals? We did not ask what their children's specific goals would be. Most respondents would not know for sure. We assume that by and large what the respondents themselves wanted most in life would be similar to what they thought their children would want.

As the results show below, the respondents were more optimistic about their children's future than they were about their own goal achievements.

For children's goal achievements, the urban–rural division is no longer a relevant factor. It seems that when people consider the future

Table 8.3 Likelihood of Achieving Own vs. Children's Goals

	OWN GOALS	CHILDREN'S GOALS
Very likely	27.4%	38.3%
Likely	61.0%	58.2%
Not very likely	9.3%	3.1%
Not likely at all	2.2%	0.4%

of their children, they are looking beyond the current policies whether they live in urban or rural areas. Rather they are taking into account an overall, albeit implicit, assessment of the prospects of the system as a whole. The most important factor turns out to be the use of media news, probably the single most important source of information that people in China have about the system in which they live. On the whole, the greater the use of news information, the more optimistic one is about the future of one's children. Of the most heavy users, 47.2 percent said their children would "very likely" be able to accomplish their goals, as compared to only 30.9 percent among those who made little use of news information. It seems that heavy users of news information have greater confidence in the future of the Chinese socioeconomic system. Education, on the other hand, seems to have a negative impact. Those who have senior high school or college education are less optimistic about their children than the two lower education levels. In the higher education group, only 33.9 percent said "very likely," versus 41.2 percent in the middle group and 40.8 percent in the lower education group.

We combined the use of media news and education into one scale to examine their cumulative effect.[2] Using "very likely" as an index, we present the results in table 8.4.

When the use of media news was high (c and d), people were more optimistic about their children's future. High education (c), however, substantially brought down this level of confidence in the future prospects of the social system. When the use of media news was low (a and b), people were less optimistic, and those who were better educated (a) were even less so. The difference between high news information/low education (d) and low news information/high education (a) was nearly 21 percent. Using "very likely" as an index, we com-

Table 8.4 Media News, Education, and Likelihood of Children to Reach Their Goals

	NEWS INFORMATION	
	Low	High
Education high	27.8% (a)	38.0% (c)
	(306)	(450)
Education low	34.4% (b)	48.7% (d)
	(642)	(559)

puted the average percentages of high use (43.9 percent) and low use (31.9 percent) of media news, yielding a difference of 12 percent. Similarly, the average percentages were 41 percent for low education and 33.9 percent for high education, leaving a gap of 7.1 percent. The use of media news information appears to be a more potent factor than education as far as perception of children's future is concerned.

Means of Success

While the nature of a good person and the kinds of goals tell us something about a culture from the perspectives of cherished personal attributes and desirable ends, the concept of success allows us to take another look at values. It illustrates what people consider to be important means to achieve their goals.

We asked: What do you think is the most important element for career success? Success here is clearly defined as career accomplishments, not in terms of such traditional Chinese concepts as family longevity or prosperous children; this qualification of success allowed us to get more focused answers. This was an open-ended question, without suggested responses. The respondents were asked to write in their own answers, which were classified into eight categories. Nearly three out of ten respondents (28.8 percent) did not answer this question.

The results, based on the 1,424 respondents who gave an answer, are presented in figure 8.6.

The most prominent element was diligence. If we include the 5.8 percent who mentioned both opportunity and diligence, then nearly half of the answers emphasized diligence. This finding confirms the traditional Chinese value of diligence and frugality as a way of life. Personal qualifications was the second prominent factor, followed by opportunity, and drive and ambition.

Diligence	43.0%
Personal qualifications	15.4%
Drive and ambition	12.2%
Opportunity	8.3%
Diligence and opportunity	5.8%
Baile (mentor)	1.5%
Connections	1.4%
Miscellaneous	12.4%

Figure 8.6 Perceived Means of Success

The others mentioned miscelleneous factors, including personal connections and a Chinese phrase known as "Baile," which may be translated as mentor. This term refers to a person who in a traditional sense recognizes the hidden potential of a protege and gives him encouragement to develop. Baile, according to legend, was a particularly talented horse trainer. At one time a horse was presented to the king as a tribute. But the horse looked frail and weak. The king was offended. Of the king's many counsellors, Baile was the only one who recognized the exceptional qualities of this horse. It is interesting that the concept of "Baile" still exists in China today. It represents a ray of hope, especially for the young who look to someone in high position who will someday recognize their talents and help them to move up in what is seen as an extremely tight arena for career advancement.

On the whole, more people mentioned intrinsic personal qualities such as diligence, drive, and qualifications, which they themselves can develop, than external contingencies such as opportunities and connections, over which one has little control.

Because the responses were open-ended, what was not mentioned as important elements of career success is probably just as interesting as what was mentioned. There was no mention of planning by our respondents. It seems that in contemporary Chinese society, where occupational mobility is rather limited, planning a career does not promote success. One simply works hard and waits for opportunities to arise. Or one hopes a Baile will one day recognize him. Planning will be of little avail. Also, planning would be quite important for a business career, but in China there are as yet very few business opportunities. During the years of the Cultural Revolution, a revolutionary class background was considered essential for any career success. If one belonged to one of the undesirable classes, one's entire future was forever doomed. These restrictions have been largely lifted. Nobody mentioned class background as important for career success, although personal connections were recognized as helpful.

Only two factors were found relevant to the concept of success. Villagers seemed to be guided more by the traditional ideas of diligence and frugality than urban dwellers: 56.6 percent in rural villages versus 34.1 percent in metropolitan Shanghai mentioned diligence alone. People in Shanghai tended to recognize the importance of opportunity (10.5 percent) and drive (14.7 percent) more than did villagers (4.1 percent and 9.7 percent respectively). Western culture seems to exert a distinct influence. Those under heavy Western influence appeared to attribute success more to external factors such as opportunities and less to intrinsic attributes such as diligence and personal qualifications than those under little influence.

Meaning of Life

We asked several questions about the general ethos of contemporary Chinese culture. One was about the meaning of life. We asked: Which one of the following do you agree with? (1.) the most important thing in one's life is to live happily. (2.) the most important thing in one's life is to make some contributions to society. This question may be regarded as a measure of individualism versus collectivism. Although "live happily" was presented first, an overwhelming majority (76.8 percent) chose the second option. This finding is in keeping with the traditionally strong concept of collectivism in Chinese culture, except that traditional Chinese collectivism was focused on the family rather than on society.

Three factors were found related to the new version of collectivism, the most prominent of which was Western cultural influence, in a clearly negative way. The stronger the Western influence, the stronger the endorsement of individualism, and conversely the weaker the attachment to collectivism. Among those exposed to little Western influence, 85.4 percent said making a contribution to society was most important, and only 14.6 percent said individual happiness was most important. As Western influence increased, this trend was gradually reversed. Among those under heavy Western influence, as many as 51 percent said individual happiness was most important! Only 49 percent considered societal contributions most important.

The relation with news media information was in the opposite direction, though very much weaker. Among the heavy users of official news information, 83.6 percent endorsed contributions to society. This endorsement slowly but steadily declined to 74.3 percent among the least frequent users of news information.

Young people (35.2 percent) were about five times as likely as old people (6.7 percent) to consider living one's life happily as the most important thing in life.

We combined the Western influence scale and news information scale into one, as we did before, in order to assess their cumulative effects. The results are presented in table 8.5.

When the Western cultural influence was high (groups c and d), more people said "live happily" is most important than when Western influence was low. The use of news information seemed to have a counterbalancing effect by bringing down the endorsement of this form of individualism, from 39.3 percent to 27.4 percent. When the Western cultural influence was low (groups a and b), fewer people preferred the "live happily" lifestyle. The heavy use of news information made this preference even lower, reducing it from 16.8 percent to ll.7 percent.

Table 8.5 Western Influence, Media News, and Living Happily As Most Important

	WESTERN INFLUENCE	
	Low	High
News low	16.8% (a)	39.3% (c)
	(579)	(382)
News high	11.7% (b)	27.4% (d)
	(429)	(595)

On the whole, we found Western cultural influence to be a much more prominent factor than the use of official news information. Using the percentage of "live happily" as an index, we computed the overall percentages of this individual lifestyle. In the high Western influence group (c and d combined), the endorsement was 32 percent, as compared to 14.6 percent in the low Western influence group (a and b). The difference was as much as 17.4 percent. In the low news information group (a and c), 25.7 percent accepted this lifestyle, as compared to 20.8 percent in the high news information group (b and d). The difference, as an index of counterbalancing effect, was only 4.9 percent.

We asked another question about the meaning of life inasmuch as it is related to work ethic. Which is more important to you—treasure your time, work as hard as possible, or life is short, enjoy it while you can? Historically, life has always been hard in China, and the Chinese people have managed to survive many hardships and tribulations simply by working hard and treasuring their time. The concept that life is short and that one should enjoy it while one can has generally been regarded as deviated thinking. Our findings confirmed the traditional views. Nearly nine out of ten respondents (89.7 percent) said "treasure your time, work as hard as possible." Only 10.3 percent said "life is short, enjoy it while you can."

When we examined the data to see who were those minority deviants that wanted to enjoy life while they could, the findings were revealing and even astonishing. The most prominent factor was Western cultural influence. Of those under little influence, only 4.6 percent said "life is short, enjoy it while you can." The endorsement of this life philosophy increased steadily with Western influence until it reached 27.5 percent among those most heavily influenced! The ratio was six to one. This new lifestyle is much more popular among the young than among the old. In the age group below 29 years old, 16.2 percent wanted to enjoy life while they could. Among those above 50 years old, only 2.9 percent expressed this feeling; 97.1 percent said "treasure your time, work as hard as possible." This finding confirmed our impression that if this question had been asked in a survey 50 years ago, nearly everybody would have said "work as hard as possible." People in metropolitan Shanghai (12.9 percent) were more inclined to say they should enjoy life than those living in a rural environment (5.1 percent).

The "work versus play" lifestyle is another one of those instances where Western cultural influence and the use of official news information have opposite effects. While Western influence was positively associated with the "enjoy life" philosophy, the use of news information tended to strengthen the "work hard" orientation although this relationship was not nearly as strong as the "enjoy life" value reinforced by Western culture. Of those who made heavy use of news information, 93.9 percent said "work as hard as possible," compared to 87.2 percent among those who made little use.

We combined the Western cultural influence scale and news information scale into one for cross tabulation with the "work versus play" lifestyle. The results are presented in table 8.6.

When the Western cultural influence was low (a and b), nearly everybody followed the traditional concept of working as hard as possible because time is precious. The acceptance of this traditional concept was slightly enhanced by the use of official news information, up from

Table 8.6 Western Influence, Media News, and Work vs. Play Lifestyle

| | WESTERN INFLUENCE | |
	Low	High
News low:		
Enjoy life	5.5% (a)	21.7% (c)
Work hard	94.5%	78.3%
	(567)	(374)
News high:		
Enjoy life	3.3% (b)	12.7% (d)
Work hard	96.7%	87.3%
	(422)	(590)

94.5 percent to 96.7 percent. Under heavy Western cultural influence, the "enjoy life" philosophy received a tremendous boost, especially when the use of news information was low (c). Under those circumstances, nearly 22 percent said enjoying life was more important. This was almost seven times as high as what prevailed when Western influence was low and the use of news information was high (b). Even when Western influence was high, the heavy use of news information brought down the percentage of "enjoying life" to around 13 percent (d).

In comparison, Western cultural influence was far more compelling than the use of news information. Using the percentage of "enjoy life" as an index, we computed the overall percentages. In the high Western influence group (c and d combined), 16.2 percent endorsed this philosophy. In the low Western influence group (a and b), it was only 4.6 percent, yielding a difference of 11.6 percent. In the low news information group (a and c) the endorsement was 11.9 percent, compared to 8.8 percent in the high news information group (b and d). The difference was only 3.1 percent.

Face

Saving face is an important cultural value to Chinese, occupying an especially significant place in interpersonal relations which in the past functioned in a familial context. In traditional China many of these relations, whether social or economic, took place within the domains of the extended kinship structure and its numerous layers of secondary connections. Even beyond the extended family, Chinese wanted to cast their relations in simulated kinship terms. Persons senior in age were referred to as "elder brothers" or "uncles" depending on the age differences and their relations with those already in the social network. A key ingredient of these relations is known as renqing, which may be translated as "personal obligations and affections." It is largely this feeling of renqing that tied together many of these basically reciprocal relations in traditional Chinese society (King, 1985). In a practical sense, a renqing network was an exchange network.

Face is a key element of renqing, which we have discussed in chapter 4. A person participated in the renqing network not merely because of the practical rewards, which were considerable, but also, perhaps just as importantly, because this was one way to maintain one's face. In one sense, face in traditional China was almost like a membership card in a huge "old boy's club." One wanted to keep this membership card in order to assure full participation and enjoy its benefits. The way to do that was to honor the expected renqing obligations. Failure to live up to such expectations would result in a loss of face. A serious loss of face would in turn impair one's standing in the "club" so to speak. An individual would find himself excluded from the renqing network.

In other words, people participated in the renqing network in order to maintain face. At the same time, they wanted to protect their face so that they could continue to participate as full members of the renqing network. Thus "face" can be considered both a means and an end. As a cultural value, "face" also borders on what Clyde Kluckholn (1951) calls the "mode" of desirable action because for whatever ends they were striving toward, the Chinese were very much concerned that they caused no damage to the face of themselves as well as of those they were dealing with. Their deep-rooted concern with face leads to a particularly valued style of action, and thus fits what Kluckholn calls the desirable mode.

Chinese society today is certainly not what it was before 1949. The extended kinship structure has lost its economic foundation, and with that, many of its former functions. It would not be incorrect to say that the traditional kinship structure does not exist in China anymore. Chinese children may still call the friends of their parents "uncles" and "aunties." But adults no longer use the formal term "elder brother" to address each other as people did before 1949 (and still do in Taiwan and Hong Kong). They call each other by the informal term of "Old Wang" or "Old Li," or "Young Chang" or "Young Chen."

Even though the utilitarian outreach of the traditional kinship-based social "club" is largely gone, within a smaller circle of immediate family members, including brothers, sisters, cousins, uncles, and aunts, some influence trade-offs are still being practiced on a limited scale whenever feasible. In that small circle renqing is still important. Failure to live up to renqing obligations may not impose as many dire consequences as it did before, but it is a matter not to be treated lightly. When asked what factors most influence interpersonal relations in Chinese society today, 22.3 percent specifically mentioned renqing and another 25.7 percent said friendship, in which renqing plays a major role. If renqing is still prominent in its own way, what about face?

We asked our respondents this question: In our society today, how do you regard the matter of face? An overwhelming majority still considered face to be either "very important" (39 percent) or "rather important" (39.1 percent), totalling 78.1 percent. The others answered "somewhat important" (15.7 percent), "not very important" (4.3 percent) and "not important at all" (2 percent). If we include "somewhat important," then nearly everybody (93.8 percent) considered face to be important. The importance of face has not diminished at all.

Three factors, urban versus rural living, education, and gender, were relevant. People living in rural villages (53.6 percent said very important) considered face to be more important than townspeople (43.5 percent) and Shanghai residents (31.7 percent). It seems that in the rural environment, where people interact more closely on personal terms, face is a much more important matter than in a big city like Shanghai, where life is more impersonal. The lower the education, the more important face is. In the high-education group, 30.2 percent said face was very important. The corresponding figure increased to 40.2 percent in the middle group and 51.8 percent in the low-education group. Women (44.2 percent said very important) attached greater importance to face then men (34.4 percent). These findings suggest that a personal social network occupies a more prominent place in the lives of women than men, and in the lives of the lower educated than the higher educated.

How our respondents answered the next question suggests that face is important to Chinese not simply because it enables one to move around in the renqing network, but also because it is a symbol of one's good moral standing in the community. When asked whether members of a family would feel they have lost face if an unmarried daughter gets pregnant, 85.4 percent said yes. In this case, it is the urban people in Shanghai (89.3 percent) and Qingpu towns (87.1 percent), who were more concerned about loss of face because of a pregnancy out of wedlock, than rural villagers (75.1 percent). We think this is because such matters are taken less seriously in rural villages where some marriages are still informally taken care of. Rather interestingly, those under heavy Western cultural influence (average 76 percent for the two top groups) were less concerned about loss of face due to this situation than those under little influence (86.7 percent).

We asked two similar questions. Will you lose face if your son-in-law asks your daughter for a divorce? Will you lose face if your daughter-in-law asks your son for a divorce?

There were no such things as divorces in traditional China. A husband had the right to dissolve a marriage for a number of reasons, including his wife's failure to produce a male heir, disobedience of her father-in-law and mother-in-law, and indecent behavior. All he had to do was to inform his wife's family. His decision would be final. It would be considered a serious loss of face for the wife's family. More often than not, this decision was made by the parents of the husband. No matter how much she was abused, the wife had no right to ask for a divorce.

Divorce is allowed and guaranteed under China's new marriage law passed in the early 1950s. Now both the husband and the wife can

Table 8.7 Divorce and Loss of Face

	DAUGHTER-IN-LAW	SON-IN-LAW
Lose face	45.4%	44.4%
No	40.6%	40.9%
Not sure	14.0%	14.8%

ask for divorce. From the way our respondents answered these two questions, however, it is clear that a divorce is by no means taken lightly by the parents. The results for the two questions are nearly identical.

While this would probably have been a very serious matter 50 years ago, now less than half of the respondents considered such a situation to be a loss of face, regardless of where the request originates. Although such a divorce request is not as morally objectionable as pregnancy out of wedlock, the tradional negative undertone associated with the dismissal of an unfit wife still seems to linger on.

The relevant factors are the same for daughters-in-law and sons-in-law. People of lower education took this far more seriously than people of higher education. If the daughter-in-law asked for divorce, 56.9 percent in the low-education group would consider it a loss of face, compared to only 35.5 percent in the high-education group. The mother-in-law is hurt more than the father-in-law: 51.9 percent of women versus 39.6 percent of men said this would be a loss of face. The findings about the son-in-law are highly similar.

Human Nature

In Confucian philosophy, human nature is believed to be good. Mencius, a disciple of Confucian teaching, was a strong advocate of this belief. His contemporary, Xun Zi, strongly argued against it. To Xun Zi, human nature is basically evil. The benign manifestations that we see, he argued, are merely a false facade that we have learned to stage. In the mainstream of Chinese philosophy, however, the orthodox Confucian teaching as advocated by Mencius prevailed. Chinese were taught to believe that human nature is good. What is the impact of some thirty years of class struggle, particularly during the years of the Cultural Revolution, when children were encouraged to denounce and even physically abuse their parents, when husbands and wives were compelled to accuse each other, and when personal survival in a mass criticism campaign meant not trusting even one's closest friends?

We asked a straightforward question: Do you think that human nature is good or evil? We gave the respondents four choices: human nature is good, human nature is evil, human nature has a good side and also an evil side, human nature is neither good nor evil.

How Chinese would have answered this question fifty years ago, we have no way of knowing. In our survey, only 2.8 percent said human nature is evil, and as many as 30.9 percent said human nature is good. The majority, 53.3 percent, said that human nature has a good side and also an evil side. Another 13 percent said human nature is neither good nor evil.

Only education and age were found to be relevant factors. The higher the education, the lower the percentage saying human nature is good. This percentage decreased from 41.0 percent in the low-education group down to 24.9 percent in the high-education group. Conversely, with higher education, more people recognized that human nature is neither good nor evil. This view was expressed by 19.2 percent in the high-education group versus 7.9 percent in the low-education group.

Age seems to have a different impact. The dividing line again appears to be between the middle-aged group and the older group, a dichotomy found with other cultural values. The old people (44.6 percent) were far more likely to believe that human nature is good than either the middle-aged group (26.7 percent) or the younger group (25.7 percent). On the other hand, the younger people (60.2 percent) and middle-aged people (56.7 percent) were more likely to see human nature as both good and evil than the old people (39.6 percent).

We were somewhat puzzled by these findings about age differences. In one sense age represents physical differences due to aging that can be reflected in different values. For example, "true love" is rather important to young people but has little appeal to those over 50. But age also embodies different life experiences. In China, because of the radical upheavals during the last forty years, such differences in life experiences can be particularly pronounced. When we compare the young and the old, one difference that promptly emerges is their experiences with class struggles. Is it possible that some Chinese have adopted a more cynical view of human nature, seeing it as both good and evil instead of the traditionally benign concept, because of their painful sufferings during the class struggles? If so, then we would expect the older and middle-aged people to share this cynical view more because they definitely have had more traumatic experiences than those now in their twenties. Most of the latter were too young to suffer during the Cultural Revolution. A person who was 25 in 1987 was only four years old when the Cultural Revolution started in 1966. If the class-struggle experience was a major factor, then we would expect the old and middle-aged people, as a group, less likely to say human nature is good and more likely to say human nature is both good and evil. This was not what we found (figure 8.7).

What we found was a clear dividing line with respect to the concept of human nature, leaving those above 50 on one side and those below 49 on the other. This dichotomy needs to be explained not just by the traumatic experiences during the Cultural Revolution, which those in their 60s, 50s, and 40s shared to some extent, but in terms of life experiences common among those above 50 and yet very different from those below 49. Such life experiences, we think, can be summed up in one phrase: sufficient socialization under the umbrella of traditional Chinese culture (figure 8.8).

The average age of the younger group and middle-aged group as a whole was around 35. People under 38 years of age in 1987 were not yet born when the Communist revolution succeeded in establishing the People's Republic in 1949. All those in the younger group and most people in the middle-aged group drew no personal experiences from a traditional China. In the older group, the average age was 58. They were already 19 years old in 1949. They had been socialized under traditional Chinese culture. We think it is this traditional socialization in the formative years that acted as a mediating factor for the older people when they tried to cope with traumatic experiences in later years, including the many struggle campaigns. Despite their intensive suffer-

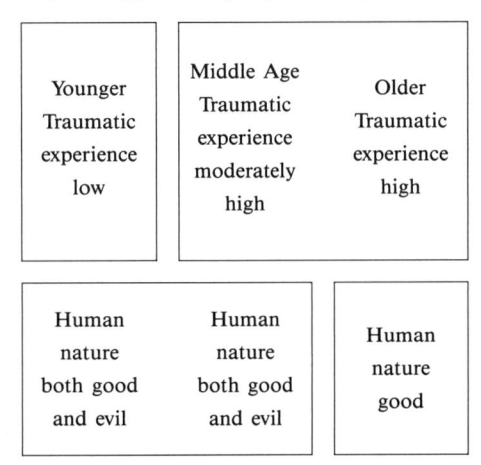

Figure 8.7 Age, Traumatic Experience, and Concept of Human Nature

Younger Socialization in traditional China: none	Middle Age Socialization in traditional China: hardly any	Older Socialization in traditional China: completed
Human nature both good and evil	Human nature both good and evil	Human nature good

Figure 8.8 Age, Socialization in Traditional China, and Concept of Human Nature

ings during the Cultural Revolution, we think, the older people still have much faith in the good side of human nature because they had assimilated a value system before the coming of Chinese communism.

This traditional socialization hypothesis is consistent with several other findings. Our research demonstrates that people above 50 years of age were more likely to consider harmonious relations within the family an important goal in life than both the middle-aged group and the younger people. As we know, harmonious family relations were extremely important in traditional China, and those who were socialized before 1949 seem to cherish this old value much more than those whose socialization experience began after 1949.

We also recall that the older group attached greater importance to contributions to society, even though this was not one of the more prominent goals for our respondents as a whole. Part of their socialization experience was the war with Japan from 1937 to 1945, which instilled a strong sense of patriotism in the Chinese people, particularly the young at that time. It seems that many in the older generation, who were young during the war, have retained this feeling of patriotism.

Discussion

One rather striking finding is that more than one-third of our respondents either did not know what was a good person or were not able to answer that question. Because those "no answers" were concentrated among the older people and metropolitan Shanghai residents, we think that it was their common traumatic experiences with the class struggles, particularly during the Cultural Revolution, that destroyed their fundamental conception of what constitutes a good person. While honesty and decency are still recognized as important, other traditional virtues like Yi (dedication to friends), social harmony and performance of good deeds have lost their meaning as valued individual traits.

A close and warm family and successful children have always been high on the list of desirable ends for Chinese, and they still are. In the aftermath of China's economic reforms and open-door policy, Chinese seem to be aspiring to important new goals, particularly career accomplishments and a comfortable life. Even though in reality these new goals are unlikely to be fulfilled in the foreseeable future, our respondents were by and large optimistic. They seemed to have an even more optimistic outlook about the future of their children. These high material aspirations and optimistic expectations are encouraging indications because they can provide energy for China's modernization. If, on the other hand, these aspirations continue to be unfulfilled for a long time to come, they can become the breeding ground for a rising wave of popular discontent and frustration.

On the positive side our findings reaffirm the meaning of life for the Chinese people. An overwhelming majority of our respondents felt that making a contribution to society far outweighs pursuing individual happiness, and that one should treasure one's time and work as hard as possible rather than entertain the idea that "life is short and let's enjoy it while we can." Behind these findings we see a reservoir of hope and potential energy for building China's new society. It is up to the ruling elite not to take steps that will dash the hope and destroy the energy.

Traditionally Chinese have been taught that human nature is good. The many years of class struggles and mutual accusations, however, seem to have diluted this concept. The majority of our respondents now see both a good side and an evil side in human nature. Face has been an important aspect of Chinese life, and its importance has remained undiminished. Because of the overriding role of personal connections in China today, which we have discussed in a previous chapter, people will have to be concerned about their "face" in order to maintain their connections in the social networks.

Among our most significant findings is the consistent and perhaps even astonishing influence of Western culture in the mass media on fundamental Chinese cultural values, considering the fact that Chinese people have been exposed to such influence through television and films for only about ten years. We get a clear picture by contrasting those under heavy Western influence with those under little influence, table 8.8.

Those under heavy Western cultural influence give much greater importance to true love and true friendship than those under little influence. They are more eager to go abroad to pursue their education, and are more venturesome and more willing to take risks. Living a life happily and enjoying it while they can is far more meaningful to them than to those not heavily exposed to Western cultural influence. In contrast, career accomplishments, working hard, and making a contribution to their country are relatively less important.

News information from China's official media seems to have the opposite impact, though much less strong than that of Western cultural influence, as summarized in table 8.9.

Career accomplishments in China's current social and economic context appear to be more important to those who make heavy use of news information from the official media than to those who make little use. Conversely, true love is less important to them as a goal in life. They are more optimistic about their children's prospect of achieving their goals, a finding consistent with their own attachment to career accomplishment. Making a contribution to society and working hard seems to be somewhat more important to them than those who make little use of official news information. Although the impact of official

Table 8.8 Influence of Western Culture on Chinese Values

ITEMS	HEAVY INFLUENCE	LITTLE INFLUENCE
Goals in life:		
Career accomplishment	51.0%	63.2%
True love	41.2%	21.2%
True friendship	27.5%	15.2%
Contribution to country	10.5%	23.5%
Go abroad to study	27.4%	4.4%
Adventure and risk taking	9.8%	1.2%
Meaning of life:		
Live happily	51.0%	14.6%
Contribute to society	49.0%	85.4%
Enjoy life	27.5%	4.6%
Work hard	72.5%	95.4%

Table 8.9 Media News and Chinese Cultural Values

ITEMS	NEWS HIGH	NEWS LOW
Goals in life:		
Career accomplishment	72.4%	53.6%
True love	25.4%	29.8%
Children's goals:		
Achievement very likely	47.2%	30.9%
Meaning of life:		
Live happily	16.4%	25.7%
Contribute to society	83.6%	74.3%
Meaning of life:		
Enjoy life	6.1%	12.8%
Work hard	93.9%	87.2%

media news appears significant, it is much less pronounced than Western cultural influence even though the official media have held a dominant position in China for four decades while Western cultural influence has been a very recent occurence.

Another look at response patterns identified by age groups clearly divides those 49 years and below from those 50 years and above. We summarize our findings in table 8.10.

In previous chapters we have contrasted the young with the old because the middle-aged group usually stands in the middle. When we look at these fundamental cultural values in this chapter, we see a different picture. The one exception is true love as a goal in life, which is usually identified with youthful passion. As far as other values are concerned, the dividing line is unambiguously marked between those 50 years and above, and those 49 years and below.

When we discussed the concept of a good person, we suggested that the many "no answers" among those 50 years old and above and those residing in metropolitan Shanghai could be due to their common traumatic experiences with the class struggles during the last few decades. Such experiences, relevant as they may be for the concept of a good person, seem no longer adequate for explaining the other consistent differences between the older people on the one hand, and the middle-aged and younger groups on the other. This is because the older and middle-aged groups shared many of these same agonizing

Table 8.10 Age Cohorts and Chinese Cultural Values

ITEMS	29–	30 TO 49	50 +
Goals in life:			
Warm family	76.1%	79.2%	84.8%
Harmonious family relations	48.9%	47.8%	68.5%
Contributions to country	15.3%	16.8%	26.6%
True love	48.5%	24.2%	10.9%
Human nature:			
Good	25.7%	26.7%	44.6%
Both good and evil	60.2%	56.7%	39.6%
Good person:			
Did not know or no answer	30.8%	33.1%	46.2%
Meaning of life:			
Live happily	35.2%	25.3%	6.7%
Contribute to society	64.8%	74.7%	93.3%
Enjoy life	16.2%	10.9%	2.9%
Work Hard	83.8%	89.1%	97.1%

experiences while the middle-aged group and younger group did not have these in common. The dividing line between 50 and 49 years of age, though arbitrary in a statistical sense, could be more convincingly explained in terms of socialization experiences in traditional Chinese society, as we have suggested earlier. Because of their early experiences, the older people are more apt to see the benign side of human nature, to treasure harmonious family relations, and to feel more keenly about making a contribution to society. Although this interpretation seems to make sense, we present it here merely as a hypothesis for further verification. If this hypothesis should be confirmed by additional research, then we will be faced with a rather disturbing spectacle of a whole new generation of Chinese who cynically view human nature, who place a high premium on the pursuit of individual happiness, and who no longer highly treasure harmonious family relations. The consequences of these newly developed cultural traits may prove disruptive for China's future.

Chapter 9

Cultural Values: Family and Children

In this chapter we examine cultural values in contemporary China in the context of family relations. A primary focus is on relations between parents and children. What are the guiding principles governing parents' expectations of their children? Can they count on their children's support when they become old? Do they expect help from their children when they are in financial need? What do they consider to be important goals of child rearing? What is the preferred means of achieving their goals of raising proper children? What are their educational and occupational aspirations for their children? Courtship and marriage are important steps for a family because they involve the introduction of a new member into the family's intimate circle. What are Chinese people's conception of male–female relations during the stage of courtship? What criteria are considered important for the selection of a marriage partner? These questions are illustrated by the data from our survey.

Family Values

An important Chinese cultural value is filial piety. Traditionally Chinese children felt a lifelong obligation to their parents, ideally exemplified by an unreserved devotion to please them in every possible way. "The Twenty-four Stories of Filial Piety," which Chinese children were required to learn as part of their growing up, contained many illustrations. In one story, a young boy was worried that mosquitoes might be disturbing his father. So every night during the summer, before his father went to bed, he would lie in his bed and let the mosquitoes feed on him until they were full. In another family, the mother wanted to eat fish on an icy winter day. The dutiful son unrobed himself and lay on a frozen pond until the ice melted, enabling him to catch a fish. These stories might sound absurd today. They illustrate, however, the deeply ingrained sense of duty and devotion which Chinese people felt toward their parents.

Few Chinese today would find behavioral models in these examples. A concrete expression of filial piety in contemporary China is the caring of aging parents by adult children. Chinese have always been expected to look after their parents in old age as a way of showing their gratitude. During the years of the Cultural Revolution, however, many young people were compelled to denounce their parents for their ideological sins. Some of the cases, publicized in the official Chinese press as political lessons for the general public, were reported in the Western media. These stories revealed concerns regarding the survival of traditional Chinese family values. In their study of village and family life in Southern China in the 1970s, Parish and Whyte (1978) found little change in familial support of and respect for the aged. In the rural areas of that part of China, the Cultural Revolution apparently did little damage to the traditional parents–children bond in Chinese family. We wanted to assess the situation in Eastern China in the late 1980s.

In our survey, we asked: Do you think old parents should be (physically) looked after by their children, or should they take care of themselves? The question was phrased in such a way that the respondent would not feel obligated to endorse the first alternative. An overwhelming majority, nearly 80 percent, said children should look after their parents. Some 7 percent said parents should take care of themselves. The remaining 13 percent either were not sure or said it would depend on circumstances.

Age was a prominent factor, in a rather unexpected manner. People of 50 years of age and above were more inclined to say that parents should take care of themselves (14.7 percent) than people under 49 (less than 5 percent). Among those under 49, some 82 percent said children should take care of their parents, versus 70.4 percent among those of 50 and above. While most Chinese endorsed this traditional cultural value, it seems that the older people would prefer to look after themselves and enjoy some degree of independence.

Another significant factor was education. The higher the education, the smaller the percentage of respondents endorsing the idea that children should look after their parents. This endorsement dropped from 85 percent in the low-education group to 73 percent in the high-education group. When age and education were combined, the endorsement of this traditional family value was highest (87.3 percent) in the group who were below 49 and had low education, and lowest (66.1 percent) in the group who were 50 and above and had high education.

Another demonstration of children's obligation is providing financial assistance. We asked: If parents face some financial difficulties, do you think they should ask their children for help, or should they first seek other means? Again, the question was phrased in such a way as not to indicate a preference for the first alternative. The same overwhelming majority, 80 percent, said parents should ask their children for help. Some 14 percent said they should seek other means first. The remaining 6 percent were not sure. Age is again the most prominent factor, in a similar way. The percentage who mentioned asking children for help was much higher among those 49 years of age or below (about 84 percent) than among those 50 years of age and above (about 69 percent). In the older group, some 22 percent said parents should seek other means first. The corresponding figures in the younger and middle-aged groups were around 11 percent. Even though younger Chinese are prepared to provide financial assistance, it seems that the older people are reluctant to impose on their children if there are alternative means.

Another relevant factor was income. This was one of the few instances where income was significantly related to a cultural value in our study, but in a way contrary to common sense expectation. Those who were better off were *less* willing to give their parents financial help. In those families where the average monthly income was Y89 or below, some 83 percent said the parents should ask their children for help. This willingness to help was expressed by only 75 percent of those whose average family income was above Y90. Among those better off respondents, some 18 percent would prefer their parents to seek other means first, as compared to less than 12 percent in the lower income families. We want to emphasize that even among the better off families, the great majority still wanted to help. But it does seem that in China's current social and economic context, where some families are beginning to earn more income and enjoy some material comfort after living a life of scarcity all these years, there may be a reluctance to divert their newly acquired income as financial relief for their parents before other alternative means are explored.

When age and income were combined, the percentage of respondents who mentioned asking children for help was the highest (86.8 percent) among those 49 years of age and below and of lower income, and the lowest (68.5 percent) among those 50 years of age and above and of higher income.

An important Chinese cultural value is family togetherness. In the extended family of the past, several generations were expected to live under the same roof. A man's most cherished wish was to live long enough to have not only grandsons, but also great-grandsons living in his same household. This was known as "four generations sharing the same hall." In comparison, other forms of accomplishments were of lesser importance. In China today, the extended family has virtually disappeared. Is family togetherness still highly valued?

We asked: After young people get married, do you think it is better for them to live with their parents, or is it better for them to live by themselves? We asked only for their preference. Whether in reality it is possible for a young couple to live with parents in a crowded city like Shanghai is another matter.

Our respondents were divided. Some 60 percent, a majority, now said it is better for the young couple to live by themselves. The remaining 40 percent thought the young couple should live with their parents. People in urban and rural areas have clearly different views. In the villages, some two-thirds (65.3 percent) still said the young couple should live with parents. In urban areas, including metropolitan Shanghai and the towns in Qingpu, the reverse is true. Over two-thirds (68.2 percent and 67 percent respectively) said it is better for the couple to live by themselves.

Education was a factor. The higher the education, the higher the preference for living away from parents. In the high-education group, some 73 percent had this preference. In the low-education group, only 44 percent said the young couple should live by themselves.

Chinese people believed in strict punishment as a way of disciplining children. Spanking was a common practice. The popular saying was: Use the rod unsparingly, and you will have dutiful children. In their study in rural villages in Southern China, Parish and Whyte (1978) found little change in the practices of corporate punishment of children. What was the situation in metropolitan Shanghai and the surrounding villages in the late 1980s?

We asked: At what age do you think it is inappropriate to spank your children? This question implied that spanking is acceptable, so that the respondents did not have to cover up their actual practice. As it turned out, only about one out of nine said children should not be spanked at all. The others felt that spanking would not be appropriate when children reached the following ages: 3, 4 years (20.4 percent), 5, 6 years (12.4 percent), 7, 8 years (18.6 percent), 9, 10 years (10 percent), ll, 12 years (6.8 percent), 13, 14 years (7.7 percent), 15, 16 years (7.4 percent), and 17, 18 years (5.5 percent). It may be noted that some 20 percent of the respondents considered spanking children a proper punishment until they became teenagers. Attitudes toward spanking appeared uniform among most of our respondents. We found no differences in terms of age, gender, education influence was a relevant factor.

We asked two questions related to child rearing that reflected Chinese cultural values. First we asked: Some people want their children to have career accomplishments, others just want their children to be good persons. Which is more important to you? The choice was between being virtuous in a society with limited career opportunities, and striving for career success against great odds. Traditionally, Chinese were taught to cultivate peace of mind even in an impoverished environment. Success was highly desirable. But if success was beyond reach, one should accept poverty and derive satisfaction from just being a good person.

We find the cultural pattern today to be quite different. Nearly seven out of ten respondents (68.2 percent) wanted their children to have career accomplishments. Only 31.8 percent would settle for their children being just good persons. The only relevant factor was education. Those with no more than elementary school were nearly evenly split between career accomplishments (52.8 percent) and just being good persons (47.2 percent). Among those with junior high school education and above, nearly three-fourths (about 73 percent) wanted their children to have career accomplishments.

We further asked: In child rearing, which is more important? To let children develop freely as much as possible, or to teach children to follow rules? The choice can be seen as between modern individualism and traditional collectivism. As it turned out, nearly two-thirds of the respondents (64.2 percent) considered it more important to teach children to follow rules. Only 35.8 percent chose "to let children develop freely as much as possible." Our findings on spanking are consistent with the view that the purpose of child rearing is to teach children to follow rules.

Two relevant factors were found: age and education. The younger the respondents, the more likely they want their children to develop freely. In the young group, 45.3 percent chose this answer, compared to 23.6 percent in the old group. Likewise, the higher the education, the higher the endorsement of allowing children freedom to develop. In the high-education group, 43.4 percent favored this idea. In the low-education group, it was only 23.2 percent. With both age and education, the gap was more than 20 percent wide.

Educational Aspirations for Children

Traditional China was a society of very limited career opportunities. By the time most Chinese entered the workforce, their life was pretty much fixed. If they were peasants, for example, they would remain peasants for the rest of their life. In some other societies, people looked to the next life. Some Chinese, particularly those of the Buddhist faith, practiced merit making so that their next life would be better. Most Chinese, however, pinned their hope on their children. Children are expected to become as glorious as "dragons," as the popular saying goes. Other than war, which opened up opportunities for a few valiant warriors, the only avenue of upward mobility in old China was education. If one passed the state examinations, one could enter the world of imperial service. Chinese people traditionally attached a great deal of importance to their children's education, that is, if the opportunity existed.

Present-day China has retained many of the former characteristics that curtailed career opportunities. During the years of the Cultural Revolution, universities were open primarily to those who had a revolutionary class background and who could demonstrate an unquestionable ideological purity. It did not matter whether they were of mediocre intelligence. This policy has been discarded, and now admission to universities is by highly competitive entrance examinations. Education has again become one of the few means of upward social mobility. What are people's educational aspirations for children today?

We asked two similar questions. If you have a son, how far will you support him in school? If you have a daughter, how far will you support her in school? The results for sons and daughters were nearly identical, table 9.1.

One is struck by the exceptionally high aspirations for children's education. More than 80 percent were willing to support their sons and daughters through either college or graduate school. Although college education is heavily subsidized by the state, which provides tuition-free education and dormitory space, food and other expenses

Table 9.1 Educational Aspirations for Sons and Daughters

	SONS	DAUGHTERS
Elementary School	0.8%	1.2%
High School	8.3%	9.8%
College	52.6%	55.9%
Graduate School	32.2%	27.6%
Others	6.0%	5.5%

Figure 9.1 College co-eds play a card game in their dorm.
(*Photo courtesy of Linus Chao*)

can run higher than Y60 a month, representing a large chunk from an average family's monthly income. Yet most respondents are willing to make that kind of sacrifice.

The same relevant factors were found for educational aspirations for sons and daughters: education, age, and urban versus rural setting. The higher the respondent's own education level, the higher the aspirations for children. In the high-education group, 40.8 percent wanted to support their sons through graduate school. For those with no more than elementary school, it was 16 percent. The corresponding figures for daughters were 33.1 percent and 15.7 percent.

Younger people have higher educational aspirations for their children. The dividing line is again between the 40-year olds and the 50-year olds. Among those 49 years old or below, 35.5 percent wanted to support their sons and 30 percent wanted to support their daughters for graduate school. Among those 50 years old and above, it was 22.2 percent for sons and 20 percent for daughters. Educational aspirations for children were highest in Shanghai and lowest in rural villages. Regarding graduate school for sons, it was 37.5 percent in Shanghai and 19.6 percent in villages. For supporting daughters through graduate school, it was 30.9 percent in Shanghai and 20.4 percent in villages. Even for rural villages, these appear to be extraordinarily high aspirations.

Occupational Aspirations for Children

Occupational aspirations are a reflection of one's goals and values. We have seen what ideal jobs our respondents would prefer if they could have a choice. The top choices were managerial positions and research or scientific work, followed by factory workers and service personnel. In present-day China, where occupational mobility is severely limited, these ideal job preferences by our respondents are largely wishful thinking. What may be slightly more practical are the occupational aspirations for their children. In the minds of most Chinese, perhaps their children might be able to achieve what they themselves have failed to accomplish.

Thus we asked: If you have a child, what would you like him (or her) to do when he (or she) grows up?

For sons, the overwhelming choice was scientific and technical work (33.2 percent), followed by factory workers (19.1 percent), teachers (9.7 percent), doctors (8.3 percent), managerial positions (7.8 percent), and military (5.9 percent). Very few people would want their sons to become Party or government cadres (3.4 percent), a career path which used to be seen as a road to success during the Cultural Revolution years. Artists (4.1 percent), the service profession (2.8 percent), farmers (2.1 percent), and self-employed occupations (0.8 percent) were not desirable career choices for sons.

For daughters, the preferences were somewhat different. Medical doctors (28.5 percent), instead of scientific and technical work (16 percent), were the first choice for most respondents, reflecting perhaps the traditional Chinese conception that women were unfit to be scientists and technicians. During the Cultural Revolution years many of the so-called "barefoot doctors" were women. This may have given some respondents the idea that medical doctors would be an ideal profession for girls. School teachers (18.9 percent) were also seen by many to be an ideal career for daughters. Artists (8.8 percent) were almost as popular as factory workers (9.9 percent). But few (1.8 percent) considered their daughters to be suitable for managerial positions. Neither Party and government cadres (1.1 percent) nor a military career were considered ideal for girls. Very few would want their daughters to be farmers (1.7 percent) or self-employed (0.2 percent).

Four factors were related to ideal job preferences for sons: education, urbanization, Western cultural influence, and age. Those who chose factory work as an ideal job for sons were clearly of low education and not much exposed to Western cultural influence. Among those of low education, 39.3 percent wanted their sons to be workers, compared to only 8 percent among those of high education. A worker's job was attractive to 28.6 percent of those least exposed to Western cultural influence. In the high-exposure group, only 2.1 percent made that choice. Those who preferred a worker's job for sons also tended to come from villages (31 percent versus 15.8 percent in Shanghai). Apparently factory workers are still an attractive choice for rural people. Respondents over 50 years old were twice (31.4 percent) as likely as those below 49 (about 16 percent) to prefer a factory worker's position for their sons.

Scientific and technical positions, on the other hand, are definitely the choices of the better educated and of those living in metropolitan Shanghai. In the high-education group, 46 percent made that choice compared to only 19.1 percent in the low-education group. In Shanghai, 42.2 percent wanted their sons to pursue those careers, more than twice as many as the 17.1 percent in rural villages. Those below 29 years old are less likely (25.2 percent) to prefer scientific and technical positions than older respondents (about 38 percent). The young were more attracted by managerial positions for their sons. Exposure to Western cultural influence made no difference.

While managerial positions for sons were not very popular, perhaps because few considered them realistic choices, they were preferred mostly by those of higher education, living in metropolitan Shanghai, and by the young. In the high-education group, 12.1 percent indicated this preference, versus 3.4 percent in the low-education group. Between Shanghai and the villages, the difference was between 10.4 percent and 3.8 percent. Those below 29 preferred it more (11.6 percent) than those above 50 (4.4 percent). If someone is heavily exposed to Western cultural influence, he (or she) is far more likely (12.8 percent) to prefer a managerial position for the son than someone least exposed (3.9 percent).

Hardly anybody outside the rural areas wanted his son to be a farmer. Among those who did, most tended to be of low education (5.2 percent versus 0.8 percent in the high-education group). Likewise, a military career for the son was attractive primarily among rural residents (9.7 percent versus 4.8 percent in Shanghai) and those of lower education (8.2 percent versus 4.8 percent in the high-education group). Becoming a doctor, on the other hand, was a parental aspiration for sons among those living in urban Shanghai and those of higher education. Regarding artists as an ideal job, the only related factor was Western cultural influence. Someone who was heavily exposed to Western cultural influence was about five times (17 percent) as likely to want his (her) son to be an artist as someone least exposed (3.3 percent).

Ideal job choices for daughters were related to the same four factors, education, Western cultural influence, age, and urbanization. Those who wanted their daughters to be factory workers were clearly of lower education, living in rural villages, not much exposed to Western cultural influence, and older. Factory workers were chosen by 21.7 percent in the low-education group versus 3.5 percent in the high-education group, by 15.4 percent of villagers versus 8.4 percent of Shanghai residents, by 15 percent of those least exposed to Western cultural influence versus 2 percent of those heavily exposed, and by 18.2 percent of those over 50 versus 6.2 percent of those below 29.

Those of higher education, living in metropolitan Shanghai, and heavily exposed to Western culture had much higher occupational aspirations for daughters. They wanted their daughters to be medical doctors. The medical profession was the choice for daughters by 38.4 percent of high education versus 17.9 percent of low education, by 34.3 percent in Shanghai versus 19.3 percent in the villages, and by 47.1 percent of those under heavy Western cultural influence versus 26.3 percent of those under little influence.

Respondents who were not heavily exposed to Western culture were more attracted (around 21 percent) by a teaching career as something ideal for daughters than the heavily exposed (11.8 percent). On the other hand, those under heavy Western cultural influence tended to want their daughters to be artists (23.5 versus 5.2 percent of the least exposed). Only those living in rural villages, particularly those of low education, considered farming to be an ideal job for daughters. Those who preferred scientific and technical jobs for their daughters tended to be better educated, older, and living in urban areas. The one clear factor, however, was Western cultural influence, in a negative way. If someone was heavily exposed to Western cultural influence, he (or she) was about half as likely (7.8 percent) to express such preferences as someone least exposed (17.7 percent). Many of those under heavy Western cultural influence wanted their daughters to be doctors and artists.

Male–Female Relations

The Chinese used to have rigid rules regulating male–female relations. They were taught to abhor any physical touching between men and women. The taboo was so rigid that Mencius was once asked how he would handle this dilemma: Suppose he saw his sister-in-law drowning. Would he extend a helping hand? For Mencius, that would be sufficient justification to break the "no touch" taboo.

Marriage was arranged by the two families. Unless they were close relatives, the first time the bride and the groom saw each other would be after the wedding ceremony, during which time the bride's face was covered by a piece of red cloth. It was only after the guests had departed and the new couple had retired to their bridal chamber, that the bridegroom was allowed to lift the red cloth. With the founding of the Chinese republic in 1912 and the influx of Western ideas, things began to change slowly. In urban centers like Shanghai, girls were allowed to go to schools exclusively for girls from middle and upper-class families. Marriages were still arranged, but young couples were allowed to get acquainted under strictly chaperoned circumstances. Major changes began to occur during the Sino–Japanese War, when many young people left their homes in the coastal areas and moved to the interior to go to school. Away from their families, many college students began to find marriage partners on their own. The general pattern in those days bordered on "going steady" in American society. After a boy and a girl were attracted to each other, they would maintain a close relationship until they were ready for an engagement or marriage. The American custom of "dating" was definitely out of the question. A girl who saw more than one man at one time would be considered indecent. Her reputation would be ruined.

In China today men and women work in mixed groups. The old taboo against physical touching has been relegated to the past. But courtship is difficult to handle. How do Chinese people feel about male–female relations before marriage? We asked two similar questions:

If you have a daughter, and she carries on with several boyfriends before she gets married, what would you think about this?

If you have a son, and he carries on with several girlfriends before he gets married, what would you think about this?

Such behavior might be called "dating" although this term does not exist in the Chinese vocabulary.

The response patterns were nearly identical for daughters and sons. An overwhelming majority, 72.9 percent for daughters and 72.1 percent for sons, would not permit this kind of behavior. One out of five, 20.4 percent for daughters and 20.8 percent for sons, said this would be all righ
t. The others were not sure. It seems that the concept of "dating" is not popularly accepted even in the Shanghai area. In their research in Chengdu, Sichuan, Xu and Whyte (1990) also found little sign of a "dating culture" emerging.

For both daughters and sons, the same relevant factors were

found. In both cases, Western cultural influence turned out to be the most prominent factor, in nearly identical ways. Among those least exposed to Western cultural influence, only some 16 percent would allow their daughters and sons to engage in "dating." As the degree of exposure increased, the percentage of endorsement steadily increased until it exceeded 40 percent (43 percent for sons and 41 percent for daughters) among those most heavily exposed to Western culture. The percentage of objection declined.

Age was a factor, but much less pronounced than Western cultural influence. The older the respondents were, the less likely they would permit this kind of "dating." For both daughters and sons, some 25 percent of those respondents under 29 years of age would permit it. This positive attitude declined to about 14 percent among those over 50 years of age.

People in metropolitan Shanghai were somewhat more liberal than those in small towns and rural villages. Women were more conservative than men.

We asked a related question: "If a man and a woman are in love, and they live together before their marriage is registered, what do you think about this situation?" This is a more serious departure from traditional behavior patterns than "dating" before marriage. Nearly nine out of ten (86 percent) rejected this kind of lifestyle. Only 10.3 percent said this would be all right. The others were not sure.

Again, Western cultural influence was the most prominent factor. Of those least exposed to Western cultural influence, only 5.4 percent said living together before marriage would be acceptable. The degree of acceptance increased steadily with exposure, and reached 33.3 percent among those most heavily exposed.

Age is clearly related to this cultural value. Among those 29 years of age or below, 18.8 percent expressed their endorsement. Among those over 50 years of age, it was only 4.6 percent.

Men (12.8 percent) found this arrangement somewhat more tolerable than women (7.5 percent).

Mate Selection Criteria

In a traditional society, where life offered relatively few choices, perhaps the most important decision in one's life was the selection of a marriage partner. The Chinese consider marriage to be a step that affects one's whole life. Once two persons get married they should stay together for the rest of their lives. Therefore criteria for mate selection would reflect some of the fundamental cultural values. In China in the past, the decision was made exclusively by the two families, not by the two young persons who were about to get married. The young people were simply informed that a mate had been chosen, and they were not allowed to raise objections. The single most important criterion was social class compatibility. The two families were supposed to have "doors matching each other," that is, share the same social status. Once that test was passed, a matchmaker would sort out the astrological suitability of the two young persons in what was known as the "eight characters." If the eight characters were not suitable to each other, there would be no match. Beyond that, individual attributes mattered very little.

What are the selection criteria in China today? We gave our respondents a list of eleven criteria and asked them to pick three that seemed to be most important among young people today. They were free to write in other criteria not on the list. Very few people (0.2 percent) did so. Our analysis was based on the eleven criteria we provided. What we asked was their perceptions, rather than their own personal criteria, so that all respondents could answer that question regardless of their own marital status. Their perceptions, however, were most likely colored by their own value judgments. The results are shown in figure 9.2 in descending order of importance.

What seems to be rather striking is the finding that family social position, which used to be the single most prominent criterion in traditional China, is now considered the least important of all. This finding is highly significant because family social position as a criterion was inherited in a peculiar way by the authorities after the founding of the People's Republic in 1949. A Party cadre, for example, would have to

High moral standards	47.4%
Emotional compatibility	45.3%
Common interests	39.9%
Education	34.8%
Looks	27.3%
Work ability	26.8%
Love	22.6%
Age	14.7%
Family financial condition	14.4%
Occupation	11.2%
Family social position	7.6%

Figure 9.2 Criteria for Mate Selection

report to his (or her) organization describing the family background of the person he (or she) wanted to marry, and official approval had to be obtained for the marriage. Such a request would be denied if the cadre had picked somebody whose father or mother happened to be, say, a former landlord, a class that was denounced after 1949. As a matter of fact, people were generally encouraged to marry those with a revolutionary family background or a peasant–worker origin. On the other hand, children from families that belonged to the "four undesirable classes," that is, former landlords, former rich peasants, anti-revolutionaries, and rightists, usually had a hard time finding a marriage partner outside their own condemned circles. Few people would want to be dragged down to such a low status through marriage. Many tragedies happened as a result of this practice. In the past decade or so, this practice has largely been discarded. Family social background has become less important. What came as a surprise was that only 7.6 percent picked this as one of the three most important criteria. While the traditional concept of "doors matching each other" is definitely gone, our finding suggests that the notion of revolutionary class background is now also rejected by the Chinese.

Rather interestingly, those who were heavily exposed to Western cultural influence were more likely to see the family social position to be an important criteria (13.7 percent) than those least exposed (5.9 percent). Obviously, they were not referring to revolutionary class background. No other relevant factors were found.

Family financial condition, which was prominent in the traditional concept of "doors matching each other," is not important any more. It ranked third from the bottom. Again it was those under heavy Western cultural influence who tended to give more weight to the family financial position.

The most highly endorsed criterion was high moral standards. If two persons are to become lifelong companions, it is only reasonable that one would choose someone highly reliable. "High moral standards" could simply mean "highly reliable." Age was definitely a factor. The older people were far more likely (62.4 percent) to see this as an important criterion than the younger and middle-aged group (about 42 percent). The difference was 20 percent. There was no difference between the younger and middle-aged groups. These findings suggest some residual effect of socialization in traditional Chinese society, similar to the findings we discussed about the concept of human nature. Most of the people in the older group grew up in traditional China before the founding of the People's Republic in 1949. High moral standards seemed to be still very important to them for the selection of a marriage partner. For most people in the middle-aged and younger groups, their socialization did not begin until after 1949. In the many mass criticism campaigns that took place during the lifetime of the middle-aged group, what counted was not moral standards, but ideological reaffirmation and the tenacious ability for survival. Even though those in the younger group did not have such intensive experience with the criticism campaigns, they grew up in a social environment where moral standards had already been diluted. Both the middle-aged and young groups considered moral standards to be much less important for mate selection.

Women (52.9 percent) were more concerned about moral standards than men (42.5). A most intriguing finding again has to do with Western cultural influence. The more heavily one is exposed to Western culture, the less likely one is to recognize high moral standards as an important criterion. Among those least exposed, 52.4 percent mentioned this criterion, twice as many as the 25.5 percent among those most heavily exposed. Most of those heavily exposed to Western culture were young. But there seems to be something else other than age that makes moral standards less important to those under heavy Western cultural influence. As a plausible hypothesis, it seems that the Western lifestyle which viewers see in American television programs and Hollywood films is having an impact.

Almost equally important as a criterion for mate selection was emotional compatibility, endorsed by 45.3 percent. This is perhaps a subdued Chinese way of saying "love." Love, on the other hand, was recognized by only 22.6 percent as important. To most Chinese, "love" is still not something they can talk about openly. In courtship one rarely says "I love you." The Chinese do not feel comfortable uttering the word "love." It is just not part of the vernacular Chinese language. The public display of affection is still considered in poor taste, and even abnormal behavior in China today. People commented: "Chinese are not supposed to behave like that; Westerners are." Therefore, it is quite understandable that "love" comes seventh in our list. This does not mean, however, that the Chinese do not want emotional attachment. By saying that emotional compatibility is important, our respondents are referring to a deeper level of love. It is still love, but the Chinese refuse to call it "love."

Recognizing emotional compatibility as a key criterion was primarily an urban phenomenon. In metropolitan Shanghai, 52.3 percent said that was important, compared to only 27 percent in rural villages. No other relevant factors were found. Love as a criterion, however, was mentioned more by rural villagers (29.8 percent) than urban dwellers (about 20 percent). As we recall, the rural respondents were much younger.

Common interest was another important criterion, recognized by 39.9 percent. It seems that if two persons are to stay together for life, it will be important for them to have some common interest. Just like emotional compatibility, common interest was primarily an urban criterion, endorsed by 44.6 percent in Shanghai compared to only 29 percent in rural villages. It was also a criterion of the better educated. Among those who have completed junior high school and beyond, some 43 percent considered that important, versus 28.3 percent among those of elementary school level.

In China today, where educational opportunities are still limited, about one-third of our respondents selected education as an important criterion. Those who were heavy users of media news information considered education to be more important (40.8 percent) than those who made the least use of media news (29.6 percent). Looks were more important to the younger people. Some 30 percent of those under 49 picked looks, compared to only 15.3 percent of those above 50. Men (32.3 percent) considered it more important than women (21.9 percent).

Work ability was as important as looks. It was more important among those of low education (34.6 percent) than those of high education (23.2 percent).

Age did not seem to matter much as a criterion for mate selection. Only 14.7 percent mentioned it. Those who considered age important tended to be rural people (29.4 percent in villages versus 8.7 percent in Shanghai), of lower education (24 percent in elementary school group versus 8.7 percent in high school and college group), and male (17.2 percent versus 11.9 percent of women).

Occupation was not considered important, chosen by only 11.2 percent. If this finding is surprising, it is largely due to the unique occupational structure in China. While nearly everybody is guaranteed some kind of employment, there is almost a total absence of occupational mobility. It is next to impossible for someone in the interior to get a transfer to Shanghai. Other than joining the army, the only way to move away from where one was born is to enroll in a university. This option is open to less than 1 percent of the population. Regardless of what job one holds, one receives pretty much the same wage, with severely limited opportunities for promotion. It is thus not surprising that occupation is not an important criterion, related to neither age, nor gender, education nor any other factors.

Discussion

Contrary to concerns raised during the height of the Cultural Revolution, Chinese family values remain largely intact and stable. The general picture that emerges from our data is consistent with the findings of Parish and Whyte (1978) in villages in Southern China. The traditional expression of filial piety may not be feasible following the social structural changes introduced by the Communist revolution. But an overwhelming majority of our respondents are willing to look after their aging parents and provide financial assistance when needed. Family togetherness, a cultural value among Chinese for centuries, is still important to most Chinese.

The age-old practice of spanking as a way of bringing up good children is largely followed even today. To most people, it is still more important to teach children to follow rules than allow them freedom to develop. A majority of our respondents wanted their children to have career success, following the traditional Chinese concept of "expecting children to become dragons," although a sizable minority would be contented to have their children become "just good persons."

We found exceptionally high educational and occupational aspirations for children. An overwhelming majority of the respondents would like to support their sons and daughters through college and even graduate school. These expectations are nearly impossible to fulfill given China's limited enrollment for universities. While factory work is still considered by many to be a desirable occupation, very few want their children to be farmers even if they themselves live in villages. Other than factory work, the preferred occupations are scientific and technical work, managerial positions, professionals such as medical doctors and artists. In reality, very few people in the younger generation would be able to fulfill these aspirations. Hardly anybody would want their sons and daughters to become Party or government cadres.

Chinese people today are basically conservative when it comes to male–female relations. Behavioral patterns that come close to "dating" before marriage are clearly not accepted. Living together before marriage is even more strongly rejected.

For mate selection, the traditional criterion of family social class compatibility is definitely no longer followed. Moral standards are considered important if two persons are to stay bound for life. So are emotional compatibility and common interest. Education, looks, and work ability are given considerable weight as selection criteria, but romantic love is not high on the list.

Exposure to official news information does not seem to be a relevant factor as far as values regarding family and children are concerned. Those who were heavy consumers of official news attached greater importance to education as a criterion for choosing a marriage partner than those least exposed. Interesting trends emerge when we look at some of the cultural values in the perspective of three prominently related factors: age, education, and Western cultural influence. We first look at age. "Young" refers to those 29 or below, and "old" refers to those 50 or above, table 9.2.

We see rather clearly that the young people in China are much less conservative on matters having to do with children and male–female relations. They attach greater importance to children's

Table 9.2 Age and Family Values in China

ITEMS	YOUNG	OLD
Way to bring up children		
develop freely	45.3%	23.5%
Several boyfriends for daughter		
all right	25.7%	13.5%
Several girlfriends for son		
all right	25.3%	14.3%
Living together before marriage		
all right	18.8%	4.6%
Support son's education		
up to graduate school	31.1%	22.2%
Support girls' education		
up to graduate school	28.4%	20.0%
Ideal jobs for sons		
workers	16.9%	31.4%
managers	11.4%	4.4%
Ideal jobs for daughters		
workers	6.2%	18.2%
artists	14.3%	2.8%
Mate selection criteria		
moral standards	42.0%	62.4%

free development than the older generation. While the majority of them are still opposed to the idea of dating and living together before marriage, their degree of tolerance is much greater than that of the older people. They have higher educational aspirations and higher occupational aspirations for their children. At the same time, they seem to be less concerned about high moral standards, as reflected in their mate selection criteria.

People of lower education present a different profile. Low education refers to those with no more than elementary school education. High education refers to those with senior high school or college education, table 9.3.

People of lower education appear to stay more closely with these traditional Chinese cultural values than those of higher education.

Table 9.3 Education and Family Values in China

ITEMS	LOW EDUCATION	HIGH EDUCATION
Caring for parents		
children care	85.0%	73.1%
Where to live after marriage		
with parents	56.5%	27.3%
Expectation for children		
be good person	47.2%	26.7%
Way to bring up children		
teach them to follow rules	76.8%	56.6%
Support education for sons		
up to graduate school	16.0%	40.8%
Support education for daughters		
up to graduate school	15.7%	33.1%
Ideal jobs for son		
workers	39.3%	8.0%
science/technology	19.1%	46.0%
managers	3.4%	12.1%
Ideal jobs for daughters		
workers	21.7%	3.5%
doctors	17.9%	38.4%

Table 9.4 Western Cultural Influence and Family Values in China

	WESTERN INFLUENCE	
Items	Low	High
Several boyfriends for daughter		
all right	15.7%	43.1%
Several girlfriends for son		
all right	16.3%	41.2%
Living together before marriage		
all right	5.4%	33.3%
Mate selection criteria:		
family social position	5.9%	13.7%
family financial position	11.9%	18.8%*
moral standards	52.4%	25.5%
Ideal jobs for son		
workers	28.6%	2.1%
artists	3.3%	17.0%
managers	3.9%	12.8%
Ideal jobs for daughters		
workers	15.0%	2.0%
artists	5.2%	23.5%
doctors	26.3%	47.1%

*average percentage of top two levels on Western cultural influence scale.

They are more ready to look after their aging parents. They seem to attach greater importance to family togetherness, by preferring their sons to live with them after they marry. To them, the traditional concept of having children who are just good persons is still very important. A large majority of them consider it more important to teach children to follow rules than to let them develop freely. They also have much lower educational aspirations for their children. Their occupational aspirations for children are "old fashioned," so to speak. To many of them, a factory worker position looks pretty good, whereas those of higher education want their children to be scientists, technicians, managers, and doctors.

    It may be noted that exposure to news information in the official media had virtually no effect on values regarding family and children. The only difference found was with regard to education as a criterion for choosing a marriage partner. Those heavily exposed to official news considered education to be more important (40.8 percent) than those least exposed (29.6 percent). In comparison, Western cultural influence in the mass media seems to have a rather profound impact, relating consistently to male–female relations and criteria of mate selection as well as occupational aspirations for children, table 9.4.

Those respondents who are heavily exposed to Western cultural influence on television, films, and radio seem to have moral standards about male–female relations rather close to what is being portrayed in Hollywood movies and American television drama. Not only is "dating" an acceptable form of courtship to many of them, but one-third would go so far as accepting an arrangement currently common in American society, by which a young couple live together before they get married.

On the other hand, they seem to be largely unconcerned about high moral standards as an important criterion for selecting a marriage partner. To put it more correctly, relatively few of them see it as important. While family social position and financial status are on the whole viewed as unimportant in China today, those under heavy Western cultural influence tend to see them much more positively than those not under such influence, reflecting, as it were, a greater materialistic inclination. Similarly, those under heavy Western cultural influence are no longer contented with factory work for their children. They have much higher occupational aspirations and want their children to be artists, managers, and doctors.

Chapter 10

Cultural Values: Traditional Precepts

Developing nations face a common problem: on their way to modernization, traditional cultural values are being challenged by new ideas and new ways of life as a result of two main factors: first, domestic economic development and the amassing of energies to press for corresponding political and social reforms; second, external influences that arrive together with modern technologies from industrialized countries, mainly the Western world. As traditional values give a nation its cultural identity and pride in its past, its tradition-minded citizens, particularly the older generation, strive to prevent their cultural heritages from being threatened by the "Western wind." Despite such efforts, however, the Western wind keeps blowing, often colliding sharply with traditional values. This has been the case for many developing nations.

In one sense China is no exception to this general trend. Western influence began to infiltrate during the final years of the Manchu Dynasty and, after an interruption of nearly thirty years under Mao's mantle, once more penetrates the social environment through China's open-door policy. The recent economic reforms have improved the material life of Chinese people after a long period of austerity and give rise to political and social aspirations that have been suppressed for decades. Changes are inevitable. In another perspective, however, China's case may be unique. It is probably the only country in Asia, if not in the entire world, where the ruling elite, under the predominant influence of one man, has mobilized the gigantic forces of the state in a deliberate attempt to destroy the old culture in order to build a new one. China is unique because the forces of modernization are compounded with the forces of revolution to alter the very nature of its traditional culture.

It would be misleading, however, to suggest that what has happened in China in the last forty years should be held responsible for all the changes that we see in Chinese traditional cultural values. These changes, in fact, started as early as the mid-19th century when China's door was forced open by the Opium War with Britain, and continued through the early 20th century. The May 4th Movement of 1919 could be called the first cultural revolution of this century. The founding of the People's Rupublic in 1949, however, forcefully commenced a new chapter in cultural change in a way unprecedented in modern Chinese history. Using all the resources at his disposal, and waging nationwide campaigns to fight what he called "old ideological values," Mao led the assault on traditional values almost as soon as his victory celebration was over. The attack reached a frantic level during the Cultural Revolution. Especially during the initial chaotic stage from mid 1966 to early 1967, millions of Red Guards bombarded the traditional Chinese cultural values from all sides (Yan and Gao, 1985). They created a period of "cultural void." Recent years have seen the return, or rather the surfacing, of some traditional cultural values, which, mixed with certain Western ways of life, are forming a semi-traditional and semi-modern culture. The old picture is no longer there. The painting of a new culture is by no means clear. China is right in the midst of radical cultural change that is as yet unfathomed.

When we designed our research, we had these questions in our mind: How are the thousand-year-old traditional Chinese cultural values being changed? Does the Great Wall of Chinese culture look as great as before? How deep are the cracks that have surfaced in this age-old cultural great wall? Is China on the verge of cultural disintegration?

This chapter assesses the current status of traditional Chinese cultural values. We collected our data by presenting our respondents with eighteen traditional values. We asked: "Of these elements of traditional Chinese culture, in your opinion which ones do you feel proud of, which ones should be discarded, and which ones are you not sure of?" The values were presented in a random order so that the way the respondents answered one question would have a minimum effect on the way they answered others. As a first step of data analysis, we used the percentage who were proud of a value, minus the percentage who said it should be discarded, to construct an index of endorsement for each of the eighteen values. The indices ranged from a positive 89.7 percent to a negative −64.0 percent. We present the traditional values and indices in a descending order before discussing them in five categories, figure 10.1.

long historical heritage	89.7%
diligence and frugality	86.2%
loyalty and devotion to state	67.5%
benevolent father, filial son	48.0%
generosity and virtues	39.8%
respect for traditions	38.5%
submission to authority	33.2%
harmony is precious	29.5%
tolerance, propriety, deference	25.3%
chastity for women	-13.5%
glory to ancestors	-23.8%
a house full of sons and grandsons	-35.5%
farmers high, merchants low	-43.3%
pleasing superiors	-48.9%
discretion for self-preservation	-55.9%
differentiation between men and women	-59.2%
way of golden mean	-59.6%
three obediences and four virtues	-64.0%

Figure 10.1 Endorsement and Rejection of Traditional Values

Traditions and Heritages

We classified the 18 traditional values into five categories. The first, under Traditions and Heritages, included three values that appear to lay for Chinese society a foundation of cultural identity. They are: long historical heritage, respect for traditions, and loyalty and devotion to the state.

Long Historical Heritage

An overwhelming majority of our respondents (91.2 percent) said they felt proud of China's long historical heritage. The endorsement was nearly universal, with no differences among the three age groups or any of the other demographic factors. Only 1.5 percent of the respondents said this value should be discarded, with another 7.4 percent unsure. The rating is encouraging to those who fear that the Chinese people, the younger generation in particular, are abandoning the country's historical roots.

The only relevant factor was exposure to official media news, with those under heavy exposure endorsing this value slightly more (92.6 percent to 95.9 percent) than those under little exposure (88.3 percent). The differences were small, but do suggest the effect of the Comunist Party-controlled media, which often appealed to the patriotic feelings of the Chinese people to support the establishment.

Indeed the Chinese have reasons to feel proud of their country's long historical heritage. China's civilization represents a history of some five thousand years dating back to the neolithic age and Chinese people have always been proud of the rich heritage of their culture, including some of the world's earliest inventions such as the compass, paper, printing, and gunpowder, and of course, its agriculture, its literature and arts, its philosophies, and its unique way of life. Ever since the First Emperor of the Qin Dynasty unified the country in 210 B.C. until 1842 when China was defeated in the Sino–British Opium War, China, meaning "the center of the world" in the Chinese language, was proud of its long history with a privileged position over what the Chinese emperors called the "barbarians" dwelling on the periphery of its geography. The modern history of China is a history of its gradual degeneration into a semifeudal and semicolonial state, subject to economic plunder and cultural humiliation by colonial powers. Chinese people found it painful to accept the fact that the former "barbarians" now had gunships and weapons superior to their own traditional weaponry with the potential to defeat the Middle Kingdom. However, this feeling of inferiority was often compensated by the sustained sense of pride that "We Chinese had a longer historical heritage than you barbarians!" So the Chinese found contentment in the past and ignored the humiliation of their contemporary situation. Generation after generation, the value of a long historical heritage was passed down without the slightest doubt.

The leaders of the People's Republic endorsed this value in order to agitate the people to march toward a common goal with a sense of pride and unity. Even during the Cultural Revolution, when many of the traditional values were swept away, the value of a long historical heritage was upheld. For forty years, the first lesson school children learned in Chinese history was the value of a long historical heritage. Today while the general populace still regards it as something to be proud of, many intellectuals question the possible negative effects of this time-honored past.

Intellectuals see a serious obstacle: this long historical heritage can burden a country's future (Li, 1987). Pride in the past obstructs a nation's efforts to change and progress. For too long, China has been resting on its enduring traditions, reluctant to make big and bold strides toward modernization. Among Chinese intellectuals today there is a strong belief that while a long historical heritage can be the source of national pride, it also has hidden negative effects.

Respect for Traditions

Respect for traditions refers to Chinese traditional values, especially those with ritualistic manifestations. Traditions came under severe attack during the May 4 Movement of 1919, when a group of prominent scholars led by Hu Shih launched the "Down with Confucius" campaign. That movement caught the imagination of young Chinese intellectuals, but was mercilessly criticized by the establishment at that time. Later Hu Shih himself acknowledged that he was excessive in his denunciation of Confucius.

After the 1949 revolution, Mao campaigned for a distinction between the genuine traditional values and the false ones. The genuine was to be retained, the false rejected. The difficulty was how to distinguish the genuine from the false. During the Cultural Revolution, anything that was associated with the past was condemned. Red Guards went on a rampage across the country destroying traditional relics, temples, and historical statures. The confusion regarding traditions during recent decades is reflected in our findings. When asked how they regarded respect for traditions, over half of our respondents (53.1 percent) said they felt pride. About one out of six (14.6 percent) wanted to discard this value. A sizable group, almost one-third of the sample (32.4 percent), were not sure. These views were uniformly held in all groups.

Loyalty and Devotion to State

A large majority of respondents (74.5 percent) said that loyalty and devotion to the state is something to be proud of. Only 7.0 percent said this value should be discarded. There were 17.1 percent who were not sure.

Media news exposure and education were two relevant factors. Mass media in China, controlled by the state, and the state-run educational institutions have consistently emphasized loyalty to the state. Not surprisingly, more people who had high exposure to media news (84.9 percent) endorsed this value than those who had little exposure (69.8 percent). Conversely, more low-exposure people than high-exposure people would either "discard" this value (9.1 percent versus 3.7

percent) or were "not sure" (21.1 percent versus 11.4 percent). We also found a higher percentage of endorsement of this value among the high-education people (77.5 percent) than among the low-education group (70.2 percent).

One of the ideals that Confucius wanted his followers to realize in their lifetime was "cultivation of self, union of family, rule of state and peace under the heaven." Although this was Confucius' philosophy of achieving a perfect social order, it demonstrated a hierarchical relationship between family and state. Loyalty to the state was considered a supreme virtue in ancient China as the state in Confucian ideology was an extension of the family. Being loyal to the state was as honored as being filial to parents. In fact, the Chinese believed that filial devotion to parents was a clear sign of loyalty to the state. And loyalty to the state was equated with loyalty to the emperor, since the emperor was the son of heaven and the highest representative of the state. It was the duty and responsibility of every subject to obey the emperor even when he made a grievously wrong decision.

There were numerous such loyal subjects throughout Chinese history, among whom the most famous included General Yue Fei (1103–1141) of the Song Dynasty. To recognize and honor his loyalty to the Song Court in the battle against the northern invaders, Emperor Gao Zong personally presented to him a battle flag inscribed "Loyal Yue Fei." That recognition, however, did not prevent Emperor Gao Zong from murdering Yue Fei when the victorious general was close to totally defeating the invaders, and thus raising the prospect of bringing back the former emperor, Gao Zong's elder brother, from captivity. If that was allowed to happen, Emperor Gao Zong would have to return the throne to his brother. All through the past eight centuries, millions upon millions of Chinese have paid tribute to Yue Fei's tomb in Hangzhou, not far from the city of Shanghai, for his loyalty and devotion to the state. Qin Kuai, the prime minister at that time, was condemned as the villain who framed Yue Fei, although it was Emperor Gao Zong himself who committed the heinous murder to save his throne.

Loyalty and devotion to the state has long been cherished among the Chinese. All Chinese governments, including the current one, have promoted this political value.

Familial Relations

Next we examine three traditional values that contribute to family cohesion. They are: benevolent father and filial son, glory to ancestors, and a house full of sons and grandsons.

Benevolent Father, Filial Son

The idea that a father should be benevolent and a son should demonstrate total filial respect was one cornerstone of Chinese family stability for centuries. Three-fifths of the respondents (60.8 percent) said they felt proud of this value. But 12.8 percent said it should be discarded! A sizable portion of the sample (26.4 percent) were not sure.

Education was the only relevant factor. We found more people who had high education (65.2 percent) feeling proud of this traditional value than those who had low education (51.6 percent). More low-education people (31.8 percent) were not sure about this value than high-education respondents (24.5 percent).

In Confucian ideology there is a basic value which is called *"xiao ti."* *"Xiao"* means being filial to parents, *"ti,"* obedience to elder brothers. Once a disciple asked Confucius about filiation. Confucius said: "No disobedience is allowed." Also according to Confucius, it was the duty and responsibility of the father to educate the son. The classical Three-Character Scripture writes: "If a son is uneducated, the father is to blame." Therefore, the value of "benevolent father, filial son" is a more balanced form of "xiao ti," which has been highly endorsed throughout Chinese history.

This traditional value became problematic during the Cultural Revolution. What should a son do toward his father if he was labeled as a class enemy and condemned by the revolution? Should he behave like a filial son and defend his father? Definitely not. The son had to draw a clear "revolutionary demarcation line" between him and his class-enemy father in order not to be "ideologically poisoned" by the father's "counter-revolutionary" ideas. In such a case, the value of "benevolent father and filial son" had to be put aside. But in normal situations, particularly among revolutionary classes of "workers, peasants, and soldiers" (called *"gongnongbin"* in Chinese), nothing was wrong with "benevolent father, filial son." As a matter of fact, in ordinary families including those with a nonrevolutionary background, and in the vast rural areas, this value has always been upheld to some degree. Even during the most difficult years of the Cultural Revolution, it was secretly observed in many troubled families.

Glory to Ancestors

Ancestors were an important part of Chinese life. Chinese people not only worshipped their ancestors, but believed that their accomplishments in life were mainly for the glory of ancestors. Glory to ancestors as a precept was thus not only a foundation of family cohesion, but also a powerful motive in task performance, and used to be accepted by nearly everyone. Among our survey respondents more than two fifths (42.3 percent) said this traditional value should be discarded! Age was the major relevant factor. The rejection was stronger among the old people (53.0 percent) than among the young (37.1 percent), which came as a surprise. Also quite a large number of people (39.2 percent) were not sure, with more young respondents (42.0 percent) feeling uncertain about it than old (32.5 percent). Those who felt proud of this traditional value accounted for only 18.5 percent. More rural residents (22.3 percent) than urbanites (17.3 percent) were still proud of this tradition.

These findings represent a major value change. Confucianism, Buddhism, and Taoism were the three main belief systems in old China. Confucianism, with its sophisticated ethical norms and rules of proprieties, had a more powerful influence on Chinese people's social attitudes and behavior even though it was not a religion per se. Most of the Confucian values and ethical norms originated from the family and the clan, and spread to other types of social relationships. Ancestors, being the ultimate symbol of authority in the family, assumed enormous importance in the life of Chinese. Even the emperor, who bowed to heaven and earth, also knelt to honor his ancestors. In that sense, ancestors may be considered the source of all authority in traditional China.

This value was severely condemned after the 1949 revolution, particularly if it involved families that were regarded as enemies of the people. Worshipping and burning incense for a former landlord who had died, for example, could be interpreted as "calling back the soul of the landlord class," a charge extremely serious during the Cultural Revolution. This condemnation was discontinued after the Cultural Revolution ended. But the lofty status of ancestors was lost. As a value, our findings suggest, glory to ancestors seems to be fading, just as ancestor worship is disappearing.

A House Full of Sons and Grandsons

Sons have always been important to a Chinese family. They prolong the family tree and take care of the parents in old age. To many people in the past, their accomplishments in life were measured not by their positions or wealth, but by "a house full of sons and grandsons." As far as children were concerned, the traditional concept was "the more the better." Daughters did not share this esteemed position. They were considered "losing propositions."

Despite the fact that China's large population has brought a nearly unsolvable problem to the country and that most people are aware of it, still one out of five respondents (20.6 percent) said they were proud of this tradition, with far more villagers (36.2 percent) feeling this way than townspeople (17.4 percent) and urbanites (14.9 percent). Over half of the sample (56.1 percent) acknowledged that this traditional value should now be discarded, with a much stronger conviction from the urban respondents (63.6 percent) and townspeople (62.2 percent) than from the villagers (34.4 percent). As many as 29.4 percent of village respondents were not sure, compared to 21.5 percent in Shanghai and 20.4 percent in Qingpu towns. These findings seem to suggest that this tradition is still valued in the countryside, relatively speaking. With the introduction of the responsibility system in rural areas, peasants need more labor force to till their allotted land and engage in other productive activities. Chinese peasants also have more money than ever before to support their children and grandchildren. One might hear villagers say, "What's wrong with having one more kid? Isn't it just to add another pair of chopsticks to the dining table?"

We found more high-education people (65. percent) wanting to discard this traditional value than low-education respondents (46.2 percent). More of the latter (28.1 percent) felt proud of it than of the former (13.7 percent). This is quite understandable. What came as a bit of a surprise was that there were far more old people (76.2 percent) than young respondents (42.7 percent) who said this traditional concept should be discarded. As many as 28.8 percent of the young were still proud of this value, compared to only 9.3 percent among the old. It is disturbing that many of the young people still want big families.

Historically, the family occupied a central position in traditional Chinese society, and so a house full of sons and grandsons indicated the prosperity of the family. But in present-day China, this "prosperity" would be hard to sustain for the majority of people, especially in urban areas, whose monthly income can barely make ends meet. The old respondents, who had gone through some very difficult times including three years of severe food shortages in the early 1960s, probably know better than the young how difficult life can be with an extended family full of children and grandchildren.

The population policy of "one family, one child" has been more closely followed in urban areas, particularly in large cities like Shanghai and Beijing, than in rural areas. Because farmers do not rely on state wages, the government has less success in enforcing the "one family, one child" policy in the villages. Quietly, the old value of a house full of sons and grandsons is moving back into the minds of the farmers. This may add to China's population problem and slow down the country's economic development in future.

Social Relational Guidelines

We examine here seven traditional values that have provided guidelines for social relations in China both within and beyond the family context. Most of these traditional values are traceable to the teachings of Confucius. They are: the Way of the Golden Mean, generosity and virtues, "tolerance, propriety, and deference," "harmony is precious," submission to authority, pleasing superiors, and discretion for self preservation.

Way of Golden Mean

As a Confucian ethical ideology, the Way of the Golden Mean refers to a middle-of-the-road attitude toward life, a denial of extremes in the negative or the positive, and a plea for moderation. Confucius says, "As a virtue, the way of the golden mean is the highest." This ideology of Confucius compares with Aristotle's *mesotes*, which shares almost the same meaning. All Chinese dynasties throughout history strongly endorsed this value, as it obviously was highly favorable to the ruling classes. One might say that the way of the golden mean held a central place in the Chinese way of life in the olden days. It is hardly surprising that many contemporary radical revolutionaries have fiercely attacked this traditional Confucian value. For example, Lu Xun, the most influential literary master in contemporary Chinese history, considered it most negatively. He wrote, "Human inertia expresses itself in various forms, of which the most popular include, Number One, submission to fate, Number Two, the way of the golden mean." Lu Xun loved the spirit of "hitting hard a drowning dog" as an antithesis to this value.

Lu Xun was a national hero for Mao Zedong who, during the war years and postwar period, called on his people time and again to learn from Lu Xun, particularly his spirit of "hitting hard a drowning dog." Chairman Mao apparently hated the way of the golden mean more than Lu Xun because he firmly believed in his class struggle theory. After 1949 and particularly during the extreme period of the Cultural Revolution, those identified with practicing the way of the golden mean were charged as class enemies. Ironically, Zhou Enlai, Mao's closest comrade-in-arms and China's premier for more than two decades, was labelled at his death bed the "master of the way of the golden mean" by the Gang of Four who had organized numerous media attacks on Confucian philosophy. Such attacks have been discontinued since the purge of the Gang. We had no idea about the effects of all these years of ideological assault on this traditional value taught since the time of Confucius.

Totally surprising was the finding that only 5.4 percent of the respondents felt proud of the way of the golden mean. As many as 65.0 percent said this traditional value should be discarded! And quite a few (29.7 percent) were not sure how to deal with it.

Remarkably, more older respondents (67.5 percent) than younger people (61.8 percent) wanted to see this Confucian value discarded. The difference was not large, but significant. Slightly more young people (6.9 percent) than old (3.8 percent) said they were proud of it. Thus, it would seem that the way of the golden mean as a traditional value is fading, and the old disapprove of it more than the young. During the Cultural Revolution and for a long period before the ten-year mass chaos, Chairman Mao wanted his people to replace the way of the golden mean with his struggle philosophy. According to Mao, class struggle was the only efficient way to maintain a "revolutionary relationship" among the people, and the way of the golden mean would only quench people's revolutionary enthusiasm and help the enemy to escape. Despite recent intellectual efforts by some Chinese scholars who argue that this traditional value could be effective in solving human conflicts, our findings suggest that many people are still influenced by Mao's struggle philosophy. Particularly the older people who have been subjected to more label-condemning propaganda (such as the campaign condemning the way of the golden mean during the Cultural Revolution) appear to be more psychologically alienated from this Confucian value than the younger Chinese who have had less exposure to the Party's media propaganda.

Generosity and Virtues

"Generosity and virtues" is one of the Confucian values given a positive rating. Over half of the respondents (55.9 percent) said they felt proud of this tradition, with more urbanites (61.5 percent) feeling positive about it than townspeople (47.4 percent) and village folks (47.7 percent). However, as many as 16.1 percent of the respondents said this traditional value should be discarded, with stronger negative feelings from town residents (20.7 percent) and village people (21.1 percent) than from urbanites (12.8 percent). Quite a few respondents (28.0 percent) were not sure about this value, with less urbanites (25.7 percent) feeling uncertain than townspeople (31.9 percent) and villagers (31.2 percent). No other factors were relevant.

Generosity and virtues were loosely defined and broadly inclusive moral standards of Confucianism. Like tolerance, propriety, and deference, this value was used to regulate and strengthen human relationships among people of various social strata. Generosity is not an entirely appropriate rendition of the original Confucian concept, which can be loosely interpreted to mean treating people with kindness and justice. A general principle, according to Confucius, was "not to do unto others what you do not want done unto yourself." Virtues referred to all the ethical and moral standards for interpersonal relations.

During the May 4 Movement early in the century, this value was severely condemned by scholars and students as serving the interests of the ruling classes and being highly hypocritical. After the People's Republic was founded, the term "generosity and virtues" ("*ren yi dao de*" in Chinese) was often used to mock the hypocrisy of the former exploiting classes. An interesting phenomenon in contemporary Chinese film-making during the Cultural Revolution years may be noted. When a scene showed a young housemaid being raped by her landlord or a sick laborer being kicked out of the house because he could no longer work, the four big Chinese characters "ren yi dao de" inscribed on a plaque was usually seen hanging over the scene. In the interpretation of the establishment, "ren yi dao de" was hypocritical, and revolutionaries were advised never to practice "ren yi dao de" toward class enemies. During the Cultural Revolution, this value was ridiculed in every way possible by the Red Guards. In recent years, some new interpretations have appeared. Some scholars argue that this value possesses a positive meaning that can be adapted by the people to create harmony in existing social relationships. The ambivalence about this value is clearly revealed in our survey findings, although on the whole the assessment is positive.

Tolerance, Propriety, Deference

These were standards of interpersonal behavior taught by Confucius as a means of achieving a perfect social order. Tolerance means to tolerate unfair treatment or even injustice; propriety means to respect the existing human relationships of a hierarchical nature; deference means to submit or yield to different or opposing views. With propriety (*li*) at the core, the three elements of this traditional value combine to mold a set of social norms and moral standards that constitute the foundation of Confucianism.

Almost half of the respondents (44.9 percent) were proud of this value. About one out of five persons (19.6 percent) said that it should be discarded. More than one-third of the respondents (35.6 percent) were not sure. Although on the whole the assessment of this tradition was still positive, signs of erosion were clearly there. Education was the only relevant factor. More high-education people (52.6 percent) felt proud of this value than low-education respondents (35.9 percent). This is another indication that education in China still retains some residual influence of Confucianism.

Tolerance, propriety, and deference are distinctively human qualities found in all societies. They serve constructive functions by endowing human relations with harmony. In this sense, they contribute toward maintenance of social order. In Chinese history, all ruling classes promoted this Confucian value as a means of achieving social stability. If overly emphasized, however, these qualities can inhibit necessary social change and prolong social injustice.

The Chinese government also used this traditional value to serve its own revolutionary purpose. However, it was clearly stated that the practice of this value was suitable only among the revolutionary ranks. No tolerance, propriety, or deference should be applied to the class enemies. This was the meaning of Mao's famous quotation that "revolution was not a dinner party," a saying that became the most popular during the Cultural Revolution. But once the Cultural Revolution was over, the government again emphasized this value among the people, hoping to restore harmony in society which was needed for keeping the people in line with the establishment. This ambivalence was reflected in our findings.

Harmony Is Precious

Although Confucius never spoke of harmony as something precious, the maintenance of harmony was a cornerstone of his concept of perfect social order. Tolerance, propriety, and deference, important elements of Confucian teachings, were all intended to contribute to building a society where harmony prevailed and conflicts were kept at a minimum. For centuries, Chinese lived in a society where the patterns of social relations promoted harmony as an ultimate goal. Thus the value of "harmony is precious" was nearly universally endorsed in the past. This traditional value, however, is the antithesis to Mao's philosophy of class struggle. Mao believed that conflicts, which he called contradictions, and struggle were the only way to carry out his model of socialist revolution and reconstruction. Indeed, for nearly three decades following the founding of the People's Republic, the Chinese endured the continuous turmoil of conflicts and struggle. Mao wanted "merciless struggle" against erroneous ideas and deeds committed by the enemies of the people. During the Cultural Revolution, even the very word "harmony" was rarely used.

How do Chinese regard the traditional value of "harmony is precious" now? We found that less than half of the respondents (46.9 percent) felt proud of this tradition, with more urbanites (54.4 percent) feeling this way than town residents (38.8 percent) and village people (33.6 percent). Not many respondents from the city proper (13.8 percent) said this traditional value should be discarded, compared to 22.0 percent in Qingpu and 22.9 percent in the villages. It is a bit surprising that as many as 43.5 percent of our village respondents said they were not sure, compared to 39.1 percent in Qingpu towns and 31.8 percent in metropolitan Shanghai. These unusually high percentages of "not sure" responses indicate Chinese awareness of the contradiction between their traditional value of harmony and Mao's philosophy of struggle.

Another relevant factor was education. More people of higher education (53.5 percent) were proud of this traditional value than people of lower education (36.6 percent). It is possible that education in China, even though under state control, may still reflect some residual influence of Confucianism. On the whole, there is no question that this traditional value, which was very important in the past, has been very much weakened in the last forty years.

Submission to Authority

According to the anthropologist Francis Hsu (1949), submission to authority was a cornerstone of traditional Chinese culture. This value was the very foundation upon which the hierarchical social order was built and cemented in China for centuries. The Three Cardinal Principles of social relations attributed to Confucius stipulated that subjects should submit to their emperor, children should submit to their father, and women should submit to their husbands. These relations were not only hierarchical but also patriarchical. As long as these principles were followed, social order would prevail. Submission to authority may be considered a way of life for Chinese people in the past.

A primary objective of the Chinese revolution was to establish an egalitarian, rather than hierarchical, social order. One of the first tasks of the revolution was to destroy the old structure of authority. Soon after the founding of the People's Republic, peasants all over the country were mobilized to challenge and condemn their landlords who had occupied positions of authority in rural China for centuries. Likewise, urban workers were organized to criticize factory owners and managers, who were eventually expropriated. Authority was taken over by Party cadres at various levels. During the initial years of the Cultural Revolution, the Party cadres themselves were condemned by the Red Guards as "capitalist roaders" and exiled to the countryside to work at manual labor. Most of them were brought back to their old positions after the Gang of Four were purged following the death of Mao.

These chaotic years of ups and downs left the concept of authority in a state of confusion. Over half of our respondents (50.3 percent) said they felt proud of the tradition of submission to authority, with no apparent differences recorded between rural and urban areas. More than one out of six (17.1 percent) said this traditional value should be discarded. As many as 32.6 percent said they were not sure, pointing to the ambivalence of Chinese people toward this important traditional value. This was one of the few occasions where the percentages of responses were more or less even among all subgroups. It may be noted that these percentages were nearly the same as those concerning respect for traditions. Similarly, for respect for traditions, we found no significant differences with any of the independent variables.

Pleasing Superiors

To people unfamiliar with traditional Chinese culture, "pleasing superiors" seems to be a concept with a negative connotation. However, to the Chinese, pleasing superiors could be a respected practice. Historically, it was an implicit part of the concept of filial obedience: children were expected to please their parents. Likewise, loyalty to the emperor required a wholehearted effort on the part of subjects to do everything possible to please the emperor, even to the point of hiding the true conditions of the state from him lest the emperor should be needlessly upset. In the Chinese world, this value was extended beyond parents and the emperor to nearly all superiors. The Chinese have adopted an ambivalent but pleasant sounding phrase for "pleasing superiors," *ying he*, that is almost beyond translation. It conveys no obviously negative tone.

During the Manchu Dynasty and even in the early years of the Republic of China, "pleasing superiors" was widely practiced. *Exposés of Chinese Bureaucracy*, a popular novel that came out in the early 1920s, described in intricate details the ingenius ways Chinese people concocted to please their superiors in order to get ahead in the bureaucracy. The revolutionary leaders of the Chinese Communist Party advocated egalitarian relations between Party officials and the common people. But in reality, many of the old practices of pleasing superiors seem to have lingered on.

We had no idea as to how people would currently rate this traditional value. As it turned out, very few people (6.9 percent) said they felt proud of it, with more villagers (12.5 percent) endorsing this value than townspeople (7.2 percent) and urban residents (4.4 percent). Over half of the respondents (55.8 percent) said this value should be discarded, with far more urbanites (60.9 percent) and townspeople (60.2 percent) feeling this way than village people (40.6 percent). Quite unexpectedly, however, almost half of the village respondents (46.9 percent) said they were not sure how to deal with this tradition, compared to 34.7 percent in Shanghai and 32.6 percent in Qingpu. The unusually high percentages of "not sure" indicate the ambivalence which people felt about this value. Also, the practice of pleasing superiors still had a stronger influence on villagers than on urban residents and townspeople.

Education was a relevant factor. We found that more high-education respondents (68.0 percent) than low-education people (44.4 percent) were not happy with this practice, saying it should be discarded. Quite a large number of low-education people (44.0 percent) were not sure if pleasing superiors was good or bad, compared to 28.8 percent among the high-education respondents. More low-education people (11.5 percent) said they felt proud of this value than high-education people (3.2 percent).

Age was also relevant here. Again the young seemed more conservative, as it were. While nearly two-thirds of the old (61.5 percent) said this value should be discarded, less than half of the young respondents (47.8 percent) agreed. Pleasing superiors might be more important to them as they begin to compete in the world of harsh realities.

This value of pleasing superiors indeed represents a major paradox for Chinese people. In principle, this practice can be viewed as lacking integrity. But in practice, it never stops functioning as a necessary tactic to get things done. Chinese society was, and still is, built on a rigid hierarchy in which an inferior obeys a superior. In such a society, it would be very difficult, if not entirely impossible, to achieve one's goals without the endorsement of one's superiors. So it became a common practice in old China that one tried to please one's superiors in order to get a favor. To justify this behavioral pattern, the term "pleasing superiors" was popularized. This paradox still exists in present-day China. In recent years, people have all along been talking about corruption in Chinese society. Pleasing superiors has been "upgraded" to bribing superiors whenever necessary. The practice is seen as inevitable because basically China remains a country still very much ruled by man, not by law. On the other hand, Mao's idea of people power, in the sense that the people of China are the true masters of the country, has probably made this practice more objectionable in the minds of most people. Our findings clearly point to a situation where people very much hate what they have to do. The practice of pleasing superiors does not seem to have changed. What has changed are people's attitudes toward that practice.

Discretion for Self-Preservation

The first part of this Chinese phrase implies an ability to distinguish between virtue and vice, between truth and falsehold. It is a kind of philosophical enlightenment that can guard against ignorance and disaster. By not getting involved in something that is false and sinful, one is actually making progress in the pursuit of virtue and truth. One preserves the integrity of self. Thus discretion for self-preservation is considered a positive value.

In practice, however, this concept means not to get unnecessarily involved with something that can get you into trouble. It means to keep silent when one should speak out. It means to look the other way when one sees acts of injustice being committed.

As many as 63.7 percent of the sample said this traditional value should be discarded, and only 7.8 percent were proud of it. Quite a sizable number of respondents (28.6 percent) were not sure. Media news exposure, education, and age were three relevant factors. More people with high media news exposure (72.4 percent) wanted to discard this value than low-exposure respondents (58.8 percent). We also found a higher percentage among the high-education respondents (68.9 percent) than among the low-education people (55.8 percent) wanting to discard this value. However, when age is examined as a factor, the outcome becomes quite unexpected: far more old people (75.6 percent) than young respondents (50.6 percent) wanted to discard this value. As many as 38.0 percent of the young said "not sure," compared to 20.6 percent among the old. Also more young respondents (11.4 percent) than the old (3.8 percent) still felt proud of this value.

Our findings clearly reflect the treatment of this value since the 1949 revolution. During the Cultural Revolution and many other ideological and criticism campaigns, it was not an option to remain silent and look the other way. Once the target of criticism had been identified, everybody was required to speak up and condemn him (or her). Nobody was allowed to stay out of the campaign. Mao wrote to criticize this concept of "discretion for self preservation" in his famous essay on "Serving the People." During the Cultural Revolution, to be accused of practicing "discretion for self preservation" was a very serious charge. Someone who avoided an active participation in the campaign must have some selfish interest to hide. After all the criticisms in the mass media in these years, it is not surprising at all that those under heavy media news exposure would have a more negative view of this traditional value. People of higher education were generally required to participate more actively in those criticism campaigns, which seemed to have an effect on them. The young people, on the other hand, had little experience with the Cultural Revolution, and interestingly, they felt less negative about this value.

Roles of Women

We examine three traditional values having to do with the roles of women, especially in their relations with men. They are: chastity for women, three obediences and four virtues, and differentiation between and men and women.

Chastity for Women

This was a traditional value imposed on Chinese women. Women must maintain their chastity under all circumstances, while men were allowed various kinds of licentious behavior. To a Chinese woman, loss of chastity was considered to be more serious than loss of life. Many communities had built "chastity statues" that paid tribute to exemplary behavior by some women to protect their chastity.

Chastity for women means that before marriage women should protect their virginity at whatever cost. It also means, in the traditional Chinese context, that after her husband died a woman was not supposed to remarry no matter how young she was. Obviously this was one of the confining moral standards set up to control women's life. Like three obediences and four virtues which we discuss later, this value was condemned during the May 4 Movement of 1919 and in many of the masterpieces in modern and contemporary Chinese literature and art forms.

This value as a whole continued to be viewed as negative after the 1949 revolution. However, so far as virginity is concerned, it is still held as a cherished value. Premarital sex is frowned upon if not socially condemned. But second marriages have become fairly common among Chinese women, old and young. Widows are encouraged to get remarried.

Now only less than one-third of the respondents (31.2 percent) said they felt proud of this value, with a much stronger endorsement from the young people (36.9 percent) than from the old (18.1 percent), at a surprisingly high two-to-one ratio. Nearly half of the respondents (44.7 percent) said the restrictive idea of chastity for women should be discarded. Again the rejection rate was much lower among young people (37.3 percent) than among the old (61.7 percent). Those who were not sure accounted for 24.2 percent. Age was the only relevant factor.

Treatment of this value in the Chinese mass media has mainly been negative in the past forty years, which presumably would have had a stronger influence on the old people's perception than on the young. The data we have presented above partly reflects this trend. That is, the old have been "better educated" than the young, so to speak. But we do not think the enormous difference between the old and the young could be entirely attributed to the effects of media propaganda. Rather, we think the traditional value of virginity is still there, and this is something the young people are very much concerned about.

Three Obediences and Four Virtues

Another traditional value that discriminated against women in China was defined by the rules of "three obediences and four virtues." The three obediences were, first, obedience to father before a woman got married; second, her obedience to husband after marriage; and third, her obedience to son after her husband died. The four virtues included *fude* (a woman's morality), *fuyan* (a woman's language), *furong* (a woman's manners), and *fugong* (a woman's work). Chinese women lived by standards of morality that kept them within the confines allowed by the traditional society. Men were not bound by the same standards. Women were expected to use a pattern of language that showed their humble nature. Their manners were controlled in such a way as to reveal their inferior status. For example, a woman was not supposed to lean her body against the back of a chair in a comfortable way; she must sit with her body leaning a bit forward to show her respect for any men present. In terms of work, women were expected to excel in certain useful skills such as knitting or embroidery.

The criticism of this traditional value has had a history that predates the Chinese Communist revolution. The principle of "three obediences and four virtues" was fiercely attacked as a feudalistic yoke on Chinese women during the May 4 Movement in 1919. Ever since it has been criticized in the works of many contemporary Chinese literary masters, such as Lu Xun, Shen Yanbin, and Ba Jin. Criticisms continued after the People's Republic was founded. While not all Chinese can identify the three obediences and four virtues, the majority relate this value to negative attitudes about women.

As many as 71.9 percent of the respondents said that this traditional value should be discarded. Only 7.9 percent said they felt proud of it. One out of five respondents (20.3 percent) were not sure. It may be noted that these percentages were very similar to those about "differentiation between men and women," which we discuss next. These were among the most negatively held traditional values cited in our survey.

Age and education were two relevant factors. Not surprisingly, more people with high education (76.6 percent) wanted to see this traditional value discarded than people with low education (64.1 percent). But rather unexpectedly, the rejection of this traditional value was considerably higher among old people than in the younger generation. In the old group, 84.7 percent said this value should be discarded, compared to 69.3 percent in the middle-aged group and 64.3 percent in the young group. This, we think, reflects in part the effect of government propaganda, to which the older people have been exposed more heavily. Older people also had more personal experiences of discrimination against women in the old society, and probably felt more strongly against it.

Differentiation between Men and Women

This traditional value was another euphemistic justification for discrimination against Chinese women. Because women are different from men, they should be treated differently. Now only about one out of ten respondents (9.9 percent) said they were proud of this tradition. Over two-thirds (69.1 percent) said it should be discarded. Quite a few respondents (21.1 percent) said they were not sure. The rejection of this traditional value seemed to be nearly universal regardless of sex, age, education, and income. Only minor differences were found between urban and rural residents. Slightly more villagers (12.7 percent) still endorsed this traditional value than urbanites in Shanghai (8.9 percent).

Traditional Chinese society was patriarchical in nature. The father was the head of the family and descent was reckoned by the male line. Children belonged to the father's clan. In such a society, men would be naturally seen as superior to women, and the long-existing tradition of male superiority gave rise to all sorts of stereotypes about the inferiority of the female sex: less intelligent than men, indecisive, shortsighted, poor taste, selfish, to name only a few. In the

Chinese language, "a woman's opinion" means an opinion that is narrow-minded or shortsighted. Even Confucius believed that women and mean-spirited men were hard to deal with. Chinese women were not only oppressed by the old social system; they were also oppressed by men.

One of the ideals of the Chinese Communist revolution was proclaimed to be the full emancipation of women and equality between men and women. The government has been fairly effective in achieving this goal. Media propaganda on women's liberation has been persistent and powerful for the past forty years. During the Cultural Revolution, when Jiang Qing, Mao's wife who was later sentenced to death, usurped the power with the three other members of the Gang of Four, Chinese women's status was raised to a high level for a time. Mao's statement that "women hold up half of heaven" became a motto for all women organizations. More women began to sit on Party's politburo and assume other important Party and government positions for a period during the Cultural Revolution. Chinese women appeared to be winning new political rights.

However, if we examine the vast rural areas, the status of women shows little improvement. Reports of female infanticides, child marriages, the selling and buying of women proliferate. In today's rural areas women are usually assigned physically harder, professionally unskilled jobs while men take care of the so-called management responsibilities that allow them to sit in offices smoking and sipping tea. After a day's work, women go to the pigsty to feed pigs and do other household chores while men wait to be served dinner. The situation for urban women is a little better, but they also live a harder life than men. Our findings showed that nearly one-third of our respondents were either still proud of the traditional discrimination against women or not sure. That nearly seven out of ten respondents felt this traditional value should be discarded was encouraging. However, it is a fallacy to say that Chinese women have won their full emancipation, politically, economically, and socially. Many have paid lip service to women's liberation. The gap between reality and ideal is yet to be bridged.

Work Ethic and Social Status

We included two traditional values on work ethic and social status. They are: diligence and frugality, and a precept known as "farmers high and merchants low."

Diligence and Frugality

A large majority of the respondents (89.1 percent) said they were proud of this element of Chinese culture. Only 2.9 percent of the sample said this value should be discarded, and another 8.1 percent responded "not sure."

The young people were less sure about this value. While nearly all the old people (96 percent) were proud of it, only about four out of five young people (82.7 percent) expressed the same positive endorsement. Other young people were either not sure (12 percent), or said this traditional value should be discarded (5.3 percent).

Western cultural influence was another relevant factor. In recent years, owing to China's open-door policy, though still rather limited in the cultural arena, Chinese people have had a fairly good exposure to Western culture communicated primarily through the mass media, especially television and films. In big cities like Shanghai, tourism and other interpersonal contacts add another form of input. We found that people who had low Western cultural exposure endorsed the value of diligence and frugality much more (91.9 percent) than those who had high exposure (74.5 percent). Also more high-exposure people (17.6 percent) felt unsure about this value than the low-exposure people (5.7 percent). This shows that Western cultural influence has produced some effect on the Chinese perception of this traditional value.

Those heavily exposed to the official media news endorsed this value slightly more (90 percent to 92 percent) than those only marginally exposed (87 percent), suggesting some limited effects of government propaganda.

China has been an agricultural country for thousands of years. Agriculture in ancient times depended largely on nature and farmers had to work diligently in order to have a bumper harvest. They had to practice frugality so that they could cope with unprepared situations. Confucian teachings also stressed diligence and frugality, whose combination was considered a virtue by ancient Chinese. This value, together with other aspects of Confucianism, was found to be highly endorsed in other East Asian countries such as Japan and Korea. So this is not only a value unique to the Chinese, but belongs to many other countries, particularly those that share part of the Confucian tradition.

However, this value has some unique significance in the current Chinese context. Soon after the Communist Party came to power, it directed its members and the general population to practice diligence and frugality as the country had virtually nothing but poverty and backwardness left over by war. China experienced more serious economic problems at the beginning of the 1960s when the country was stricken by natural disasters and ultra-leftist policies. The government persuaded the people to work harder and consume less. A campaign to "recall the bitterness of the past and taste the sweetness of the present" was launched with a view to educating the people to believe that the socialist system was good and that the practice of diligence and frugality was still necessary to overcome the mounting economic crises.

No sooner had the ten-year Cultural Revolution ended than the Chinese government realized the gravity of another legacy of Mao, the population explosion. Chairman Mao once observed: "With more people we could have more strength." But the fact was: With more people there are more mouths to feed. China had already nearly one billion mouths to feed when the Cultural Revolution came to an end. Even though China launched its one-child per family campaign in the early 1980s, the population keeps growing, more so in rural areas than in cities. This population expansion places an unshakable economic burden on the country. Suggestions that have been offered include: birth control, raising productivity, and encouraging the whole nation to practice diligence and frugality.

Based upon the above analysis, we detect a major tension: while the majority of Chinese people still believe in the value of diligence and frugality, they are also growing somewhat impatient, more and more so when watching the affluent lifestyles of their neighboring countries and regions such as Japan, South Korea, and Taiwan. The growing impatience, particularly among the younger Chinese, may add to the conflicts already existing between the people and their government. Our analysis suggests that Western cultural influence may aggravate what is already a serious situation, by raising aspirations beyond reach. Therefore, one should not feel too optimistic about the high percentage who still believe in diligence and frugality. Our findings do not imply that the people of China will always be contented with working hard without the incentive of material rewards.

Farmers High, Merchants Low

Throughout Chinese history, the ruling class maintained an uneasy relationship with merchants. Commerce and trade were necessary, but the accumulation of wealth in the hands of a group of relatively mobile people was seen as a threat to the imperial court. Material wealth must not be allied with political power. Thus during different periods of Chinese history, various measures were adopted by the ruling elite to keep the merchants under control.

Capitalism never had a chance to develop in China. For too long a time, the Chinese lived in a society where Asiatic modes of production played a dominant role in the ancient economy. Most people were farmers who lived a self-sufficient life on their own land which fed successive generations. They had little interest in commerce except on a modest scale. Trade never developed into something as important as agriculture. In the traditional Chinese mentality, merchants, considered immoral, devious, and devoid of ethics, were assigned a lower social status than farmers. This mentality became a value known as "farmers high, merchants low."

This concept was inherited by China's revolutionary leaders. The Chinese Communist revolution was by nature a peasants' revolution, hence farmers have all along been important in the eyes of the Communist Party. The farmers, together with the urban working class, formed the backbone of the revolutionary forces. Like his predecessors in history, Mao was suspicious of merchants, who were considered capitalists. He believed that only collectivization and communization could pave the way for the Chinese to improve their standard of living, an idea which was later found to be a complete failure. All through the 1960s and the Cultural Revolution, farmers (called commune members since 1958) were not permitted to engage in any kind of private trade, dubbed "the tail of capitalism," a tail which Communist leaders demanded be cut off. However, things changed soon after the Cultural Revolution was declared over. The commune system was abolished and the land redistributed among the individual farmers. The once-cut-off tail of capitalism grew again, represented by free markets in the countryside as well as in urban areas. The traditional value of "farmers high, merchants low" was being challenged.

Now over half of the respondents (53.7 percent) said the value known as "peasants high, merchants low" should be discarded. This negative feeling was equally shared by urban residents and villagers, many of them were farmers. More people with high education (61.4 percent) felt this way than low-education people (42.7 percent). More than one-third of the sample (35.9 percent) were not sure. Only one out of ten people (10.4 percent) were still "proud of" this value, with a higher percentage among the low-education people (18.1 percent) than among the high-education respondents (6.0 percent). An interesting trend reveals that those under heavy Western cultural influence rejected this traditional value more strongly than those under little influence. Among the former, 76.5 percent wanted to discard this old value and only 3.9 percent were proud of it. Among the latter, only 47.9 percent were in favor of discarding while 13.1 percent were still proud of it.

Discussion

We take another look at the 18 traditional values as a whole, using as indices the net differences between the percentages who felt proud and the percentages who wanted to discard them. We arrange these traditional values under five categories, figure 10.2.

Of the nine traditional values seen as positive, long historical heritage is the most highly regarded, followed by diligence and frugality, and loyalty to the state. Of the nine negatively viewed values, three obediences and four virtues, the way of the Golden Mean, and differentiation between men and women were most strongly rejected.

Traditions and Heritages	
Long historical heritage	89.7%
Respect for traditions	38.5%
Loyalty to state	67.5%
Familial Relations	
Benevolent father, filial son	48.0%
Glory to ancestors	-23.8%
A house full of sons and grandsons	-35.5%
Social Relational Guidelines	
Way of golden mean	-59.6%
Generosity and virtues	39.8%
Tolerance, propriety, deference	25.3%
Harmony is precious	29.5%
Submission to authority	33.2%
Pleasing superiors	-48.9%
Discretion for self-preservation	-55.9%
Roles of Women	
Chastity for women	-13.5%
Three obediences and four virtues	-64.0%
Differentiation between men and women	-59.2%
Work Ethic and Social Status	
Diligence and frugality	86.2%
Farmers high, merchants low	-43.3%

Figure 10.2 Five Categories of Traditional Values

Our data reveal just how much revolution and modernization have changed the face of China. If a similar survey had been conducted half a century ago, one would expect high and positive ratings on nearly all these traditional values. These current findings are thus nothing short of phenomenal. To many people today, Chinese or non-Chinese, negative attitudes toward such values as three obediences and four virtues seem only natural. But we recall that these values were cherished in China for thousands of years before the People's Republic was founded in 1949. It is true that some of the now negatively viewed values were subjected to criticism by intellectuals early in the century, particularly during the May 4 Movement of 1919. However, the real challenge did not come on a massive scale until the People's Republic was founded. We are inclined to believe that most changes in values and attitudes took place in the last forty years as a result of the fundamental changes in the superstructure as well as the infrastructure of the country. The Communist revolution has not only changed the nature of the economic and political systems; it has also remolded the minds of a people living under those systems. Remarkably, these fundamental changes in traditional Chinese culture have been brought about within a lifetime.

From its own perspective, the Chinese Communist Party seems to have succeeded in remaking the Chinese culture, by retaining those cultural elements that consolidated its proletarian dictatorship and discarding others that conflicted with its basic beliefs. For example, the value of long historical heritage was effectively used to give the Chinese a strong sense of cultural identity and national pride. The value of diligence and frugality adapted well to a country with a formidably large population, limited resources, and an often troubled economy. The government-controlled media never stopped educating the people on the importance of practicing diligence and frugality. The traditionally strong hardworking spirit was suppressed by the collective reward system during Mao's time. Since that system was modified in the early 1980s, Chinese farmers have once again become their diligent selves. Loyalty and devotion to the state was essential to the ruling elite, hence high on the priority list in the Party's propaganda campaigns. We think this traditional sense of loyalty to the state was one factor that helped cement what might otherwise be a frail foundation of support for the establishment. Even the value of "benevolent father and filial son," which could be condemned as feudalistic, was useful in holding the Chinese family together, and thereby maintaining social stability.

A group of traditional values, which we believed were nearly universally accepted in the past, received only marginal to moderate endorsement. Submission to authority used to be among the most important traditional values. It received a clear endorsement from only one-third of our respondents. Traditional authority began to erode in the early 1950s when landlords and others who held high positions in rural China were purged in the agrarian land reform movement. Urban capitalists were the next to go during the takeover of industries and businesses by the state in 1956. The humiliation of intellectuals, who were always highly regarded in the past, began with the Anti-Rightist movement of 1957, and continued throughout the Cultural Revolution years. They were labeled the "stinky No. 9," at the bottom of the social ladder. Until the summer of 1966, Party cadres were the only elite who occupied positions of authority. During the Cultural Revolution that followed, many of them were forced by the Red Guards to parade in the streets in humiliation before they were exiled to the countryside to clean up latrines and do other manual labor. Even though many were restored after the death of Mao, the concept of authority was cast in a state of confusion, and our findings reflected that.

Likewise, the prolonged, contentious class struggle, the acrimonious mutual accusations during ideological campaigns, and the sudden rise to power of those who knew how to manipulate the chaotic situations have torn apart the traditional moral fiber that held Chinese society together for centuries. Such traditional values as generosity and virtues, harmony, tolerance, propriety and deference have lost their cultural meanings to most Chinese. Even though their ratings were still marginally on the positive side, these values no longer seem to be prominent in the minds and life of the Chinese people.

Among the negative values, those relating to women are clearly a result of government policies that have sought to do away with some of the age-old discriminations against Chinese women. The New Marriage Law introduced in the early 1950s gave women equal status within the family. What made that equal status real rather than a pronouncement in a piece of paper was changes in the occupational structure and educational system. Men and women now work as equals, or nearly equals, in factories, government offices, and the rural countryside, in what used to be communes. Most of the top managerial positions are still held by men. But women bring home their own wages, and thus have achieved their own status in the family. They are no longer "dependents." In the school system, boys and girls enjoy equal educational opportunities up to the middle-school level. More boys than girls aspire to college education. But when girls apply, they are treated equally in the entrance examination system.

Other negative values most likely reflect both the ruling elite's ideological indoctrination and the changing social and economic environments in which Chinese live. The way of the golden mean is a good example. This value, which used to be an important element of Chinese philosophy of life, has now been clearly rejected by most people. Three factors may be noted. First, after the 1949 revolution, China was no longer a land appropriate for practicing the golden mean; instead it became a land of merciless class struggle. Chairman Mao felt threatened by this Confucian principle because if people still practiced it, they would not participate in the class struggle. So Mao led the media in fiercely attacking this time-honored value. Our survey findings are the first concrete evidence of how successful he was.

Second, even now in daily life when no class struggle is being waged, the current economic and social environments in China make the way of the golden mean impractical. In a setting of extremely scarce resources, when Chinese have to compete intensively for what little they can get, they cannot defer to a virtue of moderation and risk getting nothing. A demonstration of this situation occurred in Shanghai several years ago when the government lifted its decade-long freeze on wages and offered pay raises to a limited number of employees. In many organizations the fight for pay raises was fiercely intense. Some people resorted to violence against their supervisors when their applications for pay raises were not granted. Also, partly as a result of the class struggle, a social atmosphere of surveillance and vigilance now prevails. Most people are cautious in dealing with people around them, but if they feel their personal well-being is being jeopardized for whatever reason, their response is to fight back ferociously in order to protect themselves, rather than observing the way of the golden mean.

Third, as a prominent value in traditional Chinese culture, the golden mean did not function alone but was part of a pervasive cultural milieu that stressed harmony, tolerance, and propriety. Chinese people practiced this value in the past because other people would honor it. But now the general cultural milieu is radically changed, as our survey data show. Harmony is not considered precious. Tolerance, propriety, and deference have lost their former cultural relevance. In this drastically changed cultural context, the rejection of the way of the golden mean is to be expected. Seen in these perspectives—political, economic, social and cultural—the survival of this traditional value is simply not feasible.

The erosion of this traditional value raises a basic question about the viability of contemporary Chinese culture. Traditional Chinese culture was an intricate set of values and beliefs that evolved over a period of several thousand years, shaped by history and highly complex socioeconomic forces. For centuries it maintained a state of delicate equilibrium and fulfilled in its uniquely Chinese way the major functions of individual gratification and societal survival. This cultural equilibrium was not static but a dynamic force that accommodated change and became an integral part of Chinese history. However, never before in Chinese history has its culture undergone such radical restructuring so abruptly, as our survey findings have demonstrated. Being an integrated whole, Chinese culture cannot survive if the ruling elite continues to select certain components, such as its historical identity and loyalty to the state because they suit revolutionary purposes, and eliminate others because they were seen to be in conflict with the ideals of the revolution. Mao did not seem to realize, even with his broad revolutionary vision of history, that once he had succeeded in destroying traditional Chinese culture, Chinese people would inevitably find themselves in a "cultural void" until a new vibrant culture emerged to take its place. Currently there is no assurance that a new culture will develop. If it does not—and we think recent events since the Tiananmen incident in the summer of 1989 have raised serious doubts whether it will—then China faces the devastating prospect of a long and traumatic period of cultural disintegration.

Exposure to news information in the official media seemed to have little to do with the strength or erosion of traditional values. Those respondents who were heavily exposed to official news felt more strongly about loyalty to the state as a value (84.9 percent), as one might expect, were somewhat more proud of China's long historical heritage (92.6 percent), and were more inclined to reject the traditional value of harmony (19.1 percent) than those least exposed (69.8 percent, 88.3 percent, and 14.2 percent respectively).

Western cultural influence in the mass media has been found to be a major factor with several other aspects of Chinese culture. As far as traditional Confucian values are concerned, however, it seems to have little impact. Those under heavy Western cultural influence were less proud of diligence and frugality as a value (74.5 percent) than those under little influence (91.9 percent). This is consistent with similar findings on work ethic. Those under heavy influence also were more eager to discard the traditional value known as "farmers high and merchants low" (76.5 percent) than those under little influence (47.9 percent).

It seems that the erosion of traditional values predates Western cultural influence, which returned to China around 1979 after an absence of thirty years, and is largely unrelated to what news information people currently get from the official media in the era of economic reform. The force behind that erosion, we suggest, resides in the many ideological communication campaigns which Chairman Mao directed in the two decades from 1957 till his death in 1976. We see an indirect evidence of this hypothesis in our consistent findings on age differences.

What may seem to be a most puzzling phenomenon is the finding that young respondents (age under 29) were less "radical" than old subjects (age 50–65) in their attitudes toward the negatively viewed values, which were generally those that the establishment wanted to see disappear. Consistently, more old respondents than young people said these traditional values should be discarded, whereas more of the young felt proud or unsure of them. These findings were unexpected. The list in table 10.1 clearly shows this general trend.

With the exception of "farmers high, merchants low," and "differention between men and women," all the negatively viewed values were disapproved of more strongly among the old than the young. An easy interpretation would be that the young were more conservative than the old. But this is neither an adequate nor a plausible explanation, because it is contrary to the general trend elsewhere in the world. Based on our knowledge and understanding of the past history of the People's Republic, we view this phenomenon as an indication of the successful ideological remolding of the older people by the revolutionary elite, and of the failure of such indoctrination on the younger generation.

China completed its socialist transformation of agriculture, industry, and other businesses in 1956. With the country's infrastructure shaped into the socialist mold, the ruling elite began to tighten its control over the superstructure by launching a major ideological campaign

Table 10.1 Age and Rejection of Traditional Values

Negative values	YOUNG % Proud	Not sure	Discard	OLD % Proud	Not Sure	Discard
Way of golden mean	6.9	31.4	61.8	3.8	28.6	67.5
Three obediences and four virtues	9.4	26.3	64.3	3.8	11.5	84.7
Glory to ancestors	21.0	42.0	37.1	14.5	32.5	53.0
Chastity for women	36.9	25.9	37.3	18.1	20.2	61.7
Pleasing superiors	8.6	43.5	47.8	5.6	32.9	61.5
A house full of sons and grandsons	28.8	28.4	42.7	9.3	14.5	76.2
Discretion for self-preservation	11.4	38.0	50.6	3.8	20.6	75.6

against the so-called rightists in the following year. In that historic year of 1957, hundreds of thousands of Chinese intellectuals were being systematically persecuted. From that year on, Chinese people saw one campaign after another, big and small, each endorsing new socialist ideals and repudiating old traditional values that were seen to be in conflict with the revolutionary spirit. These campaigns continued through the Cultural Revolution as a traumatic climax and ended only in the reform period (1979–1989) following the death of Chairman Mao. Together these ideological communication campaigns, no matter how each of them was evaluated afterwards, seem to have left an enormous impact on the psychology of older people. Consider someone who was 50 years old in 1987 (the youngest in the old group). This person was 20 in 1957, old enough to be targeted in the campaign and mature enough to be influenced ideologically. Subject to consistent brainwashing for some thirty years, the old people became highly vulnerable. Their cultural resistance collapsed. They found it psychologically more comfortable to support those values that the ruling elite endorsed and cut ties with the traditional values which were condemned.

Most of our young respondents were not even born when the Cultural Revolution was started, and many were only children. They had no knowledge of the massive purges of intellectuals during the Anti-Rightist campaign of 1957. Many of them had only a vague notion about the Cultural Revolution, something their parents occasionally mentioned and something they may have read about in the "scars literature." The young group started to mature, ideologically, in the late seventies or early eighties, an era characterized by economic reforms, mounting Western influence, and increased corruption. During the reform years they witnessed two ideological campaigns. However, both the Anti-spiritual Pollution campaign of 1983-84 and the Anti-bourgeois Liberation campaign of 1987 were short-lived and left little impact.

Never confined by the ideological straitjacket which restricted their parents, these young Chinese seem to be readily susceptible to Western cultural influence. They are attracted by the material benefits promised by economic reforms but still beyond reach for most of them. Not surprisingly, this generation of young Chinese would strongly resent any attempt to imbue them with revolutionary ideologies, as our survey has shown. We are not suggesting that the young generation can be viewed as defenders of traditional values. Rather, our research findings indicate a possible counterreaction by the young to anything promoted by the establishment. Knowing that these traditional values have been condemned by the ruling elite, some of them may deliberately endorse them, as it were, to express their frustration.

In this sense, we see the young people not as more conservative, which our data may superficially indicate, but as more cynical, more rebellious and more anti-establishment than their parents.

It seems certain that the young will become more and more assertive of their own value system, which is still in the process of emerging. Even though their values are as yet unclear, they can be expected to move in a direction not desired by the establishment. This situation puts a country undergoing radical cultural change at risk. What may develop are two antagonistic groups, the young and the establishment, fighting for domination or at least survival. The ensuing conflicts may lead to mass-scale physical confrontations and even bloodshed. The Tiananmen Square incident of 1989 is a typical example of such a confrontation. Behind the bloody scene was a fierce struggle between two value systems. The same Tiananmen incident may be interpreted from different angles (Hsiung, 1989; Fei, 1989; Liu, 1989). Chinese students may have seen it as an expression of their demands for a dialogue with the government and for speeding up political reform. Deng Xiaoping and his supporters may continue to see it as a counter-revolutionary rebellion which must be suppressed by force at whatever cost. The Western media may see it as a major challenge to Communism. To us, the Tiananmen incident represented a major value confrontation dramatized in a most violent and bloody way. Now the Tiananmen incident has become a historic event and no one can predict if it will be repeated in the foreseeable future. However, value confrontations of a similar nature, whatever form they may take, are bound to recur as China enters the 21st century. How these confrontations are resolved will either hamper or stimulate China's modernization process.

Chapter 11

Belief System

The belief system of a culture consists of religious and non-religious beliefs. Here in this chapter we are concerned about religious or religion-related beliefs, whose modern variations can be seen as major indicators of cultural change in society.

China is sometimes referred to as a "society *almost* without religion" (Liang, 1963). In fact until Buddhism was introduced from India, there was no indigenous religion in China except the worship of heaven and ancestors. Taoism was fashioned after Buddhism although it took its name from the philosophy of Lao Tze. Because of the overriding influence of Confucianism, religion had relatively shallow roots in the cultural soil of China. Confucianism is not a religion per se, but a set of moral principles guiding social relationships. It is a vision of perfect social order, and as such offers a balanced meaning of life. As a code of ethics regulating day-to-day behavior and a body of rituals for ancestor worship that formed a link with the world of the unknown, Confucianism served for centuries those social and psychological needs that were generally fulfilled by religion. Buddhism was introduced to China in the East Han Dynasty around 65 A.D., but it did not take roots among the Chinese populace until the third and fourth centuries during the Jin Dynasty. The political disorder and social chaos at that time, following many years of prolonged warfare, had shaken the foundation of the Confucian social order. Chinese people lived in a state of anguish and despair. Buddhism was able to fill a spiritual void by offering hope in the next life and peace of mind in this one.

The growth of Buddhism in China, and for that matter Taoism as well, had to rely on Confucianism as a broad cognitive foundation. The Chinese saw no contradiction between ancestor worship and worship of Buddha. Chinese Buddhism is different from Indian Buddhism partly because of translation difficulties, especially during the crucial initial stage. Also, in hundreds of years of evolution (Ren, 1981), Chinese Buddhism changed many of its tenets in order to coexist peacefully with Confucianism, which would not tolerate, for example, such a practice as burning the body of a parent, an Indian Buddhist ritual. So long as a religion did not collide with the basic principles of Confucianism, whether it originated from abroad or at home, it was allowed to exist. The adaptation of Buddhism to Confucianism later developed into a mutual, interactive process. During the Song and Ming Dynasties, Neo-Confucianism incorporated Buddhist teachings as part of its philosophical foundation. Also Buddhism has left its mark on Chinese art and music. Owing to the omnipresent influence of Confucianism, religious practices in China were developed only to a moderate degree. However, as an important part of the Chinese belief system, Buddhism and other religions, as well as other related quasi-religious beliefs, did have a large influence on social life in old China, particularly in the rural areas.

In contemporary China, religious or religion-related, superstitious activities were often seen as conflicting with the basic aims of the Communist revolution. Over the years the Chinese government adopted various policies to limit religious practices among the people. In theory, the constitution of the People's Republic has never explicitly banned religious beliefs in China. Nor has it ever promoted them. In practice the Chinese government has viewed all religious activities with suspicion or even hostility. Religious activities in China have been strictly controlled since the People's Republic was founded in 1949. The philosophical position of the ruling elite toward religion has been best summarized by Ren Jiyu, a scholar who specializes in the history of Chinese Buddhism (Ren, 1981, p.16). Although Ren is commenting on Buddhism, his tone most likely reflects the official position on other religions as well.

"We do not believe in Buddhism. Nor do we accept as truth what Buddhism has propagated.... The road toward salvation offered by Buddhism is false. But the sufferings that Buddhism revealed in society were true, and we must take them seriously. The multitude of Buddhist believers in the last two thousand years were themselves victims. ... They truly believed that Buddhism could help lift them up away from the reality of sufferings. Their behavior is not to be commended, but we must sympathize with them as captives of religion."

In the last few years religious activities were reported to be coming back in China owing to the government's open-door and reform policies. Buddhist temples began to receive many worshippers. Christian churches in Shanghai were allowed to conduct regular Sunday services, attracting a good number of people, believers and nonbelievers alike. When one of the authors visited Xiamen in the spring of 1988, he attended Easter Service in a Protestant church in Gulangyu, where he used to live before 1949. The church was packed that day, with mostly older people and far more women than men. Other than the choir members, few young people were in the congregation.

Shanghai, because of its early contacts with Western missionaries and longtime interactions with people brought up in Christianity, has more Christian churches than Buddhist temples or Islamic mosques. In 1986, there were 29 Catholic churches, 23 Protestant churches (including one newly built in Wusong District), 9 Buddhist temples, 2 Taoist temples, and 5 Islamic mosques. Statistics in 1986 showed that in Shanghai there were about 100,000 Catholics and 40,000 Protestants. Each Buddhist festival in Shanghai, according to a government report, registered an average of about 30,000 worshippers burning incense at various temples in the city. There were about 2,000 people visiting Taoist temples on a regular basis. Muslims attending their festivals regularly numbered about 4,000 in Shanghai. For a metropolitan city of nearly eight millions, those who participated in religious activities on a regular basis were about 0.2 percent.[1] It is against this social and historical background that we examine a few salient points in China's current belief system.

Religious Faith

To what degree Chinese people have maintained their interest in religion, and what is the picture now after decades of restriction of religious activities, we did not know. So we asked this question: "Do you think it is necessary to have religious faith?"

Only a relatively small minority of respondents (28.4 percent) said it is necessary. Over two-fifths (42.0 percent) said religious faith was not necessary, and 29.6 percent were not sure. It is interesting, however, that villagers seemed to be more contented with their secular life than urban dwellers; almost half of our village respondents (47.1 percent) did not see religious faith as necessary, compared to 38.9 percent in metropolitan Shanghai. Town residents in Qingpu were close to rural villagers; 45.7 percent of them did not consider religious faith necessary. Only about one out of five villagers (21.9 percent) said religious faith was necessary, compared to 32.8 percent in Shanghai. Besides the area of residence, age was the only other relevant factor. Surprisingly, the older people were more atheistic than the younger generation. Among those 50 years old and above, 50.3 percent said it was not necessary to have any religious faith. The corresponding figure decreased to 43 percent in the 30–49 age bracket, and dropped further to 32 percent among those below 30 years of age. These findings, contrary to the ongoing trend elsewhere in the developing world, seem to set a consistent pattern in our survey data, as we see later.

In the above question, we were not asking whether or not our respondents themselves had religious faith. When someone says it is not necessary to have religous faith, we assume that this person most likely does not believe in any religion. But a person who says it is necessary to have religious faith may or may not have the faith himself. We then asked a question more concretely related to people's own religious activities: "How important are Buddhist festivals in the life of your family?" We asked about Buddhism, instead of any other religions, because Buddhism used to be the dominant religion in China.

Buddhist festivals used to be important days in the Chinese calendar. The birthday of Buddha, the birthday of the Goddess of Mercy, and the Ghost Festival on the seventh full moon known as Yu Lan Peng, among others, were occasions for community celebration and family worship. In areas around Shanghai, outside the small Christian population, every family observed these festivals. Now very few people (3.5 percent) considered Buddhist festivals to be "very important."

Figure 11.1 A Buddhist festival attracts a curious small crowd in Shanghai. Religion no longer occupies a central place in Chinese life. (*Photo courtesy of Linus Chao*)

Those who said "important" accounted for 5.1 percent and those who mentioned "somewhat important," 13.2 percent. An overwhelmingly large majority of our respondents (78.2 percent) said that Buddhist festivals were not important at all. For most people in our sample, Buddhism seemed to have lost its meaning. However, we see a difference between rural villagers and urban residents. While almost none of the Shanghai respondents (1.5 percent) said such festivals were very important, 8.8 percent of the villagers said they were. As many as 83.7 percent of our Shanghai sample said "not important at all," compared to only 61.4 percent in rural areas. This is quite understandable as historically there were more Buddhist believers in the countryside than in large cities.

We have a seemingly contradictory picture about religious faith and religious practices among urban and rural people. On the one hand, urban people seem to take religious faith a little more seriously than rural people. On the other hand, rural people consider Buddhist festivals somewhat more important than urban people. This apparent contradiction illustrates the typical traditional Chinese attitude toward religion, which has been noted by anthropologists like Francis Hsu. Religion to most Chinese was not a matter of rigid faith of a monotheistic nature, but constituted a mixture of festivals and rituals imbued with pragmatic characteristics. The rural people traditionally attached greater importance to the ritualistic side of Buddhism than urban residents, perhaps owing to their greater dependence on the unpredictable whims of nature, and our findings suggest that they still do. Urban residents today, our findings suggest, seem to hold on to the philosophical side of religion a bit more, seeing religion more as a matter of faith, than rural people do, even though religious faith is on the whole not very important to them either.

Education and age were also relevant factors. We found, as expected, that more people of high education (85.3 percent) than those with low education (66.2 percent) said that Buddhist festivals were "not important at all." The findings about age were not what we expected: the percentage saying "not important at all" was found to be considerably higher among the old respondents (85.5 percent) than among the young (71.0 percent). This suggests that the government's tight control of religious activities over a period of three decades from the 1950s to the early 1980s has left a stronger impact on those who grew up in that traumatic period.

In order to have something to compare with, we asked a follow-up question: "How important is the celebration of the Spring Festival in the life of your family?" "Spring Festival" is the term now used for the celebration of the Chinese lunar New Year, perhaps the single most important festival of traditional Chinese society. It was an occasion for family reunion and for thanksgiving after a year of toil in labor. It used to begin on the eighth day of the twelfth moon, when the family prepared a special rice soup made of eight ingredients, to signify the start of the celebration. This was followed by a simple ceremony a few days later to send off the kitchen god back to heaven to make a report on what the family did during the year. This was a small idol who sat in one corner of the kitchen and monitored events in the family. To make sure a favorable report would be filed, the family not only offered food but also sweetened the kitchen god by putting syrup on his lips. Women in the family spent days preparing all kinds of food for family members, relatives, and guests. On the New Year's eve, before the family sat down for a reunion dinner, the head of the family led all members in a ceremony to worship and give thanks to their ancestors. Food was offered and incense burned. After the dinner, family members and guests stayed up till after midnight to greet the New Year with fireworks. Early in the morning of the New Year's day, the whole family performed another worship of ancestors before beginning with the celebration. Children kowtowed to their parents to offer New Year's greetings and express their gratitude. The joyous celebration lasted for another fifteen days ending with the Lantern Festival on the first full moon of the lunar year. In China today, the Spring Festival is only a two-day public holiday. It is still an occasion for family reunions, with a traditional dinner on the eve of the New Year. On the Chinese New Year's day, people visit relatives and friends to offer good wishes and say happy new year. Parents buy new dresses for their children and perhaps take them to see a movie. There is no more kowtow or ancestor worship in Shanghai, and all the religious celebrations are gone. After two days people go back to work. We wondered whether the Spring Festival, with its simplified celebration, had also lost importance as had the Buddhist festivals. As the pace of life quickens in a more secularized society during a transition from rural to urban lifestyle, is it possible that people become too much preoccupied with making a living to have time for these festivals, whether religious or not? In our question for the Spring Festival we used the same response options as in the Buddhist festival question.

The picture looks quite different, table 11.1.

The Spring Festival has retained much of its traditional importance. Age was a major relevant factor. Young people seemed to enjoy the Spring Festival more than the old: 43.3 percent of the former said the festival was "very important," compared to 18.2 percent of the latter. Only 6.7 percent of our young respondents considered the Spring Festival "not important at all," compared to 21.8 percent of the old

Table 11.1 Relative Importance of Spring Festival and Buddhist Festivals

	SPRING FESTIVAL	BUDDHIST FESTIVALS
Very important	30.3%	3.5%
Important	33.9%	5.1%
Somewhat important	21.9%	13.2%
Not important at all	13.9%	78.2%

who felt that way. People of lower education were more likely to consider the Spring Festival to be very important (35.4 percent) than those of higher education (27.4 percent). No differences were found between urban and rural areas. Our findings suggest that in contemporary China, the sharp decline of Buddhist festivals is not a reflection of a general trend of urban living, but more likely a result of the government's restrictive policies on religion. With its religious components deleted, the Spring Festival still occupies an important place in the life of Chinese, in urban and rural areas alike.

As religious activities resume under the open-door policy, there have been people, though a small minority, who have paid pilgrimage visits to Buddhist temples in the past few years. Before 1949, such pilgrimage journeys were enormously popular, attracting hundreds of thousands of people to various Buddhist shrines in the general Shanghai region. How do people in general look at pilgrimages today? Do they still believe that pilgrimage visits would bring them blessings and protection? We phrased this question: "Some people often take pilgrimage trips to temples. Do you think they would receive protection?" Again a very small number of our respondents (6.6 percent) believed that pilgrimage visits to temples could give them protection, and as many as 67.6 percent of the sample responded with a clear no. The remaining one out of four (25.9 percent) were not sure.

Age, gender, and Western cultural influence were three relevant factors. What surprised us was the difference between the old and the young in their perception of pilgrimage visits to temples. While only about two out of 100 old respondents (1.8 percent) believed in pilgrimages, more than one out of ten young people (11.7 percent) felt positively about it. As many as 84.9 percent of the old said no, compared to only 54.3 percent among the young. More young people (34.0 percent) than old (13.3 percent) felt unsure about this religious practice.

Men were more negative about pilgrimage activies than women. We found 72.2 percent of men versus 62.4 percent of women saying they did not believe in pilgrimage journeys. This is not surprising, because traditionally Chinese women took these religious activities more seriously.

Western cultural influence also made a difference, in a rather unexpected way. Those who were under high exposure to Western culture (12.0 percent saying yes) seemed to be more positive about this religious activity than the low-exposure respondents (5.1 percent). We found a slightly higher percentage of low-exposure people (72.7 percent) rejecting pilgrimage journeys than among the high-exposure respondents (64.0 percent). These findings were puzzling even though the differences were not large. We cannot attribute the differences to age, because the differences remained significant after age was held constant. We have suggested earlier that those under heavy Western cultural influence are more attracted to modern amenities and less inclined to identify themselves with the current social system. It is possible that the ideas of being blessed with prosperity and material possessions from a pilgrimage visit are more appealing to them as well.

Our survey results are consistent with the earlier findings of Parish and Whyte (1978) in their study of village and family life in South China. They found little change in feasting for traditional holidays, such as the Spring Festival, and life cycle events. Superstitions and rituals clearly declined in South Chinese villages.

Fate

Religious faith is related to one's belief in fate though academically religion and fatalism are two different concepts. Fatalism used to be strong among the Chinese people. When the hardship of life became almost unbearable, Chinese people generally blamed it on fate and accepted it as unalterable. Social injustice was thus not actively contested. We assumed that low religious faith would be matched by disbelief in fate. To test this assumption, we asked: "If someone does not do well all his life, do you think this is because

> he does not work hard enough,
> or he is treated unfairly by others,
> or it is his fate?"

Attributing failure to not working hard enough is a positive approach that acknowledges one's own responsibility. To say that unfair treatment causes failure is to lay the blame on social inequity. The third response is a recognition of fatalism.

Quite consistent with their answers to the question about religious faith, only a small number of respondents (13.5 percent) said it was due to fate. More than two-thirds of the respondents (71.8 percent) attributed one's failure in life to not working hard enough. Another 14.7 percent said that unfair treatment by others made the person fail. Our findings on fatalism versus one's own efforts are similar to the results of a recent survey conducted in China (Bai and Wang, 1987). The Chinese researchers printed a questionnaire in a 1985 issue of the popular magazine *China Youth* on attitudes toward life, work and competition. More than 7,600 readers returned the questionnaires (the percentage of returns was not reported), and a subsample of 3,340 was analyzed. The results showed only 11.6 percent agreed with the statement that "it is best to leave our life to fate," 88.4 percent disagreed. Conversely, 86.8 percent agreed that "as long as one tries hard, one can improve one's situation of life." Only 13.2 percent disagreed.

In our analysis we found three independent variables to be statistically significant: Western cultural influence, education, and age. The impact of Western cultural influence manifested itself again in a rather unexpected way. An overwhelming majority of low-influence people (80.3 percent) attributed one's failure in life to the reason that "he does not work hard enough," compared to only 58.8 percent among the high-influence respondents. Only one out of ten low-influence people (10.5 percent) said it was "because he is treated unfairly," compared to 21.6 percent of the high-influence respondents. It seems that those under heavy Western cultural influence are less favorably impressed with the degree of social equity in the Chinese system. What is most surprising was the finding that 19.6 percent of the high-influence people saying "it is his fate," twice as many as the 9.1 percent of the low-influence group. These findings, as well as the higher endorsement of pilgrimages, strongly suggest that those people under heavy Western cultural influence seem to be less willing to face the realities of life under the current system. They are more tempted to engage in wishful thinking, such as pinning their hope on pilgrimage journeys, and when their efforts fail, they tend to blame it on fate.

According to our data, the attitude toward fate was significantly related to one's education. It seems that low-education people, like those under low Western cultural influence, tended to believe that a person who failed in life should be held responsible for his own failure, while high-education people, like those under heavy Western cultural influence, would attribute failure also to other factors including one's fate. As many as 80.9 percent of the low-education people attributed one's failure to not working hard enough, compared to 63.2 percent among the high-education respondents. One out of five high-education respondents (20.8 percent) believed that if someone failed it was because of unfair treatment by others. This was a rather high percentage, twice as large as the 9.8 percent among the low-education people. Fate was mentioned by 9.3 percent of low-education respondents, but by as many as 16 percent of high-education people. It seems that higher education sensitizes people to the inequitable distributions of opportunities that exist in the present Chinese system. They are more keenly aware of unfair treatments. It also seems that in the current social context in China, where unfair treatment is probably seen by those of higher education as not readily remediable, they adopt an escapist tendency and attribute failure to fate.

Surprisingly, we found far more young respondents (20.3 percent) saying "it is his fate" than old respondents (6.0 percent). Four out of five old people (81.5 percent) attributed failure to not working hard enough, compared to 67.9 percent among the young. Unfair treatment was mentioned more by the middle-aged (17.2 percent) than by either the young (11.8 percent) or the old (12.6 percent). This is one of the few rare occasions where a slight curvilinear trend was found in the data. It is possible that old respondents have been more heavily exposed to revolutionary rhetoric and therefore attach less credence to fate. Unfair treatment strikes the middle-aged people more, we think, possibly because the young are barely experiencing it and do not feel it intensely, while the old are about ready to retire.

In order to further test how fate is perceived by our subjects, we designed a related, but somewhat different question: "If your whole family works very hard on a job, but it fails, how do you feel?"

Almost nobody (1.9 percent) attributed it to fate, and the number of those who "feel very bad, will not do it again" (6.4 percent) was also very low. Most of our respondents were divided between "feeling very bad, but will try again if the opportunity arises" (38.3 percent) and "not feeling bad, will try again if the opportunity arises" (53.3 percent). On the whole our respondents had a highly positive attitude toward the tough challenges of life. In a concrete situation when the respondents' families were involved, as our data showed, even fewer people turned to fate as a way out.

Exposure to official media news was the only relevant factor. More respondents of the high news exposure group (60.4 percent) said they did "not feel bad and will try again" than those of the low-exposure group (49.0 percent). In the low-exposure group, 3.2 percent atttributed their families' failure to fate, while in the high exposure group nobody did so. This was one of the rare zero percentages we found in our data. Also, more people in the low-exposure group (7.3 percent) said they felt bad and would not try again than people in the high-exposure group (3.3 percent). Although the differences were not big, the trend was interesting. Our findings seem to suggest the possibility that exposure to media news increases one's ability to handle distress and face reality in a positive way. This hypothesis requires further testing.

Ancestor Worship

The way Chinese treated their ancestors comprised an important part of their belief system. Ancestor worship used to be practiced by all Chinese families before the 1949 revolution, not only during the New Year celebration but also on Tombs Day [*qingming*] in the spring, Ghost Festival in the autumn, and at the annual observance of deceased parents and grandparents. Ancestor worship existed even before the time of Confucius. Worshipping ancestors was a practice that reinforced the Confucian ideology of the young showing respect for the old. It served as a cognitive and ritualistic foundation of family cohesion. Chinese people believed that ancestor worship could bring protection to the family. By the same token, protecting the good name of the ancestors was a very important consideration in one's social behavior.

In order to test the strength of belief in ancestor worship, we first asked a relatively concrete question: "Do you believe that the locations of your ancestors' tombs affect the well-being of your family?" This was a test of the traditional belief of geomancy as related to ancestor worship. Chinese formerly believed that the locations of their ancestors' tombs and acquisition of merit through good deeds were two determinant factors of a family's fortune. We found only a small number of respondents (7.2 percent) who believed that the locations of their ancestors' tombs would affect the well-being of their family. An overwhelming majority (78.1 percent) said they did not believe and another 14.6 percent were not sure.

Age and education were two relevant factors. What came as a surprise was the discovery that more old people (87.8 percent) than young respondents (71.8 percent) said they did not believe. About one out of five young subjects (20.1 percent) were not sure about it, compared to 7.5 percent of the old. Is it possible that the young were more conservative than the old? We don't think so. Rather we think that the old identified with the establishment more than the young. We have discussed this point in chapter 10 and will return to it in our concluding chapter.

As one can understand, more people with high education (81.5 percent) than respondents with low-education (77.6 percent) said they did not believe in geomancy. The difference was not as large as the one we found with age.

Then we asked a more general question: "How do you think you should treat your ancestors?" Consistent with their responses to the previous question, very few people (3.5 percent) said they should burn incense and worship their ancestors in the traditional way, which Chinese people had been doing for centuries. About one out of four respondents (24.0 percent) would choose to visit and sweep tombs, with more urbanites (30.5 percent) and townspeople (22.0 percent) wanting to do so than their rural counterparts (9.7 percent). In reality, tombs no longer exist in most places in China. What the respondents were referring to was to visit the mortuaries where the ashes of their parents were kept, although out of habit the term "visit and sweep tombs" was still used by most people. A high 43.8 percent endorsed the idea of having a memorial ceremony within the family. In the Shanghai area, this usually means having a small family dinner with close relatives on the birthday of a deceased parent. It has nothing to do with the family's ancestors, and no ceremonies are performed. The sharp decline of ancestor worship in East China may come as a surprise. However, Parish and Whyte (1978) also found clear indications of less domestic ancestor worship in villages in South China. In a remote village in North China, Cohen (1990) was told that ancestor worship was still in practice, though limited to the lunar New Year and among the very rich who owned a family temple [*jiamiao*], where the annual ritual took place. In the particular village which Cohen studied, no such family temples were represented.

In our survey in East China, rural villagers favored family memorial dinners the most (67.4 percent), the townspeople (46.4 percent) preferred them less, and the Shanghai urbanites (33.3 percent) still less. What is highly significant is the finding that as many as one-third of the Shanghai residents (33.4 percent) said nothing needed to be done about ancestors at all. The corresponding percentages espousing no observance at all were lower in Qingpu (28.6 percent) and in rural villages (17.5 percent), but still these figures came as a bit of a surprise in view of the enormous importance of ancestors in traditional Chinese society.

Besides areas of residence, we found age and education to be two other relevant factors. Almost none of the old (0.8 percent) said they should burn incense and worship their ancestors in the traditional way, compared to 6.5 percent of the young who would do so. As many as 28.7 percent of the old and 18.2 percent of the young were for "visiting and sweeping tombs." As for the "memorial dinner in family," we saw more young respondents (47.8 percent) endorsing it than the old (37.4 percent). More old people (33.1 percent) than the young (27.5 percent) said nothing was required.

Over half of the low-education subjects (57.7 percent) were for family memorial dinners, compared to 35.5 percent among the high-education people. We found more high-education respondents (36.9 percent) than low-education people (20.4 percent) saying that ancestors needed no attention.

Discussion

Owing to the deep-rooted influence of Confucianism, religion never developed in China as fully as in such countries as India and Iran. In fact, China has never been a highly religious society if religion is defined as an established system of monotheistic beliefs that permit no rival interpretations of the ultimate truth. Even in the old days, there were not many hard-core believers in such established major religions as Buddhism and Taoism. And there were no religious wars in China's long history. However, quasi-religious, supernatural or superstitious activities such as ancestor worship and a variety of individual deity worship were widespread among the populace in prerevolution China.

Soon after they won the revolution in 1949, the Chinese leaders were determined to wage two protracted wars: an economic war against poverty and backwardness and an ideological war to consolidate the proletarian dictatorship. Religion soon found itself caught up in the ideological war. Believing Marx's motto that religion is the opiate of the masses, the Chinese leaders were initially uneasy about all religious activities. When they found that Catholic churches and Buddhist and Taoist temples could be used to harbor "imperialist spies" or "counterrevolutionary elements," they became very distrustful of the influence that religions could have in a socialist country, and they began to design restrictive policies to put religious activities under the tight control of the state. The government particularly wanted to prevent the younger generation from becoming religious converts, although it still allowed some limited religious functions by those old-timers who were perceived to be patriotic and supportive of the Chinese Communist Party. Since this group often involved well-known national religious figures and personalities in sensitive minority regions such as Tibet, protection of such highly visible people was useful propaganda. At the grass-roots level, however, the government's policies were much tougher. Particularly after 1958, the year of communization of the rural areas, religious activities, together with what was left of the traditional rural economic system, were nearly wiped out. During the Cultural Revolution, all churches, temples, and mosques were forced to close down and religious activities became punishable.

The Chinese government started to loosen its control over religious life when it decided to open China to the outside world. Since the beginning of the 1980s, we have seen a marginal revival of the four major religions in China: Buddhism, Taoism, Islam, and Christianity. It should be remembered, however, that the state still controls and limits religious activities to prevent violation of the Four Cardinal Principles: the principle of the leadership of the Chinese Communist Party, the principle of socialism, the principle of Marxism, and the principle of proletarian dictatorship. Although this relaxation of religious prohibitions seems illogical in the Marxist context, it is clear the state will remain in strict control of all activities related to worship.

Furthermore, it should be noted that the social structural foundation of such traditional religions as Buddhism and Taoism has been destroyed in the last forty years. Both Buddhism and Taoism had the support of the ruling class. Temples were maintained largely through the land they acquired from local communities, usually free of cost, as well as through donations from the wealthy. It was the landlords and wealthy merchants who provided funds for organizing the major annual religious festivals. Buddhist monks and Taoist priests performed vital rituals during funerals and were treated with respect even by civil officials. Some of them moved in upper class circles. Even at times of war, Buddhist and Taoist temples were usually spared. All these forms of structural support have vanished. Former landlords and wealthy merchants have been expropriated. Over the years they themselves had been subject to numerous persecutions and purges; their children were classified as social outcasts. Even though temples are allowed to reopen, their former lands now belong to the state. Monks and priests have lost their social position.

Because of a mounting political pressure and loss of social structural support, religions do not play much of a role in Chinese life any more. The majority of Chinese do not have any religious belief. The Chinese are now strictly secular, living in a world of spiritual void. Buddhism has lost its traditional significance. A major surprise was the nearly total disappearance of ancestor worship from the life of the Chinese people. Ancestor worship as a practice predates Confucius. The noted anthropologist Francis Hsu (1949) considers ancestor worship to be the cornerstone of traditional Chinese culture. In prerevolution China before 1949, even some Christian families still practiced ancestor worship on New Year's eve, and the church did not consider it necessary to intervene. Now not only has ancestor worship been discontinued as a practice, but even the concept of ancestors does not seem to exist any more. Although our data were based on a survey conducted in Shanghai and its surrounding villages, our inquiries with a number of people from various other parts in China led us to believe that the disappearance of ancestor worship was a widespread phenomenon. The findings of Parish and Whyte in rural Southern China in the 1970s pointed to the same direction. It is indeed extraordinary that a folk practice as deeply rooted as ancestor worship, which formed the core of Chinese culture for thousands of years, could be largely eliminated within two generations.

Our findings also show that fatalism no longer dominates the psychology of the Chinese. This too is a significant change accomplished over the past forty years. Fatalism does not have much influence even on people with minimum education. This is an indication of successful government education on the one hand, and general social progress on the other. Chairman Mao's teachings on self-reliance, on how the human will can overcome the obstacles of heaven, and how a "foolish old man" determined to move a mountain, have subtly influenced the minds of the Chinese people. The dismantling of old structural barriers in traditional Chinese society, as they existed in the land-tenure system, has given Chinese people more direct access to some of their basic material resources, possibly contributing to a general feeling of greater self-confidence and conversely a decline in fatalism.

The ideological indoctrination in the last few decades clearly has had a stronger effect on the old than on the young. Our data reveal, consistently, that the old identified themselves with the government's stand on religious and quasi-religious matters more closely than the young. The older people also believed less in fatalism. It may be noted that it was not the young people, who were not yet born, but the older people, who took part in the dislodging of the traditional land-tenure system that redistributed arable land to the peasants. It was the older people who lived through the many ideological communication campaigns, including those staged during the Cultural Revolution, which attacked traditional values and religious practices. In order to show these developments clearly, we present the comparisons in table 11.2.

This consistent pattern of change in beliefs appears across our survey data on religion. The overall trend is clear: Religion has lost its importance in contemporary China. But relatively speaking, the younger people are consistently a little more religious, or rather, a little less nonreligious, than their older counterparts. It is not really that the

Table 11.2 Religious Beliefs of Old versus Young Chinese

ITEMS	OLD	YOUNG
Buddhist festivals		
not important at all	85.5%	71.0%
Pilgrimages give protection		
believe	1.8%	11.7%
not believe	84.9%	54.3%
Failure in life due to fate		
believe	6.0%	20.3%
Ancestor tomb locations		
affect family fortune		
not believe	87.8%	71.8%
Worship ancestors	0.8%	6.5%

young are more conservative than the old, and the old more radical than the young. It is, rather, that the older people tend to associate themselves with government positions more closely than the younger people do. This is, we believe, largely due to the impact of the government propaganda programs, to which the older people have been exposed far more strongly. As far as the decline of fatalism is concerned, we think it is also due to the personal experiences of the older people in the early years of structural change shortly after the founding of the People's Republic. They saw how the landlord class, an age-old structure of wealth and authority in the rural countryside, could be toppled when the peasants stood up as a united force with the backing of the Party.

    The differences between the age groups raise an important question. As the Chinese government continues to ease its control over religious activities, and as the older generation passes away, is it possible that some of the traditional religions such as Buddhism may slowly return, again to fill the spiritual void during a time of political disorder and social chaos, as they once did in the past? Looking at the hundreds and sometimes even thousands of people milling around Buddhist temples during major festivals in Shanghai, one is tempted to draw a parallelism between the present conditions and those during the dark days of the Jin Dynasty. But this parallelism, we think, is more superficial than real. If all that the temples can offer is a promise of blessings of a material nature in return for one's worship, then religion is no more than a superstition. Buddhism and for that matter other religions will grow and flourish only if they endow the faithful with a spiritual vision.

During the Jin Dynasty, Buddhism took root in Chinese soil by building upon the foundation of Confucianism. Confucius taught generosity and virtue. Buddha taught mercy. Confucius preached harmony as a way of life. Buddha preached peace of mind. Confucius taught the way of the Golden Mean. Buddha taught moderation. Both Confucius and Buddha exalted the attainment of salvation, although by different means. For Confucius, salvation was to be achieved in a perfect universe in this world, through cultivation of the self. For Buddha, salvation came in the next world, through meditation and denial of the self. When a perfect universe in this world became clearly beyond reach in those dark days of the Jin Dynasty, Chinese people chose salvation in the next world. Buddhism found a readily receptive multitude. But in China today, the foundation of Confucianism has been seriously damaged and may no longer exist. The traditional value of generosity and virtue is no longer upheld. Harmony is no longer considered precious. The way of the Golden Mean has been unequivocally rejected. Struggle and contention are the order of the day. Instead of salvation, the ultimate goal is supposed to be a socialist utopia, to be achieved through the means of a proletarian dictatorship. To what extent this ideal is shared among the people of China is difficult to say. Because the cultural milieu today is so entirely different from that of the Jin Dynasty, one doubts very much whether Buddhism, or any other religion, would be able to fill the spiritual void of Chinese people as it once did in the past.

Part III

Conclusion

Chapter 12

Whither Chinese Culture

We have collected concrete data on the current status of social relations, material relations, and attitudes, values and beliefs (figure 1.1) in Chinese society. From our survey findings emerges the outline of a contemporary Chinese culture. Although there remains some limited continuity with the past, primarily in family relations, the lifestyle and values in post-Mao China today demonstrate a radical departure from the traditional Chinese culture as we have known it.

This chapter is organized into three sections. In section one, we discuss our major findings under eight characteristics of contemporary Chinese culture: (1) family stability, (2) work ethic, (3) materialism, (4) social relations, (5) submission to authority, (6) moderation and harmony, (7) belief system, (8) adventurism and risk taking. Each characteristic is reviewed in the light of concrete findings from a variety of responses that offer a high degree of consistency. We then discuss the evolving social processes by which a cultural characteristic either maintains its continuity with the past or changes from its traditional dimension into its current new manifestation. These processes reflect the changes in constraints and incentives in Chinese society in the last forty years, some structural, others ideological. The significance of continuity and change will be considered.

If traditional Chinese culture can be likened to another Great Wall, comparable to the mammoth stone structure that has guarded China's huge territories for ages against invading horsemen from the North, then the impression gained from our research suggests that this cultural Great Wall is crumbling. It seems to lie in ruins, waiting for a modern miracle to resurrect it and imbue new life to the Chinese society it has traditionally defended. We offer this impression as a hypothesis.

In section two, we review our findings from the perspective of five major factors that are clearly related to processes of cultural change in China. These are: age, Western cultural influence, education, urbanization, and use of news information in mass media, in an approximately descending order of relative weight. These relevant factors have been identified in the various specific chapters. Reviewing them here together gives us a holistic picture of the processes of change up to the present and provides a solid data base for projecting the future of contemporary Chinese culture.

In section three we step back to take an overall view of what we have learned from this comprehensive research project. Our discussion is informed by a historical perspective that reviews not only what has happened in China in the last forty years under socialism, but also China's agonizing awakening since the mid-19th century from a millennium of self-imposed confinement and painful search for a new cultural identity. If the cultural Great Wall now lies in ruins, we shall consider a few scenarios about its future resurrection or eventual disintegration.

I. Major Characteristics of New Chinese Culture

Family Ties Remain Stable

We have heard numerous stories of how the Cultural Revolution set members of the same family against each other in caustic ideological confrontation and merciless class struggle. Children denounced their parents. Husbands and wives accused and attacked each other at mass struggle rallies. We have no doubt that most of these stories were true. And it is inconceivable that such painful experiences did not impair close and warm family relations for those directly involved. Yet our findings suggest that the damage inflicted by the Cultural Revolution on the Chinese family seems to be limited and most probably short-lived.

The traditionally stable Chinese family seems to have emerged from the decades of turmoil with its basic functions more or less intact, even though its structure has been radically altered. The kinship structure, upon which the traditional Chinese family was anchored, has been formally disbanded if not totally destroyed. The landed gentry was a mainstay of the Chinese kinship structure. It had the economic resources, including land, to back up its position of authority within the kinship network. When the landlords were purged and their land holdings confiscated during the Land Reform movement in the early 1950s, the formal parameters of the kinship structure collapsed. The attack on ancestor worship, which was initially discouraged and then totally banned during the Cultural Revolution, further dealt a blow to the spiritual foundation of the kinship structure.

The restoration of individual family farming following the abolishment of the People's Communes in 1982 has raised an interesting question. Rural families now have land, but their land holdings are becoming smaller as each married son takes a piece of the family land under the custom of *fen jia*, or "divide the family." Credit for production expenses is becoming scarce and hard to get. Under those circumstances, would some individual families choose to return to the traditional extended family as a means of consolidating their economic resources? In their research in the hinterlands in Yunnan in Southwestern China, Unger and Xiong (1990) looked into this question but did not find a single instance of extended family in any of the villages they visited. It seems that once a social structural component like the extended family is destroyed, it will be difficult for it to come back and rebuild its economic foundation.

However, kinship as a concept is by no means extinct in China, even though its reaches are very much curtailed. In the villages, people having the same surname and sharing a common lineage still treat each other with a touch of special consideration, limited within the constraints of political and economic forces. Cohen (1990) has documented how people in a remote village in North China rely on their lineage organizations as social contexts for feasting and visiting during the lunar New Year and other rural festivals. In urban centers such as Shanghai, close relatives still form a small circle of their own. They help each other out whenever possible, that is, within the controls of a political environment that are more restrictive in urban areas than in the villages. But this circle no longer includes the many members of the extended family, which for all practical purposes does not exist in Shanghai any more.

The Chinese family today consists of a married couple and their children, usually no more than two. Partly because of the overly crowded housing situation, this nuclear family is often joined under the same roof by the parents of either the husband or the wife, and connected to nuclear families of other siblings through visits within the same locality. This nuclear family, rather than the extended family of the past, is the building block of contemporary Chinese society. It is this nuclear family, as our research findings show, that provides a secure basis of societal stability. A major function is socialization of the young. Spanking, a traditional form of disciplinary action, is still widely practiced. As we recall, only about 7 percent of our respondents said children should not be spanked at all. On the other hand, one out of five respondents felt it would be appropriate to spank their children anywhere from 13 up to 18 years of age. But spanking in China is not done without love and care. An overwhelming majority of our respondents (81 percent) said their parents either gave them appropriate suggestions or expressed concerns without interfering. If their own teenaged children should behave badly, for example, by smoking or drinking, most parents would only advise them against it while others would not hesitate to resort to spanking if advice alone was not enough. Only 5 percent would follow the permissive approach of letting their children correct themselves.

One indication of change is what we would characterize as a growing sign of independence on the part of children. Excluding those respondents who had no children or whose children were too small, we found two out of three respondents said their children talked back either under most circumstances, or sometimes, when they were asked to do something. This is very different from the past, when hardly any children would dare to talk back to their parents. This new independence is reflected in mate selection. While most marriages were arranged in the past, now about nine out of ten respondents would leave it to their children to find their own mates. This new responsibility on the part of the children is not to be abused. More than 70 percent of the respondents would not permit their daughters to carry on with several boyfriends. Sons were treated just as strictly as daughters. Sex mores were quite rigid. Some 86 percent would not permit a "living together" arrangement even if the young couple are in love and intend to get married.

The stability of the Chinese family and the emotional support among family members are indicated by both husband–wife relations and parents–children relations that appear to be very close. Divorces are still rare in China, though increasing in recent years. Even if a couple have great difficulty getting along, a majority in our sample would want to keep the broken marriage together for the sake of children, rather than have a divorce. The traditional concept of filial devotion, a cornerstone of Chinese family stability, is clearly present. As we recall, of the eighteen traditional values, the concept of "benevolent father and filial son" was among the few that were still highly regarded. The endorsement of this traditional value is reflected in concrete terms in several ways. Nearly 80 percent said grown-up children should physically look after their aging parents. If parents run into financial difficulty, about the same percentage said they should ask their children for help. Of those respondents whose parents were still living, two out of three were living with their parents. This is probably not entirely due to the congested housing situation in big cities like Shanghai, but reflects a desire for family togetherness because among those not living with their parents, some 45 percent were visiting their parents within the last two or three days. In Shanghai and elsewhere, we know that when young people are ready to get married, it is their parents who take out their lifetime savings to pay for the dowry and the banquets. In more than 60 percent of the families, all members gathered together everyday other than during meal time. They watched television and chatted.

The Chinese family of the past had its roots partly in the kinship structure and partly in the nuclear locus of spouses and children. The disbanding of the kinship network has apparently left no crippling impact on the nuclear family, which used to be a small unit within the kinship boundary. A number of factors appear to have contributed to the survival of the Chinese family. First and foremost, we think, is its resilient strength developed through age-old historical traditions. The family has been the single most important cornerstone of Chinese society. Family life is the core of Chinese life. The attachment between parents and children has proved to be too deeply rooted to be destroyed by the arbitrary forces of any state, even as they were powerfully amassed during those chaotic early years of the Cultural Revolution. The survival of the Chinese family, however, does not depend on its traditional cultural fortitude alone. Other core values of traditional Chinese culture do not seem to have survived, as we shall discuss later. In addition to the traditional roots of the Chinese family, we see four other relevant factors: political, economic, social, and psychological. Politically, we think the Party leadership recognized the unpredictable but potentially grave perils if the Chinese family should be destroyed. Even though during the height of the Cultural Revolution there were many cases when children were incited to accuse and denounce their parents who were branded as counter-revolutionaries, on the whole the Party has recognized the importance of the family as a building block of Chinese society. The position of parents within the nuclear family in general has rarely been under attack. Even the denunciation of parents by young ideologues proved to be a transient phenomenon.

What happened during the brief initial period of the People's Commune movement in the fall of 1958 came closest to doing away with China's family institution. Small children were put in nurseries. Older children were assigned to brigades of Little Red Soldiers. All able-bodied adults were mobilized to join the communes and work in production teams. They were encouraged to dismantle their kitchens and contribute their cooking utensils to the communes. Family members, young and old, had their meals in commune mess halls. When one of the authors paid a visit to one of the villages in Qingpu in 1987 to make preparations for the fieldwork, he passed a deserted ramshackle building. Painted on its broken door were the fading characters of "People's Commune Mess Hall." Upon inquiry, he was told that this was where people of that village went for their meals during the first few months of the commune movement. That commune experiment proved to be a colossal human disaster. Within a matter of three months, the Party had to retreat from its utopian ideals of communal life and restored the Chinese family to its time-honored functions. Since then the Party leadership has been conscious of the importance of the family, and has been careful not to destroy it.

Economically, the family has been a basic production unit throughout Chinese history. Even during the difficult years of the People's Communes, from 1958 when the communes were first established until early 1982 when they were finally abolished, rural Chinese worked in their communes and received work points, but parents and adult children lived together and shared their meager income from the communes. Family members labored on their own tiny private plots to grow vegetables and raise poultry for a little extra income. After the communes were abolished, the land was leased back to the peasants. Until the family land is divided among the married sons, members of the same family have had to work together to survive and prosper. Quite often not only immediate family members but also close relatives help each other out in order to make effective use of their limited resources.

Socially, the Chinese policy that restricts physical mobility tends to keep family members in one place. An overwhelming majority of Chinese spend their entire lives in the same general area where they were born. People born in Shanghai live their entire lives in Shanghai. People born in Qingpu stay in Qingpu. Members of the same family thus stay geographically together. A severe shortage of housing makes it a general practice for adult children to live with their parents until they get married. Even after marriage, many young couples have had to share a partitioned corner in their parents' small living quarters of one or two rooms until they can get their own housing. One family in Shanghai known to one of the authors lived in a one-room unit with three sons. Every time a son got married, a corner was partitioned off until there was virtually no space left for the parents themselves. The family had no choice but to live together.

The close family ties reflect a latent psychological motive. After years of class struggle and mass campaigns, Chinese people are naturally cautious in dealing with each other. The only people they trust best are members of their own immediate family. In one sense, the nuclear family today may have assumed even greater importance than before. Since there is little kinship support to count on any more, and since friends and co-workers are to be treated with caution, one can only turn to one's nuclear family and a few close relatives for psychological support. The family has become the last sanctuary in a life of hidden turbulences and dark uncertainties. It is hardly surprising that a warm and close family is considered the uppermost goal in life. Small and crowded as it may be, to most Chinese their home is where they can turn for love and consolation. Their family is where their psychological need of nurture and affiliation is fulfilled.

The importance of family stability in a society that has experienced some of the most traumatic convulsions in human history can hardly be overrated. The family seems to be among the few remaining buttresses that are keeping the Chinese culture from a total collapse. If China's cultural Great Wall should be rebuilt in the foreseeable future, the inner strength of reconstruction could possibly spring from the force of close family ties. That possibility will become a reality only if the broader social environment begins to reinforce the family-based values in social relations at large. It does not seem likely at the present moment. We will return to this point later.

Latent Work Ethic

Traditionally Chinese people were known for their diligence and perseverance. Living in a generally inhospitable environment of limited resources, and working with mostly simple technologies, Chinese people had to work hard just to survive. Yet there was apparently something in the collective system of Chinese communism that tended to go against the traditional hard working spirit. Even in the early days of the People's Commune movement, when collective enthusiasm and euphemism seemed to run high, Chinese peasants were reacting with a subtle form of work stoppage. A popular folk song at that time went like this:

> Commune work, drag your feet,
> When noontime comes, let's go and eat.

The Party leadership later tried to maintain work incentives by devising a system of work points and by allowing the commune members small private plots. The modified policy succeeded to a point. But it is common knowledge that throughout the years when the commune system was maintained, agricultural productivity was below par. This was the main reason why the communes were abolished in 1982. In urban areas, the same slow work pace prevailed in factories and government offices. Production campaigns and group competitions were periodically launched to stimulate work output. Model workers were praised in big character posters and paraded in public to inject some symbolic incentive into the economic system. But the impact was generally short-lived. Once a production campaign was declared a success and concluded, workers reverted to the same slow pace.

Has the traditional hard working spirit died among the Chinese? Our research findings say no. At the attitudinal level, the latent work ethic remains strong. Most of our respondents (83 percent) had a positive attitude toward work, saying they would try to do more than others. An overwhelming majority (91 percent) would prefer a workmate to be someone with high work ability even though not a close friend, and some 78 percent would prefer someone who works hard even though he may not have a sense of humor. When asked to assess the meaning of life, an equally large majority (88 percent) said people should treasure their time and work as hard as possible, rather than suggest that "life is short, enjoy it while you can." Most people would refuse to stop their work to accept an invitation from a friend for a good time. They wanted rigorous work evaluation. When asked what they considered to be the most important criterion for promotion, an overwhelming majority (88 percent) listed "diligent, hardworking" as the top consideration. Of the eighteen traditional values, "diligence and frugality" was one of the three that received a strong endorsement.

The findings are consistent and unmistakable. Despite a practice of eating from the same big pot for some thirty years, the Chinese attitudes toward hard work seem to persist. However, there is definitely a large gap between their latent attitudes and their overt behavior. We think the low work morale, widespread absenteeism in factories, and other forms of chronic organizational malaise, which many observers have noted, have been largely caused by the collective reward system, which offers little incentive for performing a job well. Once that system is modified, the traditional Chinese work ethic bounces back almost immediately. In the vast rural countryside, now that the communes are abolished, Chinese peasants have become the hardest working people one can find anywhere. In one village in Qingpu County, one of the authors was told the story of a young man who was working so hard in his own pig farm, from daybreak till late at night everyday, that he had totally neglected his wife, who wanted a divorce. Village officials were able to intervene and save their marriage.

The latent work ethic is a highly positive feature in contemporary Chinese culture. In fact, it bears a strong continuity with the past, only temporarily interrupted by the collective reward system enforced under the leftist policy of Chairman Mao. Under the current economic reform, China has now been able to work out an effective reward system for its vast rural regions. Agricultural productivity has improved significantly. China is still experimenting with the far more complicated situation in urban areas. If the urban economic reform does not succeed, we think the blame should be laid on the system itself, not on the flagging work ethic of the Chinese people.

Rising Materialism

Chinese people were traditionally known for their willingness to accept a sparse existence with few material comforts. Peasants toiled ceaselessly for a whole year, just to savor the joy of family reunion and celebration for a few brief days during the lunar New Year. After the gongs and fireworks subsided, they returned to their fields to face another year of uncertainty. This life of hardship was made tolerable by the Chinese cultural value that accepted poverty as a way of achieving a peace of mind. To the large peasant population, a life of blissful happiness meant a cow, a small piece of land, and a wife in a warm bed. Century after century, a delicate balance was thus maintained between curtailed material expectations and the harsh realities of life.

Poverty as a value was vigorously upheld by the Party leadership under Mao, especially during the years of rigid collectivism from 1958 to 1976. Accepting poverty was praised as a virtue. Aspiring to get rich was condemned as an unforgivable sin. Cadres in rural areas must be recruited from the ranks of former poor and lower-middle peasants. Children from those families would be given preferential consideration for college admission. Those who belonged to the former class of rich peasants were classified as untouchables, along with former landlords, rightists, and counter-revolutionaries.

Under the economic reform policy, the prevailing wind changed its direction. To be rich was not only acceptable, but was actually encouraged and even praised. Recognizing the difficulty of turning a poor country into a land of plentitude overnight, the Chinese government adopted a policy that would allow some areas to become rich first. Peasants who made an initial quick success were publicized as new "ten thousand yuan" families, because they earned more than ten thousand yuan a year. Suddenly, before the government realized what was happening, the entire country seemed to be preoccupied with ideas of how to strike it rich. A predominant mood, known as *"xiang qian kan,"* fascinated everybody. This was a pun which could mean either "looking forward," or "looking only at money." The praise of poverty vanished without a trace along with the Gang of Four.

Our survey findings confirmed this prevailing mood. When asked what factors influence social relations today, many (25 percent) answered frankly: money. High income was the topmost criterion (36 percent) if people could change their jobs. For ideal jobs, managerial positions received the most enthusiastic endorsement (26 percent). A manager's job means both money and status. Teachers, who used to be highly respected, were now among the least desirable, along with Party cadres, who ranked close to the bottom. A popular saying recently circulating in Shanghai, known as "Three Better," suggests how exceedingly important money can be among some young people in that metropolitan city. With the open door policy, many Americans are visiting Shanghai, including some Chinese Americans. Some have returned to the United States with their newlywed young Chinese wives, and in a few cases, newlywed young husbands. "Three Better" summarizes three principles by which some young Chinese in Shanghai select their prospective American spouses: Money, the more the better; age, the older the better; health, the poorer the better.

The preoccupation with money, in a society where few institutionalized channels exist for orderly profit seeking, has led to a social phenomenon known as "going through the back door." This practice of using personal connections to get something done in a hurry has always existed in Chinese society, but it has now reached almost epidemic proportions. When demands run high and yet opportunities and resources are severely limited, people have no scruples about pursuing every possible means in order to get what they want. Our research findings confirmed this tendency. When facing a problem, most people (72 percent) would tap their connections before following the slower normal channels.

If the traditional concept accepting poverty as a way of achieving tranquility was ever a cultural suppressant of motivation for a better livelihood, there is no doubt that this age-old ideological suppressant has finally been removed. More likely the old concept was simply a way by which Chinese people rationalized what they considered to be unchangeable. Living under rigid structural constraints, under which upward mobility was not available except for a very few, a life of misery became tolerable and even acceptable for the majority of people because it promised a peace of mind. For the first time in Chinese history, two of the major structural constraints were lifted when the Party leadership eliminated from the traditional class structure the landed gentry and urban business entrepreneurs in the 1950s. The initial response of peasants and urban workers was enthusiastic. At long last

Chinese people dared to hope for a better life, which they were told would be within reach under socialism. This enthusiasm, however, proved to be short-lived. Within a few years, a series of leftist policies guided by an unrealistic quest for a socialist utopia, culminating in the Great Leap Forward, dampened the initial high spirit.

What the Party hierarchy under Mao's leadership did was to impose a new set of structural constraints which were even more suffocating than the old. Within the collective framework, which dominated nearly all productive activities, there was no room for incentive. Outside the collective framework, any efforts by peasants to cultivate productivity from their small private plots were condemned as the "tails of capitalism," which had to be cut immediately. In villages in Qingpu County, where we did our fieldwork, a family of two was allowed to raise only one chicken. This quota was raised to two chickens for a family of three, and three chickens for a family of five. In one production team, every year following the national day of October 1 the team leader went around at night, a flashlight in hand, to search for extra chickens. Any chickens found that exceeded the quotas were seized and killed. One peasant grew chives on his private plot. It was discovered and nearly one thousand pounds of chives were destroyed. Living under that system in those days, Chinese people had no alternative but to accept poverty again, except that poverty was seen not as a way of achieving a peace of mind, but as a physical demonstration of a new revolutionary spirit. For those who knew how to manipulate the new political environment, an outward demonstration of poverty could even become a means of upward mobility.

In this historical context, the new wave of rising materialism is completely understandable. When the Party leadership in the post-Mao era declared its drive toward the Four Modernizations and encouraged Chinese people to get rich, the mass of people took it seriously. Many people, more in rural areas than in urban center, found ingenious ways of using their limited resources to increase their earnings. In this sense, the rising materialism should be seen in a positive light. As one Chinese scholar noted, one of China's problems in the past was its exceedingly low level of material aspirations. If so, that problem no longer exists. It is now possible for the Chinese people to release their long suppressed energies for achieving a level of material life which they are entitled to. The many seemingly unhealthy symptoms of materialism that we now observe, such as the prevailing mood of "xiang qian kan," the practice of "going through the back door," and even the diabolical "Three Better" attitude noted among young people in Shanghai, we believe, are mostly transient phenomena of dislocations between the rising aspirations of the people and the rigid, nonresponsive constraints of the current Chinese bureaucracy. Why would any fair-minded young maiden want to follow the principle of "Three Better" if she could marry a young Chinese who cares about her and if she could live a modestly sufficient material life in her own homeland? When these constraints are removed and replaced with appropriate structural incentives, optimistically in the next fifteen or twenty years, those unhealthy symptoms will gradually diminish.

Social Relations Becoming Superficial

The social world in traditional China was partitioned largely into two spheres: an inner circle of family members and close relatives within the kinship network, and an outer circle of friends, neighbors, and other acquaintances. Both circles were important. In fact, there was a traditional saying that "at home, one relied on one's parents; away from home, one relied on one's friends." Chinese people tended to cast social relations in the outer circle in simulated kinship terms. Friends addressed each other as "brothers." Parents of friends and acquaintances were addressed as "uncles" and "aunts." Relations in both circles were characterized by a warm reciprocity and mutual trust until someone proved he was unworthy, usually because he did something outrageously indecent. Even then, the person would generally be given a chance to atone for his misbehavior and later be welcomed back.

In a sense, friends are still important in China today. If a friend asked for help to get something done, about two-thirds of our respondents (64 percent) would do it even though they would incur some inconvenience. If the request came from a good friend, an overwhelming majority (90 percent) would offer assistance even if they were tired at day's end. But friends are less important than relatives. For the same request that would entail some inconvenience, 70 percent would help if the request was made by a relative. If a person needed money, the first place to solicit help outside the immediate family would be relatives (41 percent), followed by friends (31 percent), and finally the work unit (15 percent).

While we have no concrete data from the past for comparison, results from a parallel survey conducted in Korea (KBS, 1989) lead us to believe that friendship is losing some of its importance in China today.[1] When asked to indicate what they considered to be their important goals in life, only 19 percent of our Chinese respondents mentioned true friendship. In responding to the identical question, 34 percent of a Korean sample chose true friendship as one of their important goals in life. This wide margin of difference takes on greater significance when seen in the perspective of the equally important goal of family warmth in the two cultural groups. A warm and close family was considered to be the most important goal by both the Chinese (80 percent) and the Koreans (80 percent).

Neighbors used to be very important for Chinese. Close and harmonious relations with neighbors were highly valued. One of the coauthors grew up in Shanghai before 1949, and he remembered the very close relations his family had with people who lived next door in a small alley. They visited with each other nearly everyday. The situation is quite different now. Nearly half of our respondents said they hardly ever talked to their neighbors. Only about one out of four said they chatted with their neighbors nearly everyday. People in metropolitan Shanghai kept an even greater distance from their neighbors. As many as 56 percent in Shanghai versus 28 percent in the villages said they hardly ever talked to their neighbors. The distant social relations are indicated by the way Chinese approach people they meet for the first time. An overwhelming majority (84 percent) said they would not trust that person until they got to know him better. The trend seems fairly clear. Social relations in China outside the immediate family circle are becoming less close and more superficial. But it is not easy to identify the contributing factors behind this trend. We think urbanization is one factor, as suggested by our data. Compared to the situation in the villages, an urban lifestyle makes close interpersonal relations more difficult in China as well as elsewhere around the world. A unique factor in China, we think, can be found in people's experiences during the Cultural Revolution, especially from the many political campaigns during those ten years. A close friend today might turn out to be one's most vicious enemy tomorrow. Life outside the family simply had so many hidden pitfalls that one had to be cautious in dealing with people, including friends and neighbors. One had to be on constant alert and watch out for traps that were invisible. If the Chinese people are a pool of sand, as Dr. Sun Yat-sen at one time observed, the sand now seems to be even thinner and more inclined to sink.

Submission to Authority Weakening

A major characteristic of contemporary Chinese culture is a radical departure from the traditional value of submission to authority. According to the anthropologist Francis Hsu (1949, 1981), submission to authority was a core value in traditional China. In nearly all types of social relations Chinese behavior followed a hierarchy of superiors and subordinates. The latter were expected to submit to the authority of the former. This kind of submission is best illustrated by what is known as the Three Principles of Guidance. That is, the emperor provided guidance for his subjects, the father provided guidance for his sons, and the husband provided guidance for his wife. In other words, subjects must submit to their emperor, sons must submit to their father, and a wife must submit to her husband.

This submission was to be willingly enacted, rather than coercively enforced, partly because Chinese were taught to behave this way since childhood, and also because of its psychological and practical rewards. In a practical sense, subjects submitted to their emperor because the emperor, as a symbol of the state, offered them protection. A father brought up his sons and gave them discipline and nurture. A traditional Chinese husband rarely gave his wife anything even remotely reminiscent of love, but he at least provided her with a home, gave her children and, with that, a position in the family and the community at large. But it was the psychological reward that made submission to authority truly meaningful in traditional China. Submission was valued, in and by itself, as an expression of loyalty to the emperor, of filial piety to the father, and of wifely dedication to the husband. As a core cultural value, submission was not conditioned by the practical rewards which may or may not be forthcoming.

Closely related to submission to authority, as a concrete behavioral manifestation, was the concept of pleasing superiors. On the surface, this concept may have a negative undertone. Actually it did not. The Chinese term, *ying he*, means exactly the same in Japanese. It means "to greet" and "to harmonize." In practical terms, it implies that by anticipating the wishes of his superior and by fulfilling them realistically, a subordinate can best greet and harmonize with his superior. In fact, this was supposed to be the most gratifying way for a subject to express his dedication and loyalty to his emperor.

The spirit of the Three Principles of Guidance was applied to other social relations, in which a subordinate willingly submitted to a superior and tried hard to please him. When these same principles were extended to the entire society, both social harmony and social stability would be readily achieved. Submission to authority, in that sense, literally functioned as a cornerstone of societal integration in China. It was the most fundamental guiding principle of the Chinese social system, from the imperial court at the top down to the kinship structure on the bottom, in which everybody knew his place.

Our findings demonstrate clearly that this traditional core value is fast disappearing. Submission to authority, a cultural value presumably universally accepted in the past, was endorsed by only about one-third of our respondents. Pleasing a superior as a behavioral expression was overwhelmingly rejected as something negative. Most people still say young people should show respect for older people. But if they do not agree with someone who is senior, an overwhelming majority (94 percent) would not hesitate to express their different opinions. In fact, more than half of them (53 percent) would even argue with him, something unthinkable in the past. In their evaluation of leadership qualities, seniority was ranked close to the bottom. By a ratio of nearly nine to one, our respondents would prefer a young, capable leader, to the highly respected elder of the past.

Erosion of authority also permeates the family. As we recall, some two-thirds of parents with children old enough said their children talked back either sometimes or under most circumstances when asked to do something. This was by no means the pattern in the past, when parents held almost absolute authority within the family. Today parents seem to be giving up their authority. One example is the selection of a marriage partner for a son or daughter. Previously, this was something decided by the parents without consulting the young adult whose life was being determined. Now most parents would leave the matter up to their children.

Another concrete example is the declining authority of the husband. The old traditional value of "three obediences and four virtues" is emphatically rejected by our respondents, men and women alike. The idea that a wife could ask for a divorce was something unheard of among most Chinese half a century ago. Only the husband had the right to "dismiss" his wife if and when he should choose to do so. Now the majority of our respondents supported the idea of a divorce if the couple could not get along.

Submission to authority was a core cultural value anchored in traditional Chinese social structure based largely on the landed gentry. It symbolized a powerful structural as well as ideological constraint that regulated the hierarchical nature of Chinese society for many centuries. The rural land reform introduced by the Party leadership in the early 1950s literally wiped out the landed gentry as a social class. In fact, members of landlord families not only lost their land holdings and status of prestige and power in rural China; for some thirty years they were branded as social outcasts, a stigma that was not removed until the early 1980s. Something of a less painful nature happened to industrialists and urban business owners when the state took over their factories and businesses in 1956. For the majority of Chinese, peasants and workers alike, this drastic shift of social status lifted them out of their erstwhile subordinate positions. Persons who previously held authority were downgraded almost overnight. Some peasants and workers rose to leadership positions in their work units.

The concept of authority began to take on a different meaning. Cadres in various government and Party organizations wielded power and authority pretty much the same way officials and bureaucrats did in the past. But that new authority was not a distant authority, not one that was dressed up in rituals and formalities, especially at local levels, largely because many of the cadres came from the grassroots. One important factor behind the fading of distant authority has been China's egalitarian wage system. Except for a relatively small number of high ranking officials who still enjoy an assortment of special privileges, more so at the central and provincial government levels than at the grassroots, most others live within a rather narrow range of wage differentials. A university professor does not take home much more than a factory worker. The economic basis of social position and authority of traditional Chinese society has been largely removed.

The Cultural Revolution seemed to have dealt a crippling blow to authority in Chinese society. During the chaotic early months of the Cultural Revolution Chinese people all over the country saw their officials and cadres being humiliated, abused, and denounced by young Red Guards. Many of them were later sent down to remote villages for reform through manual labor. A favorite device of humiliation directed them to clean latrines and spittoons. A whole range of experiences between the common people and the cadres apparently further eroded the concept of authority.

Within the family the change was no less profound. The radical structural change that disbanded the landed gentry also destroyed the formal kinship structure and undermined the position of the father in the family. The father was no longer a symbol of authority within a clan-based extended family. He became little more than a subsistence provider, a position he had to share with his wife under China's new occupational system. The nearly full employment of women, who are able to earn their own wages, has changed the traditional husband–wife relations and greatly weakened the dominant position of the husband.

Rejection of the Way of Golden Mean

The erosion of submission to authority as a traditional value is accompanied by a new trend of assertiveness. This assertiveness is not merely reflected in a readiness to speak one's mind when one does not agree with someone senior, as we have just noted. It is also demonstrated in a wide range of behavioral patterns that appear to be fundamentally different from the past. Traditional Chinese behavioral patterns appeared to be just the opposite of assertiveness. They can be best described by the Confucian way of the golden mean. Whatever Confucius meant by this philosophy of life is a topic for stimulating discourse among historians and philosophers. To the average Chinese, the way of the golden mean implied a rather mundane notion of taking the middle road, being wishy-washy, and not sticking one's neck out. This kind of discretion was considered to be the best way for self-preservation in case one found oneself in the middle of conflict or controversy. This pattern of behavior is reflected in a popular saying: "Let us each sweep the snow in front of our own house, and never mind the frost on other people's roofs." In other words, mind your own business. Don't get involved. For generation after generation, Chinese were taught to practice the way of the golden mean and to use discretion for self preservation.

Our findings were thus totally unanticipated. Among the traditional values we presented to our respondents, we recall, the way of the golden mean and the value of discretion for self preservation were two of the most vehemently rejected. The rejection of these two traditional values vividly presents itself in many ways in our findings. When asked what they would do if they had different opinions with someone in their work units, the single most vocal answer was: directly confront him with the difference. Traditionally, the way of the golden mean dictated keeping silent. Also, today if a neighbor or a friend takes something illegally, most people said they would report it rather than say nothing. A large majority rejected the idea that how a local government spends its money is the government's own business, but insisted that the public has a right to know. This is very different from sweeping the snow in front of one's own house.

An overwhelming majority, nearly nine out of ten, said public affairs should not be left to those with influence and experience, but should be discussed with the people. If someone under their supervision does not work diligently, most would not remain silent or get a message to him indirectly, which was the favored behavior in the past for the purpose of preserving harmony. Today the supervisor would directly criticize this person. The traditional value of preserving harmony used to be considered enormously important. In our survey it was endorsed by less than three out of ten respondents. The Confucian virtues of tolerance, propriety, and deference, another vital cornerstone of traditional Chinese social behavior, were valued by only one out of four respondents.

Historically China has been known as a society of "rites and righteousness," where people lived by the Confucian ethic of propriety and tolerance. Our research findings strongly suggest an erosion of this traditional value. One clear manifestation is the high incidence of quarrels among family members. Friction between mothers and daughters-in-law has probably existed for as long as Chinese history. In the past, daughters-in-law submitted themselves to their mothers-in-law and quarrels were rarely allowed. Now such quarrels have forcefully come to the open, and indeed are reported as frequently as those about the overcrowded housing situation. Frequent quarrels were also reported about problems of caring for aging parents, children's education, daily expenses, and character incompatibility between married couples.

It will be interesting to compare the findings from China with parallel findings from Korea using identical questions, table 12.1.

With only two exceptions, character incompatibility and lifestyle problems, the Chinese sample reported these family disputes far more frequently than did the Korean sample. These two exceptions probably reflect different paths of social and cultural change largely due to a quicker pace of industrialization and a much higher standard of living in Korea. This point will be addressed more fully in a separate research monograph. Here, we assume that traditionally the Chinese and Korean cultures were similarly influenced by Confucian teachings. If so, then the unusually high incidences of family disputes we see in our Chinese data seem to provide one more indication of a major departure from the Confucian ethics of harmony reinforced through a teaching of rites and proprieties.

What appears remarkable—some might prefer to call it astonishing—is the distinct possibility, as suggested by our research findings,

Table 12.1 Family Disputes Reported in China and Korea

	CHINA	KOREA
Housing problems	53.4%	9.7%
Mother and daughter-in-law	54.5%	25.5%
Children's education	49.1%	32.9%
Daily expenses	34.9%	27.7%
Caring for old parents	33.0%	14.0%
Lifestyle problems	23.5%	34.2%
Character incompatibility	40.8%	50.8%
Property disputes	20.0%	16.1%
Entertainment	10.7%	4.4%

that the deep-rooted cultural heritage of harmony and moderation, which managed to survive in China for some three thousand years, is now disappearing. We do not think the dramatic changes in cultural values which we have documented are largely traceable to urbanization and industrialization. The differences we have found between industrialized urban Shanghai and neighboring rural villages are marginal. Some concrete manifestations of change, such as family disputes over housing, could be a reflection of the severe housing shortage in China, a mark of poverty if you will. However, one of the authors lived in Shanghai before Pearl Harbor. Due to the huge refugee population, housing shortage in the International Settlement was just as bad in those days, if not worse than now. He did not recall any housing disputes among his relatives. Most of the rejections of traditional values we have documented in our research do not seem to be directly related to poverty. We think the main factor behind those value changes, in as much as they appear radically different from what we understand about the past, are primarily attributable to the capricious attacks on traditional values during the countless struggle campaigns that Chairman Mao initiated during the quarter century of his rule from the early 1950s till his death in 1976. The Cultural Revolution simply brought the class struggles to a feverish climax. During those struggle sessions, children were urged to scream accusations at their parents, students were lined up to condemn and spit at their teachers, officials and scholars were put on public trials and paraded in humiliation in the streets. An atmosphere of lawlessness and anomie gripped China during the darkest days between 1966 and 1967, while Red Guards roamed the country, destroying anything reminiscent of the past which they could lay their hands on. From our data, we now see that even though the Chinese family has remained intact, Chinese culture paid an awesome price for those reckless excesses commmitted in the name of the Great Cultural Revolution.

Belief System in Doubt

Just as the traditional value of submission to authority appears to be fading away, and just as harmony and moderation no longer seem to be followed as a way of life, ancestor worship as a major cornerstone of the traditional Chinese belief system also seems to be disappearing. Ancestors had been a central part of Chinese life for thousands of years, dating back even before Confucius. Confucius once commented: "When you worship (the ancestors), behave as if they were right in our presence." Before Buddhism was introduced to China, ancestor worship was the major venue of religious life for Chinese people. Even the adoption of Buddhism from India did little to change the nearly universal adherence to this traditional religious form. Francis Hsu, whose classic study of traditional Chinese culture is entitled *Under the Ancestors' Shadow*, says he knows of no Chinese who does not practice ancestor worship. He was referring to Chinese outside the People's Republic.

According to Hsu (1981), ancestor worship was important to Chinese in at least three fundamental ways. First, Chinese believed that they owed their fortunes or misfortunes to their ancestors. If they were successful or prosperous, this was because their ancestors had done something good. If their lives had been impoverished, this did not necessarily reflect their own failure, but rather it was their fate, in part because their ancestors had not accumulated enough good deeds. Conversely, doing good deeds themselves would be one way to enhance the chance of prosperity for their offspring.

Second, ancestors were treated like gods and other spirits, but in a special way. Ancestors were believed to have needs that were not different from those of the living, and it was the duty of the descendents to take care of these needs. This is why during ancestor worship, food was always offered. Depending on the descendent's financial ability and the occasion, offerings might include the burning of paper models of clothing, furniture, sedan chairs, and even paper rickshaws. Hsu once saw paper automobiles being burned. These rituals symbolized a close bond of affinity between the ancestors and the living. Chinese people wanted to work hard not only for themselves, but also to take good care of their ancestors.

Third, because of this peculiar "social tie," Chinese people believed that their ancestors not only continued to live among them, but would protect and help them in times of crisis. Taking care of the needs of the ancestors was one way to make sure that this protection would be given to the living when needed. The living were also careful not to commit any misdeeds that might reflect badly on their ancestors' good names, lest their ancestors became angry with them.

Ancestors were a symbol of final authority in the Chinese family, and by extension in the Chinese social system at large. The head of the family was the person responsible for direct communication with the ancestors. During the worship rituals, it was he who led the family members in performing the necessary ceremony. He acted as the official representative of the ancestors, and in this role, exercised the final authority over all members of the family. If a family member committed a serious misdeed, the head of the family would lead a special ceremony in front of the ancestors' shrine, and pronounce the punishment according to the "family decree" in the name of the ancestors. Even the emperor, who was the embodiment of ultimate authority over all his subjects, must worship his ancestors who were considered to be a divine bridge between heaven and the dynasty. Each dynasty had its own decrees passed down from its ancestors.

In short, worshipping their ancestors and the beliefs regarding relations with them gave the Chinese a feeling of affinity and security, a sense of anchorage within the generations of previous family members, and a purpose in life. Ancestors offered an umbrella of spiritual protection against the unknown dark forces lurking in the environment. They could be used, even though not openly, as an excuse for failure in life. At the same time, they offered a ray of hope for a better next life. Ancestors became a source of motivation for hard work and good deeds, and functioned as a powerful mechanism against antisocial behavior. Perhaps most importantly, from a structural point of view ancestors were a symbol of ultimate authority in the family as well as in society at large, and became a spiritual foundation for societal stability.

For thousands of years, ancestors were worshipped by the people of China. They are still worshipped nearly universally in Taiwan and Hong Kong, and among people of Chinese origin in Singapore. But our survey findings show that in the larger Shanghai area, including the metropolis, the small towns and the villages, ancestor worship has now virtually disappeared. In the villages, a very small percentage of respondents still said ancestors should be worshipped, but in practice hardly any families were performing these rites as far as we could tell from a separate in-depth study conducted in the same rural community. In fact, for most people in the larger Shanghai area, the notion of ancestors no longer exists. People refer to their deceased parents only. A family dinner on the birthday of a deceased parent now seems to be a typical way to replace what used to be ritualistic ceremonies to honor the ancestors several times a year. A sizable minority in metropolitan Shanghai even reject this family occasion. They think nothing needs to be done about their ancestors (deceased parents) at all. Chinese people used to believe that whatever they accomplished was for the glory of their ancestors. A majority of our respondents felt that this traditional idea should be discarded. Another strong belief held by Chinese people was that the locations of their ancestors' tombs determined the prosperity of the family and the offspring. In fact, many people in Hong Kong and Taiwan still hold on to this belief. We found from our survey that only 7 percent of our respondents still believed this.

Other than ancestor worship, Chinese people in general have not taken religion very seriously. Until Buddhism was introduced, the people of China did not have a formal religion of their own, except for ancestor worship and its related rituals paying tribute to heaven as a symbol of the unknown. Confucianism was not a religion. Nor was Taoism as it was originally conceived by Lao Tze. Buddhism came to China at a time of widespread social disorder and political chaos, and thus was able to fill a spiritual void. With the support of the ruling class, Buddhism was readily assimilated by the Chinese into their own version of ancestor worship.

Francis Hsu (1981) considers religion in China to be polytheistic. Different religious cults such as Buddhism and Taoism by and large coexisted, though often as jealous rivals. Even though Buddhism was the major religious faith, Chinese people showed no particular interest in theological interpretation of its tenets. In fact most Chinese who professed Buddhism, including many of the monks, did not consider it necessary to study the scriptures. There were no religious wars in Chinese history. The Taiping Rebellion of the mid 19th century was not a religious war, but rather a nationalistic movement for independence from the Manchu rulers, in spite of the fact that its founder Hong Xiuquan used Christianity in a peculiar Chinese way as the spiritual foundation of his campaign.

All of this is not to suggest that religion was unimportant to Chinese people. On the contrary, religion assumed an important role in Chinese society. Chinese people have always shown reverence to that sphere of their lives that was unknown, inexplicable, and uncontrollable. Particularly because life in China was marked most of the time with an unusual degree of hardship, some general religious faith always had its appeal. Whether it was the Buddha, or the Goddess of Mercy, or a localized diety, or simply one's own ancestors, Chinese people leaned heavily on them for consolation in times of distress, and for protection in the face of danger. When faith in Buddha or some other deity failed to lessen their sufferings, Chinese people would attribute it to fate and accept their current life of misery as unalterable, rather than seek the source of their sufferings in social inequities. Once in a while, leaders of some outcast religious cults such as the Yellow Turbans of the Han Dynasty or the White Locus of the Qing Dynasty were able to arouse hungry and desperate peasants to join a mass revolt. But on the whole one might say that mainstream religion in Chinese history contributed to social stability on the one hand, and prolonged the reign of social injustice on the other.

We can see why a radical revolutionary movement, such as the one pursued by the Chinese Communist Party, would find it difficult to tolerate the existence of this brand of religion in China. Indeed various religious institutions have been under consistent attack since 1949.

What seems to be extraordinary is our findings from Shanghai and the adjacent villages that forty years of indoctrination has brought about a sharp decline of religious beliefs among Chinese people along with the virtual disappearance of ancestor worship. Some 42 percent of respondents now considered it unnecessary to have any religious faith, and another 30 percent were not sure whether religious faith was necessary or not. Only 28 percent considered it necessary to have some religious faith. In contrast, a parallel survey conducted in Korea in 1988 showed that 64 percent found it necessary to have religious faith and only 15 percent said religious faith was unnecessary. The others were not sure. While Chinese people in the past were taught to believe that a pilgrimage to the temple would give them protection, only 6 percent today still shared this belief. Buddhist festivals used to be important occasions for most Chinese. Entire communities came out to celebrate the birthday of Buddha, the day Buddha attained sainthood, the birthday of the Goddess of Mercy, the day the Goddess became a saint, and the special Buddhist festival on the seventh full moon dedicated to all the dead for their salvation. Now nearly eight out of ten respondents said Buddhist festivals were of no importance to them; fewer than 4 percent said these festivals were "very important." On the positive side, fatalism is on its way out. Only some 13 percent would blame it on fate if someone does not do well in life. An overwhelming majority, 71 percent, said that failure is due to not working hard enough.

The fading of something as fundamental as ancestor worship and the decline of Buddhism as a religious base for traditional Chinese culture do seem to be extraordinary, particularly when these cultural components remain strong in the highly industrialized societies of Taiwan and Hong Kong. They are, however, not inexplicable in the light of major events in China. The coercive force of the state against ancestor worship and Buddhism no doubt played a major role. Especially since the chaotic early days of the Cultural Revolution, ancestor worship and Buddhist practices became punishable sins. But their erosion began years before the Cultural Revolution, when the demise of the landed gentry as a social class removed a financial base of support from ancestor worship and Buddhism. Indeed this was the first time in China's long history that a political regime mounted an unreserved attack on these two religious institutions, an act that had significant psychological implications. People quickly realized, as ancestral tombs were levelled and Buddhist temples closed, that neither ancestors nor Buddha could protect them from the destructive forces of the state. People also realized that doing good deeds, a concept inherent in both ancestor worship and Buddhism, meant virtually nothing against the accusations and marathon criticism sessions during the class struggle.

In retrospect the rapid decline of ancestor worship and Buddhism thus came as no surprise.

What did come as a surprise is the distinct possibility that the removal of ancestor worship and Buddhism from China's cultural horizon may be creating a vacuum in the belief system for a population of a more than a billion people. Behind Chairman Mao's attack on ancestor worship and Buddhism was the expectation that once he destroyed the old, he would be in a strong position to rebuild something new for China's ideological landscape. He wanted to firmly establish in the minds of the Chinese a commitment to a new China founded on Marxist principles and Communist doctrines. Our survey did not include any questions on Communist ideology as a basis for a new belief system. Our impression, one gleaned from a number of questions touching on leadership qualities and promotion criteria, seems to suggest that the endorsement of Chairman Mao's revolutionary beliefs was peripheral at best. For example, revolutionary class background, a centerpiece of Chairman Mao's new ideology, was rated the least important characteristic for leadership by 87 percent of the respondents. In Chairman Mao's thinking, if someone came from a family of peasants or revolutionary soldiers, then he or she would be sure to embrace the Maoist ideology which stressed a firm belief in a future socialist utopia. This type of person would be an ideal leader for Mao's new China. An overwhelming majority of our respondents now rejected this concept. Likewise, an important criterion for promotion in the days of Mao was "to study politics seriously," again a clear demonstration of one's dedication to Maoism. This criterion is now considered to be the least important of all. In the light of massive demonstrations at Tiananmen Square in the summer of 1989 as well as recent events in Eastern Europe, we suspect that the popular endorsement of Marxism in China could be rather marginal.

What Mao probably failed to understand was the fundamental cultural differences between the traditional beliefs which he wanted to destroy and apparently succeeded in doing, and the new ideological commitment which he tried so hard to establish but failed.

Even though the origin of ancestor worship was unknown and could not be ascertained, its ritualistic ceremonies and cognitive foundation fitted neatly into China's traditional family structure and the patterns of hierarchical social relations beyond the family. It functioned as a force of societal stability, a source of motivational drive, and a haven of psychological shelter. Buddhism came from India at a time of political chaos and social anomie. It not only fulfilled a social and psychological need, but also found a niche in Chinese life which was left vacant because the Confucian tradition refused to discuss the realm of the supernatural. Buddhism simply filled that void and received enthusiastic endorsement from the Chinese populace.

In addition to their common anchorage in the supernatural, ancestor worship and Buddhism shared two important features. First, they were the products of spontaneous social processes stretching over centuries. Over this long period of time, they were continuously reinforced through behavioral enactment by Chinese people at all levels. Second, like any other religious faith, the validity of their beliefs, in ancestor worship and Buddhism alike, could not be empirically tested. Stories of miraculous protection were usually given wide circulation. When protection did not materialize for some people despite pleas to ancestors or Buddha, Chinese people would blame it on their misdeeds either in this life or in a previous life, rather than lose faith. This umbrella against an empirical test of validity was punctured only after Chairman Mao mounted his vehement attack on ancestor worship and Buddhism.

These two important features are both missing in the Maoist ideology which the Great Helmsman endeavored to establish. The sources for Mao's ideology came from outside the Chinese context, particularly from Marx and Lenin, modified by his own vision of a socialist utopia. It was then imposed on the Chinese populace by using massive communication channels organized by the Party. The Maoist ideology did not evolve from spontaneous social processes backed by a long historical tradition. What is perhaps more important is the fact that the promises entertained in Chairman Mao's vision could be readily subject to empirical verification. People were able to see for themselves whether some of his promises had become reality, or at least were about to be realized. It is thus hardly surprising that the Maoist ideology was not wholeheartedly embraced by the Chinese people. The point we want to emphasize here is that even in the unlikelihood that Mao's new belief system should someday be accepted, the destruction of ancestor worship and Buddhism would still leave the Chinese people hopelessly exposed to the unknown world of uncertainties without the protection of a religious umbrella.

Indeed, the rapid decline of religious beliefs and the disappearance of ancestor worship among Chinese today can be expected to have far-reaching societal consequences. What all this points to is a culture devoid of any meaningful anchorage in religious beliefs and supernatural underpinnings. Such a scenario would have been unthinkable to most Chinese only a couple of generations ago. Social relations now appear to function in an environment of raw, brutal force without a cushion of spiritual, nonmaterial considerations. Furthermore, when the sailing is rough, Chinese people would have no illusory hopes to turn to (do we know how important such illusory hopes are?) as if they were caught in a gigantic trapeze act without a safety net. Because the stakes are so high in an environment of scarce resources, and because there is no spiritual haven to turn to, Chinese people can be expected to enter the arena of life with a tenacity and ferocity hitherto unknown.

Adventurism and Risk Taking

One traditional Chinese cultural characteristic that seems to have changed little is a low spirit of adventurism and a reluctance to take risks. Historically Chinese life has been defined by a petty mode of peasant production, which seems to have contributed to a geographical, economic, and perhaps even political narrowmindedness. Largely earthbound, Chinese people never developed the kind of bold adventurism that drove Europeans across the oceans to explore a new world in the fifteenth century. China's dismal record in overseas adventures was not due to lack of maritime technology. In fact, a huge Chinese fleet left Fujian in 1405, under the command of Admiral Zheng Ho, for the first of seven eventful voyages that reached as far as the East African coast. This was long before any European seamen had sailed into the Atlantic and beyond. To this day, the purpose of those overseas journeys led by Admiral Zheng has remained a mystery. The overseas Chinese settlements in Southeast Asia and North America today are descendents of a very small minority from the coastal regions of Guangdong and Fujian provinces, who left China out of desperation in search of a better living.

This typical spirit of "no adventurism" can be summarized by the words of a young peasant in a poverty stricken region in interior China, as reported in the much-debated 1988 television documentary, *The River Elegy*. When asked by the television reporter why he was not leaving that village even though he saw no hope of a better life there, he said: "My parents did not give me the guts when I was born." Taking risks, *maoxian*, has the connotation of facing danger *weixian*.

Our survey findings confirmed this enduring trait. Out of 14 goals in life, "adventure and initiative" received by far the lowest endorsement. Only 2.1 percent of our respondents picked this as one of their important goals in life. In contrast, 80 percent identified a "warm and close family" as an important goal. Even though self-employment has proved to be highly profitable under the current economic reform policy, it received a very low rating among our respondents because such jobs involve many unforeseen risks. Less than 1 percent of the respondents wanted their children (0.8 percent for sons and 0.2 percent for daughters) to be self-employed. In the Korean survey, the corresponding preferences for self-employment were 30 percent for sons and 13 percent for daughters.

It seems that this traditional aversion to adventure and risk taking has been heavily reinforced under China's occupational structure, by which the state more or less guarantees a job for nearly everybody. As long as one can eat from the "big pot," there is little incentive to take any risks. We see a clear economic implication of this conservative attitude in our community study in rural Qingpu, the details of which will be reported in a separate volume. Some enterprising farmers have initially achieved remarkable success in their private ventures, such as raising ducks or operating a trucking business. Once they have made a sizable amount of money, however, they tend to keep their earnings rather than reinvest their profits in new business ventures. The bureaucratic constraints on the economy are certainly a factor. An equally important factor seems to be their reluctance to take bigger risks for bigger gains.

This attitude against adventure and risk taking can also have political implications. Unless they are pushed beyond their limits of endurance—and these limits seem to extend far into the horizon—Chinese people appear quite willing to tolerate social injustice and political oppression, as demonstrated time and again in Chinese history, rather than take the risk of challenging a despotic ruler. Only under extreme circumstances, as typified by the Chinese phrase of "driven to join the Liangshan rebels," would Chinese people stand up and fight.

II. Factors Related to Cultural Change Processes

In section one we have drawn the outline of a contemporary Chinese culture representing a radical departure from its traditional predecessor despite important threads of continuity, primarily in the stable Chinese family. We have discussed the social processes by which major changes in Chinese culture have been brought about. Some of the processes of cultural change were generated by the massive social restructuring which the Party introduced to both rural and urban China since the early 1950s. These structural changes, as embedded in the rural land reform and expropriation of urban business, radically altered the alignment of structural incentives and constraints as important underpinnings of traditional Chinese culture. The reversal of superior and subordinate relations in both cities and villages, as well as the humiliation of Party cadres during the Cultural Revolution, appears to have undermined the concept of submission to authority as a cornerstone of traditional social hierarchy. It has given rise to a new set of vertical social relations and contributed to an outgrowth of assertiveness hitherto unknown in Chinese society.

The prolonged curtailment of material incentives under the collective, "eating from the big pot" practice suppressed the behavioral expression of China's traditional work ethic. The latent work ethic, however, remains strong and bounces back when the "big pot" structural constraint is lifted. The economic reform and the open-door policy have given further impetus to a search for quick material gains among the Chinese people. Social relations have lost their traditional cultural moorings and seem to be heading in a direction dominated by material concerns.

Just as important as the social restructuring, and perhaps having even greater far reaching consequences, were the class struggles, the communication campaigns, and the new ideological parameters defined in the struggle philosophy. While the structural changes altered the relational boundaries of social interactions, thus leaving some lasting impact on Chinese culture, the effects of the struggle campaigns and the new ideological constraints appear to be even more penetrating. The ideological incentives in traditional China have lost their functional basis. Yet the new ideology advocated by Chairman Mao does not seem to have a solid foundation consistent with reality. The results seem to be a serious erosion of the very cognitive foundation of Chinese culture and cast a shadow over its basic nature of humaneness. Moderation, harmony, and propriety have given way to conflict and confrontation. The Confucian concept of the golden mean is no longer a rewarding way of dealing with a confusing social and political environment. Personal survival, generally through overt conformity, seems to override basic compassion and considerateness. Belief in the supernatural, whether in ancestor worship or Buddhism, has lost much of its meaningfulness, resulting in an ideological vacuum in the absence of popular support for the new Communist ideology.

The impact left on traditional Chinese culture by radical social restructuring and massive communication campaigns in class struggles, we believe, extends over the entire Chinese population. This is because the measures of structural change and the implementation of struggle campaigns were not limited to certain selective areas, but were carried out throughout the country. This does not mean, however, that all individuals experienced the impact of these measures evenly. We know that the conduct of the struggle campaigns was far more intensive in urban areas than in rural villages. The intellectuals were singled out for struggle and criticism in those campaigns far more pointedly than peasants and workers (Barnett, 1979). And young people, who grew up after the Cultural Revolution had peaked in the late 1960s, had quite different experiences from their parents' generation. In this section, we examine the varying impact among people from different age brackets, different educational levels, and from urban and rural residences. We also examine two particular communication media factors: the influence of Western culture and official news information in the mass media.

Different Age Group Experiences

Age is one of the key factors that differentiate many cultural variables. Yet as far as such core cultural values as submission to authority and the way of the golden mean are concerned, age surprisingly does not seem to make much difference. Whether they are young or old, the rejection of such cultural values appear to be more or less uniform, with only minor variations. We consider this to be a highly important finding. Even though most of the young people did not live through those traumatic, painful experiences which their parents had to endure during the Cultural Revolution, they nevertheless show no great attachment to those cultural values that were cherished in traditional Chinese society.

This finding is important because it was uncovered in a quasi-experimental cultural setting rarely available for observation in human history. We are able to observe what happened when the fundamental cultural values of a society were forcefully interrupted and negatively reinforced in the many communication campaigns for one whole generation, as they were in Mao's China for approximately two decades, from the Anti-Rightist Movement in 1957 until his death in 1976 brought an end to the Cultural Revolution. Is the negative impact confined only to that generation of Chinese people who directly suffered during those chaotic years? Or is the impact extended to the next generation as well? Our rather startling results seem to suggest that a full-scale assault on those fundamental cultural values could disrupt the basic socialization process for the next generation. The normal social environment in which children could learn those traditional values no longer seems to exist in China. Even though the young people did not personally experience the confrontational accusations of the Cultural Revolution, they grew up in an environment in which such traditional values as harmony, moderation, and the way of the golden mean were largely unknown. They simply were denied the opportunity to learn and inculcate these traditional values.

Growing up in such a cultural vacuum, where traditional values no longer prevail and new values have yet to be established, may do more damage to young Chinese than the impact of value denunciation their parents had to endure. This possibility is suggested by our findings on basic human nature which we have discussed in chapter 8. Old people who had completed their socialization before the establishment of the People's Republic considered human nature to be basically good. It seems that their traditional socialization in the formative years acted as a mediating factor when they tried to cope with their traumatic experiences in later years, including events during the Cultural Revolution. Despite their sufferings during the class struggle campaigns, the older people still have faith in a benevolent human nature, we think, because of the traditional values they had acquired before the coming of Chinese Communism. Young people did not have any socialization experience in this older China. They have no roots in traditional Chinese culture. They came of age at a time of anomic confusion, and therefore exhibit more skepticism and awareness of the evil in human nature.

The lack of socialization in traditional society is also reflected in the attitudes of young people toward work. By and large, we found them to be consistently much less serious about work. Only 41.3 percent of the young versus 71.4 percent of the old said they wanted to do much more than their co-workers. While more than nine out of ten of the old (92.1 percent) would decline an invitation to play before their work was finished, only 71.4 percent of the young held such a conscientious attitude. Old people (48.3 percent) would prefer a workmate with a strong sense of responsibility at a ratio of nearly two to one when compared to the young (only 25.3 percent). More young people (51.4 percent) opted for a job with no heavy responsibility than old people (37.6 percent), and attached less importance to work performance as a criterion for promotion (27.8 percent) than their elders (38.5 percent). It seems that when the young people became detached from such Confucian virtues as harmony and the way of the golden mean, they also somewhat lost touch with the traditional values of diligence and frugality. As we recall, while nearly all the old people (96 percent) were proud of diligence and frugality, only 82.7 percent of the young felt that way.

The young are more fun-oriented: 16.2 percent of the young versus only 2.9 percent of the old endorsed the idea that "life is short, enjoy it while you can." Likewise, 35.2 percent of the young versus 6.7 percent of the old considered it more important to "live happily" rather than "contribute to society." Harmonious family relations are relatively less important to the young (48.9 percent endorsement) than to the old (68.5 percent endorsement). The young seem to be more unscrupulous: when facing a problem, 75.7 percent of the young versus 54.4 percent of the old would first try going through the back door. Self-preservation, on the other hand, is more important for the young. While a net 71.8 percent of the old felt that the traditional value of discretion for self-preservation should be discarded, the corresponding figure was only 39.2 percent among the young. Pleasing superiors as a traditional value was also viewed more negatively by the old (a negative index of 55.9 percent) than the young (a negative index of 39.2 percent).

Regarding the other traditional values we measured, on the whole the young people have negative attitudes mostly similar to people in their parents' generation. However, they are clearly less negative than the old on two important values, both having to do with male–female relations. On "three obediences and four virtues," the old had a negative index of 80.9 percent, compared to a negative index of 54.9 percent among the young. On the value of "chastity for women," the difference was even more pronounced. The old had a negative index of 43.6 percent on this traditional value. For the young, the negative index was only 0.4 percent. Interestingly young men and women hold similar attitudes about this concept. It may be noted that those two traditional values are not directly related to the class struggle philosophy, but were rather pointedly attacked in the media during the Cultural Revolution. Many older people seemed to be affected by such criticisms in the media in those days, to which the younger people were not exposed.

While the old people are more apt to condemn the traditional one-sided concept of chastity for women, they seem to be more conservative about dating, mate selection, and premarital relations than the younger generation. The young people are consistently more tolerant about dating and premarital relations even though on the whole they themselves disavow such behavior. They are also less concerned about moral standards as a criterion of mate selection. We think these attitudinal differences most likely reflect a general trend of change that has little to do with class struggle. They stem largely from a loosening up of parental authority along with an increasing independence among the younger generation. Nearly half of the young (45.3 percent), as compared to only one fourth of the old (23.5 percent), said the correct way to bring up children is to let them develop freely, rather than to teach them discipline.

We note a rather puzzling trend in our data. The young, who are less exposed to ideological propaganda, seem to be less antagonistic toward religion than the old even though on the whole both are not much attracted to the supernatural. While only 1.8 percent of the old believed that pilgrimages would give one spiritual protection, as many as 11.7 percent of young held that belief. Nearly nine out of ten (87.8 percent) among the old discounted the idea that the location of ancestors' tombs would affect the family fortune. This disbelief was shared by only 71.8 percent of the young. Only 71 percent of the young, versus 85.5 percent of the old, considered Buddhist festivals to be of no importance at all. On the other hand, 20.3 percent of the young, versus 6 percent of the old, would attribute one's failure to fate. While less than 1 percent of the old would burn incense and worship their ancestors, this traditional view was expressed by 6.5 percent of the young, still a very small percentage but more than among the old. Similarly, glory to ancestors as a traditional value received a negative index of 38.5 percent among the old, compared to a much weaker negative index of 16.1 percent among the young. These findings point to the possibility, seemingly remote at this moment, that given time, perhaps some religious practices will return to favor.

Educational Background

What we consider to be noteworthy is that regardless of their educational background, the rejection of such traditional values as submission to authority, harmony, and propriety was more or less the same among our respondents. It seems that the erosion of these traditional values came as an outcome of a new social environment brought about by the radical structural change and class struggles. Although those of higher education were more strongly targeted for ideological indoctrination, the impact seems to have spread to other segments of the population as well. Whether people were of high or low education, most of them seemed to be able to grasp the futility of such traditional values in a new atmosphere of struggle and confrontation.

Those of higher education, however, did differ from those of lower education on two traditional values. They resented the concept of "pleasing superiors" much more strongly (68 percent of them versus 44.4 percent of lower education wanting this concept to be discarded). They also reacted more negatively toward the discrimination of women as advocated by the "three obediences and four virtues." More than three-fourths of the better educated (76.6 percent) wanted to discard this traditional value, as compared to 64.1 percent of the low education group.

What makes the higher education group stand out rather poignantly has to do with two politically oriented attitudes. Those of higher education (92.2 percent) emphatically rejected one's revolutionary class background as a relevant leadership qualification. The corresponding figure among those of lower education was 75.6 percent. It seems clear that this legacy of Chairman Mao's ideology has been rejected by most Chinese people. Those of higher education, however, seem to resent this arbitrary criterion more vigorously. Likewise, while "studying politics seriously" was not considered an important criterion for promotion by most people, this idea carried even less weight in the higher education group. Less than 5 percent of them endorsed it as a relevant factor, versus 17.6 percent of those with lower education. On the other hand, outstanding performance was considered far more important as a criterion for promotion by the higher education group (40.5 percent endorsement) than by the lower education group (27 percent).

In family relations, which have not been seriously affected by the revolutionary changes, education seems to make considerable difference. Those of higher education appear to be less traditional. They are more liberal-minded about divorce, and tend to give their children more freedom to choose where to live after marriage. In child rearing, they are more inclined to let children develop freely rather than teach them to follow rules. They have higher educational and occupational aspirations for their children. Four out of ten respondents with higher education wanted their sons to go on to graduate school, which is highly unlikely under China's current university system. In the lower education group, only 16 percent respondents had such high hopes. For 39.3 percent in the lower education group, getting a worker's job was good enough for their sons. Only 8 percent in the higher education group would be contented with that. Nearly half (46 percent) of them wanted their sons to get a job in science and technology, more than twice as high as the 19.1 percent in the lower education group. To those of higher education, it is not enough for their children to become just "good persons." They want their children to achieve career success.

On the whole, while education does make some difference, it does not seem to be as important a factor as age differences and Western cultural influence. This could be partly due to our sampling procedures and the way education was measured. To ensure anonymity and validity of the responses, we adopted a technique that left out illiterates. Also, in our sample there were very few college graduates, reflecting the small percentage of people who have received a college education in China. Because students currently enrolled in universities and colleges lived on campus, we did not include them in our residential sample. For statistical analysis, we have grouped the few college graduates into our "higher education" group with those of high school education. These factors reduce the variability of education as measured in our sample, resulting in what is known as a curtailed statistical distribution. It tends to lower the correlations between education and other variables.

Another factor, one which we consider to be more meaningful, has to do with the nature of college education in China. Higher education generally distinguishes a person from others with regards to values, beliefs, and attitudes, not only because of the amount of knowledge the person has acquired, but perhaps more importantly, because of the analytical ability and broader perspective that come with the experience of going to college. This is not exactly the case with college education in China. During the ten years of the Cultural Revolution, college education stressed political indoctrination more than academic learning. This situation has now been gradually corrected under an open door policy, particularly in the last few years prior to conducting our survey. The on-campus residence requirement, however, prevented us from including in our sample this particular college generation. Higher education in China, as reflected in our data, does not carry the same meaning as college education elsewhere, and may not function as an important factor of cultural change as one would normally expect.

Urban versus Rural Residency

Again we are struck with the relatively minor differences between urban and rural respondents as far as changes in the major traditional values are concerned. In view of the magnitude of the changes from what we know about the past, the urban versus rural variations in our data are indeed marginal. This provides one more evidence of the prevalence of impact of the radical structural change and ideological communication campaigns on Chinese culture.

Living in metropolitan Shanghai, with its urban lifestyle and more impersonal patterns of interaction, indicates a significant impact of its own. In family relations, urbanites are far more liberal minded about divorce than rural villagers. If a couple cannot get along, 82.9 percent in Shanghai versus 59.6 percent in villages would favor a divorce. In mate selection, emotional compatibility, which is a subdued Chinese expression of love, and common interest are more important to urban residents than to villagers. However, urban living also makes people more money conscious. Far more urban residents (30.7 percent) considered money to be a major factor behind social relations than rural villagers (16.3 percent), almost at a ratio of two to one.

Life is definitely less intimate and more impersonal in metropolitan Shanghai. While 40.3 percent of the villagers reported that they chatted and spent leisure time with their neighbors almost everyday, only 19.8 percent in Shanghai were able to do so. On the other hand, 56.1 percent in Shanghai versus 27.6 percent in the villages said they hardly ever talked to their neighbors. Urban living seems to accentuate a feeling of void, as it were, even in a social atmosphere where religion does not occupy more than a marginal place. While 47.1 percent villagers saw no need for religious faith in their lives, the corresponding figure in metropolitan Shanghai was 38.9 percent. The difference, though not large, is in a direction contrary to expectation and significant. It does suggest that when the time is ripe, perhaps some form of religion might possibly fill a vacuum in Chinese life in a meaningful way, particularly for people now living in a crowded, impersonal metropolis such as Shanghai.

Influence of Western Culture in Mass Media

Western culture began to return to China around 1980, after a politically enforced absence of thirty years. When one of the authors went back to China in late 1979, he found a land, which he had not seen since 1949, filled with blue and grey Mao jackets, for men and women alike. When he returned for his second trip in 1981, he was surprised by the changes that had occurred in less than two years. Streets in Beijing and Shanghai were lined with Western style advertising selling consumer goods. Girls had artificially curly hair and wore colorful shirts and sweaters. At a wedding party in Shanghai, the bride wore a white wedding gown and the groom a nicely tailored suit. His relatives in Shanghai all had television sets, and some were in color. None of them had one in 1979. Western films and entertainment programs on television broke the drab monotony of political indoctrination of the Cultural Revolution vintage, and seemed to be very popular. A third visit in 1984 found an even more glaring presence of Western culture. Old people were complaining about mini skirts for girls and long wavy hair for boys. Disco dance was popular at university campuses and in hotels, where customers were mostly young Chinese. Not very good on the dancing floor himself, he was amazed by the ease with which young people seemed to glide and twist along with the music. American movies drew big audiences in Shanghai. When he visited Shanghai again in the summer of 1987 in preparation for the survey fieldwork, the Shanghai Hilton was under construction next to where he was staying. Videocassette recorders, which had already swept across countries elsewhere in Asia, were beginning to enter China. Karaoke bars had sprung up in areas around hotels in Shanghai, catering mostly to local clientele. Magazines, featuring leggy girls in swim suits on the covers, attracted crowds at street-corner stalls. Sex and adultery, for centuries tabooed in Chinese literature, began to receive open treatment in short stories and even television programs. Mao jackets, a symbol of the revolutionary past, had virtually disappeared.

Western culture has been pouring into China in a variety of forms. But for most Chinese the major sources are television and movies. This was how we have measured it in our survey. The influence of the West did not arrive until after the Cultural Revolution, and we saw no reason why it should interfere with the impact of the radical social restructuring and struggle communication campaigns that took place during and before the Cultural Revolution. It is therefore hardly surprising that Western culture did not appear to influence China's traditional values. Its impact was manifested elsewhere, primarily in the work ethic, male–female relations, materialism, political attitudes, and adventurism.

Consistently, we have found those heavily exposed to Western culture to be less serious about work when compared to those who are little influenced. The differences were as large as 20 percent to 35 percent. Among those under little influence, as many as 60.3 percent wanted to do much more than their co-workers. This attitude was shared by only 33.3 percent of those heavily influenced. Among the former, 84.9 percent would decline an invitation to play. Only 54.9 percent among the latter would do so. About one-fourth (26.7 percent) of those little influenced would want to retire and live comfortably, rather than continue to work. Among those under heavy influence, more than half (51 percent) opted for the easy route, twice as many as those under little influence. As many as 71.9 percent of those under heavy influence preferred a job with little responsibility, as compared to only 41.6 percent of those little influenced. A surprisingly high percentage of the former (49 percent) would prefer a workmate who is a lot of fun but does no work versus only 12.5 percent of the latter. This was about a four to one ratio. While hardly anybody (3.9 percent) under little influence saw no need for work evaluation, this extreme attitude was held by 11.8 percent of those under heavy Western influence. The traditional value of diligence and frugality was endorsed by 91.9 percent of those under little influence, but by only 74.5 percent of those under heavy influence.

Western influence is clearly related to the respondents' conception of meaning of life. Of those under heavy influence, 51 percent said it was more important to live happily than to contribute to society, compared to only 14.6 percent of those little influenced. The ratio was more than three to one. Similarly, 27.5 percent under heavy influence said "life is short, enjoy it while you can." This hedonistic view was shared by only 4.6 percent of those under little influence. It was nearly a six to one ratio.

Rather interestingly, this kind of laissez faire attitudes toward work and pleasure-seeking lifestyle among those under heavy Western influence were accompanied by a greater leaning toward fatalism, superstition, and short cut as a way of resolving problems. If someone is not successful in life, only 9.1 percent of those under little Western influence would attribute it to fate, while as many as 19.6 percent of those under heavy influence said it was his fate. Whereas only 5.1 percent of the former believed that pilgrimages to temples would bring protection, 12 percent of the latter held such a belief. In a similar vein, 84.3 percent of those under heavy influence versus 64 percent under little influence would automatically choose the back-door tactic when faced with a problem. Social network connections were considered "very important" by 54 percent of the former versus 37.8 percent of the latter.

The differences are clear and unambiguous. What remains unproven is the direction of causality. Is it primarily those people who are not serious about work, and who are attracted to pleasure-seeking and short cutting, that are drawn to Western entertainment programs on television and Hollywood movies? Or is it because of what they have seen in Western programs that they have developed these attitudes toward work and toward life? The correlational data we have collected cannot resolve this issue in and by itself. We need longitudinal evidence to conclusively settle this question. Most likely, we think there is a two way traffic. Certain people who are somehow alienated from the current social and political system are more attracted to Western entertainment on television and in films. From our data, we see that those people are mostly young, better educated, and living in metropolitan Shanghai. What they have seen in these programs is a life of plentitude and affluence, which makes them even less inclined to endorse the current system by putting in hard work. This seems to be a plausible explanation because, as we recall, not a single person in the heavy influence group wanted to be a Communist Party cadre. This was one of those rare zero percentages sometimes encountered in survey research. Their rejection of the current system is further indicated by two related findings. As many as 58.8 percent of them, compared to only 20.2 percent under little Western influence, rejected "study politics seriously" as an important criterion for promotion. Nearly everyone in the heavy influence group (96.1 percent) considered a "revolutionary class background" to be the least important leadership attribute. In the low influence group, it was 82.8 percent.

The Western influence hypothesis is given credence by additional findings on male–female relations. Most likely because of what they have seen on television and Western movies, many of those under heavy influence felt it would be all right for their daughters to have several boyfriends (43.1 percent) and for their sons to have several girlfriends (41.2 percent). The corresponding approval ratings among those with little influence were as low as 15.7 percent and 16.3 percent respectively. For those under heavy Western influence, many (33.3 percent) would even consider it all right for a couple to live together before marriage. This arrangement was found acceptable by only 5.4 percent of those under little influence. The ratio was six to one. Conversely, only 25.5 percent of the heavy influence group, versus 52.4 percent of the little influence group, considered moral standards an important criterion for mate selection.

The impact of Western culture is not all that negative. While "adventure and initiative" is not an important cultural value to most Chinese, it is endorsed far more strongly by those under heavy Western influence (9.8 percent) than by those under little influence (1.2 percent). The former are also more assertive: 60.8 percent of them would argue with someone senior if there is disagreement, compared to 49.2 percent of those under little influence.

News Media Information

Compared to the pervasive Western cultural influence, the effects of news information in the official media seem rather limited. Although we found scattered differences that were statistically significant, the main effects of official news seem to manifest themselves in two aspects of life in China. One is related to work ethic. Those who used official news information a great deal were more willing to work harder than their co-workers (56.1 percent versus 49.5 percent in low exposure group), to have a rigorous work evaluation once a year (82.7 percent versus 74 percent in low group), and to prefer "working as hard as possible" (93.9 percent versus 87.2 percent) rather than say "life is short, enjoy it as you can." To them, career accomplishment was a more important goal (endorsed by 72.4 percent versus 53.6 percent in low group).

The other aspect of effects is with community life. The heavy consumers of official news appear to be more public-minded. They were more serious about making a contribution to society (83.6 percent versus 74.3 percent in low exposure group), and more willing to sacrifice their individual interest for the public good (95.2 percent versus 89.4 percent in the low group). They were more concerned with their community affairs (27.7 percent "quite often concerned" versus 18.8 percent in the low group) and more willing to serve on neighborhood committees (57.8 percent versus 52.3 percent in the low group). They were also more optimistic about their children's chance of achieving their goals (rated very likely by 47.3 percent versus 30.9 percent in low group). These differences, mostly not large, on the whole reflect a more positive assessment of the social and economic system in which Chinese people live, indicating some effects of the news information carried in the official media. But in view of the Party's massive programming and total control of official information in all these years, the effects seem to be rather marginal when compared to the widespread impact of Western culture reflected in the mass media for less than ten years.

III. Whither Chinese Culture?

Traditional Chinese culture, the psychocultural Great Wall of the Chinese people, first revealed signs of erosion following China's defeat by Britain in the Opium War of 1842 (Pye, 1984; Spence, 1990). China's elite suddenly awoke to the realization that their ancient civilization built upon Confucian ethics was no match for the guns of the barbarians. Courageous Chinese warriors fell like weeds in the face of Western gunfire. But Chinese intellectuals were not ready to give up their Confucian teachings. Their response, as reflected in the Self-Strengthening Movement in the mid-19th century, was to apply Western technology to the foundation of traditional Chinese culture. Engineered by the then Prime Minister Li Hongzhang, this movement ended in smoke when the modern Chinese fleet Li had put together was wiped out by smaller Japanese battleships during the first Sino–Japanese War of 1895.

The destruction of Li's fleet hastened the fall of the Manchu Dynasty. The establishment of the Republic of China in 1912, with Dr. Sun Yat-sen as its first provisional president, ushered in a period of political turmoil marked by more humiliation and unequal treaties imposed by Japanese and European imperialists. Looking for cultural roots to their political malaise, Chinese intellectuals began soul searching and heatedly debating about traditional Chinese culture. A battle cry, raised by the noted philosopher Hu Shih in the midst of the May 4th movement of 1919, was: "Down with Confucianism!" The widespread corruption and the inept bureaucracy were blamed on Confucius, or more accurately, on the rigid ideological and structural confines which the ruling elite had imposed on Chinese people in the name of Confucius. Rejecting their historical heritage in Confucianism, Chinese intellectuals looked for a new cultural identity in two Western symbolic statues, personalified by Mr. Science and Mr. Democracy.

Hu Shih and some of his contemporaries apparently failed to recognize a cardinal principle about culture. Any culture, including traditional Chinese culture, is the outcome of complex social processes over a long historical period of time. Marches, slogans, and public debates at best can direct people's attention to certain flaws in a culture. But they cannot in and by themselves change a culture.

However, two historical events altered the course of traditional Chinese culture. One was the Chinese Communist movement which had its official beginning on July 30, 1921, just two years after the May 4th movement. The manifesto declaring the founding of the Chinese Communist Party was adopted by eleven delegates, including Mao, on a sightseeing row boat in South Lake outside Shanghai. Attracting many young intellectuals who were angered by their weak and corrupt government in the face of foreign imperialism, the Chinese Communists soon established themselves in Fujian and Jiangxi provinces until they were dislodged by Kuomintang troops and started their Long March to settle in the caves of Yanan. The other was the Marco Polo Bridge incident on July 7, 1937, in which a Japanese soldier was found missing while his unit was conducting a military exercise outside the Chinese city of Wanping. The Japanese military took this as an excuse to start a fullscale invasion of China. The eight years of devastating war fought on Chinese soil led to the defeat of the Japanese by Kuomintang and Chinese Communist troops. More importantly, both the war which shook loose the structural foundation of traditional Chinese culture and the widespread corruption within Kuomintang's power structure made it easier for Mao to win the civil war and later introduce his radical structural changes.

When Hu Shih issued his call of "Down with Confucianism," he had no idea how to bring it about. Nor did anybody know how to nurture Mr. Science and Mr. Democracy on Chinese soil in place of Confucius. However, the search for a new cultural identity among Chinese intellectuals and the fever of patriotic nationalism ignited by the Japanese invasion definitely aided the Chinese Communist movement. Many young men and women who were disappointed with the Kuomintang trekked to Yanan to join the revolutionary movement of the Communists (Chen, 1991). They hoped to find in the caves of Yanan what they failed to see in the foggy city of Chongqing (Chungking). Eventually, it took Mao's revolution to destroy the ancient Chinese sage and wipe out much of his influence on Chinese culture. In doing so, ironically, Mao has nurtured neither science nor democracy, but rather has pushed China to the verge of cultural disintegration.

Great Wall in Ruins

Submission to authority, the way of the golden mean, ancestor worship, and belief in Buddhism were four pillars of traditional Chinese culture (Hsu, 1949, 1953, 1981; Chu, 1979). They helped maintain a stable social order in China for centuries, not only by reinforcing the existing authority structure and mitigating social conflict, but perhaps more significantly, by giving Chinese people a sense of belonging, a psychological sanctuary against the harsh realities of life, and even a glimmer of hope for a better future. These four pillars stood firm and unshaken for centuries against the impact of countless external forces, not the least of which were the guns of European powers. If the stone Great Wall built by Emperor Qin kept China safe from the hoofs of the invading horsemen of the north, then these cultural pillars held together a psychocultural Great Wall, as it were, under which Chinese people lived an emotionally restrained but nevertheless well-protected life. They served important *system-sustaining* functions. We now face the rather astonishing spectacle of this psychocultural Great Wall beginning to crumble. And this happens after China has lived under the legacy of Chairman Mao for only some forty years.

The Great Helmsman of the Cultural Revolution never wavered in his determination to wipe out the old traditional Chinese culture. Unless you destroy the old, he used to say over and over again, you do not stand a chance of building the new. Mao wanted to build a new Chinese culture, so much so that he chose to call those chaotic years from 1966 on the Great Proletarian Cultural Revolution. He urged his young, enthusiastic followers, the Red Guards, to destroy anything and everything reminiscent of the old. And they did it with force and vigor. Old books were burned. Scholars were abused and paraded in the streets. Ancestral tombs were leveled. Buddhist sculptures were smashed. Temples were ruined. If anyone has doubted the impact of those years of wanton rampage, these doubts can now be put to rest. Our findings show rather clearly the extent to which Mao succeeded in destroying the old, in a devastating manner unprecedented in Chinese history.

In fact, the destruction of traditional Chinese culture started long before the Cultural Revolution began in the summer of 1966. The roots of the traditional value of submission to authority were shaken loose in the early 1950s, during the Agrarian Land Reform that engulfed the entire rural countryside (Chu, 1977). The landed gentry had been a mainstay of Chinese society. They controlled the land, the most important economic resource in rural China, and held broad influence in their communities. When the land reform movement put them on public trial and confiscated all their properties, it destroyed one traditional foundation of authority in China. In the cities, the Three-anti and Five-anti movements in the early 1950s, and the Public–Private Joint Management movement of 1956 which put all private enterprises under state control, wiped out the business class as a source of influence and wealth in urban China. As a result of these movements, those who wielded power in the old society were branded as untouchables, the so-called "Five Undesirable Classes."[2] All authority was concentrated in the hands of Party cadres at various levels.

Then came the Cultural Revolution. When these same Party cadres who had exercised their power with an air of almost absolute finality were subject to all kinds of abuse and humiliation at the hands of the young Red Guards, the basis of authority in Chinese society began to fall apart. Even after the Red Guards were banished to labor exile in remote regions and many of the downgraded cadres returned to their erstwhile positions, the meaning of authority was never the same as before. Authority must still be submitted to when it controls the distribution of extremely scarce resources. But this submission is no longer willingly expressed, but reluctantly extracted and intensely resented.

Just as submission to authority began to erode in the early 1950s, so also did the way of the golden mean. For millions of peasants, it was clear during the land reform movement that there was no middle road for them to take. They must step forward to confront and accuse the landlords. In the cities, struggle campaigns began almost as soon as the nation's victory celebration was over. Initially the struggle campaigns were largely confined among office workers and intellectuals. Again, they were not allowed to remain silent, but were urged to actively participate in denouncing their ideologically corrupt colleagues. The mass criticisms reached a feverish peak during the Anti-rightist movement of 1957, when hundreds of thousands of intellectuals were singled out to be severely condemned for speaking up during the short-lived Hundred Flowers movement. The Cultural Revolution simply took a giant step forward. When rival Red Guard groups fought mercilessly, when children were urged to denounce their parents, and when husbands and wives accused each other to save their own skins, what remained of the way of the golden mean had to be set aside.

Ancestor workship was also abandoned. Ancestral tombs were leveled in most places during the Cultural Revolution, if they had not already been destroyed during the Commune movement of 1958. The slightest hint of respect for ancestors was sufficient cause for severe criticism and abuse by the Red Guards. Traditional worship of ancestors lost its meaning in those days because no longer were they able to provide even the slightest protection against the ruthless rampage of the Red Guards.

For much the same reason, Buddhism and other religious cults lost their value. Chinese people had suffered many natural calamities and endured awesome carnages in the past. But Buddhism and Taoism as established religious institutions were usually untouched and were able to provide shelter to a limited number of refugees. After the turmoils were over, those who survived could go to the temples to offer their thanks. They were the ones who kept the institutions of religion alive. During the Cultural Revolution, the temples themselves became prime targets of attacks as monks were dispersed and temples were closed. Both the institutional foundations and the psychological roots of religions in China were impaired.

If Chairman Mao has succeeded in destroying the old, he has failed demonstrably in building the new. Mao wanted to construct a new Chinese culture which knew of only selfless dedication to collective ideals according to his understanding of Communism, while the mass of people would carry on his version of class struggle to the very end. Chinese people seemed to follow his lead of class struggles dutifully when he was around, but showed little inclination of the kind of selfless dedication that he demanded. Heroes that Mao singled out for praise either were received with skepticism, such as the revolutionary martyr soldier Lei Feng, or proved to be fraudulent, such as the much publicized Dazhai Brigade leader Chen Yonggui. The legacy of Mao's policy seems to be a cultural void, in which old cultural values have been torn apart but new cultural values are yet to be formulated.

Is Cultural Rejuvenation Possible?

China's cultural Great Wall is crumbling. The weight of evidence from our survey clearly shows that. The difficult question is: Will the Chinese people be able to rebuild a new Chinese culture from the ruins? We examine the possibilities in the perspective of the three major components of Chinese culture: social relations, material relations, and the ideological domain, that is, values, attitudes, and beliefs.

Social Relations. We wonder whether the Chinese family, which has remained stable and close, has a positive role to play in the future of Chinese culture. Is it possible that the close family relations could be extended beyond to change the environment outside when young people in the next generation begin to assume their roles in society? Indeed the family is the most important institution that is keeping contemporary Chinese society from falling apart. This is a role the family has always played in China's long history. But we see an important difference between the role of the family now and the role Chinese family played in the past.

In traditional China, the family was literally the cornerstone of Chinese society. We might even say that traditional Chinese society was an extension of the Chinese family. The patterns of relations within the family and the underlying values were extended, with only minor modifications, to social relations beyond the family. Take parent–children relations and the value of filial piety as an example. Relations between superiors and subordinates outside the family, and the value of submission to authority that supported those relations were almost exact replicas of their counterparts within the family. In fact, filial piety (*xiao*) and submission (xun) are usually used together in Chinese language. But the contemporary Chinese society is no longer an extension of the contemporary Chinese family. This we consider to be among the most significant changes in Chinese culture that we have learned from our study. There seems to be a wide discontinuity between what happens within the family and what happens in the society at large. When we suggest that the family has become the last sanctuary for the Chinese people, a place where they can find nurture and support in an otherwise chaotic social environment, this discontinuity cannot be made more graphic.

At this moment it seems unlikely that the warm family relations could be extended beyond to change the environment outside, unless the restrictive environment itself begins to show signs of change. We see some tentative and initially encouraging signs of this possibility in Guangdong and Fujian, where the close family ties are beginning to play a limited but positive role in a regional economic revival, in a way similar to the roles Chinese families in Hong Kong and Taiwan have played, on a much larger scale, in the economic development there. However, if the environment remains rigidly inflexible, we may be faced with the chilling possibility that the caustic social environment in the chaotic world outside will some day eat into the warm and close family relations. The many family disputes that were reported by our respondents would seem to suggest that this unthinkable scenario is not totally impossible.

In a structural perspective, if there is one way to characterize contemporary Chinese culture, it is a potential shift from obligations to rights as the guiding principle for social relations.

Traditional Chinese culture was accentuated by pervasive and long binding obligations that held together various types of social relations. By nature these traditional obligations were diffused within a broad context of general role expectations rather than applied to particular tasks. The emperor, for example, could ask his subjects to do anything he pleased, and the subjects were required to obey. Likewise, a subordinate was expected to fulfill a wide range of obligations to his superior, even if they were beyond the confines of his duties. The concept of "pleasing superiors" best exemplifies this kind of diffuse obligation.

These obligations were rigidly hierarchical, as illustrated by the Three Principles of Guidance between the emperor and his subjects, between a father and his sons, and between a husband and his wife. The cultural value of submission to authority laid a firm psychological foundation for these obligation-based relations, so that submission did not have to be enforced, but was enacted willingly. A total unwillingness and inability to assert one's rights toward superiors was very much a part of the Chinese concept of submission to authority.

These obligations were primarily one-sided. Tradition obligated a husband to provide for his wife. But if he did not, the wife was not supposed to assert her rights. She must continue to honor her husband's wishes. The emperor was obligated (in theory at least) to look after his subjects. But if he did not—and many neglected this moral duty—his subjects were not permitted to assert their rights. Instead, they must demonstrate the same loyalty and devotion to the emperor.

Other than submitting to authority and pleasing superiors, several traditional Chinese values also provided support for these primarily obligation-based relations. One was "tolerance and deference." If one party refuses to honor his obligations, should the other party insist on asserting his rights and provoke a confrontation? In superior–subordinate relations such confrontations were rare when most people followed submission to authority and practiced pleasing superiors. In relations between equals and nearly equals, if such a confrontation was about to occur, then either one or both parties would abide by the principle of tolerance and deference. Confrontation would be avoided. The traditional cultural value of harmony, considered to be of integral importance to the societal whole, reinforced the obligation-based, hierarchical, and diffused social relations.

The current rejection of these traditional cultural values suggests a potential shift from obligations to rights as the guiding principle of social relations. We see this shift consistently in many of our findings. Rather than being submissive, Chinese today are beginning to be assertive. They no longer willingly submit to authorities in the way their forefathers did. They strongly resent the notion of having to please their superiors. They do not value harmony for its own sake or feel afraid to speak out. They are unwilling to practice tolerance and deference simply to avoid confrontation. They are not contented with taking the middle road as a way of life to fulfill the Confucian teaching of the golden mean. They are no longer hesitant to speak their minds if they do not agree with someone who is senior. They feel that they have a right to know how a local government spends its money, and believe that public affairs should be discussed with the people, rather than left to those with influence and experience. These are signs of the beginning of a fundamental shift from obligations to rights as a basis of social relations. Such a shift will be extremely important because it touches the core of traditional concept of authority as the cornerstone of Chinese society.

As of now, however, the rights are yet to be clearly defined and vocally articulated. The institutional support for this shift is not readily visible. There is a long, arduous way to go before the shift will actually take place. If it should indeed happen, this shift from obligations to rights can potentially alter the very nature of Chinese society and lay the foundation of a new Chinese culture. There is a grave danger, how-

Figure 12.1 One of the numerous private markets in Shanghai, a sign of the economic reform. *(Photo courtesy of Linus Chao)*

ever. If the traditional roots of social obligations are abandoned, and yet no firm respect of individual rights is institutionalized, social relations in China will be left to function in a normless state of disorder without commonly accepted rules. Cultural disintegration will deteriorate.

Material Relations. The preoccupation with material gains in contemporary China is partly the result of an abrupt policy change from Mao's revolution to Deng's economic reform. After a prolonged period of austerity and deprivation, Chinese people are shocked to find an outside world dazzling with modern amenities beyond their wildest imagination. Poverty is no longer a symbol of revolutionary strength, as it used to be under Mao's policies. Getting rich is now not only acceptable, but even given an official sanction under the mantle of economic reform. People do not want to accept poverty as a way of life. They want material comfort, and they want it now. Both traditional virtues and revolutionary ideals are thus pushed aside.

If part of China's cultural crisis is traceable to rising material aspirations in an atmosphere of paucity, then a remedy may be sought in Deng's economic reform. Since their initiation ten years ago, the reform programs have produced tangible results, especially in the coastal provinces of Guangdong and Fujian (*The Economist*, 1991). In 1980, Guangdong's gross industrial and agricultural output was valued at US$13.8 billion, in 1990 dollars. Ten years later it was US$44.2 billion, a real growth rate of 12.5 percent a year. Its industrial output rate rose 15 percent a year during the 1980s. Its exports reached a point where they accounted for a third of China's total exports in 1990, relying heavily on its trade with Hong Kong. Following Guangdong's example is Fujian province, just across the Taiwan Strait. In the 1970s Fujian was one of the poorest provinces in China. It now comes second only to Guangdong in terms of outside investment, mostly from Taiwan. Xiamen, the Special Economic Zone of Fujian, has grown fastest in the province. Its industrial output has increased sevenfold since 1980. Exports in 1990 went up 21 percent from 1989.

The engine for the economic growth in the whole southern China has been the more efficiently run enterprises, some private and some collective, which are financed through joint ventures and foreign capital. Provinces in inland China do not have the advantage of Guangdong and Fujian. But if their enterprises can enjoy a similar measure of autonomy, their economy will improve as well. The pressure of material scarcity on cultural values and social relations can be expected to ease to some extent.

However, we need to bear in mind China's huge population. No matter how productive the reform measures can be, the output may

Figure 12.2 Huge fish pond next to scenic Dingshan Lake, a reflection of rural economic reform. (*Photo courtesy of Linus Chao*)

not be sufficient to catch up with the rising aspirations of a population now exceeding 1.1 billion. This is not to mention the fact that China's natural resources are in a fragile state because of the damage caused by the reckless policies during the Cultural Revolution years. The devastating floods in the Yangtze River delta in the winter of 1991/1992, for example, could be traced to the disruption of ecological balance under Mao's policy of filling up huge lakeside acreages along the river in his search for more tillable land.

A fundamental dilemma, as suggested by many observers, is whether China can solve its problem of material backwardness through economic reform without a concomitant political reform. As early as 1968, during the initial stage of the Cultural Revolution, an 18-year-old high school student by the name of Yang Xiguang composed a short essay entitled "Whither China." Yang identified China's main problem as a conflict between the people and a decadent class of Party officials, which he called a "Red capitalist class" (Unger, 1991). This essay was passed hand-to-hand among Red Guards and led to Yang's imprisonment for the next ten years. The economic reform of the 1980s has aggravated this conflict, which has become the root of many of China's current problems. Deng seems to realize (Walder, 1989) that for economic reform to succeed, China needs a more open atmosphere which allows the most capable, not the most orthodox, to make key decisions. That means some kind of political reform. But after Tiananmen and subsequent events in Eastern Europe and the collapse of the Soviet Union, China's current leadership has apparently decided to put political reform on the backburner while continuing to pursue economic reform. Whether this is a viable policy option remains to be seen. The future of Chinese culture is tied to the success or failure of reform.

Ideological Domain. Major events in China in the last forty years—the massive social restructuring, the relentless ideological campaigns under the tutelage of Mao, and the economic reform and opendoor policy of Deng—have resulted in a widespread ideological confusion, if not a total cultural vacuum. The Chinese people have lost their traditional value orientations. They no longer believe in ideology. Our survey data have provided many consistent clues. One intriguing manifestation in the winter of 1991 was a sudden outburst of interest, almost a craze, among young people in Shanghai for those popular Red Guard songs that hit the nation in the hectic days of the Cultural Revolution. Those songs had not been sung for years because they reminded people of the painful, dreadful excesses committed by the Red Guards in the name of Mao's revolution. Nobody knew how or why those songs came back. It seems that the young Chinese, who knew virtually nothing about the Cultural Revolution, somehow became fascinated by the irrational, frantic search for revolutionary ideals voiced in those songs as they themselves faced a life devoid of meaning. This seemingly inexplicable espisode, we believe, is indicative of the utter frustration and deep-rooted alienation among young Chinese today.

The fascination with those revolutionary songs, however, does not change the fact that the claims of communism as a workable ideology have finally been phased out of the minds of most Chinese. We recall the survey of secondary school students (Shanghai jiaoyu keyan, 1989), in which only 6 percent still believed in communism. After faithfully following Mao's leadership in pursuing his socialist utopia for all these years, the Chinese people have now dared to think and to ask questions. They have come to understand China's current political and economic system—both its strengths and shortcomings—in a way that is possible only for those who live under that system.

In this state of ideological confusion, what is the role of China's intellectual elite, the young and educated, who may still hold on to some of their ideals about the future of China? As we recall, it was the intellectuals who started the May 4th movement in 1919 and ushered in a wave of soul-searching about traditional Chinese culture. What about the young generation today?

When we examine our data about the young people, the picture is not reassuring. Their lackluster attitudes toward work do not augur well for China's drive toward modernization. What seems rather puzzling is the pervasive impact of Western cultural influence on the young people. Western culture has many facets. What seems to be highly appealing to young Chinese, our data suggest, are a life of affluence and perhaps a "happy-go-lucky" lifestyle which viewers of American television programs and movies may easily perceive. It seems that young people in China, who grew up in a cultural vacuum so to speak, are particularly vulnerable to that kind of hedonistic lifestyle which can be readily projected onto what they see on the video tubes and cinema screens. They do not pause to think whether those images are compatible with their own cultural heritage, or to ask whether these images reflect any reality at all.

In spite of these reservations, we still see hope in China's young generation. After all, it was primarily the young who started the massive demonstrations at Tiananmen Square in the summer of 1989. It was Beijing's students who erected the Goddess of Democracy in front of the People's Great Hall. It was a lone young man who stopped a column of tanks at Tiananmen Square with nothing more than his body and his raw courage. It seems that behind their front of bewilderment and confusion, beyond their yearning for a better livelihood without the patience to work hard for it, deep down in their hearts there is something there that is both daring and noble, something that can set off a praire fire of change and unheaval. The outcome may not be entirely beneficial and desirable. But it can break the status quo of inertia and give hope a chance. In that sense, indeed, China's future is in the hands of the young.

Whither Chinese Culture?

The disruption of the *system-sustaining* mechanisms in traditional Chinese society by Mao's thirty years of class struggle seems to have left behind a rather disturbing prospect of a multitude of *system-destroying* forces of unidentified and almost unmanageable nature. Where Chinese culture is heading and whether cultural rejuvenation is feasible depends on whether the Chinese people will be able to overcome these system-destroying forces and rebuild a new structure of system-sustaining mechanisms. The trends of changes in social relations, material relations and the ideological domain in the near future will be crucial.

These trends appear to be very uncertain at this moment, and observers of events in China hold somewhat diverse views.

Because the state has played such an overwhelming role in China, the future of Chinese culture is inevitably tied to political development in the years to come. Tu Weiming, a contemporary Confucian scholar, has proposed an innovative concept which he calls "Cultural China" (Tu, 1991). This embodies three symbolic universes: mainland China, Chinese communities overseas, including Taiwan, Hong Kong, and Singapore, and scholars elsewhere in the world who are interested in China. Tu takes note of the conventional view (Su, 1990) that it will be difficult for political liberalization and democracy to take root in China for a number of reasons: the lack of a pluralistic civic society, no independent intellectual class, no independent mass media, no emerging middle class, no autonomous professional associations, and no opposition parties. On the other hand, Taiwan and Singapore used to share many of these same characteristics, and yet these Oriental societies have not only embarked on an impressive economic takeoff, but also are making significant progress in political democratization. In Tu's opinion, these Oriental societies, as part of Cultural China, have an important role to play because they can provide Chinese intellectuals an alternative reference point outside the Chinese Communist system. This can be the first step toward the formation of an autonomous intellectual force in China. The periphery may then assume the role of the center.

Dissident Chinese scholars are less optimistic. To some of them (Liu, 1991), the cultural crisis in China that began in the 1960s has now developed into a stage almost beyond repair. Moral values have eroded. There is a disregard for principles as people push for individual material gains. The traditional mutual trust in Chinese society has dissipated. Falsehood seems to have become a way of life. Crime rates have been climbing, as if people are resorting to a wanton destruction of the social order to release their frustration and anger.

Whether the future of Chinese culture lies in Cultural China, particularly in the periphery, as Tu Weiming seems to hope, or whether the situation is as grim as the one painted by some of the dissident critics, we do not know. Chinese culture seems to be on the verge of disintegration. The overall weight of evidence from our survey suggests that. But we do not think the situation is indeed beyond hope.

The root of cultural crisis in China seems to lie in a loss of rationality after all these years of revolutionary struggle (Jin, 1989). This rationality, built on the Confucian precepts of moderation and tolerance, was the soul of traditional Chinese culture and the sustaining force behind the societal integration and stability in China's long history. Mao's revolution destroyed the cultural foundation of rationality. Because the traditional Chinese rationality was founded on moral principles, not on empirical verifiability, it was able to maintain internal cohesion and social order as long as China's doors remained closed, but did not lend itself to flexible adaptation when Chinese culture was exposed to threats from the external environment.

Mao was successful in destroying the cultural influence of Confucianism. The irony is: Not only did he fail to establish a firm foundation of new Chinese culture, but his revolutionary ideals are also based on "moral" principles, not on empirical verifiability. They are just as unsuited for adaptation to a changing external environment as the traditional Confucian rationality was inadequate for meeting the challenge of Western technology during the 19th century.

The ideological thoughts of Mao are still endorsed as part of China's four cardinal principles. But when one examines the concrete policies of economic reform, it seems unlikely that China's leaders are unaware of the irrationality in Mao's revolutionary approach. The debates in the Party's top-level circles in the spring of 1992 on the direction of the economic reform suggest some soul-searching within the official hierarchy. If as a result of these debates the Chinese leadership should see its way clear to move more steadily in a direction that will gradually restore a basis of rationality in its economic policy and political structure, then it would be possible to repair the damage caused to Chinese culture by the irrational mass movements of Mao. This repair will take a long time even if it is initiated soon. It will require doing away with the major structural and ideological constraints that are a legacy of Mao, and putting in place new structural and ideological incentives that can rally the Chinese people behind a meaningful agenda of modernization. These are extremely challenging tasks and one must not belittle the obstacles. If such a course of rational policy modification is forthcoming in the near future, the peril of cultural disintegration can be averted. If not, then China's crisis will deepen and the psychocultural Great Wall will indeed collapse.

Appendix: Statistical Analysis

Chapter 3. Family Relations

Dependent Variable 1: Are you living with your parents? R = .24 (F = 28.95, df = 3, 1652, p < .001).

Independent Variables: Age (beta -.11, p < .001); Urban (beta -.14, p < .001); Income (beta -.08, p < .001). Those living with parents were younger, residing in rural areas, and of lower income.

Dependent Variable 2: If you are not living with your parents, when was the last time you visited them? R = .27 (F = 41.83, df = 1, 534, p < .001).

Independent Variable: Age (beta -.27, p < .001). Younger people visited their parents more often.

Dependent Variable 3: Is there a time during the day the whole family gets together other than having a meal? R = .15 (F = 22.75, df = 2, 1966, p < .001).

Independent Variables: Age (beta -.11, p < 001); Urban (beta -.07, p < .001). Younger people and those in rural areas reported family get-togethers more frequently.

Dependent Variable 4: Chatting in family. R = .15 (F = 23.85, df = 2, 1995, p < .001).

Independent Variables: Rural (beta -.14, p < .001); Age (beta -.10, p < .001). Urban residents and younger people reported chatting more.

Dependent Variable 5: Watching television. R = .12 (F = 9.98, df = 3, 1994, p < .001).

Independent Variables: Female (beta .08, p < .001); Age (beta .09, p < .001); Rural (beta .07, p < .001). (Female scored 2; male scored 1). Watching television was reported more by women, older people, and villagers.

Dependent Variable 6: Doing household work. R = .31 (F = 108.53, df = 2, 1995, p < .001).

Independent Variables: Rural (beta .32, p < .001); Age (beta .09, p < .001). Rural villagers reported doing household work more. Older people also did more.

Dependent Variable 7: Discussion in family. R = .07 (F = 10.76, df = 1, 1996, p < .001).

Independent Variable: News Information (beta .07, p < .001). Those more heavily exposed to news information discussed more.

Dependent Variable 8: Reading and studying in family. R = .10 (F = 12.68, df = 1, 1996, p < .001).

Independent Variable: Education (beta .10, p < .001). Those of higher education read more.

Dependent Variable 9: Playing cards, chess. R = .10 (F = 9.60, df = 2, 1995, p < .001).

Independent Variables: Rural (beta -.09, p < .001); Age (beta -.07, p < .001). Playing cards, chess was reported more by urban residents and younger people.

Dependent Variable 10: Visiting friends and relatives. R = .08 (F = 12.92, df = 1, 1996, p < .001).

Independent Variable: Urban (beta -.08, p < .001). Rural villagers and small town residents visited friends and relatives more.

Dependent Variable 11: Do your children consult you on their problems? R = .16 (F = 14.46, df = 2, 1168, p < .001).

Independent Variables: Age (beta -.12, p < .001); Female (beta .09, p < .001). Younger people and women were consulted more by their children.

Dependent Variable 12: Generally speaking, when you ask your children to do something, do they talk back? R = .11 (F = 17.80, df = 1, 1367, p < .001).

Independent Variable: Age (beta -.11, p < .001). Children of younger parents talked back more.

Dependent Variable 13: If your children behave badly, what would you do?

Discriminant Analysis for categorical responses. One function significant at .001 level. Eigenvalue = .03, variance 57.83 percent, canonical correlation .17. Lambda .95. Major independent variable on rotated standardized discriminant function: Age, coefficient 1.05. Older people were more tolerant.

Dependent Variable 14: If you have a son, will you let him find his mate, or will you find one for him? R = .09 (F = 15.63, df = 1, 1996, p < .001).

Independent Variable: Age (beta -.09, p < .001). Younger people were more liberal.

Dependent Variable 15: If you have a daughter, will you let her find her mate, or will you find one for her? R = .09 (F = 16.39, df = 1, 1996, p < .001).

Independent Variable: Age (beta -.09, p < .001). Younger people were more liberal.

Dependent Variable 16: If you have a daughter, and she wants to marry a bad character, what will you do?

Discriminant Analysis for categorical responses. Two functions significant at .001 level. First function: Eigenvalue .11, variance 81.14 percent, canonical correlation .31. Lambda .88. Major independent variable on rotated standardized discriminant function: Education, coefficient 0.61. Second function: Eigenvalue .02, variance 13.18 percent, canonical correlation .13. Lambda .97. Major independent variables on rotated standardized discriminant function: Sex, coefficient .92; Age, coefficient .54. People of higher education were more conservative. So were women. Younger people were more liberal.

Dependent Variable 17: How do your parents show their concern for you?

Discriminant Analysis for categorical responses: Two functions significant at .001 level. First function: Eigenvalue .04, variance 52.72 percent, canonical correlation .19. Lambda .93. Major independent variable on rotated standardized discriminant function: Urban, coefficient 1.09. Second function: Eigenvalue .02, variance 25.73 percent, canonical correlation .14. Lambda .97. Major independent variable on rotated standardized discriminant function: Education, coefficient 1.01. Urban residents and those of higher education were less positive about their parents.

Dependent Variable 18: Mother and daughter-in-law disputes. R = .09 (F = 17.41, df = 1, 1996, p. < .001)

Independent Variable: Education (beta .09, p < .001). More disputes reported by higher education families.

Dependent Variable 19: Disputes about housing problems. R = .16 (F = 53.47, df = 1, 1996, p < .001).

Independent Variable: Urban (beta .16, p < .001). More disputes in urban families.

Dependent Variable 20: Disputes about children's education. R = .07 (F = 9.84, df = 1, 1996, p < .001).

Independent Variable: Rural (beta -.07, p < .001). Villagers had fewer disputes.

Dependent Variable 21: Disputes due to character incompatibility. R = .14 (F = 19.00, df = 2, 1995, p < .001).

Independent Variables: Age (beta -.10, p < .001); Urban (beta -.07, p < .001). More disputes reported by younger people and rural villagers.

Dependent Variable 22: Disputes about daily expenses. R = .11 (F = 25.03, df = 1, 1996, p < .001).

Independent Variable: Rural (beta .11, p < .001). Villagers had more disputes.

Dependent Variable 23: Disputes about caring for old parents. R = .13 (F = 34.20, df = 1, 1996, p < .001).

Independent Variable: Rural (beta .13, p < .001). Villagers had more disputes.

Dependent Variable 24: Disputes due to different lifestyles. R = .08 (F = 13.58, df = 1, 1996, p < .001).

Independent Variable: Age (beta -.08, p < .001). Younger people reported more disputes.

Dependent Variable 25: Property disputes. R = .17 (F = 57.82, df = 1, 1996, p < .001).

Independent Variable: Rural (beta .17, p < .001). Villagers had more disputes.

Dependent Variable 26: Disputes about entertainment. R = .12 (F = 30.52, df = 1, 1996, P < .001).

Independent Variable: Age (beta -.12, p < .001). Younger people reported more disputes.

Dependent Variable 27: If husband and wife have great difficulty getting along and they have no children, do you think they should get a divorce? R = .31 (F = 51.16, df = 4, 1993, p < .001).

Independent Variables: Rural (beta -.15, p < .001); Education (beta .15, p < .001); Western cultural influence (beta .10, p < .001); Female (beta .07, p < .001). Urban residents, those of higher education, those under higher Western influence, and women favored divorce more when no children were involved.

Dependent Variable 28: Should they get a divorce if they have children? R = .28 (F = 32.70, df = 5, 1992, p < .001).

Independent Variables: Education (beta .13, p < .001); Western cultural influence (beta .09, p < .001); Female (beta -.09, p < .001); Rural (beta -.11, p < .001); Age (beta -.07, p < .001). Those of higher education, those under greater Western influence, urban residents and younger people still favored divorce more even when children were involved. With children, divorce became less acceptable to women.

Chapter 4. Social Relations

Dependent Variable 1: Do you have an opportunity to see relatives who do not live with you? R = .17 (F = 51.12, df = 1, 1641, p < .001).

Independent Variable: Urban (beta -.17, p < .001). Urban residents saw relatives less often.

Dependent Variable 2: What will you do if a relative wants to borrow 200 yuan from you?

Discriminant Analysis for categorical responses: Two functions significant at .001 level. First function: Eigenvalue .10, variance 74.11 percent, canonical correlation .30. Lambda .88. Major independent variable on rotated standardized discriminant function: Rural, coefficient 1.07. Second function. Eigenvalue .02, variance 12.90 percent, canonical correlation .13. Lambda .97. Major independent variable on rotated standardized discriminant function: Age, coefficient 1.14. Rural villagers and younger people were more willing to help.

Dependent Variable 3: Suppose a relative wants your help to ask someone to do something. You are able to do it, but it will give you some inconvenience. What will you do?

Discriminant Analysis for categorical responses: One function significant at .001 level. Eigenvalue .05, variance 77.05 percent, canonical correlation .23. Lambda .93. Major independent variables on rotated standardized discriminant function: Age, coefficient .88; Education, coefficient .66. Younger people and those with lower education were more willing to help.

Dependent Variable 4: What will you do if a friend wants to borrow 200 yuan from you?

Discriminant Analysis for categorical responses: Three functions significant at .001 level. First function: Eigenvalue .12, variance 69.51 percent, canonical correlation .33. Lambda .85. Major independent variable on rotated standardized discriminant function: Rural, coefficient 1.07. Second function: Eigenvalue .03, variance 15.83 percent, canonical correlation .16. Lambda .95. Major independent variable on rotated standardized discriminant function: Age, coefficient 1.11. Third function: Eigenvalue .02, variance 11.41 percent, canonical correlation .14. Lambda .97. Major independent variable on rotated standardized discriminant function: Education, coefficient 1.11. Rural villagers, younger people, and those with lower education were more willing to help.

Dependent Variable 5: Suppose a friend wants your help to ask someone to do something. You are able to do it, but it will give you some inconvenience. What will you do?

Discriminant Analysis for categorical responses: Two functions significant at .001 level. First function: Eigenvalue .05, variance 64.46 percent, canonical correlation .21. Lambda .93. Major independent variable on rotated standardized discriminant function: Age, coefficient .93. Second function: Eigenvalue .01, variance 23.74 percent, canonical correlation .13. Lambda .97. Major independent variable on rotated standardized discriminant function: Urban, coefficient .64. Villagers were more willing to help. Older people were more hesitant.

Dependent Variable 6: You are tired after a whole day's work, and you want to take a rest. A good friend comes along and wants you to do something, which is very important to him. Will you help him? $R = .07$ ($F = 9.30$, $df = 1, 1996$, $p < .001$).

Independent Variable: Female (beta .07, $p < .001$). Women were more willing to help.

Dependent Variable 7: An election is coming up. Suppose a good friend wants you to vote for someone you know nothing about. Will you agree? $R = .12$ ($F = 26.60$, $df = 1, 1996$, $p < .001$).

Independent Variable: Age (beta -.12, $p < .001$). Younger people were more ready to accommodate.

Dependent Variable 8: If you are in need of money, where would you go to borrow it?

Discriminant Analysis for categorical responses: Two functions significant at .001 level. First function: Eigenvalue .12, variance 68.42 percent, canonical correlation .33. Lambda .85. Major independent variable on rotated standardized discriminant function: Urban, coefficient .97. Second function: Eigenvalue .05, variance 30.36 percent, canonical correlation .23. Lambda .95. Major independent variables on rotated standardized discriminant function: Age, coefficient .73; Western cultural influence, coefficient -.62; Education, coefficient -.50. Villagers relied on relatives more. Younger people did not trust work units. People of lower education and people under less Western influence relied on relatives more.

Dependent Variable 9: How often do you spend leisure time with your neighbors? $R = .28$ ($F = 54.53$, $df = 3, 1994$, $p < .001$).

Independent Variables: Rural (beta .17, $p < .001$); Education (beta -.13, $p < .001$); Age (beta -.08, $p < .001$). Rural villagers, those with lower education, and younger people spent more time with neighbors.

Dependent Variable 10: If you urgently needed 70–80 yuan, could you approach your neighbors to borrow it? R = .35 (F = 284.99, df = 1, 1996, p < .001).

Independent Variable: Rural (beta .35, p < .001). Rural villagers were more ready to approach neighbors.

Dependent Variable 11: What will you do if you have a quarrel with a neighbor and receive verbal abuse?

Discriminant Analysis for categorical responses. One function significant at .001 level. Eigenvalue .06, variance 85.32 percent, canonical correlation .25. Lambda .93. Major independent variables on rotated standardized discriminant function: Age, coefficient .66; Urban, coefficient -.51. Younger people were less patient. Urban residents were more restrained.

Dependent Variable 12: Do you think that younger people should show proper respect to older people? R = .13 (F = 16.74, df = 2, 1989, p < .001).

Independent Variables: News information (beta .10, p < .001); Rural (beta .10, p < .001). Those more heavily exposed to news information and rural villagers were more respectful.

Dependent Variable 13: If you do not agree with the opinions of someone who is senior, will you express your different opinions? R = .14 (F = 19.13, df = 2, 1979, p < .001)

Independent Variables: Rural (beta .12, p < .001); News Information (beta .08, p < .001). Rural villagers and those exposed to more news information were more ready to speak up.

Dependent Variable 14: If you do not agree with what older people tell you, would you argue with them? R = .10 (F = 20.28, df = 1, 1975, p < .001).

Independent Variable: Western influence (beta .10, p < .001). Those under heavy Western influence tended to argue more.

Dependent Variable 15: During the last month have you consulted others on something? R = .27 (F = 39.00, df = 4, 1935, p < .001).

Independent Variables: Education (beta .13, p < .001); Urban (beta .16, p < .001); Female (beta -.12, p < .001); Age (beta -.08, p < .001). Those with higher education, urban residents, men, and younger people consulted more.

Dependent Variable 16: What was it that you consulted others about?

Discriminant Analysis for categorical responses: No function was significant at .001 level.

Dependent Variable 17: During the last month have other people consulted you on something? R = .27 (F = 40.11, df = 3, 1572, p < .001).

Independent Variables: Education (beta .14, p < .001); Urban (beta .13, p < .001); Western cultural influence (beta .09, p < .001). Those of higher education, urban residents, and those under more Western influence were consulted more.

Dependent Variable 18: What was it that they consulted you about?

Discriminant Analysis for categorical responses: No function was significant at .001 level.

Dependent Variable 19: In our society, what factor do you think most influences our relations with others?

Discriminant Analysis for categorical responses: Two functions significant at .001 level. First function: Eigenvalue .08, variance 65.16 percent, canonical correlation .27. Lambda .89. Major independent variable on rotated standardized discriminant function: Education, coefficient -.80. Second function: Eigenvalue .02, variance 16.40 percent, canonical correlation .14. Lambda .96. Major independent variable on rotated standardized discriminant function: Rural, coefficient .98. Urban residents and those of higher education regarded money as more important. Villagers and those of lower education valued friendship more.

Dependent Variable 20: When you meet someone for the first time, what should you do? R not significant at .001 level.

Dependent Variable 21: In our society, how important is it that we repay the kindness shown to us by others? R = .19, (F = 35.12, df = 2, 1977, p < .001).

Independent Variables: Rural (beta .18, p < .001); News information (beta .08, p < .001). Villagers and those exposed to more news information were more inclined to repay kindness.

Chapter 5. Job Preferences and Work Ethic

Dependent Variable 1: Do you like your present work? R = .28 (F = 82.14, df = 2, 1995, p < .001).

Independent Variables: Age (beta -.26, p < .001); Education (beta .07, p < .001). Younger people and those of higher education liked their jobs more.

Dependent Variable 2: If you retire now and can get enough pension to live comfortably, do you want to continue to work, or do you want to retire now? R = .23 (F = 110.35, df = 1,1986, p < .001).

Independent Variable: Rural (beta .23, p < .001). Rural villagers were more eager to continue to work.

Dependent Variable 3: Which kind of job do you prefer? A job that is boring but pays well (scored 1), or a job that is a lot of fun but pays less (scored 2)? R = .25 (F = 45.28, df = 3,1979, p < .001).

Independent Variables: Female (beta .15, p < .001); Age (beta .13, p < .001); News information (beta -.13, p < .001). Women and older people valued interest more. Those exposed to more news information valued pay more.

Dependent Variable 4: Which kind of work do you prefer? High position but heavy responsibility (scored 1), or ordinary position but responsibility not too heavy (scored 2)? R = .23 (F = 21.05, df = 4,1524, p < .001).

Independent Variables: Western cultural influence (beta .09, p < .005); Age (beta -.16, p < .001); Urban (beta .14, p < .001); News information (beta −.11, p < .001). Those under heavy Western influence, younger, and urban residents preferred ordinary positions. Those exposed to more news information preferred heavy responsibility.

Dependent Variable 5: What ideal job would you like to do?

Discriminant Analysis for categorical responses: Three functions significant at .001 level. First function: Eigenvalue .20, variance 60 percent, canonical correlation .40. Lambda .74. Major independent variable on rotated standardized discriminant function: Education, coefficient 1.12. Second function: Eivenvalue .08, variance 24 percent, canonical correlation .27. Lambda .88. Major independent variable on rotated standardized discriminant function: Rural, coefficient 1.30. Third function: Eigenvalue .03, variance 10 percent, canonical correlation .18. Lambda .95. Major independent variable on rotated standardized discriminant function: Western influence, coefficient 1.10. Urban residents preferred managerial positions. Those of higher education preferred science and research. Those under heavy Western influence rejected ordinary workers.

Dependent Variable 6: What kind of person do you prefer as your workmate? A close friend even though his work ability is low (scored 1), or someone with high work ability even though not a close friend (scored 2)? R = .12 (F = 14.84, df = 2,1989, p < .001).

Independent Variables: Age (beta .11, p < .001); News information (beta .06, p < .001). Older people and those exposed to more news information wanted high ability.

Dependent Variable 7: What is the most important quality you look for in your colleagues?

Discriminant Analysis for categorical responses: One function significant at .001 level. Eigenvalue .12, variance 93 percent, canonical correlation .32. Lambda .89. Major independent variable on rotated standardized discriminant function: Age, coefficient .70. Older people emphasized sense of responsibility. Younger people preferred friendliness.

Dependent Variable 8: If you want to pick a co-worker, which one will you prefer? Someone who works hard but has no sense of humor (scored 2), or someone who does a minimum of work but is a lot of fun (scored 1)? R = .33 (F = 82.34, df = 3,1973, p < .001).

Independent Variables: Western cultural influence (beta -.16, p < .001); Age (beta .24, p < .001); Urban (beta -.13, p < .001). Those under heavy Western influence and urban residents preferred fun. Older people valued hard work.

Dependent Variable 9: If you want to hire someone to work for you, which one will you prefer? Someone who works hard but has no sense of humor (scored 2), or someone who does a minimum of work but is a lot of fun (scored 1)? R = .18 (F = 34.56, df = 2,1977, p < .001).

Independent Variables: Age (beta .13, p < .001); Western cultural influence (beta -.10, p < .001). Older people valued hard work. Those under heavy Western influence preferred fun.

Dependent Variable 10: What is your attitude toward work? R = .26 (F = 46.31, df = 3, 1987, p < .001).

Independent Variables: Age (beta .20, p < .001); Western cultural influence (beta -.11, p < .001); News Information (beta .09, p < .001). Older people and those exposed to more news information were more serious. Those under heavy Western influence were less serious.

Dependent Variable 11: If you are doing an important job, but your friend asks you to go out and play, what will you do? R = .22 (F = 48.94, df = 2, 1986, p < .001).

Independent Variables: Age (beta .17, p < .001); Western cultural influence (beta -.10, p < .001). Older people were more serious about work. Those under heavy Western influence were less serious about work.

Dependent Variable 12: Suppose you are the leader of a unit (such as village head or factory manager). You have a lot of official business to handle. A very close friend invites you to attend his baby's "full month" celebration. Will you put down your official business and go, or will you not go? R = .13 (F = 36.59, df = 1,1996, p < .001).

Independent Variable: Age (beta -.13, p < .001). Younger people more likely to go.

Dependent Variable 13: Suppose you send someone to do a job. The job is not finished, but he has gone out to play. What will you do? R = .08 (F = 13.43, df = 1,991, p < .001).

Independent Variable: Education (beta .08, p < .001). Higher education, more likely to say "punish."

Dependent Variable 14: What is your attitude toward work evaluation? Do you support rigorous work evaluation once a year? R = .14 (F = 18.89, df = 2, 1995, p < .001).

Independent Variables: Western cultural influence (beta -.13, p < .001); News Information (beta .08, p < .001). Those under heavy Western influence were more reluctant about evaluation. Those exposed to more news information were more enthusiastic about evaluation.

Dependent Variable 15: Under the present circumstances, which of the following is the most important consideration for getting a raise in wages?

Discriminant Analysis for categorical responses: Two functions significant at .001 level. First function: Eigenvalue .03, variance 66 percent, canonical correlation .18. Lambda .95. Major independent variables on rotated standardized discriminant function: Age, coefficient 0.73; Rural, coefficient 0.58. Second function: Eigenvalue .01, variance 34 percent, canonical correlation .13. Lambda .98. Major independent variables on rotated standardized discriminant function: Urban, coefficient -.77; Sex, coefficient .77; Education, coefficient .57. Older people, men, those of lower education, and rural villagers emphasized work performance more.

Chapter 6. Organizational Relations

Dependent Variable 1: In your opinion, as we proceed with opening up to the outside world, will relations between superiors and subordinates be more tense, more harmonious, or the same as now? R = .16 (F = 17.86, df = 3, 1974, p < .001).

Independent Variables: Age (beta -.14, p < .001); Female (beta -.08, p < .001); News information (beta -.07, p < .005). Younger people, men, and those less exposed to news information were more likely to see tense relations.

Dependent Variable 2: Suppose you are working at home on something important. The leader of your unit comes and asks you to help him with something urgent. What will you do? R = .21 (F = 32.15, df = 3,1994, p < .001).

Independent Variables: Female (beta .14, p < .001); Rural (beta .15, p < .001); Age (beta .14, p < .001). Female, rural villagers and older people were more likely to help.

Dependent Variable 3: Who would you like to have as your leader? Someone old and respected, or someone young and capable, or just anybody? No independent variable was significantly related at .001 level.

Dependent Variable 4: Most important leadership qualification: technical expertise. R = .11 (F = 11.59, df = 2, 1995, p < .001).

Independent Variables: Rural (beta .08, p < .001); News information (beta .08, p < .001). Rural villagers and those more exposed to news information regarded technical expertise as more important.

Dependent Variable 5: Most important leadership qualification: being decisive, resolute. R = .23 (F = 37.94, df = 3, 1994, p < .001).

Independent Variables: Education (beta .20, p < .001); Age (beta .10, p < .001); News information (beta .07, p < .001). Those of higher education, older people, and those more exposed to news information saw being decisive as more important.

Dependent Variable 6: Most important leadership qualification: bring benefits to workers. R = .24 (F = 61.30, df = 2, 1995, p < .001).

Independent Variables: Rural (beta -.21, p < .001); Age (beta -.19, p < .001). Urban residents, younger people saw benefits as more important.

Dependent Variable 7: Most important leadership qualification: seniority. No independent variable was significantly related at .001 level.

Dependent Variable 8: Most important leadership qualification: good class background. R = .12 (F = 27.00, df = 1, 1996, p < .001).

Independent Variable: Education (beta -.12, p < .001). Those of lower education saw good class background as more important.

Dependent Variable 9: Most important leadership qualification: good outside relations, know a lot of people. R = .22 (F = 51.65, df = 2, 1995, p < .001).

Independent Variables: Rural (beta .23, p < .001); Western cultural influence (beta .08, p < .001). Rural villagers and those under heavy Western influence saw outside relations as more important.

Dependent Variable 10: Most important leadership qualification: being fair to workers. R = .12 (F = 26.97, df = 1,1996, p < .001).

Independent Variable: Education (beta -.12, p < .001). Those of lower education regarded fairness as more important.

Dependent Variable 11: Most important leadership qualification: Serious, responsible. R = .25 (F = 43.79, df = 3, 1994, p < .001).

Independent Variables: Western cultural influence (beta -.07, p < .005); Age (beta .19, p < .001); Rural (beta .16, p < .001). Those under little Western influence, older people, and rural villagers attached more importance to being serious and responsible.

Dependent Variable 12: Most important leadership qualification: respected and liked by workers. R = .12 (F = 28.34, df = 1, 1996, p < .001).

Independent Variable: Education (beta -.12, p < .001). Being respected and liked appealed more to those of lower education.

Dependent Variable 13: Suppose someone in your work unit is not qualified for the job. How would you handle the situation?

Discriminant Analysis for categorical responses: One function significant at .001 level. Eigenvalue .02. variance 55 percent, canonical correlation .14. Lambda .96. Major independent variable on rotated standardized discriminant function: Age, coefficient .97. Older people would handle this situation in a more responsible way.

Dependent Variable 14: If one of your co-workers is lazy and does not want to work, what will you do?

Discriminant Analysis for categorical responses: One function significant at .001 level. Eigenvalue .09, variance 84 percent, canonical correlation .28. Lambda .91. Major independent variables on rotated standardized discriminant function: Age, coefficient .72; Western influence, coefficient −.60. Older people and those under little Western influence would more likely talk to the co-worker.

Dependent Variable 15: If you have a difference of opinion with someone in your work unit, how would you handle it?

Discriminant Analysis for categorical responses: One function significant at .001 level. Eigenvalue .06, variance 85 percent, canonical correlation .24. Lambda .93. Major independent variables on rotated standardized discriminant function: Education, coefficient .48; Western influence, coefficient .47. Those of higher education and those under heavy Western influence were more likely to say nothing.

Chapter 7. Community Life

Dependent Variable 1: Some people say that in Chinese society, network connections have their importance. What do you think? $R = .17$ ($F = 30.47$, df $= 2, 1995$, $p < .001$).

Independent Variables: Age (beta -.13, $p < .001$); Western cultural influence (beta .08, $p < .001$). Younger people and those under heavy Western influence considered network connections to be more important.

Dependent Variable 2: Suppose you have a problem. If you follow the normal channels, it will take a long time, and the result may not be satisfactory. Do you think you should first try to go through some connections? $R = .23$ ($F = 57.56$, df $= 2, 1995$, $p < .001$).

Independent Variables: Age (beta -.17, $p < .001$); Western cultural influence (beta .12, $p < .001$). Younger people and those under heavy Western influence were more likely to try connections first.

Dependent Variable 3: People have two different views about law. Which is more important to you? Law makes people get along with each other (scored 1), or law brings justice to society (scored 2)? $R = .06$ ($F = 7.81$, df = 1, 1979, $p < .005$).

Independent Variables: Female (beta .06, $p < .005$). Women were more likely to emphasize justice.

Dependent Variable 4: Some people say how a local government spends its money is the government's own business (scored 1). Others say this is something we have a right to know (scored 2). How do you feel? $R = .13$ ($F = 17.34$, df = 2, 1975, $p < .001$).

Independent Variables: News information (beta .09, $p < .001$); Female (beta −.08, $p < .001$). Those more exposed to news information and men were more likely to say that people have a right to know.

Dependent Variable 5: Do you think that public affairs should be left to those who have influence and experience, or do you think that these matters should be discussed with the people before decisions are made? No independent variable was significantly related at .001 level.

Dependent Variable 6: Who do you think should assume responsibility for the development of your community?

Discriminant Analysis for categorical responses: Two functions significant at .001 level. First function: Eigenvalue .07, variance 68 percent, canonical correlation .26. Lambda .90. Major independent variable on rotated standardized discriminant function: Rural, coefficient .85. Second function: Eigenvalue .04, variance 32 percent, canonical correlation .18. Lambda .97. Major independent variable on rotated standardized discriminant function: Education, coefficient .89. Rural villagers were less likely to emphasize the role of government. Those of higher education were more likely to see the government's role.

Dependent Variable 7: Which one of the following do you agree with: in order to protect public interest, sometimes it is necessary to sacrifice individual interest (scored 1); or, in order to protect individual interest, sometimes it is necessary to sacrifice public interest (scored 2)? $R = .19$ ($F = 25.09$, df = 3, 1973, $p < .001$).

Independent Variables: Age (beta -.13, $p < .001$); News information (beta = −.09, $p < .001$); Western cultural influence (beta .10, $p < .001$). Younger people, those less exposed to news information, and those more exposed to Western influence were more likely to want to sacrifice public interest.

Dependent Variable 8: If other people want to elect you a member of the neighborhood committee or village committee, would you agree to serve? $R = .30$ ($F = 48.21$, df = 4, 1967, $p < .001$).

Independent Variables: Education (beta -.16, p < .001); Rural (beta .15, p < .001); News information (beta .09, p < .001); Western cultural influence (beta -.09, p < .001). Those of lower education, rural villagers, those more heavily exposed to news information, and those under little Western influence were more willing to serve.

Dependent Variable 9: Suppose your neighbors and friends illegally take something. If you do not report it, nobody will know. What will you do?

Discriminant Analysis for categorical responses: Two functions significant at .001 level. First function: Eigenvalue .21, variance 92 percent, canonical correlation .42. Lambda .81. Major independent variables on rotated standardized discriminant function: Western cultural influence, coefficient -.49; Age, coefficient .48. Second function: Eigenvalue .02, variance 8 percent, canonical correlation .14. Lambda .98. Major independent variables on rotated standardized discriminant function: Sex, coefficient -.57, Education, coefficient .46. Those under little Western influence, older people, those of lower education, and women were more likely to report the incident.

Dependent Variable 10: Have you ever been so concerned with things in your district that you really wanted to do something about them? R = .23 (F = 27.24, df = 4, 1981, p < .001).

Independent Variables: Age (beta .12, p < .001); Education (beta -.10, p < .001); News Information (beta .12, p < .001); Western cultural influence (beta –.10, p < .001). Older people, those of lower education, and those more heavily exposed to news information were more concerned. Those under heavy Western influence were less concerned.

Dependent Variable 11: Do you discuss things in your neighborhood district with your neighbors and friends? R = .15 (F = 21.70, df = 2, 1965, p < .001).

Independent Variables: Education (beta -.14, p < .001); News information (beta .08, p < .001). Those of lower education and those more heavily exposed to news information discussed more.

Dependent Variable 12: Have you ever thought about doing something good for your neighborhood? R = .20 (F = 20.08, df = 4, 1983, p < .001).

Independent Variables: Age (beta .14, p < .001); Urban (beta -.09, p < .001); News information (beta .10, p < .001); Education (beta -.08, p < .001). Older people, rural villagers, those more heavily exposed to news information, and those of lower education were more concerned.

Chapter 8. Cultural Values: General Perspectives

Dependent Variable 1: What kind of person is a good person?

Discriminant Analysis for categorical responses: No function significant at .001 level.

Dependent Variable 2: Important goal in life: warm and close family. R = .09 (F = 15.45, df = 1, 1995, p < .001).

Independent Variable: Age (beta .09, p < ,001). Older people considered a warm and close family more important.

Dependent Variable 3: Important goal in life: successful children. R = .20 (F = 41.72, df = 2, 1994, p < .001).

Independent Variables: Age (beta .17, p < .001); Female (beta .11, p < .001). Older people and women considered successful children more important.

Dependent Variable 4: Important goal in life: career accomplishments. R = .14 (F = 19.48, df = 2, 1992, p < .001).

Independent Variables: News information (beta .12, p < .001); Western cultural influence (beta -.10, p < .001). Those more heavily exposed to news information considered career accomplishments more important. Those under heavy Western influence considered career accomplishments less important.

Dependent Variable 5: Important goal in life: comfortable life. R = .09 (F = 8.07, df = 2, 1993, p < .001).

Independent Variables: Western cultural influence (beta .08, p < .001); Education (beta -.07, p < .01). Those under heavy Western influence and those of lower education considered comfortable life more important.

Dependent Variable 6: Important goal in life: harmonious family relations. R = .23 (F = 55.38, df = 2, 1994, p < .001).

Independent Variables: Female (beta .17, p <.001); Age (beta .16, p < .001). Harmonius family relations were more important to women and older people.

Dependent Variable 7: Important goal in life: true love. R = .33 (F = 78.70, df = 3, 1995, p < .001).

Independent Variables: Age (beta -.29, p < .001); Western cultural influence (beta .08, p < .001); News information (beta -.08, p < .001). True love was more important to younger people, to those under heavy Western influence, and to those not heavily exposed to news information.

Dependent Variable 8: Important goal in life: education and knowledge. R = .12 (F = 15.37, df = 2, 1994, p < .001).

Independent Variables: Education (beta .08, p < .001); Age (beta -.08, p < .001). Those of higher education and younger people considered education and knowledge more important.

Dependent Variable 9: Important goal in life: to build a house. R = .34 (F = 129.65, df = 2, 1992, p < .001).

Independent Variables: Urban (beta -.32, p < .001); News information (beta −.08, p < .001). Building a house appealed more to rural villagers and to those not heavily exposed to news information.

Dependent Variable 10: Important goal in life: true friendship. R = .08 (F = 14.22, df = 1, 1995, p < .001).

Independent Variable: Western cultural influence (beta .08, p < .001). Those under heavy Western influence considered true friendship to be more important.

Dependent Variable 11: Important goal in life: contribution to country. R = .21 (F = 30.12, df = 3, 1994, p < .001).

Independent Variables: Female (beta -.14, p < .001); Western cultural influence (beta -.10, p < .001); Age (beta .10, p < .001). Men, those under little Western influence, and older people considered contribution to their country to be more important.

Dependent Variable 12: Important goal in life: to start own business. R = .17 (F = 30.33, df = 2, 1994, p < .001).

Independent Variables: Female (beta -.14, p < .001); Age (beta -.11, p < .001). Starting one's own business was more important to men and to younger people.

Dependent Variable 13: Important goal in life: to go abroad for education. R = .26 (F = 46.79, df = 3, 1990, p < .001).

Independent Variables: Western cultural influence (beta .12, p < .001); Education (beta .14, p < .001); Age (beta -.10, p < .001). Going abroad for education as a goal was more important to those under heavy Western influence, to younger people, and to those of higher education.

Dependent Variable 14: Important goal in life: college degree. R = .15 (F = 48.13, df = 1, 1995, p < .001).

Independent Variable: Age (beta -.15, p < .001). Getting a college degree as a goal was more important to younger people.

Dependent Variable 15: Important goal in life: adventure and success. R = .09 (F = 17.67, df = 1, 1990, p < .001).

Independent Variable: Western cultural influence (beta .09, p < .001). Seeking adventure and success as a goal was more important to those under heavy Western influence.

Dependent Variable 16: How likely is it that you will be able to accomplish your goals? R = .14 (F = 20.34, df = 2, 1959, p < .001).

Independent Variables: Rural (beta .12, p < .001); Female (beta .08, p < .001). Rural villagers and women were more confident about accomplishing their goals.

Dependent Variable 17: If your children work hard, will they be able to reach their goals? R = .15 (F = 22.18, df = 2, 1953, p < .001).

Independent Variables: News information (beta .14, p < .001); Education (beta -.09, p < .001). Those more heavily exposed to news information were more confident about their children's future. Those of higher education were less confident.

Dependent Variable 18: What do you think is the most important element for career success?

Discriminant Analysis for categorical responses: Two functions significant at .001 level. First function: Eigenvalue .09, variance 67 percent, canonical correlation .28. Lambda .88. Major independent variable on rotated standardized discriminant function: Western cultural influence, coefficient .72. Second function: Eigenvalue .02, variance 18 percent, canonical correlation .15. Lambda .96. Major independent variable on rotated standardized discriminant function: Urban, coefficient .95. Those under heavy Western influence attributed success more to external factors. Rural villagers were more guided by traditional ideas of diligence and frugality.

Dependent Variable 19: Which is more important to you? Treasure your time and work as hard as possible (scored 1), or life is short so enjoy it while you can (scored 2)? R = .29 (F = 46.18, df = 4, 1946, p < .001).

Independent Variables: Western cultural influence (beta .18, p < .001); News information (beta -.12, p < .001); Age (beta -.15, p < .001); Urban (beta .12, p < .001). Those under heavy Western influence, younger people, and urban residents were more likely to say "life is short so enjoy it while you can." Those more heavily exposed to news information were more likely to say "treasure your time and work as hard as possible."

Dependent Variable 20: Which of the following do you agree with: the most important thing in one's life is to live happily (scored 1); or, the most important thing in one's life is to make some contribution to society (scored 2)? R = .33 (F = 82.46, df = 3, 1980, p < .001).

Independent Variables: Western cultural influence (beta -.22, p < .001); Age (beta .19, p < .001); News information (beta .12, p < .001). Those under heavy Western influence were more likely to say living happily is more important. Older people and those heavily exposed to news information considered making contribution to society more important.

Dependent Variable 21: In our society today, how do you regard the matter of face? R = .16 (F = 25.98, df = 2,1995, p < .001).

Independent Variables: Urban (beta -.12, p < .001); Female (beta .11, p < .001). Rural villagers and women considered face to be more important.

Dependent Variable 22: If an unmarried girl gets pregnant, do you think her family members would feel they have lost face? R = .20 (F = 40.09, df = 2, 1995, p < .001).

Independent Variables: Rural (beta -.19, p < .001); Western cultural influence (beta -.12, p < .001). Urban residents and those under little Western influence were more likely to feel a loss of face.

Dependent Variable 23: If your son-in-law wants to divorce your daughter, would you lose face? R = .15 (F = 21.90, df = 2, 1995, p < .001).

Independent Variables: Education (beta -.12, p < .001); Female (beta .08, p < .001). Those of lower education and women were more likely to lose face.

Dependent Variable 24: If your daughter-in-law wants to divorce your son, would you lose face? R = .17 (F = 30.92, df = 2,1995, p < .001).

Independent Variables: Education (beta-.13, p < .001); Female (beta .11, p < .001). Those of lower education and women were more likely to lose face.

Dependent Variable 25: Do you think that human nature is good or evil?

Discriminant Analysis for categorical responses: Two functions significant at .001 level. First function: Eigenvalue .05, variance 57 percent, canonical correlation .22. Lambda .92. Major independent variable on rotated standardized discriminant function: Age, coefficient .69. Second function: Eigenvalue .03, variance 34 percent, canonical correlation .17. Lambda .96. Major independent variable on rotated standardized discriminant function: Education, coefficient 1.06. More older people considered human nature to be good. The higher the education, the less likely they considered human nature to be good.

Chapter 9. Cultural Values: Family and Children

Dependent Variable 1: Do you think old parents should be taken care of by their children (scored 3) or should they take care of themselves (scored 1)? R = .16 (F = 26.88, df = 2, 1995, p < .001).

Independent Variables: Age (beta -.15, p < .001); Education (beta -.09, p < .001). Younger people and those of lower education were more willing to look after their parents.

Dependent Variable 2: If parents face some financial difficulties, do you think they should ask their children for help (scored 3) or should they seek other means first (scored 1)? R = .13 (F = 34.47, df = 1, 1996, p < .001).

Independent Variable: Age (beta -.13, p < .001). Younger people were more willing to provide financial help for parents.

Dependent Variable 3: After young people get married, do you think it is better for them to live with their parents (scored 1) or is it better for them to live by themselves (scored 2)? R = .30 (F = 97.56, df = 2, 1995, p < .001).

Independent Variables: Rural (beta -.22, p < .001); Education (beta .13, p < .001). Urban residents and those of higher education preferred living by themselves.

Dependent Variable 4: At what age do you think it will not be appropriate to spank your children? No independant variable is significantly related at .001 level.

Dependent Variable 5: Some people want their children to have career accomplishments (scored 2), others want their children to be just good persons (scored 1). Which is more important to you? R = .13 (F = 32.03, df = 1,1996, p < .001).

Independent Variable: Education (beta .13, p < .001). Career accomplishments are more important to those of higher education.

Dependent Variable 6: In child rearing, which is more important: let children develop freely as much as possible (scored 2), or teach children to follow rules (scored 1)? R = .23 (F = 54.15, df = 2,1977, p < .001).

Independent Variables: Age (beta -.16, p < .001); Education (beta .15, p < .001). Younger people and those of higher education would let children develop freely.

Dependent Variable 7: If you have a daughter and she carries on with several boyfriends before she gets married, what would you think about this? R = .23 (F = 27.93, df = 4, 1993, p < .001).

Independent Variables: Western cultural influence (beta .09, p < .001); Age (beta -.15, p < .001); Urban (beta .11, p < .001); Female (beta -.08, p < .001). Those under heavy Western influence, younger people, urban residents, and men were more likely to say all right.

Dependent Variable 8: If you have a son and he carries on with several girlfriends before he gets married, what would you think about this? R = .25 (F = 32.19, df = 4, 1993, p < .001).

Independent Variables: Western cultural influence (beta .08, p < .001); Female (beta -.12, p < .001); Age (beta -.15, p < .001); Urban (beta .12, p < .001). Those under heavy Western influence, men, younger people, and urban residents were more likely to say all right.

Dependent Variable 9: If a man and a woman are in love and they live together before their marriage is registered, what do think about this situation? R = .25 (F = 43.73, df = 3, 1994, p < .001).

Independent Variables: Western cultural influence (beta .18, p < .001); Age (beta -.11, p < .001); Female (beta -.08, p < .001). Those under heavy

Western influence, younger people, and men were more likely to say all right.

Dependent Variable 10: Important factor for young people when selecting a marriage partner: family social position. R = .08 (F = 12.27, df = 1,1996, p < .001).

Independent Variable: Western cultural influence (beta .08, p < .001). Those under heavy Western influence considered family social position more important.

Dependent Variable 11: Important factor for young people when selecting a marriage partner: family financial condition. R = .08 (F = 11.97, df = 1,1996, p < .001).

Independent Variable: Western cultural influence (beta .08, p < .001). Those under heavy Western cultural influence considered family financial condition more important.

Dependent Variable 12: Important factor for young people when selecting a marriage partner: high moral standards. R = .20 (F = 28.16, df = 3,1994, p < .001).

Independent Variables: Age (beta .14, p < .001); Female (beta .10, p < .001); Western cultural influence (beta -.08, p < .001). Older people and women considered high moral standards more important. Those under heavy Western influence considered high moral standards less important.

Dependent Variable 13: Important factor for young people when selecting a marriage partner: emotional compatibility. R = .21 (F = 90.75, df = 1, 1996, p < .001).

Independent Variable: Rural (beta -.21, p < .001). Rural villagers considered emotional compatibility less important.

Dependent Variable 14: Important factor for young people when selecting a marriage partner: love. R = .10 (F = 21.36, df = 1, 1996, p < 001).

Independent Variable: Rural (beta .10, p < .001). Love was more important to rural villagers.

Dependent Variable 15: Important factor for young people when selecting a marriage partner: common interest. R = .15 (F = 22.09, df = 2, 1995, p < .001).

Independent Variables: Rural (beta -.09, p < .001); Education (beta .08, p < .001). Rural villagers considered common interest less important. Those of higher education considered it more important.

Dependent Variable 16: Important factor for young people when selecting a marriage partner: education. R = .08 (F = 13.63, df = 1, 1996, p < .001).

Independent Variable: News information (beta .08, p < .001). Those heavily exposed to news information considered education more important.

Dependent Variable 17: Important factor for young people when selecting a marriage partner: looks. R = .16 (F = 26.01, df = 2, 1995, p < .001).

Independent Variables: Age (beta -.12, p < .001); Female (beta -.11, p < .001). Looks were more important to younger people and to men.

Dependent Variable 18: Important factor for young people when selecting a marriage partner: work ability. R = .09 (F = 17.51, df = 1, 1996, p < .001).

Independent Variable: Education (beta -.09, p < .001). Those of lower education considered work ability more important.

Dependent Variable 19: Important factor for young people when selecting a marriage partner: age. R = .24 (F = 124.79, df = 1,1996, p < .001).

Independent Variable: Rural (beta .24, p < .001). Age as a factor was more important to rural villagers.

Dependent Variable 20: Important factor for young people when selecting a marriage partner: occupation. No independent variable is significantly related at .001 level.

Dependent Variable 21: If you have a son, how far will you support him in school?

Discriminant Analysis for categorical responses: Two functions significant at .001 level. First function: Eigenvalue .12, variance 85 percent, canonical correlation .32. Lambda .87. Major independent variable on rotated standardized discriminant function: Education, coefficient .85; Urban, coefficient .65. Second function: Eigenvalue .01, variance 9 percent, canonical correlation .11. Lambda .98. Major independent variable on rotated standardized discriminant function: Age, coefficient .88. Those of higher education, younger people, and urban residents had higher educational aspirations for their sons.

Dependent Variable 22: If you have a daughter, how far will you support her in school?

Discriminant Analysis for categorical responses: Two functions significant at .001 level. First function: Eigenvalue .07, variance 70 percent, canonical correlation .25. Lambda .91. Major independent variable on rotated standardized discriminant function: Education, coefficient .83; Urban, coefficient .58. Second function: Eigenvalue .01, variance 13 percent, canonical correlation .11. Lambda .97. Major independent variable on rotated standardized discriminant function: Age, coefficient .72. Those of higher education, younger people, and urban residents had higher educational aspirations for their daughters.

Dependent Variable 23: If you have a child, what would you like him or her to do when your child grows up?

Discriminant Analysis for categorical responses: Two functions significant at .001 level. First function: Eigenvalue .26, variance 68 percent, canonical correlation .46. Lambda .70. Major independent variable on rotated standardized discriminant function: Education, coefficient .80; Urban, coefficient -.74. Second function: Eigenvalue .07, variance 18 percent, canonical correlation .25. Lambda .89. Major independent variable on rotated standardized discriminant function: Age, coefficient -.84; Western cultural influence, coefficient .52. Factory jobs appealed to those of lower education and those not much exposed to Western influence. Hardly anybody outside the rural areas wanted his children to be farmers. Managerial positions were chosen mostly by those of higher education, younger people, and urban residents. Those heavily exposed to Western influence preferred artists.

Chapter 10. Cultural Values: Traditional Precepts

Dependent Variable 1: Chinese traditional value: long historical heritage. R = .08 (F = 13.72, df = 1, 1996, p < .001).

Independent Variable: News information (beta .08, p < .001). Those heavily exposed to news information were more proud of China's long historical heritage.

Dependent Variable 2: Chinese traditional value: diligence and frugality. R = .19 (F = 23.70, df = 3, 1994, p < .001).

Independent Variables: Age (beta .12, p < .001); Western cultural influence (beta -.10, p < .001); News information (beta .08, p < .001). Older people, those not much exposed to Western influence, and those heavily exposed to news information were more proud of the value of diligence and frugality.

Dependent Variable 3: Chinese traditional value: Way of Golden Mean. R = .08 (F = 6.71, df = 2, 1995, p < .001).

Independent Variables: Age (beta -.08, p < .001); Urban (beta .06, p < .05).* Younger people and urban residents were less negative about this value.

Dependent Variable 4: Chinese traditional value: benevolent father, filial son. R = .10 (F = 20.45, df = 1,1996, p < .001).

Independent Variable: Education (beta .10, p < .001). Those of higher education were more proud of the value of benevolent father and filial son.

Dependent Variable 5: Chinese traditional value: loyalty to state. R = .12 (F= 15.61, df = 2, 1995, p < .001).

Independent Variables: News information (beta .09, p < .001); Education (beta .07, p < 001). Loyalty to the state as a value appealed more to those heavily exposed to news information and those of higher education.

Dependent Variable 6: Chinese traditional value: differentiation between men and women. R = .07 (F = 10.29, df = 1, 1996, p < .005).

Independent Variable: Rural (beta .07, p < .005). Rural villagers were less negative about this traditional value.

Dependent Variable 7: Chinese traditional value: three obediences and four virtues. R = .21 (F = 44.81, df = 2, 1995, p < .001).

Independent Variables: Age (beta -.17, p < .001); Education (beta -.14, p < .001). Younger people and those of lower education were less negative about this traditional value.

Dependent Variable 8: Chinese traditional value: tolerance, propriety, and deference. R = .12 (F = 29.28, df = 1, 1996, p < .001).

Independent Variable: Education (beta .12, p < .001). Those of higher education were more proud of this traditional value.

Dependent Variable 9: Chinese traditional value: glory to ancestors. R = .12 (F = 27.09, df = 1, 1996, p < .001).

Independent Variable: Age (beta -.12, p < .001). Younger people were less negative about this traditional value.

Dependent Variable 10: Chinese traditional value: peasants high, merchants low. R = .19 (F = 39.38, df = 2, 1995, p < .001).

Independent Variables: Education (beta -.15, p < .001); Western cultural influence (beta -.08, p < .001). This traditional value was endorsed more by those of lower education and those under little Western influence.

Dependent Variable 11: Chinese traditional value: chastity for women. R = .19 (F = 73.89, df = 1, 1996, p < .001).

Independent Variable: Age (beta -.19, p < .001). This traditional value appealed more to younger people.

Dependent Variable 12: Chinese traditional value: pleasing superiors. R = .26 (F = 48.51, df = 3, 1994, p < .001).

Independent Variables: Education (beta -.19, p < .001); Age (beta -.09, p < .001); Rural (beta .09, p < .001). This traditional value appealed more to those of lower education, younger people, and rural villagers.

Dependent Variable 13: Chinese traditional value: a house full of children. R = .34 (F = 86.97, df = 3, 1994, p < .001).

Independent Variables: Rural (beta .15, p < .001); Age (beta -.21, p < .001); Education (beta -.14, p < .001). This traditional value appealed more to rural villagers, younger people, and those of lower education.

Dependent Variable 14: Chinese traditional value: harmony is precious. R = .20 (F = 28.33, df= 3, 1994, p < .001).

Independent Variables: Urban (beta .17, p < .001); News information (beta -.08, p < .001); Education (beta .06, p < .01). Harmony as a value was endorsed more by urban residents, by those little exposed to news information, and by those of higher education.

Dependent Variable 15: Chinese traditional value: generosity and virtues. R = .14 (F = 42.28, df = 1,1996, p < .001).

Independent Variable: Urban (beta .14, p < .001). Urban residents considered this value more important.

Dependent Variable 16: Chinese traditional value: submission to authority. No independent variable is significantly related at .001 level.

Dependent Variable 17: Chinese traditional value: respect of tradition. No independent variable is significantly related at .001 level.

Dependent Variable 18: Chinese tradtitional value: discretion for self-preservation. R = .26 (F = 47.98, df = 3, 1994, p < .001).

Independent Variables: Age (beta -.21, p < .001); Education (beta -.15, p < .001); News information (beta -.09, p < .001). Younger people, those of lower education, and those little exposed to news information were less negative about this traditional value.

*Age reached the .001 level of significance when urban residence was included in the regression equation.

Chapter 11. Belief System

Dependent Variable 1: Do you think it is necessary to have religious faith? R = .14 (F = 19.67, df = 2, 1986, p < .001).

Independent Variables: Urban (beta .14, p < .001); Age (beta -.09, p < .001). More urban residents considered religious faith necessary. Younger people were less certain whether religious faith was necessary.

Dependent Variable 2: How important are the Buddhist festivals in the life of your family? R = .30 (F = 63.63, df = 3, 1968, p < .001).

Independent Variables: Rural (beta .16, p < .001); Education (beta -.17, p < .001); Age (beta -.09, p < .001). Buddhist festivals were seen to be more important by rural villagers, those of lower education, and younger people.

Dependent Variable 3: How important is the celebration of Spring Festival in the life of your family? R =.27 (F = 50.56, df = 2, 1989, p < .001).

Independent Variables: Age (beta -.24, p < .001); Education (beta -.10, p < .001). Spring Festival was more important to younger people and those of lower education.

Dependent Variable 4: Some people often take pilgrimage trips to temples. Do you think they will receive protection? R = .28 (F = 34.74, df = 5, 1975, p < .001).

Independent Variables: Age (beta -.25, p < .001); Female (beta .09, p < .001); Western cultural influence (beta .08, p < .001); Education (beta -.10, p < .001); Urban (beta .08, p < .005). Younger people, women, those under heavy Western influence, those of lower education, and urban residents believed in pilgrimage trips more.

Dependent Variable 5: If someone does not do well all his life, do you think it is because he does not work hard enough, because he is treated unfairly by others, or because it is his fate?

Discriminant Analysis for categorical responses: Two functions significant at .001 level. First function: Eigenvalue .08, variance 85 percent, canonical correlation .28. Lambda .91. Major independent variables on rotated standardized discriminant function: Education, coefficient -.56; Western cultural influence, coefficient -.47. Second function: Eigenvalue .02, variance 15 percent, canonical correlation .12. Lambda .98. Major independent variable on rotated standardized discriminant function: Age, coefficient .97. Those of lower education, those under little Western influence, and older people blamed laziness more. Those of higher education, those under heavy Western influence, and younger people were more likely to attribute failure to fate.

Dependent Variable 6: If your family works very hard at a job but it fails, how do you feel?

Discriminant Analysis for categorical responses: One function significant at .001 level. Eigenvalue .03, variance 69 percent, canonical correlation .17. Lambda .96. Major independent variables on rotated standardized discriminant function: News information, coefficient .64; Rural, coefficient .53. Rural villagers and those heavily exposed to news information tended not to feel bad and wanted to try again.

Dependent Variable 7: Do you believe that the location of your ancestors' tombs affects the well-being of your family? R = .15 (F = 22.82, df = 2, 1985, p < .001).

Independent Variables: Age (beta -.13, p < .001); Education (beta -.10, p < .001). Younger people and those of lower education believed in geomancy more.

Dependent Variable 8: How do you think you should treat your ancestors?

Discriminant Analysis for categorical responses: Two functions significant at .001 level. First function: Eigenvalue .12, variance 81 percent, canonical correlation .33. Lambda .87. Major independent variable on rotated standardized discriminant function: Rural, coefficient -.57. Second function: Eigenvalue .02, variance 11 percent, canonical correlation .12. Lambda .97. Major independent variables on rotated standardized discriminant function: Education, coefficient .88; Age, coefficient .82. Urban residents and those of higher education more likely saw no need for any kind of observance. Younger people preferred memorial ceremonies more than older people.

Notes

Chapter 3

1. Unless combined with news information into one scale (see note 1 in chapter 5), high Western cultural influence refers to a score of 4 on the Western cultural influence scale, low influence refers to a score of 0.

Chapter 4

1. High and low Western cultural influences refer to scores of 4 and 0 respectively on the Western cultural influence scale, same as in chapter 3.

Chapter 5

1. When combined with news information, the Western cultural influence scale was dichotomized to be as close to a 50–50 split as possible. Low Western influence refers to an original scale score of 0 (50.7percent). High Western influence refers to scale scores from 1 to 4 (49.3 percent). Similarly, the news information scale was dichotomized to be as close to a 50–50 split as possible. Low use of official news information refers to scale scores of 0 and 1 (48.5 percent). High use of official news information refers to scale scores of 2 to 4 (51.5 percent).

Chapter 6

1. High exposure to news information refers to a score of 4 on the news information scale, and low exposure refers to a score of 0.

2. High Western cultural influence refers to a score of 4 on the Western cultural influence scale, and low influence refers to a score of 0.

Chapter 7

1. Both the Western cultural influence scale and the news information scale were dichotomized to be as close to a 50–50 split as possible, same as in chapter 5.

Chapter 8

1. Both the Western cultural influence scale and the news information scale were dichotomized to be as close to a 50–50 split as possible, same as in chapter 5.

2. The use of official news information was dichotomized as before into high (scale scores 2 to 4) and low(scale scores 0 and 1), as in chapter 5. Education was dischotomized into high (high school and college) and low (junior high school and below).

Chapter 11

1. See *Shanghai Culture Yearbook*. Beijing: Chinese Encyclopaedic Publishing House, 1987, chapter on "Religion," pp. 402–407.

Chapter 12

1. Korean society shares common cultural and historical roots with China, primarily in Confucianism, which was introduced to Korea in the 4th century and officially accepted as Korea's ruling ideology for over five hundred years during the Yi Dynasty (A.D. 1392–1910). The Chinese written language was adopted at about the time Confucianism was introduced, and served as the official Korean language until the creation in 1443 of *Han'gul*, the Korean phonetic alphabets currently in use. Koreans and Chinese have shared the same family name system.

The study of contemporary Korean culture was based on a national survey of 1,500 respondents randomly drawn from Seoul, several medium size cities, and a number of villages. The fieldwork was conducted by the Institute of Broadcasting Research, Korean Broadcasting System, and jointly supervised by Dr. Won–Yong Kim and Dr. Jae–Won Lee as a cooperative research project with the Institute of Culture and Communication, East–West Center.

2. The five undesirable classes consisted of former landlords, former rich peasants, anti-revolutionaries (reactionary elements), bad elements (generally defined), and Rightists.

References

Aberle, David F., et. al. (1950) "The Functional Prerequisites of a Society," *Ethics* 60, pp. 100–110.

Almond, Gabriel A. and G. Bingham Powell (eds.) (1984) *Comparative Politics Today: A World View*. Boston: Little, Brown and Co.

Anderson, Benedict and Ruchira Mendiones. (1985) *In the Mirror—Literature and Politics in Siam in the American Era*. Bangkok: Editions Duang Kamol.

Bai, Nanfeng and Wang Xiaoqiang. (1988) *The Social Psychology of Reform: Changes and Choices*. Chengtu: Sichuan People's Publishing House, p. 120. [The research was conducted by the Social Research Unit and the Public Opinion Research Unit in the Economic System Reform Institute in Beijing.]

Ball-Rokeach, Sandra J., Milton Rokeach, and Joel W. Grube. (1984) *The Great American Values Test*. New York: The Free Press.

Barnett, A. Doak. (1979) "The Communication System in China: Some Generalizations, Hypotheses, and Questions for Research," in *Moving a Mountain: Cultural Change in China*, Godwin C. Chu and Francis L. K. Hsu (eds.). Honolulu, HI: University Press of Hawaii, pp. 386–395.

Benedict, Ruth. (1946) *The Chrysanthemum and the Sword: Patterns of Japanese Culture*. New York: New American Library.

Benedict, Ruth. (1952) "Thai Culture and Behavior: An Unpublished Wartime Study." Ithaca, NY: Cornell University, Southeast Asia Program.

Berelson, Bernard. (1952) *Content Analysis in Communication Research*. Glencoe, IL: Free Press.

Bernardi, Bernardo. (1977) "The Concept of Culture: A New Presentation," in *The Concept and Dynamics of Culture*. Bernardo Bernardi (ed.). The Hague: Mouton Publishers, pp. 75–87.

Berstein, Thomas P. (1977) *Up to the Mountain and Down to the Countryside: Transfer of Youth from Urban to Rural China*. New Haven, CT: Yale University Press.

Berstein, Thomas P. (1979) "Communication and Value Change in the Chinese Program of Sending Urban Youths to the Countryside," in *Moving a Mountain: Cultural Change in China*, pp. 363–384.

Boas, Franz. (ed.) (1938) *General Anthropology,* with contributions by Ruth Benedict, Franz Boas, Ruth Bunzel, and others. Boston: D. C. Heath & Co.
Cai, Shangsi. (1987) "Characteristics of Traditional Chinese Culture and Its Change," in *Re-evaluation of Traditional Chinese Culture.* Fudan University, Shanghai, China: People's Press, pp. 43–49.
Cai, Zhengchang. (1988) "The Shock, Right and Wrong of *Heshang* (River Elegy)." *Mainland China,* vol. 21, no. 10 (October 1988).
Cannel, Charles F. and Robert L. Kahn. (1968) "Interviewing," in *Handbook of Social Psychology,* eds. Gardner Lindzey and Elliot Aronson, 2nd ed., vol. 2. Reading, MA: Addison-Wesley Publishing Co., pp. 526–595.
Carey, James W. (1989) *Communication As Culture.* Boston: Unwin Hyman.
Cell, Charles P. (1977) *Revolution at Work: Mobilization Campaigns in China.* New York: Academic Press.
Cell, Charles P. (1984) "Communication in China's Mass Mobilization Campaigns," in Godwin C. Chu and Francis L. K. Hsu (eds.), *China's New Social Fabric.* London: Kegan Paul International, pp. 25–46.
Chamberlain, Heath G. (1987) "Party–Management Relations in Chinese Industries: Some Political Dimensions of Economic Reform," *The China Quarterly,* no. 112 (December 1987): 631–661.
Chang, Parris H. (1979) "Children's Literature and Political Socialization," in *Moving a Mountain: Cultural Change in China,* pp. 237–256.
Chen, Zhili (ed.). (1991) *A History of the Construction of the Chinese Communist Party.* Shanghai: Shanghai People's Publishing House.
Chu, Godwin C. (1964) "Problems of Cross-Cultural Communication Research," *Journalism Quarterly,* Autumn 1964, pp. 550–562.
Chu, Godwin C. (1977) *Radical Change through Communication in Mao's China.* Honolulu, HI: University Press of Hawaii.
Chu, Godwin C. (ed.). (1978) *Popular Media in China: Shaping New Cultural Patterns.* Honolulu, HI: University Press of Hawaii.
Chu, Godwin C. (1979) "Communication and Cultural Change in China: A Conceptual Framework," in *Moving a Mountain: Cultural Change in China.* pp. 2–24.
Chu, Godwin C., Alfian and Wilbur Schramm. (1985) *Satellite Television Comes to Indonesian Villages: A Study of Social Impact.* Jakarta: LEKNAS/LIPI, and Honolulu, HI: East–West Center.
Chu, Godwin C. and Gin–yao Chi. (1984) *Cultural Change in Rural Taiwan.* Taipei, Taiwan: Shangwu Commercial Press.
Chu, Godwin C. and Francis L. K. Hsu (eds.) (1979) *Moving a Mountain: Cultural Change in China.* Honolulu, Hawaii: University Press of Hawaii.
Cohen, Myron L. (1990) "Lineage Organization in North China," *The Journal of Asian Studies,* vol. 49, no. 3 (August 1990): 509–534.
Dittmer, Lowell. (1979) "Cultural Revolution and Cultural Change," in *Moving a Mountain: Cultural Change in China,* pp. 207–236.

Economist. (October 5, 1991) "The South China Miracle," 19–22.
Fei, Hsiao-tung. (1939) *Peasant Life in China*. London: Kegan Paul.
Fei, John C. H. (1989) "A Cultural Approach to the 1989 Beijing Crisis," *Asian Affairs: An American Review*, vol. 16, no. 2 (Summer 1989): 63–68.
Freeman, Derek. (1983) *Margaret Mead and Samoa: The Making and Unmaking of An Anthropological Myth*. Cambridge, MA: Harvard University Press.
Gallin, Bernard. (1966) *Hsin Hsin, Taiwan: A Chinese Village in Change*. Berkeley: University of California Press.
Goldman, Merle. (1979) "The Media Campaign as a Weapon in Political Struggle," in *Moving a Mountain: Cultural Change in China*, pp. 179–206.
Hall, Stuart, Dorothy Hobson, Andrew Lowe, and Paul Willis (eds.) (1980) *Culture, Media, Language*. London: Hutchinson.
Hayashi, Chikio. (1981) *A Statistical Method for Comparative Study of Fundamental Structure of Social Attitude*. Tokyo: Institute of Statistical Mathematics.
Hayashi, Chikio. (1987) "Statistical Study of Japanese National Character," *Journal of Japanese Statistical Society*. Special Issue, pp. 71–95.
Hayashi, Chikio, Tatsuzo Suzuki and Fumi Hayashi. (1984) "Comparative Study of Lifestyle and Quality of Life: Japan and France," *Behaviormetrika*, no. 15, pp. 1–17.
Holsti, Ole R. (1968) "Content Analysis," in *Handbook of Social Psychology*, 2nd ed., vol. 2. Reading, MA: Addision–Wesley Publishing Co., pp. 596–692.
Hsiung, James C. (1989) "From the Vantage of the Beijing Hotel: Peering into the 1989 Student Unrest in China," A*sian Affairs: An American Review*, vol. 16, no. 2 (Summer 1989): 55–62.
Hsu, Francis L. K. (1949) *Under the Ancestors' Shadow*. London: Routledge and Kegan Paul Ltd.
Hsu, Francis L. K. (1953) *Americans and Chinese: Two Ways of Life*. New York: H. Schuman.
Hsu, Francis L. K. (1981) *Americans and Chinese: Passage to Differences*. Honolulu, HI: University Press of Hawaii.
Inglehart, Ronald. (1990) *Culture Shift in Advanced Industrial Society*. Princeton, New Jersey: Princeton University Press.
Inkeles, Alex and David H. Smith. (1974) *Becoming Modern: Individual Change in Six Developing Countries*. Cambridge, MA: Harvard University Press.
Jin, Guantao. (1989) "The Spirit of Rationality in Chinese Culture—and Its Shortcomings," *The Chinese Intellectuals* (Autumn 1989): 87–96.
King, Ambrose Y. C. (1985) "The Individual and Group in Confucianism: A Relational Perspective," in *Individualism and Holism: Studies in Confucian and Taoist Values*, Donald Munro (ed.). Ann Arbor: University of Michigan Press, pp. 57–70.
King, Ambrose Y. C. (1991) "Kuan-hsi and Network Building: A Sociological Interpretation," DAEDALUS, vol. 120, no. 2 (Spring 1991): 63–84.

Klausner, William J. (1985) *Reflections on Thai Culture*. Bangkok: Siam Society.
Klausner, William J. (1989) "Notes on Participant Observation as a Fieldwork Method," personal communication.
Kluckhohn, Clyde. (1951) "Values and Value-orientations in the Theory of Actions: An Exploration in Definition and Classification," in *Toward a General Theory of Action*, Talcott Parsons and Edward A. Shils (eds.). Cambridge, MA: Harvard University Press, pp. 388–433.
Kluckhohn, Clyde and W. H. Kelly. (1945) "The Concept of Culture," in *The Science of Man in the World Crisis*, ed. Ralph Linton. New York: Columbia University Press, pp. 78–105.
Kluckhohn, Florence R. and Fred L. Strodbeck. (1961) *Variations in Value Orientations*. Evanston, IL: Row, Peterson and Co.
Kroeber, A. L. and Clyde Kluckhohn. (1952) *Culture: A Critical Review of Concepts and Definitions*. New York: Alfred A. Knopf.
KBS. (1989) *Survey of Contemporary Korean Culture*. Seoul, Korea: Korean Broadcasting System.
LaPiere, R.T. (1934) "Attitudes vs Actions," in *Social Forces*, vol. 14, pp. 230–237.
Lerner, Daniel. (1958) *The Passing of Traditional Society: Modernizing the Middle East*. Glencoe, IL: Free Press of Glencoe.
Levy, Marion. (1952) *The Structure of Society*. Princeton, New Jersey: Princeton University Press.
Li, Kan. (1987) "National Awakening in Modern China and the Destiny of Traditional Culture," in *Re-evaluation of Traditional Chinese Culture*, pp. 200–210.
Li, Pang, Ou Xiaowei, and Hou Hong (1987) "A Preliminary Exploration of University Student Group," *Nanfang qingshaonian yanjiu* [Southern Youth Research], no. 2, p. 39.
Liang, Shuming. (1963) *The Essence of Chinese Culture*. Hong Kong: Jichen Publishing Co.
Lieberthal, Kenneth G. (1984) "Communication from the Party Center: The Transmission Process for Central Committee Documents," in *China's New Social Fabric*, pp. 89–118.
Lin, Nan and Wen Xie. (1988) "Occupational Prestige in Urban China," *American Sociological Review*, vol. 93: 393–405.
Lin, Nan and Yanjie Bian. (1991) "Getting Ahead in Urban China," *American Journal of Sociology*, vol. 97, no. 3: 657–88.
Link, Perry. (1987) "The Limits of Cultural Reform in Deng Xiaoping's China," *Modern China*, vol. 13, no. 2.
Liu, Alan P.L. (1975) *Communication and National Integration in Communist China*. Berkeley, CA: University of California Press.
Liu, Binyan. (1991) "Spiritual Crisis in Mainland China," *Cheng Ming*, no. 164 (June 1991): 64–66.
Liu, William T. (1989) "A Social Study of the 1989 Beijing Crisis," *Asian Affairs: An American Review*, vol. 16, no. 2 (Summer 1989): 69–76.

Liu, Xiaobo. (1989) "The Tragedy of the Enlightenment: A Criticism of the May Fourth Movement," *Ming Bao*, vol. 269 (May 1989), pp. 37–45.

Liu, Zaifu and Gang Lin. (1988) *Tradition and the Chinese: Rethinking and Recriticizing the Main Issues of May Fourth New Culture Movement*. Beijing: Joint Publishing House.

Lu, Xinhua. (1978) "Scars" [Shang Heng], a short story published in Wenhui Bao of Shanghai, August 11, 1978. Reprinted in *Scars* [Shang Heng]: *Selections of Short Stories from Mainland China*. Taipei: Youth Culture Enterprise Publications, 1982, pp. 1–14.

Malinowski, Bronislaw. (1922) *Argonauts of the Western Pacific: An Account of Native Enterprise and Adventure in the Archipelagoes of Malanesian New Guinea*. London: G. Routledge & Sons.

Malinowski, Bronislaw. (1938) "Introduction," in *Methods of Study of Culture Contact in Africa*. International African Institute of African Languages and Cultures.

Malinowski, Bronislaw. (1945) *The Dynamics of Culture Change: An Inquiry into Race Relations in Africa*. Yale University Press, especially "Theories of Culture Change," pp. 14–26; "The Functional Theory of Culture," pp. 41–51, and "The Function and Adaptability of African Institutions," pp. 52–63.

Markarian, E. S. (1977) "The Concept of Culture in the System of Modern Sciences," in *The Concept and Dynamics of Culture*, pp. 103–118.

McGuire, William J. (1968) "The Nature of Attitudes and Attitude Change," in *Handbook of Social Psychology*, 2nd ed., vol. 3. Reading, MA: Addison-Wesley Publishing Co., pp. 136–314.

Mead, Margaret. (1928) *Coming of Age in Samoa: A Psychological Study of Primitive Youth for Western Civilization*. New York: W. Morrow & Co.

Melischek, Gabriele, Karl E. Rosengren, and James Stappers (eds.) (1984) *Cultural Indicators: An International Symposium*. Vienna: Osterreichischen Akademie der Wissenschaften.

Menghin, O. (1931) *Weltgeschichte der Steinzeit*, Vienna, cited in Kroeber and Kluckhohn, *Culture: A Critical Review of Concepts and Definitions*, pp. 182–189.

Merton, Robert K. (1961) *Social Theory and Social Structure*. Glencoe, IL: The Free Press, pp. 421–422.

Murdock, George P. (1941) "Anthropology and Human Relations," in *Sociometry*, vol. 4, pp. 140–150.

National Opinion Research Center. (1986) *General Social Surveys, 1972–1986: Cumulative Code Book*. University of Chicago.

Ogden, Suzanne. (1989) *Chinese Unresolved Issues: Politics, Development and Culture*. New Jersey: Prentice-Hall.

Parish, William L. (1979) "Communication and Changing Rural Life," in *Moving a Mountain: Cultural Change in China*, pp. 363–384.

Parish, William L. and Martin K. Whyte. (1978) *Village and Family in Contemporary China*. University of Chicago Press.

Parsons, Talcott. (1951) *The Social System*. New York: The Free Press.

Phillips, Herbert P. (1987) *Modern Thai Literature*. Honolulu: University of Hawaii Press.
Pye, Lucian W. (1984) *China: An Introduction*. Boston, MA: Little Brown & Co.
Radcliffe–Brown, A. R. (1952) *Structure and Function in Primitive Society*. London: Cohen & West. See especially, "On the Concept of Function in Social Science," pp. 178–187, and "On Social Structure," pp. 188–204.
Ren, Jiyu (ed.). (1981) *History of Chinese Buddhism* (three volumes). Beijing: China Social Science Publications.
Rokeach, Milton. (1968–69) "The Role of Values in Public Opinion Research," *Public Opinion Quarterly*, vol. 32, pp. 547–559.
Rokeach, Milton. (1969) *Beliefs, Attitudes and Values*. San Francisco: Jossey–Bass Inc., Publishers.
Rokeach, Milton. (1973) *The Nature of Human Values*. New York: The Free Press.
Rokeach, Milton. (1979) *Understanding Human Values: Individual and Societal*. New York: The Free Press.
Rosen, Stanley and David Chu. (1987) *Survey Research in the People's Republic of China*. Washington, D.C.: United States Information Agency.
Schwartz, Barton M. and Robert H. Ewald. (1968) *Culture and Society: An Introduction to Cultural Anthropology*. New York: Ronald Press Co.
Scott, William A. (1968) "Attitude Measurement," in *Handbook of Social Psychology*, 2nd ed., vol. 2. Reading, MA: Addison-Wesley Publishing Co., pp. 204–273.
Shanghai jiaoyu keyan. (1989) "An Investigation of the Values of Some Secondary School Students in Shanghai," *Shanghai jiaoyu keyan*, [Shanghai Educational Research], no. 6 (November 1989): 36.
Smelser, Neil J. (1968) "Toward a General Theory of Social Change," in Neil J. Smelser, *Essays in Sociological Explanation*. Englewood Cliffs: Prentice-Hall, pp. 192–280.
Spence, Jonathan D. (1990) *The Search for Modern China*. New York, NY: W. W. Norton & Co.
Stoetzel, Jean. (1955) *Without the Chrysanthemum and the Sword*. New York: Columbia University Press.
Su, Xiaokang. (1990) "On the Use of Traditional Resources: A Talk with Professor Tu Weiming in Paris," *Democratic China*, no. 2 (June 1990): 52–55.
Su, Xiaokang and Wang Luxiang. (1988) *The River Elegy*. A six-part television documentary. Transcript published by China Book Press, Hong Kong.
Tang, Yijie. (1987) *Modernization and Internationalization of Chinese Culture*. Beijing: International Cultural Press.
Teng, Yucheng, and Yin Qing. (1988) "An Investigation of the Choices of Professions by University Students," *Shangdong gongye daxue xuebao* [Shangdong Industrial University Journal], vol. 3, no. 4, p. 55.
Tessmann, G. (1930) *Die Indianer Nordost Perus*. Hamburg, cited in Kroeber and Kluckhohn, *Culture: A Critical Review of Concepts and Definitions*, p.

187.

Tu, Weiming (1987) "Identity and Innovation in Chinese Culture," in *Re-evaluation of Traditional Chinese Culture*, pp. 100–108.

Tu, Weiming (1991) "Cultural China: The Periphery as the Center," DAEDALUS, vol. 120, no. 2 (Spring 1991): 1–32.

Unger, Jonathan and Jean Xiong (1990). "Life in the Chinese Hinterlands under the Rural Economic Reforms," *Bulletin of Concerned Asian Scholars*, vol. 22, no. 2 (April–June 1990): 4–17.

Unger, Jonathan (1991) "Whither China? Yang Xiguang, Red Capitalists, and the Social Turmoil of the Cultural Revolution," *Modern China*, vol. 17, no. 1 (January 1991): 3–37.

Vermeersch, Etienne. (1977) "An Analysis of the Concept of Culture," in *The Concept and Dynamics of Culture*, pp. 9–73.

Walder, Andrew G. (1987) "Wage Reform and the Web of Factory Interests," *The China Quarterly*, no. 109 (March 1987): 22–41.

Walder, Andrew G. (1989) "Factory and Manager in an Era of Reform," *The China Quarterly*, no. 118 (June 1989): 242–264.

Walder, Andrew G. (1989) "Beyond the Deng Era: China's Political Dilemma," *Asian Affairs: An American Review*, vol. 16, no. 2 (Summer 1989): 83–92.

Wang, Ruoshui. (1980) "On the Issue of Alienation," *Xinwen Zhanxian* [The News Front] Vol. 8.

White, Leslie (1974) "The Concept of Culture," in *Frontier of Anthropology*, A. Montagu (ed.). New York: G. P. Putnams Sons, p. 550.

Whyte, Martin K. (1974) *Small Groups and Political Rituals in China*. Berkeley, CA: University of California Press.

Whyte, Martin K. (1979) "Small Groups and Communication in China: Ideal Forms and Imperfect Realities," in *Moving a Mountain: Cultural Change in China*, pp. 113–124.

Whyte, Martin K. (1989) "Evolutionary Changes in Chinese Culture," in *Asia-Pacific Report, Focus: China in the Reform Era*, Charles Morrison and Robert Dernberger (eds.). Honolulu, HI: East–West Center, pp. 93–101.

Whyte, William F. (1943) *Street Corner Society: The Social Structure of an Italian Slum*. Chicago: University of Chicago Press.

WuDunn, Sheryl (1991) "Divorce Rate Soars as Chinese Decide Love Is Part of Marriage," *New York Times*, April 17, 1991.

Xiao, Jifu. (1987) "A Historical Re-evaluation of the Open-door Policy," in *Re-evaluation of Traditional Chinese Culture*, pp. 378–384.

Xie, Wen and Nan Lin. (1986) "The Process of Status Attainment in Urban China." Paper presented at the annual meeting of the American Sociological Association, New York.

Xu, Xiaohe and Martin K. Whyte (1990) "Love Matches and Arranged Marriages: A Chinese Replication," *Journal of Marriage and the Family*, no. 52 (August 1990): 709–722.

Yan, Jiaqi and Gao Gao. (1985) *History of the Cultural Revolution*. Tianjin: People's Publishing House.

Yang, Haiou. (1990) "Cultural Fever: A Cultural Discourse in China's New Age," paper prepared for Workshop on Cultural Policy and National Identity, Institute of Culture and Communication, East–West Center, Honolulu, Hawaii, June, 1990.

Yi, Jiayan. (1989) "What Does *Heshang* (River Elegy) Advocate?" *People's Daily*, July 17.

Yu, Frederick T.C. (1964) *Mass Persuasion in Communist China*. New York: Praeger.

Yu, Frederick T.C. (1967) "Campaigns, Communication and Development in Communist China," in *Communication and Change in Developing Countries*, Daniel Lerner and Wilbur Schramm (eds.). Honolulu, HI: East–West Center, pp. 195–215.

Yu, Lina. (1989) "What Does *Heshang* (River Elegy) Intend to Say?: A Report of a Seminar on River Elegy." *Mainland China*, vol. 27, no. 9 (February 1989), pp. 6–21.

Zhao, Ying. (1989) "The Changes in Contemporary University Students' Views of Professions," *Gaodeng jiaoyu yanjiu* [Higher Education Research], no. 2 (December 1989): p. 93.

Index

Aberle, David F., 7
Age levels, 31–35, 41–42. *See also* Young versus old attitudes
Alfian, 20, 83
Almond, Gabriel H., 8
Ancestor worship, 9, 226–227, 262–264, 266–267, 289–295, 312–313
Anderson, Benedict, 15

"Baile" (mentor), 183–184
Ball-Rokeach, Sandra J., 5
Barnett, A. Doak, 299
Benedict, Ruth, 15, 20
Berelson, Bernard, 19
Bernardi, Bernardo, 4
Berstein, Thomas P., 51
Bian, Yanjie, 109
Boas, Franz, 5
Buddhism, 252–253, 264, 268, 291–292
  destruction of, 311, 313
  festivals, 255–256, 258, 267, 293
  karma, 9–10
  revival of, 265

Cai, Shangsi, 4
Cai, Zhengchang, 4
Cannel, Charles F., 21
Carey, James, 5
Cell, Charles P., 51
Chaffee, Steven, 43
Chang, Parris H., 51
Chen, Zhili, 310

Chi, Gin-yao, 20, 22
Chinese Communist Party, 11, 241–242, 310
  erosion of traditional values, 245–251
  family policies, 275–276
  religious opposition, 264–265
  work incentives, 277–278
Chongqing, 46
Christianity, 253–254, 265
Chrysanthemum and the Sword, The (Benedict), 15
Chu, David, 21
Chu, Godwin C., 4–5, 8, 15, 20, 22, 43–44, 51, 83, 311
Cohen, Myron L., 80, 103, 273
Community relations, 149–150, 163–168
  network connections, 150–153, 165
  public versus private interest, 156–160, 164–165, 168
  public rights and responsibility, 153–156, 163–165
  public service, 160–163, 167
Confucianism, 101, 241, 252–253, 264, 268
  the family, 225, 227
  human nature, 191
Confucius, 289–290
  on ancestors, 289
  campaigns against, 11–12, 229–230
  on the family, 225–226

Confucius *(continued)*
  on the Golden Mean, 229
  harmony, 232
Cultural change, 271–272, 297–299,
    311–313, 320–322
  adaptive functions, 11–13
  research on, 3–7
  structural-functional perspective,
    7–10
Cultural rejuvenation, 313
  ideological domain, 319–320
  material relations, 317–319
  social relations, 313–317
Cultural Revolution, 11–12, 51, 204,
    206, 319
  family relationships during, 68,
    79–81, 191–192, 200, 275, 289
  opposition to traditional values,
    224, 230–231, 234, 286, 311–312
  party cadres, 114–115
  public rights, 153, 162
  religious persecution during, 265,
    293–294
  women's liberation movement
    during, 240
Cultural values, 169, 194–198
  a good person, 170–174
  human nature, 191–194
  lifetime goals, 174–183, 196, 197
  meaning of life, 185–187, 196
  means of success, 183–184
  rising materialism, 103, 279–282,
    317–319
  saving face, 188–191
  submission to authority, 11,
    233–234, 283–286, 311–312
  way of the Golden Mean,
    229–230, 286–289
Culture
  constraining components, 8–10
  definitions, 4–7
  incentive components, 8–10
  system-destroying functions, 10,
    320
  system-sustaining functions, 10,
    311, 320

Dan wei (work organizations), 105
Deng, Xiaoping, and economic
  reforms, 12, 52, 82–85, 318–319
Dittmer, Lowell, 51
Dream of the Red Chamber, The, 18–19

East-West Center (Honolulu), 23, 43
Educational levels
  responses, 30–32, 37, 40, 54–55,
    302–304
  on community service, 167–168
  on cultural values, 200–203, 217,
    224–225, 228, 233, 235–236, 243
  on family relations, 202
  on goal of education, 173, 178, 180
  on lifetime goals, 182–183
  on occupational preferences, 116
  on religion, 256, 258, 260–264
Ewald, Robert H., 4
Exposés of Chinese Bureaucracy, 234

Face, 188–191
Family relations, 64–69, 79–85, 199,
    272–277, 313–314
  disputes, 74–77, 84–85, 287–289
  divorce, 77–79, 83, 190–191
  educational aspirations for chil-
    dren, 203–206, 215
  filial piety, 199–203, 215
  occupational aspirations for chil-
    dren, 206–208, 215
  parental concerns, 69–74
  values, 214–219
Fan Zhongyan, 156
Fei, Hsiao-tung, 15–16, 24, 46
Fei, John D. H., 251
Four Modernizations Campaign,
    103, 146
Freeman, Derek, 17
Fudan University (Shanghai), 23,
    43–44
Fujian province, 317

Gallin, Bernard, 15–16, 18
Gao Zong, Emperor, 225
Golden Lotus, The, 18–19

Goldman, Merle, 51
Great Wall
    historical, 3
    psychocultural, 3–4, 271, 277, 311, 322
Grube, Joel W., 5
Guangdong province, 317
Guanxi (network of connections), 150–153

Hall, Stuart, 5
Haoren (good person), 170–173
Hayashi, Chikio, 20, 22, 45
Hayashi, Fumi, 20
Hobson, Dorothy, 5
Holsti, Ole R., 19
Homogeneity, 46–47
Hou, Hong, 69
Hsiung, James C., 251
Hsu, Francis L. K., 4, 15–16, 18, 43, 46, 63, 233, 265, 283, 290, 292, 311
Hu Shih, 19, 224, 309–310

Indonesia, 20
Inglehart, Ronald, 5, 20
Inkeles, Alex, 20
Islam, 265

Japan, 20
Jiang, Qing, 240
Jin Dynasty, 267–268
Jin, Guantao, 321
Ju, Yanan, 43–44

Kahn, Robert L., 21
Kelly, W. H., 16
King, Ambrose, 43, 188
Klausner, William, 15, 18
Kluckhohn, Clyde, 4–5, 16, 169, 189
Kluckhohn, Florence, 20
Korea, 282-283, 288
Kroeber, A. L., 4–5
Kuomintang, 4, 310

Land reform, 11, 311–312
Lao Tze, 252, 292

LaPiere, R. T., 21
Lei, Feng, 313
Lerner, Daniel, 20
Levy, Marion, 7
Liang, Shuming, 252
Lieberthal, Kenneth G., 51
Li Hongzhang, 309
Li, Kan, 4, 224
Li, Pang, 69
Lin, Gang, 4
Lin, Nan, 109–110
Link, Perry, 4
Liu, Allan P. L., 51
Liu, Binyan, 321
Liu, William T., 251
Liu, Xiaobo, 4
Liu, Zaifu, 4
Lowe, Andrew, 5
Lu, Xinhua, 63
Lu, Xun, 229

McGuire, William J., 21
Malinowski, Bronislaw, 8
Manchu Dynasty, 4, 309
Mao Zedong, 11–12 15, 51, 243, 311–313, 322
    attacks on religion, 294–295
    opposition to traditional values, 12, 229–230, 232–233, 236, 243, 248
    population policy, 242
    praise for poverty, 279–281
Marco Polo Bridge incident, 310
Markarian, E. S., 4
Marriage, 209–210
    mate selection, 71–72, 210–215, 219
May 4 Movement, 224, 231, 237–238, 319
Mead, Margaret, 17
Media news influence, 47, 52–57, 308–309
    on community service, 161–163, 167
    on cultural values, 196–197, 224, 236, 261
    on individualism, 158–159

Media news influence *(continued)*
  on lifetime goals, 175–179, 182–183, 186–188
  on work, 124, 127, 146, 241
Melischek, Gabriele, 5
Men
  education, 36–37
  occupational status, 38–40
Mencius, 191, 208–209
Mendiones, Ruchira, 15
Menghin, O., 5–6
Meng Jiangnu, 3
Merton, Robert K., 7
Murdock George P., 6

National Opinion Research Center (NORC), 20

Occupational preferences, 106–117, 126–127
  ideal workmates, 117–120
Occupations, 37–40, 42
Ogden, Suzanne, 4
Ou Xiaowei, 69

Parish, William L., 51, 71, 96, 200, 215, 259, 266
Parsons, Talcott, 7–8
Passing of Traditional Society (Lerner), 20
People's Commune movement, 275–278
People's Daily, 47
Phillips, Herbert, 15
Powell, G. Bingham, 8
Public-private Joint Management, 46
Pye, Lucian W., 309

Qin, Emperor, 3, 223, 311
Qingpu Town, 278
  as research site, 24–25, 27–33

Radcliffe-Browne, A. R., 7
Rationality, 321–322
Religion, 252–255, 264–268, 292–296
  fatalism, 259–262, 266

festivals, 255–258, 262. *See also* Ancestor worship, Buddhism, Christianity, Confucianism, Taoism
Ren, Jiyu, 253
Renqing relations, 88, 90–91, 188–189
Research methods, 14–23
  data analysis, 45–60
  participant observation, 14–15, 16–18
  sample composition, 29–45
  sites, 24–29
  surveys, 20–23
  written materials, 15–16, 18–20
River Elegy, The, 4, 296
Rokeach, Milton, 4–5, 169
Rosen, Stanley, 21
Rosengren, Karl E., 5

"Scars, The," 63
Schramm, Wilbur, 20, 83
Schwartz, Barton M., 4
Scott, William A., 21
Shanghai, 46, 49, 253–254
  as research site, 24–27, 29–33
Sino-Japanese War, 4, 35, 46, 309
Smelser, Neil J., 8
Smith, David, 20
Social relations, 86, 98–104
  with friends, 89–92
  with neighbors, 93–96
  with older people, 96–98
  with relatives, 86–89
Song Jiang, 172
Spence, Jonathan D., 309
Stappers, James, 5
Stoetzel, Jean, 20
Strodtbeck, Fred, 20
Su, Xiaokang, 4
Sun Yat-sen, 283, 309
Suzuki, Tatsuzo, 20

Taiping Rebellion, 292
Taiwan, 15–16, 20, 22, 173, 291, 293
Tang, Yijie, 4
Taoism, 252, 264–265, 292

Teng, Yucheng, 116
Television, 66–67, 82–85
Tessman, G., 5–6
Thailand, 15, 18
Tiananmen incident, 251, 320
Traditional values, 220–228, 244–251
  Golden Mean, 229–230, 286–289, 311–312
  risk taking, 296–297
  social status, 242–243
  submission to authority, 11, 233–234, 283–286, 311–312
  women's roles, 237–240
  work ethic, 240
Tu Weiming, 4, 321

Under the Ancestors' Shadow (Hsu), 15
Unger, Jonathan, 273, 318
Urban and rural differences, 29–33, 37, 49–51, 304–305
  mass media, 154
  Western influence, 56

Vermeersch, Etienne, 4

Walder, Andrew G., 145, 318
Wang, Gungwu, 43
Wang, Luxiang, 4
Wang, Ruoshui, 4
Water Margin, 172
Western influence, 11, 13, 53–57, 98, 305–308
  on community service, 160–162
  on family relationships, 83–85, 212, 218–219
  on individualism, 157–160
  on job preferences, 116–117, 206–208
  on leadership qualities, 137
  on marriage, 209–210, 212–213, 218–219
  on network connections, 151–152, 166
  on religion, 258–260
  on social relationships, 102
  on lifetime goals, 175–179, 185–188
  on values, 185–188, 195, 248, 250
  on work attitudes, 121–124, 127–130, 138–140, 147–148, 241–242
White, Leslie, 6
Whyte, Martin K., 4, 12, 51, 71, 96, 200, 215, 259, 266
Whyte, William F., 18
Willis, Paul, 5
Without the Chrysanthemum and the Sword (Stoetzel), 20
Women, 35–37, 110
  chastity, 237–238
  discrimination against, 239–240
  education, 34–37
  obedience, 238, 239
  occupational status, 38–42, 49, 80–81
Work ethic, 105–106, 120–123, 126–130, 241–242, 277–282, 308
  evaluation of, 123–126
  ideal workmates, 117–120
  job preferences, 106–117
Work organizations, 131
  collegial relations, 138–140, 145–147
  leadership qualities, 131–138, 145
  promotion criteria, 140–146
Wu Dunn, Sheryl, 77

Xiang qian kan, 279–280
Xiao, Jifu, 4
Xie, Wen, 110
Xinhua News Agency, 47
Xiong, Jean, 273
Xun Zi, 191

Yang, Haiou, 4
Yi (devoted friendship), 172
Yi, Jiayan, 4
Yin, Qing, 116
Young versus old attitudes, 299–302
  on ancestor worship, 262–264
  on cultural values, 165–166, 200, 203, 216, 230, 235–236, 249

Young vs. old attitudes *(continued)*
    on education, 205
    on family, 216
    on human nature, 192–194, 197–198
    on marriage, 210
    on religion, 256–258, 261–264, 266–267
    on work, 127–128, 146–147

Yu, Anthony, 43
Yu, Frederick T. C., 51
Yu, Linda, 4
Yue Fei, 225

Zhao, Ying, 115
Zheng Ho, 296
Zhou Enlai, 229
Zhujiajiao Town, 27–28